TEACHING UNDERGRADUATE ECONOMICS

a handbook for instructors

William B. Walstad
University of Nebraska

Phillip Saunders
Indiana University

Irwin
McGraw-Hill

Boston   Burr Ridge, IL   Dubuque, IA   Madison, WI   New York   San Francisco   St. Louis
Bangkok   Bogotá   Caracas   Lisbon   London   Madrid   Mexico City   Milan   New Delhi
Seoul   Singapore   Sydney   Taipei   Toronto

Irwin/McGraw-Hill

A Division of The McGraw-Hill Companies

TEACHING UNDERGRADUATE ECONOMICS: A HANDBOOK FOR INSTRUCTORS

3 4 5 6 7 8 9 0 QSR QSR 0 9 8 7 6 5 4 3

ISBN 0-07-290246-9

http://www.mhhe.com

CONTENTS

PART II. FOUNDATIONS FOR TEACHING

PART III. INSTRUCTIONAL METHODS IN ECONOMICS

LECTURES AND TEXTBOOKS

DISCUSSION, WRITING, AND ACTIVE LEARNING

EXPERIMENTS AND TECHNOLOGY

PART IV. EVALUATION OF INSTRUCTION

TESTING

TEACHING

FOREWORD

Paul A. Samuelson

"Poets are the unacknowledged legislators of the World." It was a poet who said that, exercising occupational license. Some sage, it may have been I, declared in similar vein: "I don't care who writes a nation's laws—or crafts its advanced treatises—if I can write its economic textbooks." The first lick is the privileged one, impinging on the beginner's *tabula rasa* at its most impressionable state.

Nonetheless, reality in the university displays a different form. A kind of Gresham's Law prevails in which, left to themselves, professors will compete for the most advanced courses attended by the fewest students. A generation of professors even presided over the liquidation of their own undergraduate schools of business, save where the iron purse of the legislature vetoed the immolation.

It was not always so. And, as I shall argue, there are persuasive reasons for a rise in the prestige of the elementary economics classroom. In the 1890s, President Francis Walker saved for himself the privilege of giving MIT's introductory lectures in economics. And this was a time when General Walker was at the peak of his international fame. Generations of Yale men recalled in later life the economic lectures they heard from President Arthur Hadley. When Yale does something, can Harvard lag behind? Frank Taussig, the spiritual dean of American economics between the Wars, started the pre-World-War-I elite off on their understanding of the economic world. At Madison, William Kiekhofer lectured weekly to a thousand sons and daughters of the middle border, not beginning his sermons on supply and demand until self-elected cheer leaders had given him a Wisconsin locomotive. Ira Cross may not have been Berkeley's most prolific scholar, but it was his name that was on the lips of ten thousand alumni returning to twenty-fifth reunions at Old Cal.

Stuart Mill wrote the definitive textbook of classical economics. Alfred Marshall, Knut Wicksell, Gustav Cassel, Irving Fisher, and Frank Taussig did the same for neoclassical economics. (Fairchild, Furnis and Buck, the best-seller in the pre-Samuelson age, textual research will confirm, was Irving Fisher writ large and packaged for administration to Yale students one eye-drop at a time.) William James in psychology, Richard Courant in mathematics, Linus Pauling in chemistry, and Richard Feynman in physics carried on the great tradition in which leaders at the frontiers of science wrote also for the beginning students.

It would be quixotic for me to claim arguments that would successfully persuade teachers to stop lusting for the advanced seminar. My major point is that, along with those advanced courses, there is personal pleasure to be had from the very first level. My old master, Joseph Schumpeter, reveled in lecturing to large audiences—the more the merrier. But he knew he lacked the self-discipline to take on the task of providing basic foundations. Otto Eckstein, of blessed memory, created Harvard's largest undergraduate course and it is in this same vineyard that Martin Feldstein toils. When Jack Gurley appears before St. Peter, the testimonies of the many Stanford students he introduced to economics will speed him on his way.

Taussig and Hadley and Mill had an easier task than we face today in teaching undergraduate economics courses. Good sense was all they had to tell. Now economics has become a complicated subject. What not to snow students with has become as important as deciding what to emphasize. The present *Handbook*, complied from experienced authors by wise editors, is particularly prized in these complicated and exciting times.

Paul A Samuelson, MIT
Cambridge, Massachusetts
March, 1997

ACKNOWLEDGMENTS

There are several organizations and people who must be recognized for their valuable contribution to the publication of this book. Credit must first be given to McGraw-Hill for its financial and publication support of this volume. McGraw-Hill wanted us to prepare an instructional volume to be a service to economics faculty, and their support was provided without any obligation. We were given complete control over the selection of chapter authors and contents for the book. We are especially thankful for the help of Lucille Sutton, senior editor for economics at McGraw-Hill, who made all of the arrangements for the book's publication.

We must also acknowledge the advice and help of members of the American Economic Association's Committee on Economic Education. Michael Salemi, John Siegfried, and W. Lee Hansen have all served as chairs of that committee and encouraged us in our efforts to prepare the *Handbook*. Each has displayed his commitment by contributing one or two chapters to this volume. Others who have served on the AEA Committee and who have written chapters include Robin Bartlett, William Becker, Michael Boskin, Marianne Ferber, Campbell McConnell, Michael Watts, and Arthur Welsh.

Both the University of Nebraska-Lincoln and Indiana University-Bloomington have supported our work on this project. Sharon Nemeth at the National Center for Research in Economic Education at the University of Nebraska-Lincoln prepared all chapters for publication, proofed the manuscript, and compiled the index. H.L. Darby of the Department of Economics at Indiana University-Bloomington assisted in typing and preparing chapters. We greatly appreciate their work on our behalf and also the in-kind support that we received from our universities.

The National Council on Economic Education has long been interested in the improvement of the teaching of college economics. This volume draws its inspiration from ideas first presented in Teacher Training Programs (TTPs) that the National Council has sponsored since the 1970s.

We gratefully acknowledge the permissions from three publishers to use materials for this volume. Holt Reinhart and Winston allowed us to reprint Figure 8-1 and the MacMillan Company let us reprint Table 8-1. Heldref Publications, publisher of the *Journal of Economic Education*, gave us permission to use portions of articles originally published in the *Journal* for the chapter by Michael Boskin.

Finally, and most important, we are most appreciative of the support that we have received from Tammie Fischer and Nancy Saunders as we completed work on this project.

William B. Walstad
Phillip Saunders
March 1997

LIST OF CONTRIBUTORS

Robin L. Bartlett, Professor of Economics, Denison University. Member, Board of Editors, *Journal of Economic Education*. Former member of the American Economic Association's Committee on Economic Education and Chair of its Committee on the Status of Women in the Economics Profession.

William E. Becker, Professor of Economics, Indiana University-Bloomington. Editor of the *Journal of Economic Education*.

Michael J. Boskin, T. M. Friedman Professor of Economics, Stanford University and Senior Fellow, Hoover Institution. Former Chairman, President's Council of Economic Advisors.

William Bosshardt, Assistant Professor of Economics, Florida Atlantic University. Director of the Florida Atlantic University Center for Economic Education.

Beverly Cameron, Associate Professor of Economics, University of Manitoba.

Alexander J. Cowell, Graduate Assistant, Department of Economics, University of North Carolina, Chapel Hill.

George Davis, Professor of Economics, Miami University.

Wayne Edwards, Graduate Assistant, Department of Economics, University of Nebraska-Lincoln.

Kenneth G. Elzinga, Professor of Economics and Cavaliers' Distinguished Teaching Professor, University of Virginia, Charlottesville. Past President of the Southern Economics Association, 1991.

O. Homer Erekson, Professor of Economics, Miami University.

Ann Harper Fender, Professor of Economics, Gettysburg College.

Marianne A. Ferber, Professor of Economics, Emerita, University of Illinois at Urbana-Champaign. Former President of the Midwest Economics Association and the International Association for Feminist Economics.

Jean Fletcher, Associate Professor of Economics, Gettysburg College.

Robert H. Frank, Goldwin Smith Professor of Economics, Cornell University.

W. Lee Hansen, Professor of Economics and Education Policy Studies, University of Wisconsin, Madison. Former Chair of the American Economic Association's Committee on Economic Education.

Charles A. Holt, Chair and Merrill Bankard Professor of Economics, University of Virginia, Charlottesville.

Campbell R. McConnell, Professor of Economics, Emeritus, University of Nebraska-Lincoln.

Tanga McDaniel, Research Fellow at the University of Amsterdam's Center for Research in Experimental Economics and Political Decision-making.

Jerry L. Petr, Professor of Economics, University of Nebraska-Lincoln.

Michael K. Salemi, Zachary Smith Professor of Economics, University of North Carolina, Chapel Hill. Chair of the American Economic Association's Committee on Economic Education.

Paul A. Samuelson, Institute Professor of Economics, Emeritus, Massachusetts Institute of Technology. Nobel Laureate in Economic Science, 1970.

Phillip Saunders, Professor of Economics, Indiana University-Bloomington. Director of the Indiana University Center for Economic Education.

John J. Siegfried, Professor of Economics, Vanderbilt University. Secretary-Treasurer of the American Economic Association and Former Chair of the AEA Committee on Economic Education.

William B. Walstad, Professor of Economics, University of Nebraska-Lincoln. Director of the National Center for Research in Economic Education. Associate Editor of the *Journal of Economic Education*.

Michael Watts, Professor of Economics, Purdue University. Director of the Purdue University Center for Economic Education. Associate Editor of the *Journal of Economic Education*.

Arthur L. Welsh, Professor of Economics, Pennsylvania State University. Former Vice President and Director of the College and University Program of the Joint Council on Economic Education.

CHAPTER 1

THE TEACHING OF ECONOMICS: AN INTRODUCTION

William B. Walstad
Phillip Saunders

Teaching undergraduate economics has become more important in the work of economics faculty in recent years. Colleges and universities are giving more scrutiny to teaching because of student, parent, and public concerns about the high cost of education and what students are receiving from faculty in the classroom. The composition of most campus student bodies has changed, which means the students now sitting in economics classes are more diverse and have different interests than the student population in past decades. Economics departments have experienced declines in enrollments in economics courses and in the number of economics majors in recent years. Certainly, these trends and developments that are affecting higher education in general and economics in particular are forcing many economics professors to rethink what they are doing in the classroom. Economics departments are also seeking new ways to attract students and motivate them in their study of the subject. This book is designed to help economics faculty and departments meet these challenges.

Some History

It would be inaccurate to state that the economics profession has not been interested in the teaching of economics, but interest in teaching seems to have

spurts. As Paul Samuelson states in the foreword to this volume, top
ts and leaders of the profession have frequently taken an interest in the
challenges of teaching or writing economics textbooks, especially for principles
courses, and there has been periodic renewals of interest in the problems of teaching
economics in every decade since the end of World War II. During the late 1940s,
a special committee of the American Economic Association that was headed by
Horace Taylor of Columbia University studied the teaching of undergraduate
economics and issued an extensive report that was published as a special
supplement to the *American Economic Review* (Taylor, et al., 1950). In 1957, the
economics department at Grinnell College conducted a survey of instructional
methods in principles courses. In 1958 they hosted a conference on the teaching of
economics that resulted in a proceedings volume on the topic (Knopf and Strauss,
1960). During the 1960s, two conferences on new developments in the teaching of
economics, one in 1966 and the other in 1968, were held at Stanford University.
The proceedings from those conferences were published in the form of two books
edited by Keith Lumsden (1967, 1970). In the 1970s, the Federal Reserve Bank of
Minneapolis published a volume on the goals and objectives for the principles
course (Larsen and Nappi, 1976) that was widely distributed to colleges and
universities and went through a number of printings.

The 1970s was also the formative period for the development of the Teaching
Training Program (TTP) that was sponsored by the Joint Council on Economic
Education (now the National Council) and conducted at major universities
throughout the nation during that decade and into the 1980s (Hansen, Saunders,
Welsh, 1980). The TTP resource manual also served as the inspiration for the
development of a stand-alone and comprehensive volume for economics professors
and graduate students, *The Principles of Economics Course: A Handbook for
Instructors* (Saunders and Walstad, 1990). Six reviews of it in the *Journal of
Economic Education* (Fall 1990) were very positive, and about 6,000 copies were
shipped by McGraw-Hill to economics faculty, graduate students and departments
for use at colleges and universities. When the TTP was revived again during a
series of 1992–1994 national workshops, the *Handbook* served as the workshop
textbook (Salemi, Saunders, and Walstad, 1996).

By 1995, the *Handbook* had become dated, so a decision was made to thoroughly
revise and update it to make it useful to economics faculty teaching in the late
1990s and into the next century. That work has been accomplished in this current
version of the *Handbook*. For readers familiar with the original publication, the
changes are substantial. The chapters have been organized into four main sections
instead of three. There are new chapters on micro principles, the qualities of an
effective teacher, gender and diversity, active and cooperative learning, experimental economics, using technology, student and faculty evaluation, the intermediate
course, and the major. In fact, nine of the twenty-one chapters that follow this one
are new. The other eleven chapters have been revised, some quite extensively, and
new material has been added.

Purpose

The new *Handbook* book should be of value to anyone teaching a course in undergraduate economics, whether the person is a new graduate student teaching a principles of economics course for the first time or a senior professor with twenty years of classroom experience who teaches advanced courses. Each instructor should be able to read this book and gather ideas that will make him or her a better teacher of the course he or she has been assigned to teach. The new graduate teaching assistant should get many tips on how to organize and teach the first principles of economics course. The experienced professor should read the book and reflect on what he or she is doing in the classroom and consider new approaches for teaching familiar content.

The contents of the book are directly applicable to economics teaching at all levels of undergraduate instruction—principles, intermediate, and advanced. The earlier version of this book focussed almost exclusively on the principles of economics course because that was the one course that most instructors teach. In this version of the *Handbook*, however, the coverage has been broadened to the teaching of all undergraduate economics courses. The reason for the change was that several reviews in the *Journal of Economic Education* stated that the value of the book went beyond principles. For example, one stated that the book should be "required reading for any professor or graduate student who wants to improve his or her teaching of economics (not just principles)" (Lillydahl, 1990, p. 436). These comments reinforced the need to broaden coverage and show wider application to all economics courses. Consequently, several chapters were added on intermediate economics courses and the economics major, and all chapter authors were asked, wherever possible, to discuss teaching or give examples beyond just principles. Thus, the title of the *Handbook* has been changed.

The four sections of the *Handbook* cover the main teaching issues that most instructors face. The first section discusses the goals and objectives of economics instruction in principles and intermediate economics courses, and for the economics major. The second section covers topics that create the foundation for effective teaching and learning in economics, such as instructor responsibilities, insights from learning theory, gender and diversity issues, the use of graphs and statistics, and research on teaching college economics. The third and longest section explores different methods and materials for economics instruction, some traditional and some new, such as lectures, textbooks, discussion, writing, active learning, experiments, and technology. Specific examples are given in these chapters to show how the teaching method or material can be used to enhance undergraduate economics instruction. The fourth and final section focuses on the evaluation of students through classroom tests and the assessment of teaching by the instructor, students, or faculty colleagues. What follows is a further explanation of the section rationale and a brief overview of the contents of each chapter.

﹍꜀ꞁꞁomics faculty must decide what they want their students to learn from economics instruction. Accordingly, the first part of the book discusses the basic goals and objectives of principles of economics, intermediate economic theory courses, and also the economics major. Instructional goals and objectives are important for any economics professor to think about because they determine the economic content taught, the weight given to each part of the course content, and the methods used for teaching. Five perspectives on the goals and objectives issue are offered, three on the principles of economics courses, one on intermediate economics theory courses, and one on the collection of courses that constitute the economics major.

In Chapter 2, Robert Frank presents what he thinks is the best way to teach an introductory course in principles of microeconomics. He advocates the use of a short list of economic propositions that are applied in many different contexts. The short list ensures that students are not overwhelmed by the numerous economic concepts that fill many principles textbooks, and focuses only on those that are important for giving students new insights into their world given the time constraints for the course. This approach works according to Frank because students learn best through examples and repetition of how basic economics concepts can be used to explain the many facets of human behavior. Students in his course at Cornell University are encouraged to think like economists and become "economic naturalists" to answer such puzzling questions as "Why is airline food so bad?" or "Why are Australian films so good?". Frank ends his essay with four interesting examples of the type of three-page papers that he asks students to write using economic reasoning to answer perplexing questions from life experience.

Chapter 3 turns to the principles of macroeconomics course and offers the views of Michael Boskin, a professor of economics at Stanford University, on how this course should be taught. According to Boskin, the primary focus of the course should be on economic policy. He thinks that instructors should discuss the standards of performance for measuring policy achievement and stress how these standards have changed over time. Another point emphasized throughout his chapter is the need to include an international dimension throughout the course so that students do not have to wait until the end to learn about the role of international trade and finance. A large part of the chapter is devoted to problems in the typical principles textbook such as the limitations in the content coverage, especially international economics, and organizational confusion. Many of the problems cited by Professor Boskin are given further attention in Chapter 13 because the textbook has a major influence on what instructors teach and students learn.

In Chapter 4, Campbell McConnell offers his reflections on the principles course based on his experience at the University of Nebraska and as author of a principles of economics textbook now in its thirteenth edition. He begins with a look at the evolution of the course and the observation that the content has become more comprehensive and sophisticated over the years while at the same time student abilities to handle the reading and the quantitative material have probably diminished. Compounding this learning problem is the poor preparation of instructors to teach the course and the lack of interest among many senior staff in teaching principles. McConnell also discusses both sides of the controversy over content coverage, and whether instructors should use a short-list as Frank advocates or whether there should be broader coverage, as McConnell prefers. The chapter also discusses which course inputs and which outputs are most influential in instruction. In fact, some issues raised in this section are examined later in Chapter 8 and Chapter 11. He concludes the chapter with the insightful observation that we may expect too much from the principles course: our dissatisfaction arises from the difference between our aspirations for the course and our accomplishments with it.

With Chapter 5 the discussion of goals and objectives moves from the principles to the intermediate level of economics instruction. In this chapter, George Davis and Homer Erekson discuss their experiences with teaching intermediate microeconomic and macroeconomic theory courses at Miami University. They identify six content and pedagogical issues affecting the teaching of intermediate theory courses. These issues cover a range of content and pedagogical concerns such as the degree of formalism in the course, the place of intermediate courses in the economics curriculum, the sequence of theory course (micro or macro first), the coverage of content (breadth or depth), keeping content current, and motivating students to learn. The final parts of the chapter discuss the content design of intermediate microeconomic and macroeconomic theory courses and differences in the textbooks published for these courses.

Economics remains a popular major with students even though there has been a substantial decline in the number of majors in recent years. John Siegfried, a professor of economics at Vanderbilt, offers a comprehensive review of the economics major in Chapter 6. He begins by stating that the primary goal of the major is to get students to understand how to "think like economists," and then proceeds to explain in detail what that goal means. The second part of his chapter turns to the reality of the economic major and explains how it is delivered through coursework from the principles to the intermediate to the advanced level of instruction. The final parts of the chapter assess the strengths and weaknesses of the economics major, make recommendations for what the series of courses that constitute the major should be, and outline how to make the ideal economics major work. This discussion of goals and objectives for the economics major should be helpful for faculty members or department chairs considering improvements in the major at their institutions.

Foundations for Teaching Economics

Effective instruction in economics depends on more than deciding what content to teach or the selection of course objectives. Teaching places demands on professors that they must fully understand and accept if they are to become good teachers. Some knowledge of learning theory will assist instructors in guiding instructional practices and motivating students. The characteristics, backgrounds, and interests of students differ, so there must also be an awareness of how to address these individual differences. Professors must know how to make the best use of mathematics, graphs, and statistics as tools for teaching economics instead of having them be roadblocks to learning. Finally, instructors will want to know what insights can be gleaned from research on the teaching of economics. Each of these topics is discussed in this section of the *Handbook*.

Good teaching of economics requires hard work as Kenneth Elzinga clearly and persuasively explains in Chapter 7. Elzinga, a professor of economics at the University of Virginia, believes that a major goal for the economics teacher is to inspire students so they have a lasting appreciation of the subject and want to learn more about it. To make this happen requires a great deal of time and effort—inspiration requires perspiration. Economics instructors need to understand their teaching style and use it to full advantage. They must direct their energy into the careful preparation and delivery of lectures, the most commonly used method of instruction. They have to assess course content and decide on a short list of economic principles that can be meaningfully taught given the time constraints. They need to understand the characteristics of students, figure out how to relate to them and get them to own the vocabulary of economics. In short, the chapter reminds economics professors of the responsibilities they have if they want to inspire students through their teaching.

In Chapter 8, Phillip Saunders, a professor of economics at Indiana University, reviews some major findings from learning theory that have the most relevance for undergraduate economics instruction. He begins the chapter by defining learning and outlining the cognitive and affective domains of learning. He then describes four major "schools" of learning theory, emphasizing the increasing acceptance of the information processing theory. The major part of the chapter presents four propositions from learning theory—the limited capacity of the human mind to process information, the importance of prior experience, the importance of motivation, and the dominance of visual over verbal material—together with the implications for acquiring, retaining, and transferring knowledge in economics courses. Final attention is devoted to instructional objectives and the distinction between the cognitive and affective domains in setting learning objectives for students.

Chapter 9 turns to the topic of student differences, in particular gender, and discusses how they affect both course content and pedagogy. Robin Bartlett, a professor of economics at Denison University, and Marianne Ferber, a professor of economics at the University of Illinois, begin their chapter by documenting how women are underrepresented in higher education in general and economics in particular. They then examine the traditional content of economics courses, especially principles courses, fault them for their lack of coverage of topics related to or important for women and minorities, and make recommendations for changes to "humanize" economics content and classroom instruction. This analysis covers how to include gender topics in courses, instructional methods that seem most effective, handling differences in the learning styles of students, and creating a positive environment for learning in the classroom. Their set of recommendations is extensive and worth considering by all instructors.

The use of mathematics and statistics in economics teaching is the subject of Chapter 10 by William Becker, a professor of economics at Indiana University. He first argues that the mathematical notation typically used by economics professors is not conducive to helping students learn economics because this mathematical shorthand is not consistent with the symbolism used in other courses. The chapter then discusses the use of graphs in the teaching of economics and presents practical advice on their classroom use. Becker also identifies many mathematical, quantitative, and statistical skills that are essential for students to learn if they are to understand economics based on their importance for understanding articles in the popular press or economic policy debates. He suggests specific ways for making notation consistent with the notation students use in their other courses.

The final chapter of the foundations section is a review of the research literature on the teaching of college economics by John Siegfried and by William Walstad, a professor of economics at the University of Nebraska. After a brief historical overview, the main sections of the chapter discuss the relationship between student characteristics and economics teaching and the influence of course format on student learning. A final section reviews research on the economics major. The chapter is not a technical one, but is designed to describe for economic professors what research work has been conducted in economics education over the past thirty-five years. The authors draw major conclusions from the research literature that have implications for the teaching and learning of economics and should be of interest to administrators.

Instructional Methods

The third section of this *Handbook* covers subjects related to how instruction should be conducted. As might be expected, this part of the book is the longest because there are a multitude of instructional methods and teaching practices that can be used to improve economics teaching. This section focuses on seven main topics—lectures, textbooks, student writing, active and cooperative learning, classroom experiments, and the use of technology. Although this section provides instructors with several practical teaching tips, its main purpose is to provide an in-depth discussion of the major educational methods that can be used in teaching undergraduate economics courses.

Lectures are the most widely-used method of instruction by economics professors and, unfortunately for students, the one most professors think they know all about. In Chapter 12, Phillip Saunders and Arthur Welsh, a professor of economics at Penn State University, discuss this traditional method of teaching. They provide the new and even the most experienced lecturer with important ideas and techniques for more effective lecturing. They emphasize that planning and organizing the lectures are central elements of lecture preparation. They stress the need for professors to evaluate lectures so they can figure out if students are actually learning something from this form of one-way communication. These activities are just as important as lecture delivery. Ways of overcoming two common criticisms of the lecture method are also discussed in the chapter, as are seven things to help instructors improve their lecture presentations.

Chapter 13 is devoted to an examination of the principles textbook because it is the one pedagogical feature that is used, along with the lecture, in almost all principles courses and because there is a large publishing industry providing products for the principles market. In the chapter, William Walstad, Michael Watts, an economics professor at Purdue University, and William Bosshardt, an economics professor at Florida Atlantic University, offer insights about this central instructional resource. They first provide a brief history of the use of textbooks for teaching principles from the days of Adam Smith to the publication of Paul Samuelson's influential text to give instructors a sense of how textbooks have evolved. They then describe the economic structure of the market for principles textbooks and highlight several criticisms of current texts, some of which were raised by Michael Boskin in Chapter 3. The chapter also presents a detailed content analysis of some leading principles textbooks across concept clusters. What emerges from the analysis are data to support the conclusion that there is a high degree of standardization in the principles textbook market, which can either be characterized as monopolistically competitive or oligopolistic. The final section of the chapter offers practical suggestions for the selection and use of a principles textbook that will help instructors make better use of this educational resource.

Classroom discussion can be a very powerful method for teaching economics if instructors know how to use it. In Chapter 14, W. Lee Hansen, a professor of economics at the University of Wisconsin, and Michael Salemi, a professor of economics at the University of North Carolina, offer their insights for how to use classroom discussion to get students to "think like economists" and become active participants in the learning process. They emphasize the importance of using two-way talk in the classroom, and discuss each of the five elements that underlie effective classroom discussions: making discussions an important part of course planning; selecting discussion material; preparing discussion questions; creating a contract for effective discussion; and the actual conduct of the discussion itself. Many instructors should find their matrix showing a two-way classification of discussion questions and their specific examples helpful in improving discussions in their own classes.

In Chapter 11, the close relationship between writing and thinking is explored by Jerry L. Petr, a professor of economics at the University of Nebraska. Emphasizing writing as a way to create learning rather than a way to evaluate it, Petr discusses a variety of different forms of student writing including notetaking, compiling an economic issues notebook, cartoon analysis, and problem sets and data interpretation in addition to more traditional out-of-class papers or in-class essay examinations. Petr offers many specific examples and suggestions from his own experience which should prove useful to instructors interested in helping their students learn economics through writing, as well as those interested in improving student writing skills.

Passive instruction seems to be the norm in economics, which is an unfortunate state of affairs given what can be done in the classroom to encourage active learning. Beverly Cameron, an economics professor at the University of Manitoba, offers many intriguing suggestions for active and cooperative learning techniques that economics professors can use in Chapter 16. The ideas include one-minute papers, buzz groups, simulations, and directed discussions, all of which ask students to participate actively in their learning by thinking, writing, talking, or reflecting on economic content rather than being a passive spectator who simply listens to the professor pontificate on a topic. Groups can also be used in many different ways to promote collaborative learning as Cameron illustrates in the second part of the chapter. Collaborative learning groups are not informal ones formed just for one activity or a class period, but instead ones where students work together as a team over time to solve problems, discuss issues, make presentations, and give feedback. She cites specific examples of projects and assignments that an economic instructor can use to promote collaborative learning and offers guidelines on how to make it work.

One of the most exciting advances in economics and for the teaching of economics has been experimental economics. Economists now regularly use experiments to gain insights and test theories about economic decision-making in such situations as auctions, bargaining, games, and markets. Many of these experiments can be incorporated into classroom instruction to help students understand important economic concepts and promote student interest. In Chapter 17, Charles Holt, a professor of economics at the University of Virginia, and Tanga McDaniel, of the University of Amsterdam, give several examples of experiments and games and explain how to conduct them with students. They also offer practical suggestions for using experiments and games to stimulate interest in economics and reinforce traditional instruction. No special skill or expertise in experimental research is required, however, should an instructor wish to adopt this approach to active learning.

New technology constantly becomes available for teaching economics and other subjects. The problem for the economics professor is how to make the best use of technology to improve student understanding. In Chapter 18, William Walstad, Ann Fender and Jean Fletcher, economics professors at Gettysburg College, and Wayne Edwards, an economics graduate student at the University of Nebraska, discuss this problem based on their experiences in using technology for teaching. The authors focus on three types of technology that are being used—television, microcomputer software, and the Internet. Television is not especially high-tech relative to the Internet, but it does permit the instructor to bring the "real" world to the classroom. Microcomputer software in the form of spreadsheets, simulations, and tutorials lets students conduct experiments and get immediate feedback on their thinking. The Internet gives students access to extensive information resources and immediate communication. The authors offer specific classroom suggestions for each technology so that teaching will be more effective and student learning is enhanced. The chapter also provides a historical and realistic perspective on the promises of technology for teaching economics lest a professor think that it will revolutionize economics instruction or eliminate jobs.

Evaluation of Instruction

In the final section of the *Handbook*, the focus shifts to the evaluation of instruction in its several forms. There may be evaluation *of students* to find out what they have learned in a course, which is most often accomplished through classroom tests. There can also be evaluation *by students* to find out what they think about an instructor or a course. Instructors may also conduct an evaluation *of themselves* either by having their classes videotaped or having their students complete course questionnaires. Finally, there is evaluation *by other faculty,* such as peers or administrators, who may use the information to make important personnel decisions about salary, promotion, or tenure.

The two basic tools used by most instructors to find out what students learn are the multiple choice test and the essay test. Careful development and use of these assessment instruments are needed if they are to provide accurate measurement of student performance in economics courses. In Chapter 19, William Walstad makes the case for multiple choice testing by citing reasons why this assessment procedure is considered superior to that of the essay test by test and measurement experts. He then provides a detailed explanation of how to construct multiple choice tests for classroom use, and identifies pitfalls to avoid in writing items or selecting items from test banks. The final section of the chapter describes basic statistics for analyzing individual items and overall test results, explains how to interpret the data, and how to use tests to promote active learning.

The assessment position is reversed in Chapter 20 where Arthur Welsh and Phillip Saunders make the case for essay questions and tests. They review the strengths and weaknesses of essay examinations, and explore situations in which essay questions can be used to advantage. General guidelines to use in preparing questions and tests and suggestions for grading student answers are offered in the belief that careful preparation and grading can overcome some of the weaknesses of essay examinations and improve their strengths.

In Chapter 21, Michael Salemi and Alex Cowell, a graduate student in economics at the University of North Carolina, discuss the advantages of using videotape for teacher development and self evaluation. Many economics faculty and graduate student instructors who have had themselves videotaped and conducted a self-analysis of their performance have found the experience to be one of the most effective for giving insights about teaching. Salemi and Cowell explain three other ways in which videotape can help improve instruction in addition to critiquing actual classroom presentations: the use of "trigger tapes" to initiate discussion of selected problems; the use of video to illustrate various teaching techniques; and the use of videotape to master particular skills in "micro teaching" situations; and they offer several suggestions for implementing a successful critiquing program. The chapter concludes with a five step approach to using videotape for self-evaluation for those instructors who do not want to involve another person in the critiquing process.

William Walstad and Phillip Saunders conclude the *Handbook* with an examination of student and faculty evaluation of instruction in Chapter 22. They recommend that instructors get feedback from students long before end-of-course evaluations are given to students, and suggest a variety of classroom assessment strategies for getting current information about what students think or what they are learning. They also discuss how to interpret data from evaluation questionnaires, and factors that positively and negatively affect these evaluations. The second part of the chapter turns to faculty evaluation of instruction, either by faculty themselves or by peers and administrators. Again in this part of the chapter, the authors provide many suggestions for using either self or peer analysis to improve instruction. Evaluation of teaching will not be effective, however, unless economics teachers are committed to review their classroom practices and are willing to make changes in light of feedback on their performance. It is this commitment to a continual assessment of teaching behavior and practices that will improve economics instruction.

Conclusion

The teaching of undergraduate economics is far too important to be left to chance or poor instruction. The material summarized above, and elaborated in detail in the chapters which follow, makes clear that it is possible to improve significantly the quantity and quality of student learning in undergraduate economics courses. Effective course planning and effective teaching are skills that faculty can learn and develop through study and practice of what is currently known by leaders in the field. It is our hope that this volume will serve as a useful and continuing reference for departments and instructors who take seriously their responsibilities for educating millions of students in the vital subject of economics.

REFERENCES

Hansen, W.L., Saunders, P., and Welsh, A.L. (1980). Teacher training programs in college economics: Their development, current status, and future prospects. *Journal of Economic Education*, 11(2), (Spring), 1-9.

Knopf, K. and Strauss, J.H. (Eds.). (1960). *The teaching of elementary economics.* New York: Holt Rinehart, and Winston.

Larsen, A.F. and Nappi, A.T. (Eds.). (1976). *Goals and objectives of the introductory college-level course in economics*. Minneapolis: Federal Reserve Bank of Minneapolis.

Lillydahl, J. (1990). Review of *The principles of economics course: A handbook for instructors*. *Journal of Economic Education*, 21(4), (Fall), 436-439.

Lumsden, K. (Ed.). (1967). *New developments in the teaching of economics*. Englewood Cliffs, New Jersey: Prentice-Hall.

Lunsden, K. (Ed.). (1970). *Recent research in economic education*. Englewood Cliffs, New Jersey: Prentice-Hall.

Salemi, M.K., Saunders, P., and Walstad, W.B. (1996). Teacher training programs in economics: Past, present, and future. *American Economic Review*, 86(2), (May), 460-464.

Saunders, P. and Walstad, W.B. (1990). *The principles of economics course: A handbook for instructors*. New York: McGraw-Hill.

Taylor, H., et al. (1950). The teaching of undergraduate economics, Report of the Committee on Undergraduate Teaching of Economics and the Training of Economists. *American Economic Review, Supplement*, (40), December, 1-226.

CHAPTER 2

SOME THOUGHTS ON THE
MICRO PRINCIPLES COURSE

Robert H. Frank

The best way to teach introductory microeconomics—or any subject, for that matter—is to expose students to repeated applications of a short list of the core ideas of the discipline. But *whose* short list? If we asked a thousand economists to provide their own versions, we'd get a thousand different lists. Yet to dwell on their differences would be to miss their essential similarities. Indeed, almost all would contain variants of most of the following propositions:

- The optimal decision equates the relevant costs and benefits at the margin.

- Some costs (e.g., opportunity costs) matter, others (e.g., sunk costs) don't.

- A market is in equilibrium when no opportunities for individual advantage remain.

- Market equilibrium is sometimes optimal (the invisible hand often works), and sometimes not (e.g., the tragedy of the commons).

- Everyone does best when each person does whatever he or she does best in relative terms (the principle of comparative advantage).

- Incentives matter, in the design of both private contracts and public policy.

My point is not that this is the *best* short list, but that the introductory course will be taught most effectively if it begins with a well articulated short list of *some* sort, and then doggedly hammers away at it, illustrating and applying each principle in context after context. (See also Chapters 4, and 6–8.)

Most introductory economics textbooks, of course, do nothing of the sort. Oh, the core principles are found in these books, all right. But so is virtually every other economic principle that has surfaced over the last 200 years. The mind-boggling detail of these books—thousand-plus page encyclopedic reference tomes, many of them—could not have been purposely designed to more effectively camouflage the short list of principles that really matter.

Needless to say, the many distinguished and talented authors of these books did not deliberately set out to overwhelm students with detail. Indeed, the process by which the current introductory texts evolved to their current form is itself a telling illustration of the principle that rational individual actions often generate an equilibrium that is far from optimal.

An important feature of this process is that adoption decisions are often made by committee. When five busy faculty members meet to consider textbooks, broad philosophical and methodological discussions quickly give way to detailed comparisons of the topic coverage. Each committee member, of course, has his or her own favorite set of topics. And from the individual faculty member's perspective, one of the most costly mistakes is to choose a text that omits several of her favorite topics. Choosing such a book means that she will either have to abandon those topics when she teaches the course, or else have to prepare supplementary readings or special handouts in order to cover it. Time is short and, for many, the tenure clock is ticking.

Thus it is no surprise that, given two otherwise equally attractive texts, the one with broader topic coverage has a clear edge. Book publishers know this, of course, and have become understandably reluctant to invest in texts with limited topic coverage. Without exception, the best-selling introductory texts now follow the encyclopedic format. (See also Chapters 3 and 13.)

At one level, this might seem the most sensible compromise since, after all, professors can always pick and choose from the topics available in the text. Yet, as a practical matter, few of us attempt to fine-tune our assignments in this way. ("In chapter 4, read sections 4.1, 4.3, 4.4-4.6, 4.8, pages 231-233 of section 4.9, pages 245-247 of section 4.11, and sections 4.14-4.16.") In most cases, professors either assign the entire text, or else attempt to cover, in sequence, as many chapters as time permits. On the rare occasion when a professor does take the trouble to assign only excerpts from one of the encyclopedic texts, his students invariably complain about having been forced to spend so much for a book that was used so sparingly.

When the dust settles, most students leave the introductory course never having fully grasped the essence of microeconomics. Thus the opportunity cost concept, so utterly central to our understanding of what it means to think like an economist, is but one among hundreds of other concepts that go by in a blur. Opportunity cost is more important than, say, the idea that the short-run average cost curve is tangent to the long-run average cost curve at the output level for which capacity is at the optimal level. But students would never realize that from the relative emphasis these topics receive in many of our introductory textbooks.

The simple fact is that most of us learn best by example and repetition. We absorb ideas more quickly and retain them longer when the material is concrete rather than abstract. One clear explanation is often sufficient to enable a bright student to grasp a complex concept. But there is a deep difference between merely understanding a concept—in the sense of being able to answer a test question about it the next day—and really *knowing* it. Even the very brightest students never fully internalize a concept unless they use it repeatedly.

Someone who accepts this principle must therefore ask the following kind of question about the design of an economics course: Would it be more valuable to expose students to yet another application of the opportunity cost concept, or to yet another application of one of the other fundamental concepts—or would the same time be better spent discussing why the average fixed cost curve is asymptotic to the quantity axis? At *some* point the answer to that question is that it is better to move on to the technical properties of the average fixed cost curve. But in my view that point does not come during the student's first course in microeconomics.

The guiding principle for my micro principles course at Cornell is that each section should contribute equally at the margin to the student's ability to think like an economist. By "think like an economist" I mean not just to be *able* to apply the core principles to observations and experience, but also to have an *inclination* to do so. Both my topic coverage and mode of presentation are shaped by this objective.

To help identify which ideas are most important, I take cues from research showing that people often systematically violate the prescriptions of the rational choice model. For example, whereas the model says that rational persons will ignore sunk costs when making decisions, many people are in fact strongly influenced by them. Thus, someone who has purchased a basketball ticket for $50 dollars is more likely to drive through a snowstorm to get to the game than is an equally avid fan who won her ticket in a raffle. A rational ticket holder should weigh the benefit of attending the game against the cost of driving through the storm when deciding whether to make the trip—and if the former is larger, she should go, no matter how she came to acquire the ticket.

Especially in my lectures on consumer behavior, I call students' attention to situations in which they themselves are likely to make similarly irrational choices. Because student resources are limited, it makes sense to focus on precisely those issues for which knowing price theory is most likely to be helpful.

It may seem natural to wonder whether discussing examples of irrational choices might confuse students who are struggling to master the details of the rational choice model. Ironically, however, my experience has been exactly to the contrary. Such examples actually underscore the normative message of the traditional theory. Students who are exposed to them invariably gain a deeper standing of the basic theoretical principles at issue. Indeed, they often seem to take an almost conspiratorial pride in being able to see through their roommates' errors of judgment.

Another highly effective device for stimulating interest in microeconomics is to train students to become "economic naturalists." Studying biology enables people to observe and marvel at many details of life that would otherwise have escaped notice. For the naturalist, a walk in a quiet woods becomes an adventure. In much the same way, studying microeconomics can enable students to see the mundane details of ordinary existence in a sharp new light. Throughout my course, I try to develop economic intuition by means of examples and applications drawn from everyday experience. My aim is to teach students to see each feature of the manmade landscape as the reflection of an implicit or explicit cost-benefit calculation.

To illustrate, the economic naturalist is someone who ponders questions like, "Why do most cars with manual transmissions have five forward speeds while those with automatics have only three or four?" The more speeds a transmission has—manual or automatic—the better a car's performance and fuel economy will be. So why fewer speeds on automatics? The reason is that performance and fuel economy are not all we care about. We also want to keep the price of the car within limits. Automatic transmissions are more complex than manual ones, and the cost of adding an extra speed is accordingly greater. The benefits of adding an extra speed, by contrast, are roughly the same in both cases. If car makers follow the rule, "Add an extra speed if its benefits outweigh its costs," then automatics will have fewer speeds than manuals.

I try, whenever possible, to use a simple drawing or other illustration that relates in some way to the examples I discuss. For instance, when discussing the automobile transmission question, I generally display a slide of a five-speed gear shift knob on the screen. For reasons that learning theorists could probably explain (see Chapter 8), this practice seems to help root the examples more firmly in the student's mind, even though the illustrations themselves typically contain no specific economic content.

My goal of training students to become economic naturalists has also helped dictate which topics to cover and which to leave out. Other things equal, the more a topic enables us to make sense of our observations and experience, the stronger the case for including it. Thus, I find it astonishing that many people receive college degrees without ever once having been exposed to ideas like the prisoner's dilemma or the tragedy of the commons. These and other simple applications of game theory are not only ideal vehicles for illustrating several of the core ideas of microeconomics, but they also have enormous power to explain events in the world.

Some instructors may ask how a less-is-more version of the introductory course can find time to include such topics, which, after all, do not even make it into some of the encyclopedic texts. The answer is that there is plenty of time, provided we eschew topics like the distinction between long- and short-run cost curves. This means that introductory students will not learn that a perfectly competitive firm should shut down in the short-run if the market price fails to cover average variable costs. But this is a small price to pay for the opportunity to learn a general principle that explains, among other things, why urban freeways are too crowded, why whales have been hunted to near extinction, why the North Atlantic is overfished, why the ozone layer is in danger, why many fail to vote, and why the National Hockey League has a helmet rule.

No matter how lively and engaging our lectures may be, students won't really learn the principles of price theory unless they use them actively—by solving problems that both test and extend their understanding. Most of the material I present in lectures is imbedded in the context of specific examples that illustrate and apply the core principles. These examples prepare students for the kinds of questions they will encounter on exams and problem sets.

The world is a more competitive place now than it was when I started teaching in 1972. In arena after arena, business as usual is no longer good enough. Whereas baseball players used to drink beer and go fishing during the off season, they now lift weights and ride exercise bicycles. And whereas my fellow assistant professors and I used to work on our houses on weekends, the current crop spends its weekends at the office. The competition for student attention has grown similarly more intense. There are many tempting courses in the typical college curriculum, and even more tempting diversions outside the classroom. Students are freer than ever to pick and choose.

Yet many of us seem to operate under the illusion that most freshmen arrive with a burning desire to become economics majors. And many of us seem not yet to have recognized that students' cognitive abilities and powers of concentration are scarce resources. To hold our ground we must become not only more selective in what we teach, but also more effective as advocates for our discipline. We must persuade students that we offer something of value.

A well conceived and well executed introductory course can teach them more about human behavior in a single term than virtually any other course in the university. This course can and should be an intellectual adventure of the first order. Not all students who take the kind of course I propose will go on to become economics majors. But many will, and even those who do not will leave with a sense of admiration for the power of economic ideas.

A salesman knows that he gets only one chance to make a good first impression on a potential customer. The introductory micro course is our discipline's one shot at making a good impression on students. By trying to teach them everything we know, we often squander this opportunity.

To judge from comments on student course evaluations, one of the most successful learning devices in my course are the two brief term papers I assign. I conclude this essay with a copy of the handout I distribute to my class to help prepare students for writing these papers as shown in Appendix 1-1.

APPENDIX 1-1

Assignment: Three-Page Term Paper on Economic Naturalism

Your goal is to begin with a question based on some observation from your own experience, and then use economic reasoning in an attempt to answer it. You should plan on writing no more than three pages (750 words), and bear in mind that some of the best papers are shorter. Try to include a simple drawing or other illustration that relates in some way to your topic. Here are some examples:

Why do kitchens in modern American houses often occupy more than 30 percent of the ground floor area, compared to less than half that percentage in houses built near the turn of the century?

People untutored in the art of economic naturalism sometimes mention the "deepening love affair" between Americans and their kitchens. Or they may speculate that we build bigger kitchens because we spend more time in the kitchen than we used to. But although these responses are not wrong in any strict sense, neither are they explanations. Economic naturalists want to know what *causes* the growing affinity for kitchens. And the first explanation they search for is a significant change in the prices we face.

Perhaps the most important such change has been the rising price of our time. As wages grow, the implicit cost of the time we spend on nonwork activities grows. For example, when the wage rate is $30 per hour, the cost of taking an hour off to run an errand is ten times what it was when the wage was only $3 per hour. Time also becomes more costly as more and more families have both spouses at work. Rising real wages and the growing percentage of two-earner families have made it more attractive to do larger, but less frequent, shopping trips, and buying groceries in larger batches naturally creates a demand for more kitchen space to store them.

Technological changes have also contributed to growing kitchen size. The proliferation of automobile ownership has made it easier to transport large quantities of groceries; and refrigeration, freezing, special packaging, and the like have made it possible to store food for much longer periods. Economic naturalists recognize in these factors the seeds of plausible hypotheses about why modern kitchens are so much larger. They spend little energy investigating deepening love affairs for kitchens.

Why is airline food so bad?

Everyone complains about airline food. Indeed, if any serious restaurant dared to serve such food, it would go bankrupt. Our complaints seem to take for granted that airline meals should be just as good as the ones we eat in restaurants.

But why should they? The cost-benefit perspective makes clear that airlines should increase the quality of their meals if and only if the benefits would outweigh the costs of doing so. The benefits of better food are probably well measured by what passengers would be willing to pay for it, in the form of higher ticket prices.

If a restaurant-quality meal could be had for a mere $5 increase in costs, most people would probably be delighted to pay it. The difficulty, however, is that it would be much more costly than that to prepare significantly better meals at 39,000 feet in a tiny galley with virtually no time. It could be done, of course. An airline could remove 20 seats from the plane, install a modern, well-equipped kitchen, hire extra staff, spend more on ingredients, and so on. But these extra costs would be more like $50 per passenger than $5.

For all our complaints about the low quality of airline food, few of us would be willing to bear this extra burden. The sad result is that airline food is destined to remain unpalatable because the costs of making it better outweigh the benefits.

Many of us respond warmly to the maxim, "Anything worth doing is worth doing well." After all, it encourages a certain pride of workmanship that is often sadly lacking. As the airline food example makes clear, however, when the maxim is interpreted literally, it makes no sense. It is completely unmindful of the need to weigh costs against benefits. To do something well means to devote time, effort, and expense to it. But time, effort, and expense are scarce. To devote them to one activity makes them unavailable for another. Increasing the quality of one of the things we do thus necessarily means to reduce the quality of others—yet another application of the concept of opportunity cost. Every intelligent decision must be mindful of this tradeoff.

Everything we see in life is the result of some such compromise. For Steffi Graf to play tennis as well as she does means that she cannot become a concert pianist. And yet this obviously does not mean that she shouldn't spend *any* time playing the piano. It just means that she should hold herself to a lower standard there than in the tennis arena.

Why have paper towels replaced hot-air hand dryers in public restrooms?

In the 1950s and 1960s, paper towel dispensers were replaced by electric hot-air hand dryers in many public restrooms. More recently, however, it is the hot-air dryers themselves that are being replaced by paper towel dispensers.

The explanation for these movements naturally has to do with the costs and benefits of the different methods of drying hands. The hot-air dryers made their original appearance on the heels of a steady decline in the price of electricity. When power became cheap, as it did in the '50s and '60s, electric dryers became less expensive to operate and maintain than the traditional paper towel dispensers. With the Arab oil embargoes of the 1970s, however, the price of energy rose dramatically, making paper towels once again the hand-drying method of choice.

Some economic naturalists may also find it amusing to speculate about why the paper towel dispensers of today are so different from the earlier ones. Most current designs feature a continuous hand crank. The paper is inside on a roll, and the longer you turn the crank the longer sheet of paper towel you get. Older designs also had a roll of paper inside, but you had to pull the paper out by hand. Most of the older models would also release only a limited amount of paper with each pull. To get more, you had to reset the release mechanism on the front of the dispenser.

The advantage of the older design, from the establishment's point of view, was that it induced people to use less paper. Indeed, if your hands were wet enough it was difficult to get any paper at all because, when you pulled, the wet paper would simply tear away in your hands.

But if establishments saved on paper with the old design, why have they switched to the new? The answer is that saving on paper is not their only objective. They also want satisfied customers. Incomes are higher now than they were 30 years ago, and customers are willing to pay more for a more convenient way of drying their hands. The current design may use a little more paper, but it is so much less frustrating that customers seem happy to pay more for their meals or their gasoline in order to cover the extra costs.

Some people may respond that the old design, infuriating though it was, was better because of its paper-saving property. These people feel that it is wrong to waste paper, and that we ought to be willing to tolerate plenty of inconvenience to avoid doing so. The same people also often lament the thousands of trees that must be cut down in order to print each Sunday's *New York Times*. But trees are a renewable resource, which means there is no reason to treat them differently from any other scarce but renewable resource. When the demand for paper is high, we cut down more trees, to be sure. But the market also provides a strong incentive to plant new ones. The irony here is that the more paper we use, the more trees we have. If every metropolitan newspaper were to cease publication tomorrow, we would ultimately have *fewer* acres of forest, not more.

Why are Australian films so good?

Critics often remark with surprise that the Australian films shown in the U.S.— *Breaker Morant, Gallipoli, My Brilliant Career, Mad Max, Crocodile Dundee, The Last Wave, Picnic at Hanging Rock, Strictly Ballroom,* and others—are so much better than the average American film. On a moment's reflection, however, this is just what we ought to have expected. To see why, note the criteria by which people decide whether to see a film: Is it by a well-known director? Does it feature a favorite actor or actress? Has it gotten rave reviews in the media? Have friends who have seen it had good things to say about it? The one thing these early Australian films had in common was that few Americans had ever heard of the people who made or starred in them. Although Peter Weir, Paul Hogan, Judy Davis, Mel Gibson, and a few other Australian directors and actors have since gone on to fame in the U.S., they were virtually unknown at the time their films were first shown here. So the investors who were trying to decide which Australian films to book into U.S. theaters knew that their only chance for success lay in films that would generate good reviews and strong word-of-mouth—in a word, only the very best films. Anything less simply would not justify the heavy investments required to launch a movie in the American market. The economics of information thus tells us not that Australian films are of uniformly high quality, but that only the very highest-quality Australian films can hope make money in the U.S. market.

CHAPTER 3

SOME THOUGHTS ON TEACHING PRINCIPLES OF MACROECONOMICS

Michael J. Boskin

In this chapter I will discuss my views on teaching principles of macroeconomic with particular attention to the role of textbooks in this process.

In teaching at the principles level, the procedure we should follow in evaluating current macroeconomic policy is to define the current policy; define the state of the economy; measure our macroeconomic performance against what we believe to be appropriate norms; and then ask, "Can the government contribute to an improved performance? If it can, how? If it is hindering performance by its policy, what should it stop doing? What are the levers that government has for quick and decisive action when policy makers believe there is going to be a long and severe recession or a pronounced rampant inflation? How do we decide when to activate policies?" Monetary and fiscal *fine-tuning* measures are of little value, and cumulatively are probably harmful. But *if* the economy is *way* out of kilter, how can we tell when the circumstances are right for *gross* tuning?

It is within this framework that I wish to comment on what I think deserves increasing emphasis in our principles courses. First, I should observe that it is remarkable how much our performance standards for the economy have changed. In the mid 1980s it was not uncommon to view an unemployment rate between 6 percent and 7 percent as acceptable if accompanied by "modest" growth and a "low" inflation rate of about 4 percent. In the mid-1990s, 2½% real growth and a little under 6% unemployment, combined with stable 3% inflation, appear to be about all the economy can deliver with its current structure. Viewed in an historical perspective, one is prompted to ask, "Are those standards and goals the right ones?" What happened to the 4-4-1 we used to hear—4 percent growth, 4 percent unemployment, and 1 percent inflation—as our goals? A variety of reasons, including structural and demographic changes in the labor market and a long and sustained slowdown in productivity, probably make those goals unattainable today. One might also recall that it was only recently that a large number of economists, of a certain persuasion, suggested that high single-digit, or even low double-digit, inflation was not harmful to the economy, particularly if various contracts were indexed. To their credit, many economists fought hard against acceptance of high inflation rates as harmless. They pointed out that high inflation almost certainly means fluctuations in the inflation rate because it is very hard to sustain a stable 10 percent or 15 percent inflation rate. Inflation interacts insidiously with our tax system to erode incentives, and it distorts relative prices, as well as increasing their uncertainty. Some of the policy responses have been shown to be costly in themselves. Alan Blinder has suggested that the wage and price controls of the Nixon administration actually worsened the permanent inflation rate by about 1 1/2 percent. Most economists, myself included, believe that incomes policies would be no more successful.

The disinflation that began in 1981 was, indeed, very costly, although perhaps much less so than was anticipated. A common prediction in 1980 was that for each percentage-point reduction in inflation, we would bear a $220 billion loss (1980 dollars) in real output. That is at least double what the actual cumulative real output loss appears to have been. The rise in unemployment was severe in the 1981–82 recession, but the loss of output was much less than a rise of that size normally entails.

A most important and remarkable feature of the 1981–82 recession was the fact that almost *half* of the decline in real GNP was in our net exports. In the early 1990s, much of GDP growth was the increase in our net exports. This is probably the single most important fact to stress, for it reflects the internationalization of our economy, its trade and capital flows. I cannot overemphasize the implications of this development for what we teach in our principles courses. We can no longer teach them in the traditional way, that is, assuming a closed economy and leaving international trade and finance to the end, without sufficient time for serious treatment or integration into the macroeconomics. Although only a tenth of our economy is in exports and imports, most goods are traded on world markets *at the margin*.

Even more significant for macroeconomics are the until-recently unimaginable size of federal budget deficits, and the financing of about half of these deficits through capital imports. We are now obliged to place higher priority on our international economic activity, integrating it in to the mainline teaching of macroeconomics theory and policy. Macroeconomic/monetary policy can no longer be properly understood by our students without some familiarity with international trade and finance.

Let me turn now to a few further comments on how and what to teach in the elementary macroeconomics course and the role of textbooks in our teaching. The new classical macroeconomics, rational expectations, equilibrium models of the business cycle, Ricardian equivalence theorems, and the new theoretical refinements have important grains of truth in them. But I do not think that we have a perfect set of markets with perfect information that adjust instantaneously or that there are no price rigidities or wage rigidities or other types of problems that preclude the potential for any Keynesianesque macro policy action, ever. Nevertheless, I think that the types of stimuli we can expect are sharply curtailed because of the internationalization of our economy. We should be more cautious and modest in teaching about the range and efficacy of macropolicies.

We must also take pains to incorporate the rest of the world into our description of the process by which domestic macroeconomic policies affect the domestic and world economies. And we must be more realistic and cautious in our use of the traditional diagrams. We typically draw the aggregate supply and demand on the blackboard or on a transparency. We then say, "Now let's suppose we have a tax cut," and we shift the aggregate demand up by 20 percent. We assume a particular marginal propensity to save and a huge multiplier, and lo and behold, GNP is doubled! Deep down in our hearts, most of us would undoubtedly be delighted if the overwhelming majority of our students could simply identify the right sign, the right direction of change. But consider the subconscious misconceptions we introduce when we shift GNP so casually by, say, 50 percent without assigning and emphasizing realistic slopes and values and correct positions for the curves. It denigrates the seriousness of economic policy and does a great disservice. I have resolved that the next time I teach principles of economics I am going to redraw the curves more realistically.

In this quest for greater realism, how do we get our students to start thinking beyond the simple cash-flow analysis typical of the explanations of what drives consumption and investment spending, as depicted in the simple Keynesian "range" of the aggregate curves? I find it convenient to focus on three things: expectations, incentives, and time horizons. Students seem to find it intuitively plausible to relate consumption decisions to expectations. As aspiring medical students or engineers or lawyers, the students find the ideas of consuming out of permanent income or some longer-term average income plausible. They can readily understand the significance of expectations about future income, future interest rates, and future rates of inflation as determinants of consumption spending. I also find it tremendously convenient and effective to introduce some microeconomic concepts about incentives in order to develop their role in macroeconomics. The role of incentives helps to explain the macroeconomic composition of output between net exports and investment—the interest-sensitive parts of our economy—and consumer and government purchases; also, it helps us to understand the uses of income among saving and consumption of nondurable and durables. The three concepts—expectations, incentives, and time horizon—can be integrated as we gradually lengthen the time horizon of expectations about inflation or future income and explain how incentives translate our expectations into behavioral decisions. This permits us to build in and apply these concepts into explanations of how the private sector reacts to what they expect the public sector to do through monetary and fiscal actions. We may then raise the warranted questions about the efficacy of monetary and fiscal policy in this framework.

Let me sum up this part of the chapter by stating that I, like most economists, have rejected fine tuning. I won't pretend to know exactly where the distinction between fine and gross tuning should be drawn. However, I do want to indicate that it is my view that there is a modern eclectic macroeconomics in practice. In our teaching, we must try to give students an idea of what is at stake in different points of view, and upon what empirical information these views ultimately depend. We must also recognize that we are not at all certain of the full consequences of a large tax cut or major monetary expansion in any particular environment. They may very well depend on things that we do not control, and this has become especially true as our own macroeconomy has become internationalized.

We also should be teaching the most basic analysis, facts, historical episodes, and current events concerning the United States and world economies. We need to focus on why trade occurs, opportunity costs, arbitrage, supply and demand, the equaling of national income to the sum of its components, a brief factual overview of the economy such as the composition of spending on major categories of goods, the share of resources devoted to investment versus consumption, the differences between the average and marginal propensities to consume and import, marginal analysis, the distribution of income, measurement of economic well-being, the role of the price system as the primary and usually most efficient method of allocating resources, the role of profit rates as opposed to the absolute nominal dollar amount of profit in determining the allocation of the capital stock among uses, and so on.

In brief, I set as my goal helping my students to achieve mastery of enough simple analysis and descriptive overview that they can read the newspaper intelligently and critically. In addition, I hope they enjoy the process enough so that they will—or at least a substantial fraction of them will—keep up their interest in economics and economic events. If so, they can offset, at least partially, the decay of the knowledge they crammed into their brains in the short period of time they were in my course. An auxiliary goal is to paint a mural of the economy etched well enough in their minds to assist them in rejecting spurious analysis and claims, with due respect for the fact that the mural changes, sometimes rapidly.

A Framework for Thinking About Principles Textbooks

I believe that the single most important place to start thinking about the role of textbooks in principles courses is to realize that the textbook is part of a portfolio of inputs used to produce whatever output we produce. Other inputs in the portfolio include the supplementary study guide and similar materials that usually accompany textbooks, lectures, section meetings, examinations, and, increasingly, computer-assisted tutorials. Given the mix of these inputs (some universities offer them all, or each in varying proportions), the role of the textbook may acquire increasing or decreasing importance. I believe the textbook is important and will remain important for a substantial length of time. First, even the best students—and Stanford certainly has its share of them—need a ready reference beyond daily lectures. Second, the textbook should be an invaluable resource and reference for at least several years beyond the principles course. Third, many students absorb information better by reading than by listening or by interacting with a computer or a teaching assistant. Finally, the increasing preponderance of foreign graduate students with limited English language skills is straining the traditional role of the teaching assistant. For all of these reasons, modern technology is not likely to relegate the principles of economics textbook to the scrap heap.

It is also important to note that there are a huge number of principles of economics textbooks from which to choose. Although a large fraction of them follow in what has come to be called the Samuelson tradition, that is, an encyclopedia of at least first cuts at providing coverage of virtually all topics in economics, not all attempt to be so encyclopedic. They differ in length, topic coverage, level, quality of writing, visual effects, and a variety of other attributes. The overwhelming bulk adequately cover the 70 percent of common material we all tend to cover in our principles courses. (See Chapter 13.) Thus, although I have opinions about individual books, I believe that the segmentation of the market is socially desirable and that *matching* the type of textbook with the desired emphasis or complementary focus of the instructor, and the nature of the students in the course, is extremely important.

With this general perspective concerning the textbook and the principles course in mind, I turn now to several potential problems with principles textbooks as one of the inputs used in principles of economics courses.[1]

Potential Problems

At virtually every university, enormous heterogeneity exists in the class of students taking principles of economics. This heterogeneity occurs because of student differences with respect to interest in economics, intelligence, motivation, classroom experience, time input (which may be driven by other academic and nonacademic demands), and, as mentioned above, the ability to learn via alternative media (listening to lectures, reading, etc.). The heterogeneity poses a fundamental dilemma to anyone teaching principles, particularly those teaching at the introductory level (presumably, when one moves further along in the economics major, selection and other processes are at work in rendering classes less heterogeneous). The same issues that arise with respect to the level at which one pitches the lecture —lowest common denominator, median student, best students, and so on—and the costs and benefits of each also apply to the method by which each principles textbook is used, and indeed, written. Many principles textbooks have optional, more advanced appendixes, special exercises, and so on, for students who are doing well and who are well motivated. Some even have remedial chapters or sections within chapters. The ability to write textbook material that is simultaneously intelligible to the bulk of the students yet challenging to the brightest of them is probably the single most important characteristic by which we all evaluate, or at least pretend to evaluate, textbooks. I have no magic answers as to how to do better, but I can assure you that from the standpoint of a teacher who has used many textbooks, the ability to deal with this heterogeneity in the textbook is the driving force behind the use of other resources, such as computer-assisted tutorials and extensive and expensive faculty and graduate assistant time.

I personally believe that current textbooks do a better job segmenting the market by reading ability, mathematical ability, and so on, into a high, middle, and lower end than they do in dealing with heterogeneity within each group.

Second, by the *n*th edition of their textbook, most successful textbook authors have added various topical and timely material but have usually deleted precious little. Some resemble my notoriously cluttered office or bedroom closet. The fundamental economics concepts such as choice subject to constraints appear to be insufficiently enforced by authors and editors.

Third, keeping a textbook current not only by topic but by useful information is a major problem with textbooks. Typically published on a three-year cycle, an edition will have data that may be four or five years old. This can be partly redressed by having professors provide the data and update particular tables, charts, or trend graphs in the textbook for their own lectures, but to be honest, I believe that I spent way too much of my time having to do so. Perhaps teaching graduate students with some information from several years ago and commenting in your lectures about what has happened in the interim is sufficient, but the visual impact in the textbook is often of paramount importance to a freshman or sophomore. Worse yet, examples are often historically dated. Most students taking principles this academic year have parents who were themselves college students at the time of the Kennedy tax cuts, were not yet born during the Arab oil embargo, and were in pre-school during the 1981–82 recession. We are increasingly less likely to be teaching children whose parents lived through the Great Depression and who have had substantial family discussion of this major economic disruption.

In the electronic age, there ought to be much more advantage taken of the opportunity to provide updated information. Often, instructors like to incorporate current events into the course. Although there is no substitute for this practice, students are sometimes confused by differences in data presented in class and in the textbook.

Fourth, too many instructors allow a textbook to set an agenda *beyond* the basic economics upon which we all can agree. This problem is partially ameliorated by the wide variety of textbooks and by the latitude instructors have in combining the textbook with other inputs. Instructors can supplement or de-emphasize the particular topic, approach, and agenda of a given textbook by using alternative material (e.g., historical analysis). Nevertheless, the topics and approaches of textbooks are often followed very closely by instructors. This practice may be easy on the instructors and students, but many opportunities for value-added are missed.

Fifth, the encyclopedia-like structure of most principles textbooks tends almost de facto to underemphasize basic economic concepts such as scarcity, opportunity cost, and marginality. (See also Chapters 2, 4, and 7.) This style of textbook may have been less of a problem in the late 1940s and 1950s when Samuelson's pathbreaking textbook, along with others, set the tone for what was to follow. At that time, it was more reasonable to presume that a fairly large fraction of instructors in principles of economics courses knew a fairly substantial fraction of close-to-the-frontier economic knowledge. But since then, there has been an unprecedented explosion and extension of economic theory and data and, therefore, empirical analyses of the economy. The recent increase in specialization of knowledge by subdiscipline also means that a much smaller percentage of economists are likely to possess a large percentage of close-to-the-frontier knowledge in any but their own subdiscipline. In today's job market for Ph.D. candidates, for example, it is not unlikely that one will interview a prospective assistant professor whose main field of expertise is the economics of information. With all due respect to the importance of this body of knowledge, a decade ago that same person would have described himself or herself as an applied micro theorist or an industrial organization specialist. The incredible expansion and specialization of knowledge within subfields in economics means that a very small fraction of instructors of economics can be close to the frontier of knowledge in any but their own subdiscipline. This occurs because of both advances in economic knowledge and the fundamental changes in the economy, only some of which can be closely followed by today's specialist. Consider just the changes in the tax laws or the conduct of monetary policy and how quickly a teacher who is not a public finance specialist or monetary economist can lose command of the essentials.

To take another example mentioned above, the role of expectations is fundamental to discussion of macroeconomic events, theory, and policy. Two decades ago, most introductory macroeconomics lectures could mention expectations only anecdotally. Today, that would be wholly inadequate. What fraction of principles of economics students have had an introductory probability/statistics course? Thus, we are forced to develop some simple concepts from another discipline that are used as inputs into economic analysis, and thereby crowd out some other material. Yet, as mentioned above, in most textbooks, little has been crowded out. Material has just been slapped on in additional chapters, paragraphs, or subsections. Although the structure of these encyclopedia-like textbooks generally provides discussion relating to virtually all of the issues presented by instructors in lectures, the extensive scope of textbooks can limit their effectiveness as a teaching aid, unless very carefully monitored by instructors, section leaders, and students.

Chapters in textbooks are often assigned to supplement the instructor's lectures, when they do not closely coincide. However, the coverage of material in each chapter is often so extensive in the encyclopedia-like format that students have difficulty in determining which parts of the chapters are most important. In many cases, the side issues can be distracting or confusing for a large subset of the students.

Finally, let me add that, in my opinion, a variety of topics are underemphasized in principles of economics books in addition to the internationalization of trade and capital flows. I am certain that future editions of existing books will redress some of these shortcomings. Let me just mention the following six examples:

1 The post–World War II Keynesian emphasis on short-run demand management has relegated long-run growth problems, technical change, and productivity to the last part of introductory textbooks (usually not reached because we fall behind the class schedule). They deserve better. The productivity slowdown cannot be just put off as an aftermath of the oil shocks of the 1970s. Compounding these lower growth rates has a huge effect on the likely incomes, for example, of the current crop of principles students by the time they hit their peak earnings years.

2 Generally, there is very little said about what it means for economic agents to be rational. Because a form of rationality is often assumed in economics, it would be helpful to discuss the importance of maximizing behavior and the limitations of the assumption of rationality for households, firms, or governments. The public choice approach has provided a useful counterpoint to the assumption that government is working in the national interest. A related problem is that, although many students understand marginality, a large fraction fail to grasp the similarity in the optimizing procedures used in many different economic problems.

3 Discussion of alternative mechanisms for allocating resources (e.g., central planning and rationing) prior to the detailed discussion of the market system would be helpful from a conceptual point of view. Too often, these alternatives are discussed very briefly in a concluding chapter of the textbook. Yet the students should keep the market mechanism in perspective as one of a range of allocation schemes, others of which have been (some still are or threaten to return) used extensively in other countries as well as historically in the United States.

4 I find it distressing that micro- and macroeconomics are often still treated as two distinct types of economic analysis. While I do not believe, as some extremists do, that macroeconomics is simply a question of appropriate aggregation of micro behavior, the similarities and relationships between the two branches of economic analysis are often not well developed. It would help to unify the subject matter in the introductory course if the common elements of micro and macro, as well as their differences, were developed more fully.

5 Although most textbooks highlight various points of view, especially in macroeconomics, and although this is a useful pedagogical device, too much attention is paid to the disputes themselves rather than to the reasons for them (e.g., assumptions concerning behavior, empirical estimates of various parameters, etc.). A related point is that even the grossest historical evidence is often ignored in coming to a *conclusion* about such debates. For example, (1) the deficit experiments of the 1980s that coincided with a fall in the saving rate would seem to be an indictment of the Ricardian equivalence conjecture; (2) the collapse of velocity in the early 1980s and again in the early 1990s was not too kind to mechanical monetarism; and (3) the real GNP loss accompanying the post 1981 disinflation was much less than most neo-Keynesian Phillips-curve-augmented macro models were predicting.

6 Finally, although different points of view are legitimate, and a modern eclectic macroeconomics combining elements of Keynesian fixed-price models with some insights from monetarism, rational expectations, and the legitimate part of supply-side economics is emerging, there is need for neither nihilism nor apology. We should not expect the precision of the natural sciences, but we *must* establish reasonable or plausible bounds within which to operate. Although a blend of various macro theories is emerging, it is not permissible to choose parts of each approach and combine them in one's own experimental recipe (the original 1981 "Claremont" forecast, for example, required an astounding increase in velocity to be consistent; although this was not absolutely impossible, it was implausible).

Yet it is increasingly clear that these topics are far more important than the attention they receive in introductory textbooks.

My conclusion is simple: Although our attempts at objective measurement leave much room for interpretation, the net marginal social benefit of improved economic understanding may well be enormous. The extent to which the principles of economics course has somehow failed to imbue successive cohorts of students with these principles is open to question. I personally do not believe that we have failed in that undertaking, but I do believe we can and should do better. The textbook is but one item in the portfolio of inputs, and although over some range it substitutes for lectures, sections, and computer-assisted tutorials, for many students those substitution possibilities are limited. Thus, in the design and presentation of the economic textbook, my major concern is *emphasis of basics*: that most of the students leave the course with some real understanding of marginal cost, opportunity cost, basic material on the current economy, and so forth. Further I hope the instructor has stimulated in them enough of an interest in economic events that they will keep the textbook as a potentially valuable reference later on. Finally, we should take advantage of rapidly changing technology in microelectronics to make the material in the textbook more up to date, provide alternative learning environments in electronic classrooms for our students, and better integrate this material with traditional textbooks to increase our productivity—to enable more students to learn and retain more principles of economics.

NOTES

*This chapter is an edited combination of two articles that appeared in the *Journal of Economic Education* in the Fall of 1986 and the Spring of 1988.

1. Throughout this part of the chapter, I refer to the collection of principles of economics textbooks and what I perceive to be central tendencies in the collection. Virtually every criticism levied or praise heaped upon the collection will be inaccurate with respect to some members of the set.

CHAPTER 4

REFLECTIONS ON THE PRINCIPLES COURSE

Campbell R. McConnell

An invitation to reflect upon the character of, and some of the problems associated with, the principles of economics course is irresistible. But the breadth of the topic also obligates one to ponder his or her qualifications in responding. Mine, I find, are far from impeccable. However, they do include (1) almost four decades of university teaching, much of it at the principles level; (2) some very modest research contributions to the field of economic education; and (3) the authorship of a principles text which has remained viable for almost four decades. The latter—the writing and revision of an introductory text over an extended period—has had a considerable impact upon my thinking about the principles course as will become quite evident in the ensuing commentary.

It is not my goal to summarize research findings relevant to the principles course; that task has been admirably accomplished elsewhere. Nor do I propose to offer a comprehensive evaluation or critique of the course. Rather, taking full advantage of the latitude explicit in my assigned topic, I intend to offer a subjective and impressionistic series of observations and questions which I associate with the introductory course. These will focus upon the evolution of the principles course; the effectiveness with which the course is taught; its appropriate scope; the potential roles of student and institutional inputs in determining student achievement; and, finally, a consideration of the goals or outputs which might be associated with the course.

Comprehensiveness and Sophistication

Perhaps the most obvious point to be made is that over the years principles of economics has become much more comprehensive in terms of content and more sophisticated with respect to level of analysis. There is more in the course and the concepts are more demanding. The unprecedented knowledge explosion in economics since World War II has simply added a plethora of new concepts, theories, and empirical analyses which call out for inclusion in the introductory course. If one is willing to accept the assumption that course content is fairly accurately mirrored in textbooks, it becomes a fascinating exercise to compare current texts with pre-Samuelson texts. The quantum leap in content, of course, was the addition of formal macroeconomics achieved successfully by Samuelson in 1948. Since then such topics as economic growth, monetarism, the new classical economics and public choice theory, to mention only a few, have been added to the list of core topics. And, with the great expansion of international trade and finance, the trend toward internationalization of the course has spurred increased emphasis upon topics and concepts which previously were assigned a more secondary role. The amount of "crowding out" has not been great, with the result that the array of subjects confronting students has expanded significantly. (See Chapter 13.)

Although levels of analytical difficulty are not easily compared, it is my impression that it has increased significantly. It is striking that geometric analysis was extremely limited in pre-Samuelson texts. For example, the two-volume, 1150 page Taussig (1946) text contained about a dozen diagrams as compared to perhaps 150 or 200 in a present-day mainstream text. In my judgement one finds nothing as demanding in the pre-Samuelson texts as, for example, the long-run aggregate supply analysis or the international repercussions of budgetary deficits and macro policies which are now becoming common to modern texts. Furthermore, a casual perusal of pre-Samuelson texts makes it clear that easy-to-understand historical, institutional, and anecdotal material was much more in evidence than it is today. My impression is that the limited amount of crowding-out which has occurred in principles texts and courses has been in these "soft" areas. I confess that the thought has crossed my mind that the compression of such non-theory material has perhaps gone too far.

Has student understanding grown apace with the content and sophistication of the principles course? At the conclusion of the course does the student of 1997 know more about the economic system than did the student of, say, 1947 or 1967? I do not profess to know the answer to this question, but I am doubtful. We know that during much of the 1970s and into the early 1980s the communicative and quantitative skills of high school students, as measured by college-entrance examinations, declined and have essentially stagnated since then. Furthermore, demographic considerations brought about a diminished pool of potential college students and perhaps eroded admission standards. Hence, we may be confronting the challenge of teaching in increasingly difficult subject matter to students who, on the average, may possess diminished capability for college-level work. If this "sophistication-ability squeeze" does in fact exist, it may help explain why the principles course is often a source of frustration for both students and instructors.

Is the Course Well Taught?

There can be no question that there are many superb teachers—including internationally known research scholars—who are deeply committed to the introductory course. Yet it is reasonable to question whether principles students in general are well-served in the classroom. This is a disturbing assertion, but consider the following supporting points.

First, most economics departments tend to assign their least-experienced staff to the principles course. Indeed, at most Ph.D.-granting institutions, the principles course is heavily staffed by inexperienced teaching assistants (TAs). Inexperience inevitably is conducive to mistakes, an absence of depth of subject matter understanding, a restricted range of knowledge, and a constrained grasp of effective pedagogical techniques. It should be added that TAs are undergoing a very demanding and stressful educational process at unenviable rates of pay. Neither consideration is conducive to placing a high-priority on classroom performance. Furthermore, approximately one-third of all graduate students—and I would presume TAs—in the United States are foreign born. This has often posed communication problems that have become a serious source of dissatisfaction among principles students at many Ph.D.-granting universities.

Second, the propensity of most permanent staff to opt for the principles course is probably not high. Suppose you are an associate or full professor and your department chair poses these teaching options for you. "Option one: teach principles of economics. You will be confronted with a relatively large number of students whose backgrounds, interests, and motivations are highly diverse. Many students take the course simply because it is required. The subject matter is varied and far-reaching, covering many topics in which you have minimal background and preparation. Hence, rather than being complementary with your research agenda, your teaching will tend to be competitive. Your student evaluation at the end of the semester will tend to be low because evidence indicates that, *ceteris paribus*, student ratings vary directly with course level." Now consider a second option: "Teach an intermediate or advanced course in one of your areas of specialty. Because of self-selection and student attrition, you will have fewer students and they will be more interested in the subject matter and motivated to perform well. The subject matter is your specialty and therefore complementary to your research interests. Your student evaluations will benefit from the aforementioned direct relationship between such ratings and class level." While my statement of options is overdrawn and somewhat facetious, it is clear that option two will clearly be preferable to most instructors. In short, I would surmise that comparatively few senior staff will be found in the principles classroom.

Furthermore, the increased specialization which has occurred in graduate training may not bode well for teaching in the principles course. A new assistant professor, who a decade ago would describe herself as a specialist in applied microeconomics or industrial-organization, is now a specialist in the economics of information. This increased fractionalization of the discipline suggests that most new college and university teachers are less and less likely to be near the frontiers of knowledge of the array of specialties which comprise the principles course.

I have one modest suggestion which *might* improve instruction in the principles course and undergraduate teaching in general. And that is to accept the notion of specialization in accordance with comparative advantage as it might apply to our academic endeavors. It is a curious spectacle to observe economists preaching the virtues of specialization based on comparative advantage in their classrooms and then, in formulating faculty policies, insist that staff members be nonspecialists. That is, we demand that all staff members, with rare exceptions, allocate significant portions of their efforts to teaching, research, and service. This insistence is not arbitrary; it is based upon a plausible rationale. But it also seems eminently sensible to let the superb teachers devote the bulk, if not all, of their time to teaching and the exemplary researchers to spend most of their time in research. If our profession practiced the specialization it preaches, might it not be possible to obtain both a higher level of economic literacy for students and the generation of more new knowledge from a given quantity of academic inputs? In short, might we not collectively be more productive?

Aside from issues of staffing, there is perhaps a more pervasive consideration which makes effective teaching of the principles course difficult to achieve. To the extent that they exist, the aspirations of students are often such that they expect the course will provide them with clear-cut and unassailable answers to current socioeconomic problems. Given the inherent nature of the course—it is merely an introduction, after all—it quickly becomes apparent to students that their aspirations will not be fulfilled. Students frequently encounter a sense of disappointment during the course, even though they may be learning a great deal.

Why can't we provide the definitive answers which student seek? In the first place, in many critical instances we simply don't have the answers. For example, despite a substantial research effort, the profession has not as yet provided a convincing and generally accepted explanation of the productivity slowdown of the past two or three decades. Second, good answers to many current socioeconomic problems frequently require a substantial box of analytical tools which exceeds that provided by the introductory course. Finally, answers frequently transcend the discipline of economics. Economic analysis alone is inadequate to explain the persistence of poverty in an affluent society or why certain less-developed countries have achieved remarkable growth while others confront declining living standards.

Course Scope: Short-List or Long-List?

There has been a great deal of controversy—dating at least back to the early 1950s—as to the proper scope of the principles course. (See Chapters 2, 3, 7, and 8.) Should students examine intensively a relatively few topics or devote less time to each of a longer list of topics? Certainly complaints persist that the principles course is too ambitious, too comprehensive, too encyclopedic. Those who feel this is the case advocate a "short list" of core topics which are to be taught carefully and in depth. Supporters of the "short list" view contend that a "long list" of topics dooms the course to comparative failure. They argue that the long list is simply too much for students to handle. As a consequence of receiving fleeting exposure to a wide variety of concepts, theories, problems, and institutional considerations, students come away from the course with no real understanding of economic logic. Hence, students will be ill-equipped to analyze economic problems they will encounter as citizens or in business some five or ten years after the final examination. In brief, the "short list" position is that a concept or theory must be learned well or students will simple not retain it. The "long list" approach attempts to accomplish too much and, as a consequence, those who use it achieve too little.

The counterview is that the short-list approach provides no assurance that student understanding will be enhanced. Perhaps the learning process for individual concepts or theories may be subject to rapidly diminishing returns. If, for example, a student cannot grasp the concept of comparative advantage on the basis of a one-hour lecture-discussion, then he or she is not likely to be further enlightened if the time devoted to the topic is extended. One might even contend, for example, that if a student does not fully grasp the MR = MC profit-maximization rule in a reasonable period of time, it might be advisable to turn to other topics in the hope that, when the MRP = MRC input rule is encountered later, the student will comprehend the latter and come to understand that the logic underlying both rules is identical.

Another potential problem with the short-list approach is that the list itself is typically comprised of all the theoretical concepts associated with the course and little else. If one of the objectives of the course is to create and sustain interest in the discipline, one may question whether an uninterrupted diet of economic theory will foster this goal. It may be injudicious to lead students through the desert of analysis up to the oasis of real-world applications and issues and then not allow them to drink.

Finally, one may argue that it simply may be equally or more desirable to fulfill rather ambitious goals partially than to achieve modest ones more fully. To my knowledge the hypothesis that the principles course is "overloaded" has never been substantiated. In any event, this remains an important issue. As an aside, given the surfeit of "encyclopedic" principles texts and the paucity of "bare bones" books, it would seem clear that publishers and authors have favored—or at least supported—the long-list approach. The extent to which this reflects marketing considerations as opposed to consumer (instructor) preferences is open to debate.

I must admit to considerable ambivalence on the short-list versus long-list controversy. Specifically, I am sympathetic to the short-list position in the sense that I question the *level* of analytical sophistication upon which some instructors and departments insist. Some years ago an exemplary teacher pinpointed this problem and its implications as follows:

> Most of us are simply giving the students too many 'principles.' Every year, it seems, more and more concepts, which previously had been reserved for the intermediate theory or even the advanced theory sequences, are being taught in principles courses. In fact, I have an uneasy feeling that there is enough in several of today's principles texts to warrant their use in certain graduate courses. For example, indifference curves and isoquants, with all their ramifications, are frequently taught as part of elementary economics. We find ourselves enmeshed by envelope curves and saddle points. We are caught up by accelerators and even LaGrange multipliers and set theory. Then we spend the rest of the undergraduate program, and a good deal of the graduate program, repeating the same material. The results are predictable. The poor students are hopelessly swamped in the principles course, and the best students are turned off in later courses, when they find that they are getting very little new material. (Mandelstamm, 1971, p. 43)

On the other hand, I wonder whether the notion that the problems associated with the principles course stem largely from its encyclopedic character is not overdrawn. I find some merit in the aforestated arguments on behalf of the long-list approach. "Smorgasbord" should not necessarily be deemed a pejorative term. In short, the central question may not be the *length* of the list of topics included in the introductory course, but rather the *depth* at which we choose to pursue each of those topics.

Which Inputs Matter Most?

It is an intriguing mental exercise to reflect upon the many inputs which might affect a student's achievement in the principles course. It would be fascinating if we were able somehow to construct a complex educational production function for the principles course wherein we could assess the marginal contributions of a multitude of inputs to an output somehow accurately measured as, say, "enhanced student understanding" of the discipline. A useful taxonomy is to classify inputs as (a) student inputs and (b) institutional inputs. The former refers to the bundle of characteristics—such as genetic endowment, gender, age, previous educational experience, socioeconomic background, motivation, and so forth—which a student brings to the principles course. Institutional inputs, as we shall see momentarily, designate a variety of inputs which are determined or controlled by the college or university. (See also Chapter 11.)

Student Inputs The most obvious question is: What is the relative importance of the two types of inputs in determining output? There is some evidence which implies that student inputs may be more important than institutional inputs. For example, some of the literature on human development suggests that an individual's future academic achievement may be determined in the first several years of one's life. You may also recall Coleman's (1966) admittedly controversial conclusion that family background is the critical determinant of achievement and that school inputs are of relatively little importance. Similarly, studies of earnings differences by level of education suggest that a significant portion of observed earnings differences are attributable to differences in "ability" and family environment, rather than formal education. If this reasoning is accurate, then as teachers we face considerable constraints as to what we might accomplish.

Institutional Inputs As noted, institutional inputs are those which—subject to obvious budget constraints—can be manipulated by the educational institution or the individual instructor. Here a wide spectrum of questions come to mind. Do instructional techniques have a significant impact upon student achievement? Does it make much difference whether students are taught by a conventional lecture-discussion technique, by closed-circuit television, by video cassettes, by computer, by the Keller Plan, or by some other method? It is to the credit of economic educators that the past several decades have been characterized by considerable experimentation with new techniques and approaches to instruction in the principles course. From the students' vantage point these attempts at "product differentiation" would seem to be desirable. After all, the economist's own theory of consumer behavior suggests that, within limits, a wider range of consumer choice tends to increase consumer welfare. Hence, it would seem worthwhile for a department to offer its principles course through several options.

But there may be attendant problems. First, student-consumers are only in the 'market' once for the course in its various guises. They therefore lack information ex ante with respect to the satisfaction (accomplishment) which they may derive from each of the various options. How can we achieve the most efficient allocation of students among the various pedagogical options being offered? Second, it is fair to ask whether the availability of instructional options is the result of a department's interest in the welfare of its student clientele or rather a reflection of its desire to utilize its available resources to maximize the profession's perception of its quality. Does an economics department offer its introductory course via television or the Keller Plan because those are pedagogically superior approaches for some students? Or are these means for reducing teaching loads to provide more time for highly-visible research?

What about class size? Are large classes per se an impediment to learning as the conventional wisdom suggests? Should institutions with large enrollments establish an array of introductory courses for various clienteles? Should potential majors and business students be sorted into one course and all other students into a separate and distinct course? Should special courses be offered for engineers or journalism students? Is it a valid hypothesis that the more a course is fashioned to the interests and background of a particular clientele, the greater will be student motivation and hence achievement? Should we make an attempt to allocate students into sections on the basis of ability as measured by SAT scores or GPAs? Will homogeneity stimulate competition and enhance student performance? Or in a heterogeneous class will the recognition of superiority provide a positive reinforcement for the better students, while the less capable students strive to emulate the top students?

What is the optimal sequencing of material? In particular, should macroeconomics precede microeconomics or vice versa? Advocates of a macro-micro sequence point to the apparent logic of providing a "big picture" overview of the level of national output before analyzing and explaining its composition. There is also the more pragmatic argument that many students take only one semester of a two-semester principles sequence and macroeconomics is perhaps more helpful to students in understanding current events. The opposing view is that the increasing importance of the micro-foundations of macroeconomics calls for a micro-macro sequence. Furthermore, students need to understand marginal analysis before they can appreciate the incessant controversies over the legitimacy and scope of macroeconomic policies. Or is sequencing a matter of little consequence?

To what degree, if any, do instructor characteristics influence student achievement? Does it make a difference whether an instructor has his or her degree from a more- or less- prestigious institution? Is there a positive relationship between the years of experience of the instructor and student achievement? Or do newer faculty bring greater enthusiasm and approachability to the classroom which more than compensates for inexperience? On balance, are teaching effectiveness and research productivity complementary or competing endeavors?

The sometimes lengthy deliberations and machinations of textbook selection committees imply that choice of textbook has an important influence upon student performance. But there seems to be little evidence on the matter. The more widely used texts are accompanied by student workbooks, programmed materials, and computer software. What contributions, if any, do these make to student understanding? And, more particularly, do the added benefits exceed the associated costs?

Student Motivation   Student motivation is a peculiar consideration in that it is both a student and an institutional input. Learning theory clearly suggests that a student's motivation and effort are important determinants of the amount of learning achieved. (See Chapter 8.) In the absence of effective student motivation, little learning will occur. Lydall (1976) has suggested that intelligence might interact multiplicatively with what he calls the "D-factor" (representing drive, dynamism, and determination) to explain the skewness found in the distribution of earnings. One cannot help but wonder if an analogous explanation might be applied to the distribution of achievement among principles students.

Given the critical role which motivation may play in determining student achievement, it is interesting to ponder whether the traditional orientation of the principles course is conducive to student motivation. The principles course typically focuses upon "economics for citizenship" and treats broad social questions rooted in efficiency, stability, growth, and so forth. The benefits of such knowledge are largely social, rather than private or personal. In comparison, students might be more motivated in vocationally-oriented courses wherein benefits are primarily private rather than social. Bluntly put, a student might be more highly motivated in an accounting or finance course wherein the subject matter directly enhances career opportunities and expected future earnings than in an economics course which seeks to render the student a more intelligent citizen.

What Outputs Do We Seek?

What are the objectives or goals of the principles course? At the most general level, we would perhaps all agree that we seek to achieve (1) a usable level of economic literacy for those students who do not go beyond the principles course and (2) a viable foundation of economic understanding for those who will pursue upper-division courses.

But there are also a number of more elusive non-cognitive outcomes which are necessarily involved. At the most mundane level, we seek to generate continuing interest in economic issues and problems. At a more nebulous level, we might hope that the principles course will contribute significantly to the overall scholarly maturation of students and also impact upon their value systems. For example, one can plausibly argue that a highly significant outcome of the principles course is enhanced student ability to grasp and manipulate abstractions. Piaget's theory of human intellectual development distinguishes between the lower "concrete level" of mental achievement which involves specific facts or experiences and the higher "formal level" of achievement which entails analytical reasoning about hypotheses, the mental manipulation of abstractions, and the understanding of contrary-to-fact situations. The distinction may be particularly relevant for the principles course because the most baffling concepts of economics tend to be those which are the most abstract. Instructors often respond to student complaints about the abstractness of economics by pointing out that economics is formalized common sense. But this is only partly true. The concept of comparative advantage and the multiple-lending capacity of the banking system are contrary to common sense and intuitively incorrect in the minds of students.

If the principles course is instrumental in upgrading the mental capacities of students from the concrete to the formal (abstract) level, we might expect a number of desirable payoffs. First, cognitive achievement should be enhanced. Second, the teaching-learning process should become more efficient. For example, students will come to recognize that markets for products, labor, money, foreign exchange, and property rights are not distinct analytical constructs to be learned separately, but are rather variations of a common tool. They will also understand that the rule for maximizing consumer utility and the rule for realizing the least-cost combination of inputs entail a common logic. Third, if students are more able to grasp abstractions, their affinity for economics should be enhanced. Finally, an important spillover benefit for students is that they can apply their greater capacity to reason formally to other disciplines and to the real world.

Perry's[1] theory of intellectual development envisions a first stage which is "dualistic" in that students think in terms of polarities. Answers are either "right" or "wrong"; value statements are either "good" or "bad." Furthermore, the "right" answers and the "good" values are determined by authority. At a second and higher stage, dualistic thinking and the role of authority are replaced by relativism, that is, by the legitimization of uncertainty and diversity. It is also recognized that authorities embrace conflicting views as to what is "right" and "good." Knowledge and values come to be relativistic and contextual. In a third and final stage students become committed to social and moral values and to political, religious, and intellectual viewpoints. Decisions are made as to vocational choice, interpersonal relationships, and overall lifestyle. Do the pedagogical inputs which comprise the principles of economics course contribute to this maturation process?

The point to be made is that the principles course contributes to affective as well as to cognitive outcomes. The ability to grasp and manipulate abstractions, shifts in student attitudes from closed- to open-mindedness, and the maturation of student values are equally or perhaps more important than gains in TUCE scores in judging the success of the course.

I would be remiss not to mention that the role of textbook authors and publishers in promoting the overall maturation of students has not been without blemishes. I refer in particular to the issue of textbook readability. Perhaps in response to low and declining student reading levels, there has been a corresponding tendency of some authors and publishers to lower the reading level of their products. You may have endured the curious phenomenon of a publisher's representative praising a text because it embodied a ninth or tenth grade reading level. My point, of course, is that the provision of texts at or below the students' actual reading levels may be insufficiently challenging and students may miss an opportunity to improve their reading and linguistic abilities. Furthermore, one cannot help but wonder about cause and effect; some authorities feel that the diminished reading levels of widely used elementary and high school texts are a cause of declining student verbal scores.

A similar point might be made with respect to the widespread use of behavioral objectives. The presumption underlining the use of behavioral objectives seems to be that it is inefficient for instructors and students to engage in a cat-and-mouse game of determining what is important in a course. The argument is that students should be clearly and explicitly told what must be accomplished and provided with a mechanism for determining whether they have achieved that objective. For example, we should tell students that they must understand the average and marginal propensity to consume concepts and indicate that this knowledge can be demonstrated by computing the APC and MPC from given income-consumption data. Equipped with such guidance, it is hoped that a given amount of student study time will generate more educational output. My concern is that, if the development of a student's ability to discern the important from the inconsequential is a vital component of the learning process, the use of behavioral objectives may undermine that process. I also wonder if the use of behavioral objectives entails a subtle bias wherein we emphasize quantifiable relationships which permit unambiguous responses at the expense of less-explicit concepts and more debatable issues. For example, it may be easier to construct a behavioral objective concerning the nature of the Lorenz curve than one pertaining to the shortcomings of income distribution data. The latter point may be of as much consequence as the former. Do learning objectives dilute the learning process and give us a somewhat distorted picture of what is important? (See also Chapter 8.)

Unrealistic Expectations?

The preceding comments touch on a number of problems associated with the principles course. For example, the content of the course has increased in scope and perhaps in level of difficulty at a time when student capabilities may be stagnant or eroding. The processes of teacher assignment and selection may not be conducive to high quality instruction in the course. Furthermore, some observers feel that the encyclopedic character of the course necessitates that it will impart little of lasting value to students. The reader, I am certain, could readily add to this list.

While there can be little question that these and a host of other problems are causes for concern, I feel that much of our lingering frustration concerning the introductory course has different roots. As I have argued elsewhere, we may simply expect too much of our students. Marginalism, elasticity concepts, comparative advantage, allocative efficiency, externalities, and the other baggage which constitutes the course may all be commonplace and self-evident to professional economists who are imparting this wisdom to their charges for the tenth or twentieth time. But we must always be cognizant that these concepts are abstract, esoteric, and quite mystifying to most freshmen and sophomores. It is not reasonable to expect the basic tool kit of economics to be swallowed and digested in two semesters.

It is sometimes pointed out that the difference between aspirations and accomplishment is dissatisfaction. One cannot help but wonder whether some portion of our dissatisfaction with the principles course is due to our aspirations being unrealistically lofty rather than our level of accomplishment being low. All in all, we may be doing a quite commendable job in the principles course. Our more-or-less chronic discontent may stem from the possibility that we expect too much.

NOTES

I want to express my indebtedness to Professors Jerry Petr and William Walstad for their helpful comments.

1. See Perry, 1970, and Heffernan, 1975, p. 493.

REFERENCES

Bach, G.L. (1976). What should a principles course in economics be? In A.F. Larsen and A.T. Nappi (eds.), *Goals and objectives of the introductory college-level course in economics* (pp. 15-18). Federal Reserve Bank of Minneapolis.

Boskin, M.J. (1988). Observations on the use of textbooks in the teaching of principles of economics. *Journal of Economic Education*, (Spring), 161.

Coleman, J.S. (1966). *Equality of educational opportunity.* Washington: U.S. Department of Health, Education, and Welfare.

Fels, R. (1969). Hard research on a soft subject: Hypothesis-testing in economic education. *Southern Economic Journal*, (July), 7.

Heffernan, J.M. (1975). An analytical framework for planning and research in higher education. *Liberal Education*, (December), 493.

Lydall, H.F. (1976). Theories of the distribution of earnings. In A.B. Atkinson (ed.), *The personal distribution of income* (p. 35). Boulder, Colorado: Westview Press.

Mandelstamm, A.B. (1971). The principles course revisited. *Journal of Economic Education*, (Fall), 43.

McConnell, C.R. (1980). Economics 101: Where do we stand? *Journal of Economic Education*, (Winter), 21.

Perry, W.G., Jr. (1970). *Forms of intellectual and ethical development in the college years: A scheme.* New York: Holt, Rinehart, Winston.

Siegfried, J.J. and Fels, R. (1979). Research on teaching college economics. *Journal of Economic Literature*, (September), 923-969.

Taubman, P. (1978). *Income distribution and redistribution.* Reading, Massachusetts: Addison-Wesley Publishing Company, 102.

Taussig, F.W. (1946). *Principles of economics.* New York: The MacMillan Company.

CHAPTER 5

TEACHING INTERMEDIATE ECONOMIC THEORY

George Davis

O. Homer Erekson

Intermediate theory courses are key courses in establishing the foundation for the economics major, developing the "rigor and elegance of economic theory." In these courses students learn how economic models are constructed and gain theoretical building blocks useful for advanced economics electives and graduate training. They enable students "to think in a disciplined way about important and often-discussed economic problems" such as unemployment and wage discrimination (Erekson, Raynold, and Salemi, 1996).

However, some criticize the intermediate theory courses for emphasizing axiomatic theory without confronting resulting hypotheses with empirical verification. For instance, Siegfried, et al. (1991, p. 216) argue that intermediate theory courses should "establish explicit connections between theory and its empirical counterparts, to help students appraise the importance of theoretical constructs, provide a basis for selecting assumptions, and show that theory is relevant."[1]

Besides the direct learning objectives, intermediate theory courses also may serve other objectives. Intermediate theory courses play a role in faculty development by requiring that faculty remain current with professional literature, such as with applications of game theory or with real business cycle analysis. And in an era where economics majors are quite scarce, the courses may even play a recruiting function, convincing students at the margin to major in economics or not.

In this chapter, we will consider various issues related to teaching intermediate microeconomics and macroeconomics. In the first section, we will identify basic areas of agreement shared by most economists with respect to the intermediate courses, and will consider the role and importance of intermediate theory courses in the undergraduate economics curriculum. Then, we will identify the basic challenges facing instructors in designing intermediate theory courses, first for microeconomics and then for macroeconomics. The central place that intermediate theory courses play in an economics curriculum make consideration of pedagogical issues in designing and teaching them of crucial importance.

What Do We Agree Upon?

To begin, let us list the traits of the intermediate course on which almost everyone can agree. First, it is not the initial course in economics for the student. Most students have had two three hour principles courses or one four to five hour course before they register for an intermediate course. Many have taken additional economics courses that do not have intermediate theory as a prerequisite. There are a small number of students who have garnered advanced placement credit for one or both principles courses, for whom their first college experience with economics may be one of the intermediate theory courses. But, typically, even these students have had some prior exposure to economics in high school.

For most of the students in intermediate theory courses, the course will not be their last in economics. This contrasts with the principles courses where they are often terminal experiences. In fact, the intermediate theory courses are often prerequisites or corequisites for many upper level courses.

A related point is that the class is heavily populated with economics majors. Figure 5-1 provides data on the enrollment of economics majors (and minors) in intermediate theory classes in comparison to non-majors at Miami University for the 1991–92 and 1995–96 academic years. As is true for most departments nationally, the number of majors has declined. But, of particular interest here is the population of majors versus non-majors in the intermediate theory courses. In 1991–92, approximately 65–70 percent of the students enrolled in intermediate courses were economics majors. By 1995–96, this percentage has dropped to just over 50 percent. However, when economics minors are included with the majors, the percentage once again increases to well over 65–70 percent.[2] Thus, although it might appear that the intermediate theory courses are serving majors to a lesser extent relatively in comparison to five years prior, with the minors we believe it is safe to still conclude that these courses primarily serve students with a strong interest in economics.

FIGURE 5-1

Enrollment in Intermediate Theory Classes at Miami University

Course	Majors	Minors	Non-Majors	Majors	Minors	Non-Majors
	Fall 1995			Spring 1996		
Intermediate Microeconomics	28	9	21	18	5	16
Intermediate Macroeconomics	20	11	21	28	10	22
Total	48	20	42	46	15	38
Percent Majors	53.3%			54.8%		
Percent Majors + Minors	75.6%			72.6%		
	Fall 1991			Spring 1992		
Intermediate Microeconomics	67		25	31		15
Intermediate Macroeconomics	46		17	42		24
Total	113		42	73		39
Percent Majors	72.9%			65.2%		

We may summarize then as follows. The intermediate theory classes are:

- not the first student experience with economics
- not the terminal course for most students in economics
- taken primarily by economics majors or minors
- prerequisites for many upper level courses.

Pedagogical Principles of Intermediate Theory Courses

What are the implications of these traits for the intermediate theory courses? In this section, we present a series of observations that follow from the discussion above.

Principle 1:   The Economic Approach and the Emphasis on Formalism
Siegfried, et al. (1991, 216) argue that "the preoccupation with formalism rather than a focus on logically rigorous analysis of economic issues" has been a barrier to "enhancing the effectiveness of intermediate theory courses." Indeed, many economists are concerned that the use of highly technical and formal modeling in intermediate theory discourages students' interest in economics. Others argue for less mathematical orientation for intermediate theory courses and more policy application. For instance, Marks and Rukstad (1996) argue for using case studies in teaching intermediate macroeconomic theory. They argue that cases "convey information about qualitative tradeoffs and the complex environment" that deductive modeling cannot.

Although there is a danger in teaching intermediate theory with overly formalistic and technical tools, we believe that students should develop rigorous critical thinking skills in intermediate theory courses. This is not to say that the courses should require advanced calculus skills. But rather, the courses should develop formal model building skills for students.

Since students have self-selected into the course, they are in most cases already convinced that the subject matter is important. They also very likely believe that the "economic approach" to these problems is sensible. If either of these two conditions does not generally hold, it is difficult to see why the student would elect to take the intermediate courses. The self-motivation of the students reduces the need to "cheerlead" or to "sugarcoat" that can be such a large part of the principles experience.

The intermediate theory classes are primarily designed to serve majors and it is here where students should be exposed to how economists go about their business. The origin of problems and how the problems are solved should be emphasized. For example, prior to the use of indifference curve analysis, economists puzzled over the shape of the labor supply curve. Knight argued that it was positively sloped because an increase in the real wage increased the reward to work effort and would so induce a greater supply of labor. On the other hand, Robbins argued that the labor supply curve may well be negatively sloped since a higher wage meant that a worker could labor fewer hours and still bring home a higher income (Blaug 1978). Both stories seem reasonable within the context of indifference curve analysis because an increase in the real wage induces both a substitution effect and an income effect. The puzzle is thus resolved. The answer depends upon the relative strengths of income and substitution effects.

The intermediate theory classes should not only pose puzzles, but must also convey the method economists pursue in solving them. There seems to be a standard sequence. A question is posed. What is the shape of the labor supply curve? Why is consumption smoother than income? Why are some industries characterized by many small firms and others just a few large ones? A model is constructed with choice theoretic foundations. The insights and predictions gleaned from the model are judged against empirical regularities. The model is modified to improve its usefulness. Thus, economic thought develops endogenously in the sense that the answer, or attempt to answer, one question often leads to another. For example, the answer to the labor supply curve puzzle naturally leads to the question of what determines the relative sizes of the income and substitution effects.

The intermediate theory classes serve the primary function of sharpening the logic of the analysis. Often the intermediate microeconomic theory classes devote little if any course time to extensive consideration of empirical findings and their validity. Empirical regularities and policy considerations typically command more attention in intermediate macroeconomic courses. However, it is our contention that the primary purpose of the intermediate theory courses is to develop the ability of students to ask interesting questions about the world they live in (e.g., Should an author accept royalties or a fixed fee for writing a book? Should monetary policy or fiscal policy be used as instruments to provide long-term incentives for the economy?) and to learn to approach those questions using the economic way of model building.

Principle 2: Place Within the Economics Curriculum Appropriate design of intermediate theory courses is essential to an effective undergraduate economics curriculum. Siegfried, et al. (1991, p. 215) emphasize the need for departments "to coordinate the content of intermediate theory courses to insure that they establish a foundation of knowledge and skills," rather than leaving their design to individual instructors.

The place of intermediate theory courses within an economics curriculum is rather standardized. As shown in Figure 5-2, the basic structure of the curriculum is similar. Principles of microeconomics and macroeconomics both precede intermediate theory in a somewhat parallel fashion and electives in a somewhat parallel fashion. Students may take some electives that do not require intermediate theory prerequisites directly after completing principles. Other electives require an intermediate theory prerequisite. The courses that require intermediate theory are not common across various institutions of higher education. For instance, an industrial organization elective may require an intermediate microtheory prerequisite at some institutions, but not at others. Figure 5-3 shows the distribution of upper-division elective courses offered at Miami University categorized by the presence or absence of intermediate theory prerequisites.

But there are other differences that are quite significant in thinking about the design of the intermediate theory courses. The biggest differences arise in considering the electives more closely. First, there are typically far more microeconomics electives than macroeconomic electives. Further the microeconomic electives tend to build on a well-established set of microeconomic principles and concepts that can be assumed to have been covered by the instructor. This standard coverage is reflected in the intermediate microeconomic textbooks which tend to be relatively standardized.

However, the story for macroeconomics electives is quite different. The instructor of an upper division macroeconomic elective is less sure of the prior training in macroeconomics, especially at the intermediate macro level. Davis (1996) notes that textbooks for macroeconomics elective courses differ significantly depending upon the macroeconomic theory base assumed. For instance, Champ and Freeman (1994) and McCandless and Wallace (1991) develop monetary models from overlapping generations model, while Laidler (1985) takes a more traditional approach.

We believe that departments should think carefully about the role of intermediate theory courses within the context of the entire economics curriculum. If it is true, by design or historical accident, that the paucity of macroelectives has resulted in the significant variation in macroeconomic courses, perhaps the number of macroelective offerings should be increased and the macrotheory course should emphasize the construction of a basic model to understand empirical regularities, as opposed to an emphasis on competing models and policy proposals. It is "too expensive to teach a new set of equations and the rules for manipulating them anytime we want to entertain a new hypothesis about how the macroeconomy works" (Erekson, Raynold, and Salemi, 1996).

FIGURE 5-2   **Economics Curriculum Design**

Principles of Microeconomics	Principles of Macroeconomics
Intermediate Microeconomic Theory	Intermediate Macroeconomic Theory
Micro Electives (With Intermediate Prerequisites)	Macro Electives (With Intermediate Prerequisites)

Other Electives
(e.g., Econometrics)

Micro Electives	Macro Electives
Labor	Money and Banking
Industrial Organization	Monetary Theory and Policy
Public Sector Economics	International Monetary
Environmental Economics	Economic Growth
Urban and Regional	Business Cycles and Forecasting
Health Economics	
Game Theory	
International Trade	
Managerial Economics	
Government and Business	

FIGURE 5-3

Intermediate Prerequisites and Economic Elective Courses

Electives with Intermediate Theory Prerequisites	Electives without Intermediate Theory Prerequisites
Introduction to Econometrics[1]	Money and Banking
Mathematical Microeconomics	Economics Institutions and the
Topics in Microeconomics	Competitive System
Topics in Macroeconomics	Economic Analysis of Law
Monetary Theory and Policy	Public Sector Economics
Business Cycles	Economic History of Modern Europe
History of Economic Analysis	Comparative Economic Systems
The Great Depression Revisited	The Economy of Modern China
International Trade and Commercial	International Economic Relations
Policy	Economic Development
International Monetary Relations	Poverty and Income Distribution
Economic History	Labor Economics
Industrial Organization and Public	Current Economic Problems
Policy	Government and Business
Economics of Compensation,	Managerial Economics
Discrimination, and Unionization	Environmental Economics
Game Theory with Economic	Urban and Regional Economics
Applications	Topics in Regulation
	Sustainability Perspectives in Resources
	and Business

[1] Intermediate Theory Courses may be taken as corequisites or prerequisites.

Principle 3: Ordering of Intermediate Theory Courses Macroeconomics is built upon a foundation of microeconomic concepts and principles. Salemi (1996) has argued that four microeconomic competencies are especially important for mastery of intermediate macroeconomic theory:

- Students should be able to solve a two-variable constrained optimization problem, such that they can work with a two-space budget set, indifference map diagram.
- Students should appreciate that relative, not absolute prices, matter to rational decision makers.
- Students should be able to characterize the optimal use of a durable input (capital).

• Students should understand the difference between partial and general equilibrium analysis, and have an appreciation that general equilibrium analysis may be used to determine equilibrium relative prices.

Students are introduced to these concepts to some degree in principles classes. However, indifference curve analysis, optimal use of a durable input, and general equilibrium analysis are concepts often omitted in principles courses. In fact, it is not unusual to see the latter two concepts slighted in an intermediate theory class.

We believe that thorough grounding in microfoundations is important enough that intermediate microeconomic theory should be a prerequisite for intermediate macroeconomic theory. If staffing limitations or other curricular inflexibilities make it impossible for all intermediate macroeconomics students to have the intermediate microtheory course first, the instructor should provide supplemental out-of-class learning opportunities to assure that students have firm grounding in the necessary microfoundations.

Principle 4: Intermediate Theory Emphasis on Depth, not Breadth Students will typically take several more economics courses after intermediate theory. As a result, the coverage of topics in the theory class need not be broad. For example, if market structure does not get detailed coverage in the intermediate microeconomic theory class, the interested student can explore this topic more in an industrial organization class. Or if monetary policy is not covered in depth in intermediate macroeconomics, it can be so treated in a money and banking or policy class. This is not the case in the principles class, where a topic foregone is likely lost forever.

By depth we mean the repeated use of the same model or tool in successively more complex or realistic settings. For example, budget constraints can at first be constructed by numerical example and indifference curves used to find the optimal consumption of, say, cotton candy and hot dogs. The analysis can then be generalized to any two goods, prices, and income. From there the analysis can be applied to intertemporal choice where the notion of time preference and subjective rates of discount can be introduced. Budget constraints and indifference curves could further be used to analyze household choice in the presence of a food stamp program, the labor-leisure trade-off could be studied in the presence of a guaranteed income, and the intertemporal model could be extended to examine the implications of differing borrowing and lending rates of interest. These and other applications can be motivated by empirical questions. Why is there a black market for food stamps? Why are people on welfare for extended periods? Why are many households neither borrowers nor lenders?

In intermediate macro, depth could be obtained by building a coherent model that progressively incorporates more aspects of the macroeconomy. For example, a basic model may only include consumption and work effort choices and be used to study the effects of so-called supply shocks to the economy. The model could then be extended to included investment choice and money demand. Next fiscal policy could be introduced. The basic working of the model could and should remain the same in these evermore complex settings. Again each step in the progression could be motivated by an empirical question? Why is consumption procyclical? Why have real interest rates shown little if any trend over time, while output has a pronounced positive trend? What determines the long run rate of inflation? Why is output unusually high during wars?

We should emphasize that teaching fundamentals in depth does not imply that these basic models or tools are the end of the story. The standard model of consumer choice has a very difficult time explaining why people take the time to vote.[3] The basic models in macro have a difficult time explaining the non-neutrality of money.[4] These shortcomings should be admitted and can motivate more advanced discussion either toward the end of the semester or in more advanced electives. For example, many economists assign money a prominent role in causing recessions, but a basic model with money neutrality does not allow this possibility. What assumptions must be changed for money to be able to cause recessions? This type of question can lead into the various possibilities: prices or wages fail to adjust because of contracts or menu costs, information is costly and therefore agents are imperfectly informed, or distribution effects matter. Here it is important to remember that intermediate theory courses are not generally terminal courses and important extensions and qualifications remain for later classes. The details and policy implications may wait for future courses.

Principle 5: Adaptability of Course Content Economic theory is not static. Moreover, the long-lead times in textbook production, along with the sometimes even longer time for emergence of agreement about the validity of certain approaches and concepts, almost assures that the course content for intermediate theory courses must be adaptable to current trends in the profession not captured in textbook.

While, as argued below, the intermediate microtheory classes have a rather well-accepted basic set of core concepts, newer concepts and approaches are often given scant attention. Thus, in applications such as industrial organization topics, instructors are unfortunately likely to see as much attention in textbooks given to outdated concepts like the kinked-demand curve as they will to sufficient treatment of game theoretic approaches to strategic market behavior.

In macroeconomic theory courses, instructors are often faced with new concepts that have not received sufficient acceptance in the profession to justify authors modifying textbooks. For instance, modern macroeconomics courses should reflect new developments like real business cycle models and endogenous growth theory that may receive little coverage in many macroeconomics textbooks.

Principle 6: Stimulation of Student Learning Effective learning requires that students participate actively in the learning process. Intermediate theory instructors increasingly are utilizing active learning techniques. In microeconomics classes, experimental economics laboratory exercises are being used to demonstrate interdependent market behavior and the dynamics of an equilibrating market (King and LaRoe, 1991; Wells, 1991). In macroeconomics classes, historical episodes and case studies are being used to pose policy scenarios and encourage recognition of economic principles in historical context. In addition, instructors are increasingly using alternative learning pedagogies such as structuring assignments using real-world data in homework problems and on more substantial research and paper assignments, using interpretive questions that require students to use higher-order cognitive skills together with data or readings to more fully interpret a reading, and various cooperative learning formats where students confront problems in groups. (See Chapters 14–16.)

These active learning techniques dovetail well with our sense that depth is more important than breadth for intermediate theory courses. While we would encourage their use, it is important for instructors to realize they are time intensive, and that, while aiding in the depth of understanding of concepts they are applied to, their use may result in limiting the content material that may be covered.

Designing the Intermediate Microeconomic Theory Course

Intermediate microeconomic instructors are fortunate in that there exists a commonly agreed upon core of concepts that should be covered in any intermediate microeconomic theory course. This core includes the familiar topics such as optimization techniques, consumer theory (including indifference curve analysis, utility maximization, derivation of demand, and elasticity), production and cost theory, profit maximization and competitive market analysis, imperfect competition and strategic market behavior, factor market theory, and general equilibrium analysis. One can safely assume that these topics are covered, at least to some extent, in intermediate theory courses. However, the coverage may be slight. For instance, Salemi (1996) argues that the typical intermediate microtheory course "pays too little attention to optimal employment of durable inputs and far too little attention to general equilibrium theory."

This potential slighting of important topics may occur for several reasons. The typical intermediate microeconomics textbook is now 600–750 pages in length. To facilitate student learning (or is it to effectively market their book?), authors attempt to be comprehensive in the topics they cover and to provide numerous applications for students to apply microtheory. Instructors may have special interest or expertise in certain topics and spend excessive time on these topics. Moreover, the "core topics" for microeconomics are increasing significantly with the presumption that students will be introduced to topics such as game theory, uncertainty, and asymmetric information in the intermediate theory course. We would reemphasize the centrality of the intermediate theory course within an overall economics curriculum and the desirability of choosing topics to serve broader curricular goals within a department.

Textbooks   There are numerous intermediate theory textbooks available to serve different curricular approaches and tastes by instructors. Generally, the books have a significant degree of commonality in the degree to which they cover the core microtheory concepts. However, they differ with respect to analytical rigor, use of mathematical and graphical analysis, inclusion of advanced topics, the use of applications, and the timing of topics within the text.

To facilitate discussion here, we have chosen seven textbooks that reflect the somewhat different approaches instructors may choose. With respect to analytical rigor, all of the books are appropriately rigorous and convey core microtheory in a thorough and consistent fashion. Instructors who prefer a book accessible to students with modest mathematical training and abilities may find Browning and Zupan (1996), Katz and Rosen (1991), Frank (1994), and Pindyck and Rubinfeld (1995) to their liking. However, instructors who prefer a more mathematically-demanding text may choose either the Nicholson (1997) algebra-intensive book, the Nicholson (1996) calculus-intensive book, or the Varian (1996) highly structured and axiomatic book.

The books differ significantly with respect to the use of applications and in the inclusion and emphasis of certain topics. Browning and Zupan (1996) emphasize applications, devoting four chapters to policy applications with numerous other applications sprinkled liberally throughout the book. Frank (1994) also gives many examples and applications based on everyday life to help students to become "economic naturalists" in evaluating the costs or benefits of decisions. (See also Chapter 2.) In contrast, although Nicholson (1997) includes applications, he adopts a "bare-bones" approach and clearly intends that students spend their time becoming comfortable in navigating graphical and algebraic exercises. Katz and Rosen (1991) and Pindyck and Rubinfeld (1995) represent somewhat of a middle ground with their inclusion of frequent managerial or public policy applications, while Varian (1996) emphasizes formal derivation of theory to a much greater extent. The books vary in their inclusion and emphasis of newly emerging topics within microeconomics. Katz and Rosen (1991), Pindyck and Rubinfeld (1995) and Varian (1996) all include thorough discussions of uncertainty, game theory, and asymmetric information. In fact, Pindyck and Rubinfeld place a high priority on these topics with multiple chapters devoted to them.

While still maintaining more similarity than dissimilarity, the books do vary with respect to organization of topics to a degree. For instance, general equilibrium theory is introduced in very different ways. Browning and Zupan (1996) introduce general equilibrium theory in chapter 5, while Katz and Rosen (1991) do so in chapter 11, Nicholson (1997) in chapter 13, Frank (1994) in chapter 17, and Varian (1996) in chapter 28. The treatment of factor markets differs among the books as well. Browning and Zupan devote three separate chapters to input markets, whereas Katz and Rosen introduce input markets first as part of household behavior and the supply of labor.

Although instructors will generally find great similarity in the coverage of basic intermediate microeconomic core concepts in most micro textbooks, the books mentioned above and others offer some degree of product differentiation. Again we suggest that the instructor be mindful of the role the course is serving within the department's overall curriculum and choose a book that will serve student needs best, not serve the personal interests of the instructor.

Designing the Intermediate Macroeconomic Theory Course

Modern macroeconomics begins with a set of stylized facts to explain. This is, for example, how Blanchard and Fischer (1989) begin their advanced text. Such facts are usually in the form of correlations, trends, or relative volatilities. This information can be conveyed clearly by diagrams and so does not require any significant statistical background. For instance, macroeconomists might agree on the following set of stylized facts:

* consumption is procyclical
* investment is procyclical
* consumption has a smoother trajectory than income
* work effort is procyclical
* real wages are mildly procyclical
* long run inflation is a monetary phenomenon.

While there is general agreement about these fundamental issues, macroeconomists approach these issues with widely divergent modeling strategies. Davis (1996) suggests that the intermediate theory course should focus on a basic, well-understood model to address the stylized facts. Choice theoretic foundations should underpin the building blocks of the model: consumption demand, labor demand and supply, money demand, and investment demand. One consistent model should be used to integrate the building blocks into a simple general equilibrium model and the predictions of this basic model could be confronted with the facts. Fiscal policy would then be integrated into the model and the predictions of the model compared to outcomes in historical episodes. The inability of the model to explain all of the stylized facts would serve as the motivation to modify certain aspects of the basic model to the extent that time would permit, and to encourage students to pursue these areas in advanced macroeconomic electives.

Textbooks Intermediate macroeconomics textbooks do not adhere to the basic uniformity described above for intermediate microeconomic textbooks. For instance, policy plays a far more prominent role in macroeconomics textbooks, with early chapters often devoted almost entirely to policy. For example, Dornbusch and Fischer (1994) entitle their chapter 5, "Monetary and Fiscal Policy." In fact, the pages listed in the typical index under monetary policy are far greater than the combined total for antitrust and regulation in a typical microeconomics textbook.

There are two general issues to consider when examining macroeconomics texts. First, when and how does the text present in detail the microfoundations. A useful gauge is the placement of the two-period model of consumption choice and the permanent income hypothesis. Sachs and Larrain (1993) treat consumption beginning on page 78, Dornbusch and Fischer (1994) begin on page 297, and Gordon (1993) begins on page 548. We suggest that the microfoundations be laid before the model is constructed. Besides placement of the topic, the details of the treatment vary significantly. Sachs and Larrain (1993) develop the two-period model of consumption choice, writing down the intertemporal budget constraint, constructing the Fisherian diagram, and carrying out the comparative static analysis using the model. In contrast, Dornbusch and Fischer skip the formal intertemporal analysis and treat consumption primarily from an empirical point of view.

The second issue is the choice of the basic model. There are three possibilities: the infinite horizon model, the overlapping generations model, or some variant of the IS-LM-AD-AS model. The first two models are well understood and are the workhorse models for research in macroeconomics.[5]

Barro (1993) develops choice theoretic foundations early and adopts the infinite horizon model as the basic model.[6] Auerbach and Kotlikoff (1995) also employ choice models early, but they use an overlapping generations model.[7] Abel and Bernanke (1995), for the most part, provide microfoundations prior to the analysis of a model. For the model they rely on an IS-LM-AD-AS framework. Dornbusch and Fischer (1994), Gordon (1993), Mankiw (1994), and Hall and Taylor (1991) take the traditional approach of setting out the IS-LM-AD-AS model with policy discussions and then returning to the details of the choice theoretic underpinnings later.

Conclusion

Intermediate theory courses are an integral part of any economics department curriculum. Properly designed, they should offer students the opportunity to see the power of advanced economic thinking, train them to ask insightful questions, and equip them with the tools to apply rigorous economic analysis to them. The courses also should enable students to link economic theory to empirical regularities, and to develop an appreciation for the ongoing development of economics as a cumulative progressive discipline. Accomplishment of these objectives is a tall order for the intermediate theory courses, for an entire economics major, or indeed for an entire undergraduate and graduate economics program.

In this chapter, we have offered what we believe to be a set of common areas of agreement and principles for any intermediate theory course. We then have discussed the content and pedagogical challenges facing the design of effective intermediate microeconomic and macroeconomic theory courses. Throughout we have emphasized the need to view these courses within the context of the overall economics curriculum of the department.

NOTES

1. For references to Siegfried, et al. (1991) throughout this chapter, see also Chapter 6 which is a modified version of that article.

2. Miami University introduced a minor in Economics effective Spring 1995. It is not clear the degree to which minors in economics represent new students focusing on economics, as opposed to students who would otherwise be majors. However, our first impression is that the 51 students currently enrolled as minors represent net new students with a significant interest in economics who would otherwise not be majors.

3. See, for example, Romer (1996).

4. By basic models we mean the models that macroeconomists use as their starting points—best illustrated by Blanchard and Fischer (1989) chapters 2–4. It is very difficult to find a macroeconomic article in recent journals that does not begin from one of these models.

5. It is questionable whether the IS-LM-AD-AS framework is well understood and different texts have different interpretations of it. See Davis (1996, p. 131) and the references cited there for more on this issue.

6. It is sometimes argued that this approach is too difficult. However, this is a matter of how the material is treated. Davis (1995) provides an example of how this material can be made approachable at the principles level.

7. That is, Barro adapts the model in Blanchard and Fischer chapter 2 to the task, while Auerbach and Kotlikoff prefer the model in chapter 3. In both cases they employ a "workhorse" model of the practicing macroeconomist.

REFERENCES

General

Blanchard, O.J. and Fischer, S. (1989). *Lectures on macroeconomics*. Cambridge, MA: The MIT Press.

Blaug, M. (1978). *Economic theory in retrospect*. Homewood, IL: Richard D. Irwin, Inc.

Champ, B. and Freeman, S. (1994). *Modeling monetary economies*. New York: Wiley.

Davis, G. (1995). *The fundamentals of macroeconomics*. Loveland, OH: Ross Publishing.

Davis, G. (1996). The macroeconomics curriculum: A proposal for change. *Journal of Economic Education*, 27, (Spring), 126-138.

Erekson, O.H., Raynold, P., and Salemi, M.K. (1996). Pedagogical issues in teaching macroeconomics. *Journal of Economic Education*, 27, (Spring), 100-107.

King, P.G. and LaRoe, R.M. (1991). The laboratory-based economics curriculum. *Journal of Economic Education*, 22, (Summer), 285-292.

Laidler, D.E.W. (1985). *The demand for money: Theories, evidence, problems*. New York: Harper and Row.

Marks, S.G. and Rukstad, M.G. (1996). Teaching macroeconomics by the case method. *Journal of Economic Education*, 27, (Spring), 139-147.

McCandless, G.T. and Wallace, N. (1991). *Introduction to dynamic macroeconomic theory: An overlapping generations approach*. Cambridge, MA: Harvard University Press.

Romer, P. (1996). Preferences, promises, and the politics of entitlement. In V. Fuchs (ed.), *Individual and social responsibility*. Chicago, IL: The University of Chicago Press.

Salemi, M.K. (1996). Microeconomic concepts students should learn before intermediate macroeconomics. *Journal of Economic Education*, 27, (Spring), 116-125.

Siegfried, J.J., Bartlett, R.L., Hansen, W.L., Kelley, A.C., McCloskey, D.N., and Tietenberg, T.H. (1991). The status and prospects of the economics major. *Journal of Economic Education*, 22, (Summer), 197-224.

Wells, D.A., (1991). Laboratory experiments for undergraduate instruction in economics. *Journal of Economic Education*, 22, (Summer), 293-300.

Microeconomic Textbooks

Browning, E.K. and Zupan, M.A. (1996). *Microeconomic theory and applications*, 5th ed. New York: HarperCollins College Publishers.

Frank, R. H. (1994). *Microeconomics and behavior*, 2nd ed. New York: McGraw-Hill.

Katz, M.L. and Rosen, H.S. (1991). *Microeconomics*. Homewood, IL: Irwin.

Nicholson, W. (1996). *Microeconomic theory: Basic principles and extensions*, 6th ed. Fort Worth: The Dryden Press.

Nicholson, W. (1997). *Intermediate microeconomics and its application*, 7th ed. Fort Worth: The Dryden Press.

Pindyck, R.S. and Rubinfeld, D.L. (1995). *Microeconomics*, 3rd ed. Englewood Cliffs, NJ: Prentice Hall.

Varian, H.R. (1996). *Intermediate microeconomics: A modern approach*, 4th ed. New York: W. W. Norton.

Macroeconomic Textbooks

Abel, A.B. and Bernanke, B.S. (1995). *Macroeconomics*. Reading, MA: Addison-Wesley.

Auerbach, A. and Kotlikoff, L. (1995). *Macroeconomics: An integrated approach*. Cincinnati, OH: South-Western.

Barro, R. (1993). *Macroeconomics*. New York: Wiley.

Dornbusch, R. and Fischer, S. (1994). *Macroeconomics*. New York: McGraw-Hill.

Gordon, R.J. (1993). *Macreconomics*. New York: Harper Collins.

Hall, R.E. and Taylor, J.B. (1991). *Macroeconomics*. New York: W.W. Norton.

Mankiw, N.G. (1994). *Macroeconomics*. New York: Worth.

Sachs, J.D. and Larrain, F.B. (1993). *Macroeconomics in the global economy*. Englewood Cliffs, NJ: Prentice Hall.

CHAPTER 6

THE GOALS AND OBJECTIVES OF THE ECONOMICS MAJOR

John J. Siegfried

Economics is a popular major, constituting about two percent of the national total (Margo and Siegfried, 1996). About 32,000 economics majors graduate annually from the approximately 900 universities and colleges that offer students the opportunity to concentrate their baccalaureate degree studies in economics (Siegfried and Wilkinson, 1982). The number of degrees awarded grew slowly but steadily from 1982–83 to 1991–92 at about 1 percent annually. Between 1992 and 1994, however, the annual number of economics degrees plummeted about 20 percent (Siegfried, 1995). This decline is not unprecedented (Margo and Siegfried, 1996), however. It appears that undergraduate economics degree programs recover from such shocks, although it could take as long as a decade to return to equilibrium.

Administratively, economics departments are divided among colleges of arts and sciences (65 percent), schools of business (30 percent), and a few which are scattered in other administrative units, e.g., school of social sciences or administrative science. What economics students study, however, does not seem to depend on the department's administrative location (Siegfried and Wilkinson, 1982, p. 132).

Most students who major in economics plan to continue their education beyond the baccalaureate level, but fewer than half actually do. Of those who do continue their education, about half pursue an MBA and most of the rest enroll in law school; only a few (less than three percent of the 32,000 annual graduates) enroll in economics Ph.D. programs. Those who enter the labor force directly after graduation go into a wide variety of occupations in a diverse set of industries, government agencies, and not-for-profit organizations. Few describe their employment as an "economist" (Siegfried and Raymond, 1984).

Purpose of the Economics Major

There is broad consensus among economics faculty that enabling students to understand how to "think like an economist" is the overarching goal of economics education.[1] All other virtues follow. But what does it mean to think like an economist? Do our students understand the diverse approaches of different economists and the limitations of the prevailing paradigm? How can we be assured that our students can really think more like an economist by the time they walk across the graduation platform?

The typical response from an economics professor is that thinking like an economist involves using chains of deductive reasoning in conjunction with simplified models—such as supply and demand, marginal analysis, benefit-cost analysis, and comparative advantage—to help understand economic phenomena. It involves identifying trade-offs in the context of constraints, distinguishing positive (what is) from normative (what should be) analysis, recognizing incentives, tracing the behavioral implications of some change while abstracting from other aspects of reality, and exploring the consequences of aggregation (e.g., the fallacy of composition). It also involves describing the redistributive implications of changes in economic institutions and policies, amassing data to evaluate and refine our understanding of the economy, and testing alternative hypotheses about how consumers and producers make economic choices and how the economic system works.

Thinking like an economist includes several distinctive elements. One is problem-solving skills that emphasize analytical reasoning using the techniques and principles of economics. This can increase understanding of economic behavior and improve a student's ability to predict the consequences of changes in economic forces. Equally important are creative skills that help determine how to frame questions, what tools and principles apply to particular problems, what data and information are pertinent to those problems, and how to understand or explain surprising or unexpected results. Each of these is elaborated in turn.

Thinking like an economist involves an approach to problem-solving that has several distinguishing features. First, it emphasizes *deductive reasoning*. What insights can be derived logically from a set of premises?

Second, because most problems are complex and deductive reasoning is limited in its capacity to examine many forces simultaneously, there is an emphasis on *parsimonious models*—models which help us focus on the more important behavioral relationships in our complex world. To some people, economists tend to abstract too much from the richness of human behavior and reality; to many economists, the strength of our analysis is the provision of focus, and thus clarity of thought and analysis.

Third, the fundamental *principles* of economics *are* thought to be *universal*. While a Marxian economist sees a much different world than a neo-classical economist, each embraces a well-defined caricature of the economy that *they believe* reveals behaviors which transcend fields and problems.

Fourth, the economic approach emphasizes *decision making* techniques, perspectives on how choices are made, and the consequences of these choices. This, in turn, orients economists toward (1) the examination of *tradeoffs*, a comparison of alternatives; (2) measuring the costs of one choice in terms of the foregone benefits of another, or *opportunity costs*; (3) formulations involving *constrained maximization* with carefully specified constraints (necessitated by scarcity); and (4) issues relating to *efficiency*, getting the most out of limited resources. Finally, while all economic problems involve normative issues, there is a strong bias toward an analytical approach that abstracts from or downplays "value" issues and focuses on positive issues.

Understanding economic relationships is the central goal. This involves formulating hypotheses to explain these relationships, constructing models that capture their essential features, assembling empirical observations bearing on these relationships, and then testing the hypotheses using quantitative techniques. Such testing not only increases the understanding of economic phenomena, but it also promotes ever more effective predictions of the consequences of changes in our evolving world. In essence this is the form of scientific method that is used in many disciplines, but economists usually must conduct their hypothesis tests without the luxury of controlled experiments.

Thinking like an economist also involves creative skills. Identifying economic issues and problems, framing them in ways other people do not see, devising novel policy proposals for dealing with problems, analyzing both the intended and unintended effects of policies, and devising innovative methods to estimate the magnitude of these effects—all are as central to the discipline as is the development of logically coherent theories. Understanding complex problems can require considerable abstraction, or at least, decomposing problems into manageable components. Meaningful abstraction and decomposition represent the stock in trade of economic thinking, and require sophisticated analysis, extensive practice and training, hard work, and a dose of good luck. The economics approach involves isolating important "feedbacks" and interrelationships that can alter the analysis of outcomes and predictions. Finally, the specification of "constraints" and the articulation of a strategy to manage best within those constraints involves creative judgment. What is a constraint in one problem can be a mechanism for change in another; what is and should be maximized in one problem may be of little relevance to another. To think like an economist involves a highly disciplined "mind set," yet one that is creative—willing to speculate about alternative relationships and to examine their implications.

Thinking like an economist is facilitated by practice in applying the deductive and creative skills to a wide variety of economic issues, problems, and policies in diverse economic, political and social settings. It is only through continued and extensive practice that the process of thinking like an economist becomes internalized and thus an integral component of the intellectual equipment of the economics major.

Thinking like an economist is also facilitated by breadth and depth of knowledge and by the general forms of human reasoning that cut across the disciplines. An understanding of economic institutions and the historical context in which they developed is an essential ingredient of economic analysis. An economic argument contains not only logic and facts, but also analogies and stories. Facts and logic alone rarely suffice. Context is important.

The construction of economic arguments can help connect the study of economics with the rest of what students learn. Similar arguments are employed across disciplines. The equilibrium achieved in the world market for copper has striking similarities to the equilibrium achieved in a chemical reaction or the equilibrium achieved in *Hamlet*, Act V, scene 2. Ecological models of animal behavior and economic models of human behavior also exhibit striking similarities. What is important and what is shared across fields in the liberal arts curriculum is argument. Fields as different as literature, chemistry and economics do not share much content, in the sense of special facts, but they do share general forms of human reasoning.

In the economics major we share with other disciplines a desire to empower students with a self-sustaining capacity to think and learn, and to take an active role in their own education. They should know how to pose questions, collect information, identify and use an appropriate framework to analyze that information, and come to some conclusion. The end result is to qualify our students to make more informed decisions about their lives and communities long after their college experience.

The Reality of the Economics Major

Both the structure of the economics discipline and the major itself can be likened to a giant tree. The major is rooted in the introductory courses which introduce students to economic thinking and its applicability to a variety of issues. The trunk is a core of principles, analytical methods, and quantitative skills that are widely accepted in the profession. The branches of the tree, extending out in all directions, represent the array of sub-disciplinary fields, ranging from monetary economics to industrial organization. These subfields reflect the main points of interest and research in economics, and generate the problems to which principles and quantitative approaches can be fruitfully applied.

These two characteristics of economics—a central core of theoretical and empirical knowledge, combined with opportunities to extend that knowledge to a wide variety of topics—differentiate it from the structure of other social science disciplines. Whereas economics can be likened to a tree, other social sciences have a more hedge-like structure of separate and largely independent subfields with their own content and methodology. The hedge-like structure of other social sciences implies that it is just as challenging, for example, to study local politics as international relations, or social disorganization as small group behavior. At the same time, a hedge-like structure can sometimes obscure connections among the separate areas of inquiry within the discipline.

Looked at another way, the economics major is a helix—plowing the same ground repeatedly but at progressively greater depth. It goes beyond a simple accumulation of exposure to successively more topics. Basic principles introduced in the beginning courses are reinforced and refined in intermediate theory courses and then rediscovered and extended in elective courses. This repetition and apparent redundancy is essential since "application" of economic principles (in contrast to the learning of economic "technique") is very difficult to master, and pedagogically it requires practice over an extended period of time, and across several courses. Indeed, arguments first made in an introductory course are often not fully grasped until the senior year (or beyond).

The curriculum for an economics major (Siegfried and Wilkinson, 1982) typically begins with a two-semester sequence in principles of macroeconomics and microeconomics or sometimes with a single-semester introductory course combining macro and micro. These introductory courses enroll students who ultimately major in economics, students in other majors such as political science or business administration, and students fulfilling general education requirements. With over a million students enrolled annually in introductory economics courses and only 32,000 graduating majors, it is obvious that only a few of the students enrolled in most introductory economics courses are going to be majors.

Following the introductory courses, most majors take two intermediate theory courses (macroeconomics and microeconomics) and a course in basic quantitative methods. In the intermediate theory courses ideas introduced in the first course are re-examined, usually with more powerful (and less restrictive) analytical tools.

Intermediate theory courses accomplish three goals. First, they show how economists use theory, how rigorous thinking can illuminate economic phenomena, and how theory and real world events interact to produce new knowledge, concepts, and theories about the economy and how it works. Second, they provide prerequisite tools required to undertake economic analyses in elective courses. Third, they offer important signals to students: what the major is like, what content must be mastered, what skills must be developed, and what standards of performance must be met.

The quantitative methods course usually emphasizes statistics and hypothesis testing. Only a few programs also require a course in econometrics.

Finally, in junior-senior level electives—such as international trade and finance, economic history, public finance, industrial organization, labor, urban and regional economics, monetary economics, environmental economics, comparative economic systems, and economic development—students acquire substantive knowledge. These courses bring economic principles, analytical methods, and quantitative skills to bear on problems in diverse institutional contexts. Seldom are particular elective courses prescribed.

The typical economics curriculum rarely provides any kind of culminating experience. A few programs, mostly located in selective liberal arts colleges, require a major research paper or thesis, the final stage in a student's transition from neophyte to independent thinker. The comprehensive senior examination is found mainly in small liberal arts colleges, and in only a quarter of them. Even less common is the senior seminar, offering students the opportunity to integrate their ideas gathered from various courses.

There is little doubt that mathematical aptitude and skills are useful to an undergraduate economics major. The relationship between incremental and average values, for example, is pervasive in economics. Mathematics can clarify relationships and improve student understanding. Consequently economics majors sometimes are required to take calculus to prepare for their intermediate theory courses. The important principles in intermediate macro and micro, however, can be learned without the use of calculus. While many undergraduate economics departments require their majors to take some calculus,[2] how much calculus is actually used in undergraduate economics courses remains unknown.

If calculus is not used in subsequent economics courses, the link between the mathematics and economics is obscured, both lessening students' incentives to understand calculus when it is first introduced and, depending on the quality of the calculus course itself, discouraging students from majoring in economics. Since the typical general calculus course contains much material unrelated to the economics major, it may be impossible to reinforce the link sufficiently to motivate economics students to learn the calculus well. A calculus course that serves economics students well should cover partial and total differentiation, constrained and unconstrained maximization, and integration, and it should emphasize application and interpretation rather than drills in computational skills or formal proofs of theorems.

Calculus is not essential for all undergraduate economics majors. Few intend to pursue graduate study in economics, and those who do will need to supplement their economics education with a grounding in mathematics that extends well beyond basic calculus. Though calculus can help some students understand economics concepts, all too often the mathematics becomes an end in itself rather than a means to facilitate the learning, and a deeper understanding, of economics. Lamentably, the calculus tempts instructors to emphasize algebraic manipulation at the expense of intuitive explanations of economic behavior. It is relatively easy to "teach" formal tools and technique, but it is difficult to provide students with the capacity to use these tools. It is this latter goal, however, that constitutes the rationale for the mathematics requirement in economics.

Similar problems sometimes haunt the quantitative methods requirement. Originally conceived as a means of providing students with a sufficient empirical foundation to enrich their understanding and facilitate their active participation in applied courses, the requirement all too often fails to fulfill this purpose. Although the purpose of the quantitative methods requirement presupposes the development of skills in working with real data, contrived numerical examples are more common in these courses. Instructors of elective courses frequently complain that students come to them ill-equipped to interpret empirical evidence, much less to conduct their own empirical studies. These courses are often overloaded and taught at too fast a pace to adequately prepare students for the empirical dimension of elective courses. Frequently data appraisal (e.g., survey design, sampling procedures, data accuracy) is squeezed out of the course, and some quantitative methods courses fail to cover adequately the philosophy, appropriate use, and limitations of hypothesis testing and regression analysis. Sophistication in empirical work requires more than just training in statistics. It requires attention to observation skills, measurement problems and empirical judgment. Students need guidance on how to judge the quality of data, and how to identify evidence that would help to resolve an empirical dispute. Too often a superficial exposure to (but not an understanding of) more sophisticated techniques is emphasized at the expense of a more *thorough* understanding of basic concepts.

Economics majors are rarely systematically exposed to conflicting values in their economics classes, a feature with mixed blessings. Introductory students are likely to be taught early that economists are concerned with positive and not normative issues. It is said that markets determine who will work and for how much, and what will be produced and for whom. Advanced students are introduced to subtleties such as why different people have different productivities, or why income is distributed unequally. While economics courses routinely discuss the sources of poverty and the possible consequences of adopting different policies to alleviate it, usually little is said about what kind of commitment *should* be made by individuals, groups, or perhaps the government. Economists feel more comfortable describing the origins of the disadvantaged than grappling with the extent of society's responsibility to improve their lot. Since the exposure of students to such problems in other courses is typically value-oriented, economics provides a useful balance and an alternative, even if limited, perspective.

The premise that economics is purely a positive science is illusory. Students learn implicitly a good deal about values and ethics: that the value of a person's services is determined by the market; that if certain people had higher opportunity costs, they would be paid more; that the value of some people's work in the market is fixed when they stay home to raise children; and so forth. An apparently "positive" idea such as opportunity cost carries normative connotations, for example, when earnings are used as a measure of "worth." The implicit values ought to be made explicit, and they seldom are. Thus many students learn that efficiency is more important than fairness without ever questioning the idea.

Generalizing about the success of the major is difficult because in spite of widespread agreement about the course requirements for an economics major, great variety exists in what actually goes on in individual courses, with sharp differences between university departments whose majors often number in the hundreds and small liberal arts colleges where student-faculty interaction is more intense. Students in these latter departments are more likely to be in smaller rather than larger classes. As a consequence, they enjoy more classroom discussion opportunities and are more likely to demonstrate their learning through essay rather than multiple choice exams and through writing substantial papers.[3]

Considerable evidence suggests that *introductory* college economics courses are effective in the sense that students understand economic processes considerably better after taking one (Siegfried and Fels, 1979; Chapter 11). It also appears that the effects persist over time (Saunders, 1980; Walstad, 1997). By contrast, comparable evidence on the major is sparse (see, e.g., Hartman, 1978). And we know relatively little about whether any real success is achieved in enabling students to learn after they leave college, or to equip them to analyze contemporary economic problems of the kind they will read about in the press, encounter in their work, or deal with as citizens (Walstad, 1997).

An Assessment of the Major

The overriding strength of the economics major is its well-defined and commonly accepted core of analytical principles. Depth in economics should therefore be somewhat easier to define and assess than in majors that lack a common core.

The common core also facilitates communication among students and faculty in different fields within economics. Students can use their common understanding of principles to bridge institutional or chronological gaps. Because there is widespread agreement about the structure and content of the undergraduate curriculum, little faculty energy is dissipated in debates about course requirements. Differences of opinion about the curriculum manifest themselves largely as differences in what is taught in courses of the same title and how it is taught. A laissez-faire attitude toward content and method within courses often results in considerably more variety offered to economics students than is apparent from catalog course descriptions. When this variety penetrates the core curriculum, however, it can lead to confusion and frustration in the elective courses, which depend on the core to establish a uniform foundation for all students.

Because the basic principles of economics apply to a wide array of problems, majors are usually exposed to different types of inquiry, all within courses that comprise the traditional major. The commonality of the principles offers opportunities to make connections by spanning apparently dissimilar subjects. The sequential curriculum facilitates study at progressively greater depths; the common core of principles, coupled with their wide applicability, allows the use of repetition to reinforce important ideas, making it easier for students to carry their learning forward after graduation.

Finally, the enthusiasm of most academic economists for their discipline and their work is a great asset. It often leads to inspired teaching and a meaningful learning experience for majors in economics.

The economics major is not without problems, however. Economics courses are usually above average in size. Large classes may be one reason economics instructors frequently adopt a lecture approach, emphasizing passive learning, narrow forms of evaluation, few or no writing assignments, and a reliance on textbooks (rather than real books) and routine problem sets; all of these practices limit the intellectual stimulation of the major (Siegfried and Kennedy, 1995).

In our enthusiasm for teaching students how to "think like economists" we sometimes teach as doctrine that everyone *should* think like an economist, and that such thinking is possible only with the use of marginal analysis. The neoclassical paradigm in economics stresses "marginality," examining relatively small changes while holding other factors constant. Most tools of economics are appropriate to this perspective, and this dictates the types of problems selected for analysis, as well as the approach to them. Many problems, however, require solutions involving *large* changes, structural changes in the jargon of economics. The discipline is less well equipped to analyze such changes, and the capacity of economics students to use such a broader mind set can thus be limited.

Increased sensitivity to the normative nature of various paradigms might induce us to help students *evaluate* the contribution and limitations of thinking like an economist. The scant attention from the economics profession to the place of the discipline within the liberal arts curriculum produces little guidance for students to connect economics to the information and methods provided by other disciplines. This presumably unintended arrogance nurtures occasional over-confidence which, when exposed, can undermine the effectiveness of the whole enterprise.

Finally, the amount and type of student writing assignments and oral presentations in many programs not only fail to prepare students for the demands they will encounter after graduation, but they also limit the ability of students to demonstrate their mastery of economics while still in college.

Recommendations

1 *Foundations* The foundations of the major rest on three sets of courses: introductory macro and micro, intermediate macro and micro, and quantitative methods.

Introductory Macro and Micro. These courses offer breadth to the major, and, more importantly, introduce students to the fundamental concepts of economics and methods of *applying* economic theory to interesting and novel situations. This approach reveals the power of economic analysis and its practical utility. These courses tend to be encyclopedic, and all too often oriented toward formalization of theory. *The introductory courses should emphasize the application of a limited number of important concepts and theoretical tools to a variety of problems, at the expense of some of the existing formal and detailed elaboration of theoretical constructs or complete coverage of the vast array of topics included in most textbooks.* (See also Chapters 2–4 and 7–8.)

Intermediate Macro and Micro. The two semester intermediate theory sequence can be improved in several ways. (See also Chapter 5.) First, departments have often, by default, relinquished control of these courses to those who teach them. *Departments need to coordinate the content of the intermediate theory courses to insure that they establish a consistent foundation of knowledge and skills on which other courses and instructors can rely.*

While most intermediate macro and micro courses develop well the rigor and elegance of economic theory, they tend to slight its evaluation. In particular, the "usefulness" of theoretical topics and paradigms, largely assessed by confronting theory with data, applying models to various problems, and comparing the outcomes of alternative theoretical constructs, merits greater emphasis. These courses should *establish explicit connections between theory and its empirical counterparts, to help students appraise the importance of theoretical constructs, provide a basis for selecting assumptions, and show that theory is relevant.*

To achieve the overall objective of the major the intermediate macro and micro courses must *emphasize active student learning, practice in applying what students learn, and the exercise of critical judgment.* Much of this can be accomplished by increasing the number of carefully structured writing assignments that demonstrate the power of application.

Quantitative Methods. Economics is an empirically oriented discipline. The focus is on explaining and testing our understanding of economic phenomena. Hence, students need an appreciation for and an ability to deal with empirical matters. Rather than view this as a matter of learning statistics, we need to ask what it is that students must know to function as economists. The foundation in empirical methods depends on (1) knowing something about the measurement of economic variables (methods of data collection, reliability, etc.), (2) being able to organize, work with, and manipulate data for purposes of comparison, (3) the capacity to test hypotheses with empirical data, and (4) knowing how to interpret the results of various statistical procedures. We recommend that *the quantitative methods course be reoriented from its almost singular statistical focus to emphasize this wider range of quantitative methods employed by economics.*

2 Breadth Requirement

A respectable economics major requires at least five (three credit hour) courses beyond the foundations to provide sufficient opportunities for students to appreciate the art of applying economic principles and concepts in different institutional contexts. *The chosen electives should be distributed to ensure an appreciation for the historical, international, and political context of economics.* Such breadth will help students avoid a narrow parochial perspective based solely on marginalist thinking and should prepare them to deal sensibly with problems that involve other than atomistic models of individual choice.

Contextual inquiry includes courses in economic history (where connections between economics and history are explicit), history of economic thought (where different modes of thought are exposed), comparative economic systems (where social/political/cultural dimensions that influence distinctive economic systems are compared), and area studies (where synthetic analyses of countries and regions are explored). Such courses illuminate the importance of context and structure—initial conditions and constraints—and take the edge off narrow thinking about economics.

International courses include not only trade and finance, but also economic development, area studies, and comparative systems; other courses may fit too (e.g., the multi-national corporation). Such courses place students in a stronger position to use their tools of economic inquiry in a world that is rapidly becoming more integrated.

Public sector economics courses include not only public expenditure analysis and taxation, but also some offerings in theory (stressing public goods, externalities, collective decision-making, and market failure), labor economics (stressing aspects of regulation), and the like. Students should gain greater appreciation for methods of collective choice, including non-market options for resource allocation. These dimensions of decision making account for one-third to almost all resource allocations in most countries, and they are just too important to relegate to a few weeks of exploration in the foundation courses.

All elective courses should forge explicit links to both economic theory and empirical methods. Students should be expected to fit theoretical principles to the particular institutions studied in the field courses. Assignments should reinforce students' understanding of empirical methods acquired in the core quantitative methods course.

All *courses that can satisfy the breadth requirement should contain a substantial active-learning component,* such as oral and/or written reports, interactive computer simulations, class discussions or laboratory exercises, and *should draw on a broad array of source materials.* (See also Chapters 14–18.)

3 Depth Requirement

To complete the process of intellectual maturation, *every student should be required to apply what (s)he has learned to an economic problem, and in the process acquire experience really "doing economics."* For a particular intellectual encounter to accomplish this goal, *it should involve considerable responsibility on the student's part for formulating questions, gathering information, structuring and analyzing information, and drawing and communicating conclusions to others in an oral and/or written form.* The depth requirement should be implemented in each elective course and complemented through the establishment of "capstone experiences" such as special seminars or traditional opportunities for senior theses, honors research projects, and independent studies.

How to Make it Work

A respectable economics major that teaches students to "think like an economist" in a way that has lasting benefits requires considerable instructional resources, especially if, as we argue, students must obtain extensive practice at really *doing* economics. At a minimum, such a major is characterized by:

- A strong introductory sequence that stresses the application of economic tools to a variety of problems.
- Rigorous intermediate theory courses, typically taught in relatively small classes (20–25 students), that actively engage students in doing economic analysis.
- Background courses in mathematics and quantitative methods stressing the application of techniques *used* in economics.
- A minimum of five economics electives, three of which provide breadth to the major in terms of a contextual, international, and public-economics perspective. These courses should emphasize writing, oral presentations, research projects, argumentation, and feedback.
- A "capstone experience" that synthesizes the applications, encourages students to integrate economics with the rest of their college learning experience, and accords opportunities for creative writing.

Such a major is not inexpensive. It is our argument, however, that unless an experience is offered to economics majors of the type described above, the *minimum* mastery level of understanding how to "think like an economist" is sacrificed. Compromises that significantly reduce this goal invariably result in majors simply being superficially exposed to economics in varying degrees, and as a result the lasting effects of the experience are diminished, if not foregone.

How is it possible to make such a major work? The answer seems painfully simple: ration access to the major to fit the resources available while maintaining quality standards and fulfilling the responsibilities of each college or university. Placing a limit on the number of economics majors will conflict with the "philoso-phy" of many institutions. But unconstrained access to a major without concomitant resources, resulting in sufficiently diminished standards so as to compromise the intellectual integrity of the enterprise is also at variance with prevailing educational philosophy. Responsible educational planning requires "living within one's budget" of instructional resources, and the issue of *how* to ration access to the major then becomes paramount. (I am *not* arguing for *more* resources being devoted to economics instruction, although in some cases that may be appropriate.)

The method of rationing may vary from school to school, depending on the institution's policies and procedures (e.g., some preclude the use of minimum grades in prior courses as a prerequisite to select a popular major). Whatever method is used, however, rationing should be *educationally sound* with respect to the *goals* of the major. One option is to offer intellectually challenging intermediate macro and micro and quantitative methods courses whose "reputation" insures that the number of students intending to major does not exceed capacity.[4]

What does and does not constitute "intellectual challenge" in such courses must be spelled out. It does *not* require the use of formal (and seemingly difficult or sophisticated) tools (mainly mathematics) which can constitute a barrier to learning; and it does *not* involve the use of unfair or "tough" grading standards, unreasonable assignments, or "scare tactics" as techniques to discourage enrollments. It *does* involve holding students to the standard of properly *applying* reasonably sophisticated economic ideas to a variety of unfamiliar problems. This standard is intellectually more demanding than facility with formal tools *per se*, and it is, in fact, the best early indicator as to whether a student has the ability to come to grips with the major—to understand how to "think like an economist."

NOTES

This chapter is a modified version of "The Status and Prospects of the Economics Major," *Journal of Economic Education* (Summer 1991), which I co-authored with Robin L. Bartlett (Denison University), W. Lee Hansen (University of Wisconsin), Allen C. Kelley (Duke University), Dierdra N. McCloskey (University of Iowa), and Thomas H. Tietenberg (Colby College). Each of the co-authors made substantial contributions to parts of the original paper that are reproduced here.

The original report was completed in cooperation with a national review of arts and science majors initiated by the Association of American Colleges (1991). Funding for that project was provided by the Fund for the Improvement of Postsecondary Education and the Ford Foundation.

1. In order to evaluate the conclusions in this essay, a survey of 83 colleges and universities was conducted in May 1990. The questionnaire was sent to 127 institutions, generating a 65 percent response rate. Respondents were asked to react to statements in our report on a scale of 1 to 5, ranging from strong disagreement to strong agreement. Sixty-eight of 80 respondents either agreed or strongly agreed (ratings 4 or 5) with this statement of purpose. None of the 74 respondents reported that they disagreed or strongly disagreed (ratings 2 or 1) with the statement.

2. In 1980 about a quarter of undergraduate economics departments required their majors to take a course in calculus; in contrast, 81 percent of the institutions in our 1990 survey reported that calculus was a prerequisite either for their major or a course in it.

3. In the 1990 survey of 83 colleges and universities conducted in conjunction with this project, only 77 percent reported that a typical graduating economics major would have written at least one major paper in economics. Students typically write more than two major papers at only 22 percent of the institutions; at another 21 percent, including mostly large universities, the typical economics major did not write a single major economics paper.

4. Introductory courses should not be used to ration access to the major since such courses should be widely accessible to non-majors and students of diverse backgrounds and goals.

REFERENCES

Association of American Colleges. (1991). Liberal learning in the arts and science major. *Reports from the Fields* (2). Washington, D.C.: Association of American Colleges.

Hartman, D.G. (1978). What do economics majors learn? *American Economic Review*, 68, (May), 17-22.

Margo, R.A. and Siegfried, J.J. (1996). Long-run trends in economics bachelor's degrees. *Journal of Economic Education*, 27, (Fall), 326-336.

National Center for Education Statistics. (1988). *Digest of Education Statistics 1988.* Washington, D.C.: U.S. Department of Education Office of Educational Research and Improvement.

Saunders, P. (1980). The lasting effects of introductory economics courses. *Journal of Economic Education*, 12, (Winter), 1-14.

Siegfried, J.J. (1995). Trends in undergraduate economics degrees: A 1993–94 update. *Journal of Economic Education*, 26, (Summer), 282-287.

Siegfried, J.J. and Fels, R. (1979). Research on teaching college economics: A survey. *Journal of Economic Literature*, 17, (September), 923-969.

Siegfried, J.J. and Kennedy, P. (1995). Does pedagogy vary with class size in introductory economics? *American Economic Review*, 85, (May), 347-351.

Siegfried, J.J. and Raymond, J.E. (1984). A profile of senior economics majors in the United States. *American Economic Review*, 74, (May), 19-25.

Siegfried, J.J. and Wilkinson, J.T. (1982). The economics curriculum in the United States. *American Economic Review*, 72, (May), 125-142.

Walstad, W.B. (forthcoming, 1997). The effect of economic knowledge on public opinion of economic issues. *Journal of Economic Education*.

CHAPTER 7

TEACHING ECONOMICS: INSPIRATION AND PERSPIRATION

Kenneth G. Elzinga

Sidney Hook—writing about his professor exemplar Morris Cohen at the College of the City of New York—argued that the first principle of good teaching is the ability to inspire in students a dedication to the subject: by whatever pedagogical means. Inspiration, Hook explained, meant giving students a lasting appreciation for a subject; and inducing them to learn more about it (1981, p. 24).

A teacher of the dismal science who seeks to inspire students faces a substantial challenge at the outset: most students, especially entry-level ones, have little idea what the subject of economics is all about. Many think economics will teach them how to make a great deal of money in the stock market. Or how to start a business. Or how to balance a checkbook. Many students take economics because they believe it will confirm pre-existing policy views they have, whatever these may be, about the federal deficit or trade with Mexico. It is a tall order just to combat these illusions, much less inspire a lasting appreciation for what the subject really is about.

Most teaching of economics involves a combination of capital and labor inputs: a classroom, two or three weekly lectures, faculty office hours, a textbook, outside readings, problem sets, and possibly recitation sections. A library may be required for term paper research or small group projects. Economists, for the most part, use educational inputs quite conventionally and rather uniformly, at least in undergraduate teaching (Becker and Watts, 1996).

For many students in economics, a great deal is learned outside the lecture setting. So books and libraries are important. But for those students who are

73

inspired by the subject—who develop an abiding appreciation for economics or whose appetite for more study is whetted—typically it is the labor input, not capital equipment, that provokes the inspiration. It is the inspired teacher who makes for inspired students.

How does such inspiration happen? The inspiration is often the byproduct of the teacher's perspiration. Students who develop an affection or respect for a subject do so because of a teacher's hard work—and because that teacher's efforts are channeled through some basic principles of classroom teaching and course development.

Classroom Teaching: The Pedagogical Spectrum

When all is said and done, and an awful lot has been said and done, there are two basic styles of classroom teaching: Apollonian and Dionysian.[1]

Apollo, of course, was the Greek sun god. He thought rationality was a virtue. Dionysus was the Greek god of wine. He liked ecstasy. In today's world, Apollo would be the god of prudent consumption, saving for the future, and hard work. Dionysus would be the god of sex, drugs, and rock and roll.

Apollonian teachers identify with their discipline. Dionysian teachers identify with their students. Apollonian teachers want to be respected by their students. Dionysian teachers want to be liked by their students. An Apollonian teacher lectures with rectitude and understatement; a Dionysian teacher with flair and exaggeration. The Apollonian's examples are just outside the student's current experience. The Dionysian's examples are hip and relevant.

It is tempting to believe that faculty members who inspire their students are those with a classroom teaching style that mimics students' tastes—in their music, their humor, their attire, their language, or what they ingest. But great teachers have come in all styles and points along the Dionysian-Apollonian pedagogical spectrum.[2]

This should be an encouragement to economics teachers since most economists cannot teach in full-blown Dionysian style. This probably has something to do with the nature of the subject. As Kenneth Arrow reminds us, economists are the guardians of rationality (1974, p. 16). Dressing economics up in Dionysian pedagogy may seem like putting neon lights on a Corinthian column. But it would be misleading to contend that economics cannot be taught in Dionysian fashion. Professor William Kiekhofer taught economic principles in a Dionysian style at the University of Wisconsin—and did so effectively. According to a colleague of mine who was a student of Kiekhofer in the late 1930's, "It was customary for the students to start off his class with a 'skyrocket'—it went something like this; 'Sisss Boom AHHHH, Kiekhofer!' The professor would not start the class until the skyrocket was complete, and sometimes the students would taunt him by delaying it a little." The nickname "Wild Bill" bears testimony to his classroom demeanor.[3]

The master teacher is one who chooses a lecture style somewhere along the Dionysian-Apollonian spectrum that fits his or her persona and dovetails with the discipline being taught. There is no one style that fits all. What *is* common to all master teachers is a mastery of the material. Great teachers, without exception, know their subject—and they like to talk about it.

The Classroom as Focal Point

Talking about economics with students can take place in an office, a hallway, a dorm lounge, during a meal, even in a teacher's home. But most of the talking takes place in the classroom. To inspire students, the most powerful and memorable means an economics teacher has available is the classroom lecture setting.

Great classroom lectures are a function of teacher talent. But this talent, for most teachers, is not a natural gift. It is not at all like being born with great hand-eye coordination or peripheral vision. Teaching talent is not an exogenous variable. Teaching talent is an endogenous variable, involving hard work, that gets channeled into the lecture's preparation and delivery. (See also Chapter 12.)

Preparing the Lecture

Lectures themselves are like refrigerators. They need to be regularly emptied of items that have gotten stale or are no longer palatable. A strategic time to evaluate any lecture and consider how to improve it is right after it is delivered. It may seem tedious to revise a lecture right on the heels of giving it. But unless the lecture turned out to be brilliant, there is never a better time to remedy that lecture's weak spots.

How does one know if a lecture was brilliant, requiring no future revision? William Breit once proposed to me a tangible benchmark. A brilliant lecture—one to be filed away unrevised for next year's class—is one where students respond by carrying you out of the lecture hall on their shoulders and parade you around the campus.

For veteran teachers, much of the lecture material in an economics course will be the same from year to year. The formula for own-price elasticity, for example, never changes. But the lecture material about elasticity, and other important tools in the economist's toolkit, must be kept fresh for a lecture to work well. What provides the input for keeping lectures fresh? In the teaching of economics, it is real world examples involving applications of the theoretical tools that reveal the subject's hidden logic.

What I call examples, Joanna Wayland Woos calls "stories"—classroom illustrations that bring relevance and fresh perspective to the lecture (1992, p. 197). To develop and maintain informative and captivating examples involves watching for them in reading material that ranges from scholarly journals to out-of-town newspapers encountered while traveling. One surveys these sources always asking: is there anything useful here for illuminating economic analysis in a classroom lecture?

A corollary to finding good illustrations is having them at hand when the lecture is being developed or improved. A photographic memory comes in handy here. If this is unavailable, a filing system is required in order to retrieve, say, that wonderful example of opportunity cost encountered in the *Financial Times* last summer.

The Delivery of the Lecture

Some professors will bleed and die over academic freedom. The world of books and ideas is in their debt. Good teaching requires a different kind of zeal: a willingness to bleed and die over audio and visual technology, over lighting, and over classroom ventilation. It may seem too banal to put in print, but students need to *hear* the lecture. Part of the "hearing" process is the result of good capital equipment. Part comes through eye contact. Part comes through diction.

Watching my mentor, Walter Adams, began the process of teaching me about diction. It is as important as good examples. If anyone wonders about the quality of his or her lecturing clarity, there is a reliable, albeit potentially sobering, test that can be self-administered. Tape three or four lectures and then listen to them. Awkward speech patterns—slurred words, interspersed "uhhhs" between sentences—will be so embarrassingly revealed that a cure usually follows this examination.[4]

A parenthetical remark on the use of humor in lecturing: one does not have to be a comedian to teach the dismal science successfully. It is neither a necessary nor a sufficient condition. Oscar Handlin at Harvard offers proof from a different discipline: "Never did I make an effort to amuse or entertain. All such techniques seemed to me to diminish from the seriousness of our enterprise, to divert attention from the ultimate goal." (1996, p. 52)

Humor can be a helpful classroom lubricant. But in an age of political correctness and heightened sensitivities, the use of humor might entail snares. The safest use of classroom humor is when the teacher is the object of it. For those who cannot tell a joke well, they can substitute a famous quotation on the board or screen each day and identify the author.

The Subject Matter

The examples economists choose to illustrate their lectures are like the colors an artist chooses to adorn a canvas. But the lecture's *contents* are the shapes and forms on the canvas. When it comes to what gets taught (and what doesn't), many economics classes could be improved by adopting a variation of E. F. Schumacher's (1973) dictum that *Small is Beautiful*: namely, less is better than more.

In economics, we usually teach that more is to be preferred to less. But when it comes to teaching undergraduate economics, generally, economists teach too much. Gresham's law of teaching economics is that the newest trends drive out the basic principles. Only a few principles of economics can be taught and applied effectively in the course of an undergraduate semester. Introductory textbooks, themselves, reinforce the excess of material because of their encyclopedia-like scope. The review process for principles texts then compounds the problem. One reviewer may report, "It's great, but include something on job search theory." Another may recommend a different pet topic. If these suggestions are followed, the textbook becomes a collection of pet topics. (See also Chapters 2–4.)

All this leads to a distortion in the testing process, particularly in introductory courses. For example, the archetypical introductory course today is one in which an "A" student can recite the conditions of Pareto optimality, the "D" student cannot, yet neither student knows how markets discipline input users to promote consumer welfare. The "A" student can diagram the kinked oligopoly demand curve, the "D" student cannot, yet neither student can recognize on the evening news a political application of the concept of opportunity cost.

There is no greater personal pedagogical struggle I face than persuading my students that economics is, as Keynes described it, an "engine of analysis," and not an array of curves and intersections to wrestle into memorized submission. I tell them the graphs are not the economics. But when they watch me teach, they wonder if my actions don't belie my words.

A common rationale offered for teaching fewer principles is based on how little is remembered anyway from the classroom experience. A different rationale pivots on an economic principle that should be transparent to economists but often eludes us in the way we teach our material. The principle is *consumer sovereignty.* Just as the owner of a good restaurant heeds customer reactions, teaching economics involves paying attention to student/customer feedback. What is it students want to learn?

To be sure, many economics students do not know "what to order" in an economics class. Victims of bounded rationality, they are unaware of what preferences to reveal relative to what economics can offer. As surrogates for a market test of consumer sovereignty, let me suggest two feedback mechanisms for an undergraduate economics class.

The first is to ask students on the first day of class to put in writing what they want out of the course. Then tell them, as the semester goes on, how the material being presented responds to those requests, explaining as well why some requests—such as how to choose hot stocks and how to avoid paying taxes—cannot be met.[5]

The second feedback device is to ask students, about one-third of the way through the term, to respond in writing to "What is the one thing you want me to do to improve the course?" and, "What is the one thing you want the other students to do to improve the course?"[6] The feedback data that faculty traditionally receive—

namely, end-of-the-semester teacher evaluations—arrive too late to improve that course. Soliciting feedback early on enables mid-term corrections. Moreover, the signal this exercise gives to students is always positive, particularly if the information is acted upon in a way transparent to students.

The Mind-Numbing Details

Shouldering the responsibility to teach economics involves much more than giving lectures to students. Lecturing is only the visible, above-ground activity. The other part of the endeavor is less visible, even subterranean: administering the course itself. This task cannot be ignored. As Mies Van De Rohe said about architecture, "God is in the details." The same is true about teaching. Attention to details—syllabus design, test construction, care in grading, and the like—are the nuts and bolts of an economics class about which some students care in mind-numbing degree.

Van De Rohe's concern with details should ring true with economists. After all, we teach a subject matter in which tails wag dogs and not the other way around. What happens at the margin, we believe, matters, and we believe it matters more than any other social science. So care in grading, posting of office hours, syllabus design, test construction [spelling, punctuation, grammar, alignment, choice of fonts]—it all matters. The subterranean portion of an economics class profoundly affects output quality.

Teaching the Talk: The Importance of Vocabulary

One of my colleagues in the Department of English encountered the following sentence written by a student in response to an exam question. "To Hawthorne, adultery was a major digression." This was a student who no doubt had read *The Scarlet Letter*, but the student did not own the word "digression" (or the word "transgression," for that matter).

Economists think of themselves as teaching principles. Just as much, we also are teaching *vocabulary*. And just as it is important that students learn the principles, it is important they own (or at a minimum, lease) the jargon we use.

Students like using the vocabulary of economics. It is a way to show off their knowledge of the dismal science to other undergraduates. The expression "alternative opportunity cost" can roll off the lips of a student deciding whether or not to attend a movie in a way that distinguishes the student from his or her peers. Students learning economics enjoy the banter of economics' elegant lingo of maximizing and optimizing. Principal-agent problems, invisible hand, residual income claimant, sunk costs, time value of money, costs and benefits, bounded rationality, asymmetric information, externalities, short-run/long-run, intertemporal transfers: these relate to topics that abound in other classes. Giving students an ownership of the vocabulary—through the teacher's careful and congenial use of the language—inspires students toward what Sidney Hook associated with great teaching: students who have a lasting appreciation of the subject.

Most students who show up in an economics course will not become economists. Practicing economists can be grateful for this. But if these students take away a continuing sense of the subject, it will be because they own a portion of the discipline's terminology as a peg on which they hang the principles of the subject.[7]

The Master-Servant Mentality

Just as there are two basic styles of teaching, Apollonian and Dionysian, when all is said and done, there also are two basic styles of relating to students, two mindsets a teacher can adopt toward students. These are the teacher-as-servant mindset and the teacher-as-master mindset.

The Teutonic "Herr Doktor Professor," famed for brusqueness and distance, illustrates the teacher-as-master. Jesus Christ illustrates the teacher as servant, particularly the story of His washing the feet of those who called Him Rabbi (or Teacher).[8]

The pedagogical style of teacher-as-master can be an effective way of relating to students. To refer again to Oscar Handlin: he successfully taught history this way at Harvard. He reports, "In 1963 when the attendance in my course in American Social History got up above the four hundred mark, I ceased to offer it. I did not believe that an earnest desire for that kind of knowledge really moved that many undergraduates; and I feared that these lectures had become one of those experiences into which people drifted out of habit or reputation. Therefore, I chose subjects which on the face of it were not likely to draw crowds; I insisted on a whole year's commitment, non-divisible; and I offered my courses at an hour that required students either to postpone or skip their lunch." (1996, p. 52). Morris Cohen also was a master of this approach.

On the other hand, the teacher exemplar may be one who turns the normal classroom hierarchy upside down and becomes the servant. Not the doormat, mind you, but the servant: one who counts others better than himself.

In the matter of relating to students, there is no one size that fits all. Indeed great teachers sometimes, somehow, mix the two contrasting elements.[9] They are authority figures—because mastery of the material gives them that stature. But they do not teach by authoritarian methods. They show their concern for their students not by self-ingratiating imitation of student speech or dress, or grade inflation, or adopting the academy's political correctness *du jour*. Rather, the great teachers care about their discipline and flowing from this they show they care about their students—like the model lieutenant who is very much in command, but is at the same time genuinely devoted to her troops.

It is not possible to be a servant to a multitude or even a small batch of students. But if students witness—or see signaled to them—that the professor is willing to serve the needs of the class, only a fraction will step forward asking for particular, special privilege. For the most part, adverse selection will not prevail. The students served will be those most in need of special attention. Signals of a teacher's willingness to serve may include: allowing students to call at home, being available after a lecture as long as there are students with questions, and not ending office hours until the student queue is exhausted.

Outside Reading

It is not irrational (or unusual) for an economics teacher to be like the farmer who puzzled the county extension agent because he did not want more information on how to farm. The farmer explained: "I already know how to farm better than I do." Many economists know how to teach better then they do. But for those who don't yet teach to the level of their calling, there are materials to read that can enhance their prospects for making the dismal science less dismal. Three sources of potentially useful techniques and helpful ideas would be: the monthly *The Teaching Professor*, the bi-monthly *National Teaching & Learning Forum*, and the paperback *Teaching College*. This list is not exhaustive. The items on it are best read in modest doses.

Many colleges and universities also have in-house teaching resource centers that afford useful ideas, forums, and materials. For input specific to the instruction of economics, three reliable sources are the *Journal of Economic Perspectives*, the *Journal of Economic Education*, and *The Economist*.

To Sum Up

A faculty member's marginal propensity to inspire is not derived from anything very fancy or costly, except in the form of instructor time and diligence—what I've tagged perspiration. The perspiration is the result of diligent preparation, directed to the most visible part of teaching, the lecture, and to the subterranean components, like test preparation. Good teaching requires no extraordinary self-confidence or unique gifts.

Alfred North Whitehead conceded that when he lectured, he experienced "a curious mixture of being immensely at ease and stage fright" (Brennan, 1981, p. 48). Mere mortals can be permitted the same. Phyllis Whitney, the grande dame and Grand Master of American detective fiction, during a rare public interview, was told by an admiring and effusive fan how Ms. Whitney is "so gifted as a writer." No doubt about it. But Ms. Whitney saw the encomium as a cheap shot. She replied, "My writing is no gift. It's very hard work."[10] No doubt about that too, and the same truth applies to quality teaching.

Good teaching requires no radical change in curriculum; no special flair that the teacher must possess; and no great change in educational technology. Lecturing that inspires students, and provokes them to take additional work in economics, requires selecting what theoretical tools are to be pulled from the economist's toolkit and attaching memorable illustrations and stories to their use. Master teachers give their lectures with clarity of expression and seek out classrooms and other capital equipment suitable for the pedagogical task at hand.

Master teachers view their labor as a calling. The difference between a job and a calling is illustrated by two masons at work on a church building. When asked what they are doing, one says, "I'm laying bricks." The other replies, "I'm building a cathedral." Great lecturers—across schools and disciplines—are faculty members for whom the perspiration behind preparation and delivery is not a burdensome task. The faculty member for whom education is a calling will be one for whom students are a trust and not a burden. Such a teacher will pay heed to student preferences, when doing so helps the bottom line of inspiring students.

Lionel Trilling, in his short story "Of This Time, of That Place," described college teaching as a "lawful seizure of power." That was in 1943. I doubt that Trilling would characterize teaching today in precisely the same way. But today's economics teacher retains sizable discretion about how to teach the dismal science. A teacher's "lawful seizure of power" should entail setting the proper agenda for the class—a task ill-suited for all but the rarest of undergraduates. But great teachers rarely wear this mantle of authority in an authoritarian way. They realize it is exceedingly difficult to force anyone to learn anything. One can only hope to inspire learning to take place.

For most teachers, inspiration does not occur because the muse of economics decided to light upon their students. Inspiration takes place when perspiration precedes it. In one sense, the very title of this chapter, "Teaching Economics," misleads. Model teachers do not teach economics. They teach students.

NOTES

The author is indebted to Walter Adams, Pauline Adams, Marva Barnett, Phillip Saunders and William C. Wood for comments on an earlier draft of this paper.

1. The terms are from Friedrich Nietzsche (1993). To Nietzsche, Apollonian and Dionysian were the point and counterpoint of Greek culture. Nietzsche saw rational thought as Apollonian because it involved individuals weighing distinctions; ecstasy is Dionysian because it involved an individual succumbing to the emotions of others. In art, a Michelangelo sculpture would be Apollonian: a Jackson Pollack painting, Dionysian.

2. For evidence, see Joseph Epstein (1981).

3. My sources are Paul A. Samuelson, personal interviews for Kenneth G. Elzinga (1992) and Raymond Bice (1996).

4. Audio tape dominates video tape for this purpose. As useful as video tape is, only audio reveals diction most clearly (and cruelly).

5. In my own microeconomics class, I long resisted requests from students to lecture on how to make money in the stock market. With a shrug, I told students this was not a course in the stock market. But consumer sovereignty prevailed. Reflecting on the many such

requests over the years, I realized eventually that a lecture based on the economics of financial markets, particularly the Efficient Markets Hypothesis and the Random Walk Hypothesis, would be responsive in an indirect way to the revealed preferences of my students. I now lecture on what economics teaches about how to avoid fallacious ways to get rich. A fifty-minute summary of *A Random Walk Down Wall Street* (Malkiel, 1990) and a variety of EMH stories from the *Wall Street Journal* has become one of my favorite lectures, as I believe it is for my students.

6. See Nancy Loevinger (1993).

7. An interesting exercise to test the relevance of a principles of economics course is to assess the familiarity a student would have, upon completion of an introductory macro-micro sequence, with a glossary of terms associated with economics. One best-selling "list" (E.D. Hirsch, 1988) purports to embrace what a culturally literate person should know about "Business and Economics." Diligent students of a principles class will become familiar with most of the entries on this list. But not all. Problematic terms would be from accounting and finance (e.g., escrow, lien). In addition, many principles students today could not identify the personalities Hirsch spotlights (e.g., Andrew Carnegie, Lee Iacocca) and certain cultural concepts (e.g., the affluent society, bourgeoisie).

8. The servant concept is pre-Christian: Socrates saw the teacher-student relationship as one of *agape* love.

9. Robert E. Shoenberg (1994) offers a four-fold taxonomy: didactic (or "Listen to me"); apprentice (or "Follow me"); collegial (or "Be my junior colleague"); and friendship ("Be my friend").

10. Phyllis Whitney at 93, interview at the Virginia Festival of the Book, Charlottesville, VA, March 30, 1996.

REFERENCES

Arrow, K.J. (1974). *The limits of organization.* New York: Norton.

Becker, W.E. and Watts, M. (1996). Chalk and talk: A national survey on teaching economics. *American Economic Review Papers and Proceedings*, (86), May, 448-453.

Bice, R. (1996). Personal correspondence with the author, March 14.

Brennan, J.G. (1981). Alfred North Whitehead: Plato's lost dialogue. In J. Epstein (ed.), *Masters: Portraits of great teachers* (pp. 47-68). New York: Basic Books.

Elzinga, K.G. (1992). The eleven principles of economics. *Southern Economic Journal*, (58), April, 871-879.

Epstein, J. (Ed.). (1981). *Masters: Portraits of great teachers.* New York: Basic Books.

Handlin, O. (1996). A career at Harvard. *The American Scholar*, (Winter), 47-59.

Hirsch, E.D. (1988). *The dictionary of cultural literacy.* Boston: Houghton Mifflin.

Hook, S.H. (1981). Morris Cohen. In J. Epstein (ed.), *Masters: Portraits of great teachers* (pp. 24-46). New York: Basic Books.

Loevinger, N. (1993). Teaching idea: Using a mid-term evaluation to give students responsibility for the course. *Teaching Concerns*, Newsletter of the University of Virginia Teaching Resource Center, (January), 1.

Malkiel, B. (1990). *A random walk down Wall Street.* New York: Norton.

National Teaching & Learning FORUM. Phoenix, Arizona: The Oryx Press.

Neff, R.A. and Weimer, M. (Eds.). *Teaching college: Collected readings for the new institute.* Madison, Wisconsin: Magna Publications.

Nietzsche, F. (1993). *The birth of tragedy*. New York: Penguin.

Schumacher, E.F. (1973). *Small is beautiful*. New York: Harper & Row.

Shoenberg, R.E. (1994). Time shortened degrees. *The Teaching Professor*, (8), December, 1-2.

The teaching professor. Madison, Wisconsin: Magna Publications.

Woos, J.W. (1992). From graduate student to liberal arts professor. In D. Colander and R. Brenner (eds.), *Educating economists* (pp. 193-199). Ann Arbor: University of Michigan Press.

CHAPTER 8

LEARNING THEORY AND INSTRUCTIONAL OBJECTIVES

Phillip Saunders

An understanding of how humans learn should help us do a better job of teaching. Clearly established "laws" or "principles" of learning would be an invaluable aid in planning, presenting, and evaluating instruction in college classrooms. Unfortunately, there is at present no single, generally accepted theory of learning that can be used as an infallible guide to teaching. Indeed, there is some evidence that there are different types of learning, and David Kolb (1981) and others argue that students have different "learning styles" and that different academic disciplines have different "learning demands." Nevertheless, an understanding of what psychologists and others have discovered to date about human learning should still be of some value in helping us do a better job of helping our students learn more about undergraduate economics.

This chapter will discuss some of the findings that my review of psychological and educational literature indicates have the most relevance for teaching economics at the college level. The chapter begins with a general definition of learning that incorporates both what educators have termed the "cognitive domain" and the "affective domain." A brief review of the major "schools" of learning theory in modern psychology is followed by a discussion of four generally accepted propositions about human learning. Separate attention is then paid to the acquisition, retention, and transfer of knowledge, and the importance of focusing on clearly thought out instructional objectives is emphasized at the end of the chapter.

What is Meant by Learning?

While admitting the possibility and usefulness of many other definitions of the learning process, I offer the following: *Learning is the acquisition and retention of knowledge and habits of thought in a way that permits them to be employed in a useful way after the initial exposure has been terminated.* Learning in this sense takes place when we gain an understanding of a process, situation, fact or thing that we did not previously possess and when we can retain this understanding in a manner that permits us to apply it to new situations. Basically, this definition contains three elements: *acquisition, retention* and *transfer.* (We should probably also add a fourth element—*evaluation,* or some internal intellectual mechanism of checking to see if we have used our knowledge in a sensible way by judging whether or not we have made an appropriate response or behaved in a plausible manner.)

Gagne has identified and described five major categories of learning outcomes which he labels: intellectual skills; verbal information; cognitive strategies; motor skills; and attitudes. And he states: "Not only do these differ in the human performances they make possible; they also differ in the conditions most favorable to their learning" (Gagne, 1985, p. 67). If it is true that there are different types of learning, it may not be possible to develop a single theory that effectively encompasses all of the different varieties of learning. Further, the work of the Swiss psychologist Jean Piaget and the American educator William G. Perry, Jr. indicates that humans move through different stages of intellectual development wherein the modes of thinking are distinctly different.[1] Thus, the task of developing a single theory of human learning that can be applied to all types of learning at all stages of intellectual development is a formidable, if not an impossible, one. If we focus on student learning of the type of material typically presented in undergraduate college courses, however, it is useful to formulate our objectives in terms of *both* what educators have termed the "cognitive domain" and the "affective domain."

The Cognitive Domain The cognitive domain deals with intellectual outcomes such as knowledge, understanding, and thinking skills. Examples of cognitive objectives are: defines basic terms; interprets charts and graphs; recognizes logical fallacies in reasoning; predicts the outcome of an action involving economic principles. Benjamin S. Bloom and others published the *Taxonomy of Educational Objectives: Cognitive Domain* in 1956. This book describes six cognitive categories in detail and presents illustrative objectives and test items for each category. The categories in ascending order are (1) knowledge (2) comprehension, (3) application, (4) analysis, (5) synthesis, and (6) evaluation.

The Affective Domain The affective domain deals with feelings and emotions such as interest, attitude, and appreciation. Examples of affective objectives are: listens attentively; completes assigned homework; participates in class discussions;

shows interest in economics; appreciates the importance of economics in everyday life. David R. Krathwohl and others published the *Taxonomy of Educational Objectives: Affective Domain* in 1964. This book describes five affective categories in detail and presents illustrative objectives and test items for each category. The categories in ascending order are (1) receiving, (2) responding, (3) valuing, (4) organization, and (5) characterization by a value or value complex.

It should be noted that the categories in each domain of these taxonomies are arranged in hierarchical order. Thus, the term "taxonomy." Each category is assumed to include the behavior at the lower levels. Thus "application" includes behavior at the "comprehension" and "knowledge" levels, and "valuing" includes behavior at both the "responding" and "receiving" levels. An excellent brief summary of the Bloom and Krathwol material is contained in Norman E. Gronlund (1985). Appendices 8-1 and 8-2 at the end of this chapter are adapted from four more comprehensive tables in this source. These appendices give a brief one sentence definition of each of the categories in the cognitive and the affective taxonomies, and a few verbs specifying illustrative student behaviors are shown after each definition.

Much of the traditional learning theory research has focused on cognitive behaviors but, as we will see, the importance of motivation in human learning implies that we must not ignore the affective domain if we want our students to acquire, retain, and use cognitive skills.

Major "Schools" of Learning Theory

In recent years, information-processing approaches to human learning have come to supersede and blur previous distinctions between empirically oriented, behavioral-associatioinist or "stimulus-response" approaches to learning and less empirical, more intuitive "cognitive-structuralist" approaches. Thus, in the 1989 *Annual Review of Psychology*, Glaser and Bassok (1989, p. 631) could state: "Instructional psychology has become a vigorous part of the mainstream of research on human cognition and development."[2]

The Stimulus-Response School This school traditionally focused on learning as the reinforcement of associations between overt stimuli and responses, and it placed a strong emphasis on the direct observation of overt behavior. The terms "empiricists," "associationists" and "behaviorists" are sometimes used to represent the psychologists who emphasize this approach to learning. Teaching machines and programmed learning are instructional devices stemming from this school. These techniques are designed to reinforce or reward students for making the correct response (answer) to each stimulus (question). B.F. Skinner is frequently identified as the most prominent recent spokesman of the stimulus-response school. (See Skinner, 1968.)

The Cognitive-Structuralist School This school stems from the experiments of the German psychologist Wolfgang Kohler with chimpanzees who learned to stack boxes and use short sticks to rake in long sticks so that they could obtain food that was otherwise out of their reach. This school emphasizes the introspective rearrangement of previous ideas and experience into new patterns of thought, and focuses on learning as "insight" or the perception of new relationships. The terms "gestalt" (the German word for configuration) and "field" theorists are sometimes used to represent the psychologists who emphasize this approach to learning. The discovery method of instruction stems from this school of learning theory, and Jerome Bruner is a prominent recent spokesman. (See Bruner, 1966.)

The Information Processing School While stimulus-response and cognitive-structuralist theories do not agree about what goes on in a person's mind when something is "learned," neither has a very elaborate approach to the internal processing involved when compared to more recent learning theories based on formulations from computer science, linguistics, and attempts to represent the learning process by mathematical equations. These newer "information processing" theories propose a very elaborate set of internal processes, transformations, and structures to account for the events of human learning, and they imply that several distinct phases of processing occur during a single act of learning.[3]
A good recent example of an attempt to summarize and apply the information processing view of learning to the problems of instruction is provided by Robert M. Gagne in the 1985 (4th) edition of his book, *The Conditions of Learning*. Figure 8-1 is reproduced from page 71 of this book. Using italics to refer to *structures* and quotations to refer to "processes," my very condensed summary of Gagne's explanation of this figure is contained in the next two paragraphs.

The lower parts of Figure 8-1 indicate that information received from the environment is transformed into neural information by *receptors* and entered into the *sensory register* where a process of "selective perception" either allows it to die or, if it is attended to, be transformed into a new kind of input into the *short term memory*. The transformed information can persist in short-term memory for only a limited period (perhaps up to 20 seconds), but this interval can be extended by a process of *silent mental repetition* called "rehearsal." Rehearsal may also aid the "encoding" of information for input into the *long-term memory*. Encoding is a process of meaningful organization which permits the information to be stored in long-term memory. Once stored in long-term memory, we say that information is "learned" if it can be retrieved and returned to the short-term memory or used to activate a *response generator*. Information retrieved from the long-term memory into the short-term memory can be combined with other inputs to form new encodings for long-term memory or to activate a response generator. Once a response generator has been activated, some sort of performance is effected that can be observed externally and used to verify that learning has occurred.

Figure 8-1: Information Processing Model of Learning

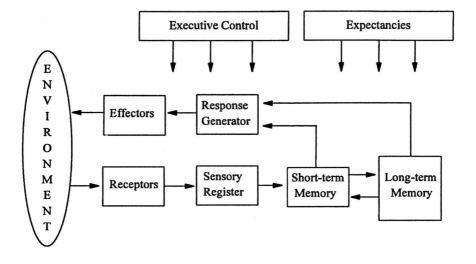

Source: Figure 4.1 from *The Conditions of Learning and the Theory of Instruction*, 4th ed., by Robert M. Gagne, copyright © 1985 by Holt, Rinehart and Winston, Inc. Reprinted by permission of the publisher.

The top parts of Figure 8-1 labelled "executive control" and "expectancies" are used to represent aspects of previous learning that are capable of affecting any or all of the phases of the information flow depicted in the lower parts of the figure. Since executive control and expectancies are the result of previous learning, they can be viewed as separate portions of long-term memory that are different from simple information storage. Control processes and expectancies are crucial parts of the learning process in determining how the attention of the learner is directed, how the information is encoded, how it is retrieved, and how it is expressed in organized responses. The terms "meta cognition" and "learning strategies" are sometimes used to refer to learners' knowledge about and control over their cognitive processes. (See Weinstein and Mayer, 1986.)

From the standpoint of learning, the most important phase of information processing is the "encoding" that meaningfully organizes the material passing from short-term memory to long-term memory. Wittrock (1974, 1978) has developed a model of learning as a generative process in which new information is related to information, concepts, and schemas already in long term memory. Creating connections between new information and previously learned information is a key step in encoding information in a meaningful learning set rather than a rote learning set.

Four Generally Accepted Propositions

Despite different conceptions of the basic learning process, there are some things that are generally accepted by most psychologists today with only relatively minor reservations.   Fortunately, each of these generally accepted propositions has implications for helping college students learn economics. Unfortunately, not all of these implications have been empirically tested and verified in undergraduate economics courses to the extent one would like, and most require some generalizing beyond the actual situations in which the research was conducted.

Limited Capacity to Process Information The limited capacity of the human mind to process information has been recognized for a long time. McKeachie (1963, p. 1120) has quoted the Moravian bishop and educational reformer Comenius (1592–1620) as stating:

If we take a jar with a narrow mouth, for to this we may compare a boy's intellect, and attempt to pour a quantity of water into it violently, instead of allowing it to trickle in drop by drop what will be the result? Without doubt, the greater part of the liquid will flow over the side, and ultimately the jar will contain less than if the operation had taken place gradually. Quite as foolish is the action of those who try to reach the pupils, not as much as they can assimilate, but as much as they themselves wish.

Over 300 years after Comenius made the preceding observation in his *Great Didactic*, the German-Swedish psychologist David Katz (1950) coined the term "mental dazzle" as a result of several experiments demonstrating that, beyond a certain point, adding elements in an intellectual task causes confusion and inefficiency.   And in 1956 George A. Miller published an important paper indicating that the number of "chunks" of independent information that an adult can keep in mind at the same time is about seven, plus or minus two. These "chunks" can vary in complexity, but the basic limitation now appears to be due to the relatively fragile nature of short-term or conscious memory compared to long-term memory.   Unlike long-term memory, which has a relatively unlimited storage capacity for "encoded" or meaningful information, new items entering the short-term memory "push out" old items once the limited capacity of short term memory has been reached. While the process of "rehearsal" mentioned above can extend the time interval that information can be stored in short-term memory, and while rehearsal may also aid in meaningfully encoding information for input into long-term memory, the number of items stored in short-term memory is not increased by rehearsal. "Overloading" short-term memory, therefore, interferes with meaningful learning and long-term memory.

The implications of the evidence on the limited capacity of the human mind to process information are clear, even if they are difficult to follow. As teachers, we must constantly resist pressure to "cover the field"—particularly in principles courses. *It is not what the instructor "covers," but what the student learns that counts.* Rather than dragging or pushing our students on a roller skate tour through the 30–, 40–, or perhaps even 50–room mansion of our discipline, everyone might be better off if we spend more time examining the foundations on which the whole superstructure rests. We should force ourselves to settle for a few things (the most important things) done well, rather than try to "cover the waterfront" in a manner that all, or most is washed away by the tides that sweep through the lives of students after final exams have been completed. Before outlining our courses or, indeed, before each class meeting we should ask ourselves: "What will the student learn today that will make a difference in his or her life five years or more from now?" An indication of how difficult it may be to follow this advice is given by the fact that the following statement appeared in a special supplement to the *American Economic Review* in 1950! "... the content of the elementary course has expanded beyond all possibility of adequate comprehension and assimilation by a student in one year of three class hours a week." (p. 56) Why we haven't made any progress in reducing the content of the principles course is also suggested in the same report: "... the fundamental error in current practice in the teaching of the first course in economics can be summarized in one word—'indecision'." (p. 56) Hopefully, some of the discussion of instructional objectives later in this chapter will help you reduce the indecision involved in dealing with this crucial issue in your own courses.

Importance of Prior Experience or "Learning Set" There is now a general recognition of the hierarchial arrangement of thought, and the importance of prior experience and current knowledge in establishing a student's "learning set." Whether prior learning is viewed as reinforced associations, configurations in the mind, or information stored in long-term memory, it is important that the demands we make on our students are not so unrelated to their prior experience that they are impossible to achieve.

Since most students' current knowledge and prior experiences are likely to be quite different from those of the instructor, we must be careful not to assume that the information that we give them will be interpreted and mentally filed away in the same way that it is stored in our own minds. Much that is "obvious" to the instructor may be incomprehensible or meaningless to the uninitiated student because of differences in assumptions, gaps in knowledge, and other differences in the "learning set."

The notion of "set" argues strongly for *pre-testing*, so that we can get a better idea of where our students are before we attempt to take them some place else. This is particularly true in economics where terms like "demand," and "investment" are given precise meanings that are often at variance with what non-economists "know" these terms mean. Ruth Beard (1972, p. 74) notes: "People differ in their capacity to relinquish 'sets,' some doing so fairly readily, whereas others will distort information they receive, forcing it to fit familiar interpretation until the weight of contradictions obliges them to a change." (p. 74) Anyone who has dealt with people who "know" that the value of money is determined by its gold backing, that "investment" is buying a share of common stock, etc., etc. will appreciate the truth of this statement. In some cases we may have to devote some time to overcoming erroneous interpretations and getting peoples minds "up" to zero, before we can begin getting them to accept new ways of looking at things. Whenever possible, therefore, we should use pre-tests to establish where our students are with respect to the learning set we want to establish. Nothing is more frustrating to a student than to be "completely in the dark." Students are unlikely to understand or retain material that is not meaningful, and new material is meaningful only if it fits in with what an individual already knows.

Carefully constructed homework problems can also be used to establish a common learning set that can help reduce much of the heterogeneity that plagues principles of economics classes by focusing student attention on a carefully structured set of questions. If students try to work the problems before coming to class, they can provide a context in which the instructors presentation and answers to student questions can be more meaningful to more students than they would be if no such problems were used.

Importance of Motivation The learner's motivation is a crucial variable in determining how much people learn. Interest in the material to be learned and an "intent to learn" are powerful motivating factors, and the desire for self-esteem and the stimulation or satisfaction of curiosity are motivations that can also be used in the college classroom. There is also some support for the proposition that a perceived usefulness of the material or, even better, an ability to use it, stimulates student interest and intent to learn. While it is no doubt true that not all students are deeply interested in everything their teachers want them to learn, there appears to be no reason for assuming that student motives are fixed. Before we point too many fingers at uninspired students, let us first ask ourselves: "What have we done to interest them in our courses?" Beyond attempting to demonstrate the usefulness of our material to our students, we should also recognize that there is some hard evidence pointing to the value of an *enthusiastic teacher* in generating interest in a subject. Along with a host of other studies on this point, Thistlewaite (1960) has reported that National Merit scholars consider instructor enthusiasm to have been one of the most critical variables influencing their choice of a field. Mastin (1963) found that 19 of 20 classes scored higher on a multiple choice exam after an "enthusiastic" presentation than after an "indifferent" presentation of material on ancient Egypt and ancient Rome and Pompeii, and Coats and Smidchens (1966) found sizable differences in immediate recall of lecture material on classroom interaction analysis when the lecture was delivered with "dynamism" (vocal inflection, gesturing, eye contact and animation) as compared to when the same lecture was read with good diction and sufficient volume.

With respect to "*intent to learn*" as a motivating device, an early study by Myers (1913) asked students to count the number of zeroes distributed among letters printed in color on colored paper. Later, the students were asked questions about what other letters were present and about the color of the paper and the letters. Their poor answers to these questions indicated that they had not learned much of the material to which they had been exposed but not explicitly told to learn. There have been several subsequent studies indicating the superiority of "intentional" learning; and Dressel and Mayhew (1954) have shown that even "critical thinking" can be significantly increased when it is taken as a primary objective by students. If we can generalize from such studies, carefully worded instructions, homework exercises, and exam questions can be used to encourage students to learn those aspects of our subjects we most want them to learn. The teacher who tests on the memorization of details, for example, encourages students to memorize details. But, if students believe that their grades are going to be based on their ability to integrate and apply principles, they will be motivated to acquire such ability. A carefully designed course syllabus that goes beyond a simple listing of dates and chapters in a textbook and contains a clearly stated set of cognitive objectives is probably the best way to stimulate intentional learning on the part of your students—particularly if you plan to test them on skills beyond the first two levels of Blooms Taxonomy. An efficient way of presenting a list of cognitive objectives that can be used for a unit in economics, or even a whole principles course, is discussed below.

With regard to students' *self esteem*, it often helps a great deal if instructors learn and use their names as soon a possible. The use of students' names indicates that you take an interest in them and that they "belong" in your classroom. Self esteem is also closely related to experiencing success and avoiding failure with respect to one's level of aspiration. The German psychologist F. Hoppe noted that a person tends to raise his or her goals after success and to lower them after failure. This process prevents one from continual failure or from too easy achievement, neither of which provides a feeling of accomplishment. An important motivating role for an instructor, therefore, is to help students set goals form themselves that are "challenging but attainable," and we should try to keep our instruction within the range of students' ability to deal with it without making it *either* too difficult or too easy. For students whose "motive to achieve success is stronger than their motive to avoid failure," Atkinson and Litwin (1960, p. 52) found that they were "most attracted to tasks of intermediate difficulty where the subjective probability of success is .50. Here the resultant positive motivation is strongest."

Similar to Atkinson and Litwin's finding that motivation may be highest in situations of moderate difficulty are D.E. Berlyne's indications that curiosity is highest in situations of moderate novelty. Berlyne contends that the interplay between the familiar and the novel is a significant factor in the development of curiosity, and he has stated:

Our theory of curiosity implies that patterns will be most curiosity-arousing at an intermediate state of familiarity. If they are too unlike anything with which the subject is acquainted, the symbolic response tendencies aroused will be too few and too feeble to provide much conflict, while too much familiarity will have removed conflict by making the particular combination an expected one. (Berlyne, 1953, p. 189)

Berlyne has also emphasized the "curiosity-inducing role of questions" and has defined "epistemic curiosity" as "a drive which is aroused by a question and reduced by rehearsing its answer." (Berlyne, 1954, p. 256) He found that using a pre-questionnaire aroused curiosity and increased the probability of college students recalling factual statements about animals. Statements recognized as answers to questions on the pre-questionnaire were more likely than others to be recalled on a post-questionnaire, and "surprising" statements were more likely to be recalled as answers on the post-questionnaire than others. Frick and Coffer (1972) later repeated the Berlyne study with a better control on the test items and obtained the same results.

Somewhat related to Berlyne's results with pre-questionnaires are the results of a number of studies that indicate that the insertion of questions in written prose materials facilitates learning. Rather than explaining these results in terms of curiosity, however, Rothkopf (1965 and 1970) has hypothesized that inserted questions give rise to "inspective behavior" or "mathemagenic activities" which "give birth to learning." In this connection, Watts and Anderson (1971) have found that inserted questions requiring application of principles to new examples were more effective than questions simply involving recall, and they argued that:

> answering application questions facilitates later performance by encouraging students to process the content of the instruction more thoroughly, in fact to transform it, in the effort to apply it in a new situation. (p. 393)

This process of using questions to encourage students to transform information is consistent with Wittrock's model of generative learning, and in 1982 MacKenzie and White tested predictions from Wittrock's model in a geography class with impressive results.

Dominance of Visual Over Verbal Bower and Hilgard (1981, p. 440) report: "A large number of learning experiments have now been done indicating that imaginal or pictorial representations of information usually facilitates memory, by factors ranging from 1.5 to 3 or so." In trying to explain why "imagery techniques" are so effective in facilitating recall of word lists, Paivio (1969 and 1971) has proposed a "two process theory of associative meaning" in which verbal information and visual information are processed or "coded" differently; and he argues that only verbal codes can be employed for abstract words whereas both visual and verbal codes can be employed for concrete words and pictures. And, in answer to their question "Why are pictures, then images, and then concrete words remembered in that order, with all remembered so much better than abstract words?", Bower and Hilgard (1981, p. 440) state:

> The current conjecture is what is called the "dual trace" hypothesis ... So a word (or word pair) that is imaged or a picture that is named has the advantage of having two, redundant copies of the memory trace laid down. The redundancy prolongs memory in comparison to abstract items, since the second, imaginal trace is likely to survive

after the initial, verbal trace has decayed. That is, not only are there two traces, but the one in the imaginal system seems more resistant to forgetting.[4]

This clearly implies that visual aids in the classroom are much more than a "gimmick." Carefully planned use of visual aids can be a valuable aid to student learning and retention. Not only do they add novelty and variation to our presentations, they also can add a concrete visual dimension to our verbal communications, and permit students to process and encode information in a more meaningful learning set.

Given these generally accepted principles on the limited capacity of the human mind, the importance of prior experience or learning "set," the importance of motivation, and the dominance of visual over verbal, let us now return to the three elements of our definition of learning. There is some evidence that the things that promote acquisition also facilitate retention and, to a lesser extent, transfer. Nevertheless, there is probably an expository advantage in discussing each of these elements separately.

Acquisition

As indicated by some of the comments above on the importance of an "intent to learn" as a motivating device, one of the most useful things that we can do to help our students acquire new knowledge is to let them know exactly what it is that they are supposed to learn. Ausubel (1963 and 1968), in particular, has argued that providing students with *"advanced organizers"* facilitates the learning of meaningful verbal material. These "organizers" are usually brief written passages which the students are supposed to read before studying new material, and they are designed to compare and contrast the new material with what the student already knows in order to provide "ideational scaffolding" to help students integrate new material into their existing "cognitive structure." A series of experiments involving material on Buddhism, endocrinology, and interpretations of the Civil War have supported the effectiveness of advanced organizers, and Wylie Anderson's experiment with a unit on supply and demand in college introductory economics classes found:

> Organizing concepts placed immediately prior (preorganizers) to a learning unit result in significantly better retention of the concepts involved than is the case where organizing concepts are positioned following a learning unit (postorganizer). (Anderson, 1974, p. 63)

The studies of the advantages of advanced organizers in classroom learning are consistent with earlier laboratory experiments that emphasized the importance of the "meaningfulness" of items in verbal word lists. Meaningfulness has traditionally been described in terms of the number of associations stimulated or the amount of "structure" that can be imposed on new material, and there is considerable evidence that initial instructions, elaboration directions, and suggested mnemonic devices can have a strong influence on rote memory tasks. The power of "mental imagery," has been discussed above. Not all mnemonic devices involve mental imagery, however, and most of us are aware of the advantages of remembering the months of the year that have a particular number of days by citing the rhyme, "Thirty days hath September, April, June and November, ..." or recalling rules governing the placement of "i" and "e" by citing, "'i' before 'e' except after 'c,' or when sounded like 'a' as in neighbor and weigh."

Since much knowledge in economics tends to be cumulative, and since some rote learning of new terms is necessary for later retention and transfer, any mnemonic devices that we can give students at the acquisition stage should provide helpful, in part because they tend to concretize (thereby making more familiar) the abstract terms or concepts they signify. Writing out "**I** nelastic" and "**E** lastic" in this manner, for example, has proven helpful to many beginning students and beginning instructors alike.

Once material has been presented and students have tried to learn it, "*feedback*," or "*knowledge of results*" has long been regarded as a powerful aid to learning, and there is a considerable body of laboratory evidence indicating the advantage of active as opposed to passive learning and the importance of *recitation* or *verbalization* in memorizing word lists. Unsuccessful attempts to slavishly apply these findings to the construction of learning programs or "teaching machines," however, indicate that there can be too much of a good thing, and Anderson (1967, p. 137) has noted: "Rather often programmed instruction research gives results at odds with the results obtained from other media, materials or techniques." In some programs, with low probability of error on each succeeding "frame," knowledge of results may not really convey much information; and, if the responses required are not relevant to the crucial content, requiring active responses may actually disrupt thoughtful reading habits. With regard to the usefulness of feedback, McKeachie (1974, p. 186) has stated:

> Knowledge of results, I would aver, *is* important for learning when the knowledge provides information and the learner knows how to correct his behavior; it doesn't make much difference if the learner already has a pretty good idea of how well he has done or doesn't know what to do differently.

And, with regard to the usefulness of active responses, Anderson (1967, pp. 139-141) has stated:

> Requiring an overt response from students is helpful only if the response is relevant to what is to be learned ... When a lesson entails technical language or foreign vocabulary, for instance, response learning becomes more important ... Clearly, an overt, constructed response should be required from a student if he is expected to be able to emit an unfamiliar, technical term ... overt responding works best with difficult, unfamiliar material.

Given the nature of most economics courses taught in the United States today, these comments indicate that we should give our students every opportunity to "respond" and "get involved" by having them complete homework problems and other assignments that are carefully graded and promptly returned with constructive comments and suggestions for improvement. There is some long standing evidence that reward is a stronger inducement to learning than punishment. Hurlock (1925), for example, was one of the first to indicate that students show large and consistent improvement when praised for their performance, but adverse effects when reproved or ignored. So in writing comments on papers, make an effort to find some things that you can praise.

In going over homework problems and/or other examples in class, one should also be aware of the principles of "guidance." On this point Hovland (1951, p. 644) has stated:

> Guidance given early apparently helps to establish the correct habits right from the start. Since, however, the learner will later have to perform the task without help, guidance must not continue too long, for the learner may become overly dependent upon outside assistance.

Although Hovland's observation was not based on the teaching of academic subjects in the college classroom, it suggests that, after students have a broad overview and sense of perspective on the entire course, perhaps a "lecture—work example—let student work a different example" sequence may be useful in the early stages until the students have accumulated enough "tools" to work for themselves. But at a later stage of the course it is probably important to put students in problem-solving situations on their own. At this stage, we must develop patience and resist the temptation to "tell them the answer." We must let them mull it over and work it out for themselves. Cameron's Chapter 16 below also outlines several active or collaborative learning activities that can be employed to get students more involved in their own learning.

Retention

As has been indicated previously, the things that promote acquisition also promote retention of new knowledge. Indeed, one can not remember what one has not learned in the first place, and most tests of acquisition require the use of memory. The single most important thing in retention, therefore, is the *degree of initial learning*. Material learned by rote is not remembered as well as "meaningful" or "organized" material, and material that is used and applied is remembered much better than material that is not. In addition to an emphasis on organization, structure, and application in their initial presentations, therefore, classroom teachers can also use *repetition* and *review* to combat disuse of important ideas and concepts. In this connection, studies of verbal learning have found that "*overlearning*"—or learning beyond simple mastery—aids retention. Since getting students to the point of simple mastery is a difficult task in itself, this finding might not seem like much of a help. Yet it is probably related to the common statement among graduate students, who have just passed their qualifying exams and begun to teach at the introductory level, that only when they tried to teach their subject to others did they *really* begin to understand what it was all about themselves. Perhaps similar experiences can be provided in briefer and simpler form at the undergraduate level by having students give class reports or summaries of term papers. Such practices may help to induce overlearning in key areas carefully selected for these purposes. (See Petr's Chapter 15 on writing.)

The forgetting of material that is not used or applied has usually been explained by "decay" or "displacement." In addition, "interference theory" has also been invoked by psychologists to explain the often observed "*serial position effect*" that material presented in the middle of a sequence is not remembered as well as material presented at the beginning or at the end of a sequence. This observation can be explained as due to interference from other material in the sequence. Interference from material presented earlier is called "proactive interference," and interference from material presented later is called "retroactive interference." Material presented first in a sequence is subject only to retroactive interference. Material presented last in a sequence is subject only to proactive interference. But material presented in the middle is subject to both kinds of interference. The implication of this for classroom lectures is clear. *It is important to make your major points at the beginning and/or at the end of your presentation and not bury them in the middle.*

In addition to decay, displacement, and interference, the information processing approach to learning has focused on still another approach to forgetting which can be called "cue dependent forgetting" to deal with situations in which the information sought for is available in the long-term memory store but is inaccessible because of inadequate retrieval cues. There is some evidence that "*priming*" can stimulate relevant recall, presumably by activating otherwise dormant retrieval cues. A study by Johnson (1965), for example, indicated the efficacy of priming in stimulating relevant recall when a group of high school seniors who had completed a unit in a physics course were given the task of solving ten problems. Half of the students were given a two minute word association pretest in which the stimulus words named concepts necessary for the solution of the subsequent problems. A significantly larger number of problem solutions were attained by the group given the prior association test than by the unprimed group.

Recalling the comments on "guidance" above, however, one should not overly rely on priming or prompting if one wants students to develop methods of recalling material on their own. Anderson, Faust, and Roderick (1968), for example, compared a heavily prompted version of an instructional program with a standard version and found that students made higher achievement scores with the latter version. So overprompting can lead to a reduction in learning effectiveness.

Transfer

Transfer of learning from one situation to another has sometimes been referred to as "learning to learn." From a very early date, verbal learning experiments have indicated that the transfer of learning involves more than repetitive practice of the initial learning exercise. Indeed, without *overt stress on underlying principles*, most learning habits are apparently highly specific to the situation in which they are practiced. With regard to memory training, the experience of William James (1890) is often cited in support of this point. After memorizing the first part of a poem by Hugo, he then practiced memorizing a poem by Milton. But, upon returning to memorizing the last part of Hugo's poem, James found that it was no easier, and indeed it took him longer to memorize the second 158 lines of the "Satyr" than it did the first 158 lines. He concluded that this sort of practice did not result in any general improvement in memorizing ability. Later, Woodrow (1927) reasoned that, if subjects were given systematic instruction in how to memorize, the improvement would have been more marked. Accordingly, he set up a study for two experimental groups and one control group. One group devoted itself to intensive memorizing of poetry and non-word syllables. The second group spent the same amount of time but divided it between receiving instruction in good methods of memorizing and performing exercises in using these methods. The group that spent all the time in practice performed little better than the control group on subsequent memory tests, but the group given instruction in methods of efficient memory showed marked improvement.

Going beyond simple memory work, another pair of early studies indicated that in one situation in which an arithmetic teacher stressed neatness in the papers handed in by students, a gradual improvement was noted in the neatness of these papers, but no transfer was found with respect to the neatness of papers turned in by these students in other subjects. (See Bagley, 1905.) When the experiment was repeated with another group of students, however, the teacher who emphasized neatness in arithmetic also stressed the general importance of neatness in dress, business, and the home. Under these conditions, improvement was obtained in the neatness of papers, not only in arithmetic, but in other subjects as well. (See Ruediger, 1908.)

The main point here seems to be that *transfer is facilitated when the initial learning can be formulated in terms of general principles applicable to new learning*. It offers little support for the doctrine of "mental discipline" *per se*, for there is no evidence that courses in formal logic alone, for example, are likely to make people more logical in other areas. But, if students can learn "what to look for" in solving certain kinds of problems, there is some hope that exposure to a *variety* of particular problems may lead eventually to a more general problem-solving ability. In a famous experiment involving shooting at targets under water, Judd (1908) set up two groups. One group was first taught the principles of light refraction, the other was not. Both groups were then given practice in shooting at submerged targets. By trial and error both groups learned about equally well to adjust for refractive errors. But, when the depth of the target was changed, the group previously taught about refraction learned to correct their aim for the new conditions much faster than did the other group. Katona's later experiments with geometric puzzles, card, and match tricks offer further evidence on this point (Katona, 1940), and in a recent review Bransford, Sherwood, Vye, and Rieser cite a number of studies that "provide evidence that an emphasis on executive or metacognitive processes can result in improvements in thinking and problem solving" (1986, p. 1083).

The studies of transfer of learning have implications not only for how problem solving material is presented but also for how homework or practice problems are designed. Practice problems that emphasize computation rather than interpretation and application may not only encourage the student to relate the material to a rote learning set rather than a meaningful learning set, they may also have limiting effects on the future study behavior of the student. If we want to develop in our students the capacity for meaningful (as opposed to rote) understanding and broad (as opposed to narrow) transfer, we must design our instructions and homework problems accordingly.

Importance of Instructional Objectives

The preceding, admittedly selective review the results of several theoretical and applied experiments in human learning indicate the importance of carefully thinking through exactly what it is we want our students to be able to do after our courses, teaching units, lectures, discussion sessions, etc. Human learning is complex. There can be different degrees of understanding or knowledge of the same concepts. The key role of motivation in human learning also underlines the importance of the affective domain as well as the cognitive domain.

Clearly specified instructional objectives can provide helpful guidance for (1) student study efforts, (2) instructor teaching efforts, and (3) testing and evaluation efforts. Yet writing long lists of objectives for every single thing we want students to learn can often run into diminishing returns rather quickly. One way to deal with this problem is to state three or four general objectives such as "knows basic terms," "understands concepts and principles," "applies basic concepts and principles to new situations" and then follow each general objective with a *representative sample* of specific illustrative behaviors. The illustrative examples should begin with a verb that specifies observable *student* behavior, and the illustrative verbs should have the most precise meaning possible—"use," "know," "*really* know" are less precise than "identify," "describe," "construct," "distinguish." Gronlund (1985, p. xx) offers a good illustration of how this technique can be applied to a principles of economic course or a unit in such a course. If presented in a format similar to Table 8-1, an outline of the cognitive objectives for your whole course can be presented on a single page in your course syllabus.

Table 8-1: Objectives for a Course (Or Unit) in Economics

These objectives can be applied to various content areas depending on the length of the course/unit.)

1. Knows basic terms.

    1.1 Relates terms that have the same meaning.
    1.2 Selects the term that best fits a particular definition.
    1.3 Identifies terms used in reference to particular economic problems.
    1.4 Uses terms correctly in describing economic problems.

2. Understands economic concepts and principles.

    2.1 Identifies examples of economic concepts and principles.
    2.2 Describes economic concepts and principles in own words.
    2.3 Points out the interrelationship of economic principles.
    2.4 Explains changes in economic conditions in terms of the economic concepts and principles involved.

3. Applies economic principles to new situations.

    3.1 Identifies the economic principles needed to solve a practical problem.
    3.2 Predicts the probable outcome of an action involving economic principles.
    3.3 Describes how to solve a practical economic problem in terms of the economic principles involved.
    3.4 Distinguishes between probable and improbable economic forecasts.

4. Interprets economic data.

    4.1 Differentiates between relevant and irrelevant information.
    4.2 Differentiates between facts and inferences.
    4.3 Identifies cause-effect relations in data.
    4.4 Describes the trends in data.
    4.5 Distinguishes between warranted and unwarranted conclusions drawn from data.
    4.6 Makes proper qualifications when describing data.

How to Write and Use Instructional Objectives, 5th ed., by Gronlund © 1995. Adapted by permission of Prentice-Hall, Inc., Upper Saddle River, NJ.

Note that the statements of specific behaviors listed under each general objective in Table 8-1 describe how the student is expected to react toward the subject matter in economics, but they do not describe the specific subject matter toward which he or she is to react. (For example, the specific behaviors listed under "knows basic terms" describe what is meant by "knowing," not what terms the student should know.) Such statements make it possible to relate the same instructional objectives to different content units, and they can serve as a highly useful guide to students and to instructors in focusing their learning and teaching efforts and in preparing for exams and evaluations.

Completely Stated Objectives

The learning outcome or the *behavior* that the *student* should be able to demonstrate is the most important part of an instructional objective. Educators correctly point out, however, that a statement of what the student must do is only one component of a completely stated objective. To be complete, an instructional objective should also contain a statement of the *conditions* in which the student should be able to do it, and a statement of the *criteria* that will be used to judge how well it is done. The three basic components of a completely stated objective—conditions, behavior, and criteria—are sometimes summarized in the three basic questions of *when? what?* and *how well?*

After attending the appropriate lecture, the student should be able to define the term "induced investment" with 100% accuracy.

Given 13 years of time series data on GNP, the stock of money, the Consumer's Price Index, and the unemployment rate, and with the aid of calculators being permitted, the student should be able to correctly compute the income velocity of circulation to two decimal places for four selected years in a five minute period.

Given a hypothetical newspaper clipping with three erroneous interpretations of an economic event, the student should be able to correctly identify two of the three errors and explain fully the reason why they are wrong.

Yet it is important to keep *conditions* and *criteria* in mind when deciding what it is we want our students to be able to do. Comparing the performance of different students or different groups on the same test, for example, is not appropriate if the conditions are not similar. Considerations such as whether or not students are allowed to consult notes and books and the amount of time allowed to work are also important in deciding what criteria to use in evaluating responses.[5]

Conclusions

The conclusions that emerge from the preceding discussion of learning theory and instructional objectives can be summarized in the following nine (7 + 2) points. If you practice these behaviors, your students should learn more in your economics course than if you do not practice these behaviors.

1 Formulate clear objectives in both the cognitive and the affective domain, and use your course syllabus and other devices to let your students know what is expected of them.

2 If you expect students to learn concepts up to the applications level, you must design presentations and exercises that go beyond recall and memory and stress transfer. You should remember the limited capacity of the human mind to process information, and concentrate on a selected number of the most important concepts rather than trying to "cover the waterfront."

3 Remember the importance of "learning set," and use pretests or questionnaires to make sure that you know where your students are starting from. As the course progresses, use carefully structured homework problems to focus student's "set", and don't be afraid to repeat and review frequently if major points are not being understood or cannot be applied.

4 Remember the importance of student motivation, and demonstrate enthusiasm, use clear directions to establish an "intent to learn," try to create situations of moderate difficulty and moderate novelty, and use students' names whenever possible. Also try to help students establish learning goals for themselves that are neither so low as to be unfulfilling or so high as to be impossible of attainment.

5 Try to use variety in your presentations, and use visual aids whenever possible to activate both visual and verbal processing activities in your students.

6 Begin your presentations of new material with "advanced organizers," and try to link new material to old. Also try to begin your lectures with memorable, thought provoking questions, and make sure that your main points are emphasized at the beginning and the end of your presentation.

7 Provide students with an opportunity to actively respond and verbalize difficult points, and provide prompt and accurate feedback on major learning exercises. In providing feedback, try to emphasize the positive, and write comments of what you can praise on papers.

8 Try to teach for transfer by emphasizing the potential usefulness of the most important general principles, and develop problems and examples that apply principles to a *wide variety* of situations.

9 In helping students with problems, use priming or cuing if necessary, but don't over prompt or provide too much guidance if you want students to develop understandings and applications on their own.

NOTES

1. Although he regarded the ages as only approximations, Piaget labeled his stages of intellectual development as: sensorimotor (birth to 2 years); preoperational (2–7 years); concrete operational (7–11 years); and formal operations (11 years and older). For more information on Piaget's ideas, which have been very influential, see Ginsburg and Opper, 1969.

Although Piaget assumed that the stage of formal operational thought is reached in the early adolescent years, his work did not extend much beyond that age group. William G. Perry, Jr. later worked out a scheme that classified various stages of intellectual and ethical development in the college years. Perry's scheme outlines a process of intellectual maturation wherein college students develop from an initial stage of "basic duality" in which absolutes and authority are viewed as either totally right or totally wrong, through stages of relativism in which diversity and uncertainty are increasingly recognized and accepted, to a final stage in which students become committed to the understandings and values that determine their subsequent life style. (See Perry, 1970.)

2. For a review of the evolution of the field of instructional psychology see Menges and Girard (1983).

3. Gagne (1985, p. 70) notes: "The processes and structures described by learning theories are inferred from empirical studies of learning. Presumably, these processes and structures reflect the action of the human central nervous system and are compatible with what is known about the neurophysiology of the nervous system. The structures and their activities remain as postulated entities, however, since they have not yet been related to particular locations or operations of the brain."

4. Bower (1970) has also offered an excellent, brief discussion of dual processing systems in nontechnical terms in the latter part of his "Analysis of a Mnemonic Device."

5. An excellent brief treatment of all three aspects of a completely stated objective is Robert F. Mager (1962). Written in a format that permits you to practice and test yourself as you go along, this entire book can be completed in about one hour.

Another brief programmed approach to formulating instructional objectives is Donald L. Troyer (1977). The second part of Troyer's chapter (pp. 116-143) goes beyond writing objectives to evaluating them in terms of "worth," "fit," and "match."

REFERENCES

Anderson, B.W. (1974). A comparison of pre- versus postorganizers upon retention of economic concepts. *Journal of Economic Education*, 6, 61-64.

Anderson, R.C. (1967). Education psychology. *Annual Review of Psychology*, 129-164. Palo Alto: Annual Reviews, Inc.

Anderson, R.C., Faust, G.W., and Roderick, M.C. (1968). Overprompting in programmed instruction. *Journal of Education Psychology*, 59, 88-93.

Atkinson, J.W. and Litwin, G.H. (1960). Achievement motive and test anxiety conceived as motive to approach success and motive to avoid failure. *Journal of Abnormal and Social Psychology*, 60, 52-63.

Ausubel, D.P. (1963). *The psychology of meaningful verbal learning*. New York: Grune & Stratton.

Ausubel, D.P. (1968). *Educational psychology: A cognitive view*. New York: Holt, Rinehart & Winston.

Bagley, W.C. (1905). *The educative process*. New York: Macmillan.

Beard, R. (1972). *Teaching and learning in higher education*, 2nd ed. Baltimore: Penguin Books.

Berlyne, D.E. (1953). A theory of human curiosity. *British Journal of Psychology*, 45, 180-191.

Berlyne, D.E. (1954). An experimental study of human curiosity. *British Journal of Psychology*, 45, 256-265.

Bower, G.H. (1970). Analysis of a mnemonic device. *American Scientist*, 58, 496-510.

Bower, G.H. and Hilgard, E.R. (1981). *Theories of learning*, 5th ed. Englewood Cliffs: Prentice-Hall.

Bransford, J., Sherwood, R., Vye, N., and Rieser, J. (1986). Teaching thinking and problem solving: Research foundations. *American Psychologist*, 41, 1078-1089.

Bruner, J.S. (1966). *Toward a theory of instruction*. Cambridge: Belknap Press.

Coats, W.D. and Smidchens, U. (1966). Audience recall as a function of speaker dynamism. *Journal of Educational Psychology*, 57, 189-191.

Committee on the Undergraduate Teaching of Economics and the Training of Economists. (1950). The teaching of undergraduate economics. *American Economic Review: Supplement*, 40(5), Part 2, December.

Davies, I.K. (1981). *Instructional technique*. New York: McGraw-Hill.

Dressel, P.L. and Mayhew, L.B. (1954). *General education: Explorations in evaluation.* Washington: American Council on Education.

Frick, J.W. and Cofer, C.N. (1972). Berlyne's demonstration of epistemic curiosity: An experimental re-evaluation. *British Journal of Psychology*, 63, 221-228.

Gagne, R.M. (1985). *The conditions of learning and the theory of instruction*, 4th ed. New York: Holt, Rinehart and Winston.

Gagne, R.M. and Rohwer, W.D., Jr. (1969). Instructional psychology. *Annual Review of Psychology*, 382-418. Palo Alto: Annual Reviews, Inc.

Ginsberg, H. and Opper, S. (1969). *Piaget's theory of intellectual development: An introduction.* Englewood Cliffs: Prentice-Hall.

Glaser, R. and Bassok, M. (1989). Learning theory and the theory of instruction. *Annual Review of Psychology*, 631-666. Palo Alto: Annual Reviews, Inc.

Gronlund, N.E. (1995). *How to write and use instructional objectives*, 5th ed. Englewood Cliffs, NJ: Merrill / Prentice-Hall.

Hovland, C.I. (1951). Human learning and retention. In S.S. Stevens (ed.), *Handbook of experimental psychology* (pp. 613-689). New York: John Wiley and Sons.

Hurlock, E.B. (1925). An evaluation of certain incentives used in school work. *Journal of Educational Psychology*, 16, 145-159.

James, W. (1890). *The principles of psychology.* New York: Holt.

Johnson, P.E. (1965). Word relatedness and problem solving in high school physics. *Journal of Educational Psychology*, 56, 217-224.

Judd, C.H. (1908). The relation of special training to general intelligence. *Educational Review*, 36, 28-42.

Katona, G. (1940). *Organizing and memorizing*. New York: Columbia University.

Katz, D. (1950). *Gestalt psychology*. New York: Ronald.

Kolb, D.A. (1981). Learning styles and disciplinary difference. In A.W. Chickering and Associates, *The modern American college* (pp. 232-255). San Francisco: Jossey-Bass.

MacKenzie, A.W. and White, R.T. (1982). Fieldwork in geography and long-term memory structures. *American Education Research Journal*, 19, 623-632.

Mager, R.F. (1962). *Preparing instructional objectives*. Belmont, CA: Fearon Publishers.

Mastin, V.E. (1963). Teacher enthusiasm. *Journal of Educational Research*, 56, 385-386.

McKeachie, W.J. (1963). Research on teaching at the college and university level. In N.L. Gage (ed.), *Handbook of research on teaching* (pp. 1118-1172). Chicago: Rand-McNally.

McKeachie, W.J. (1974). Instructional psychology. *Annual Review of Psychology*, 161-193. Palo Alto: Annual Reviews, Inc.

Menges, R.J. and Girard, D.E. (1983). Development of a research specialty: Instructional psychology portrayed in the *Annual Review of Psychology*. *Instructional Science*, 12, 83-98.

Miller, G.A. (1956). The magical number seven, plus or minus two: Some limits on our capacity for processing information. *Psychological Review*, 63, 81-97.

Myers, G.C. (1913). A study in incidental memory. *Archives of Psychology*, 26, (February).

Paivio, A. (1969). Mental imagery in associative learning and memory. *Psychological Review*, 76, 241-263.

Paivio, A. (1971). *Imagery and Verbal Processes*. New York: Holt, Rinehart and Winston.

Perry, W.G. (1970). *Forms of intellectual and ethical development in the college years: A scheme*. New York: Holt, Rinehart and Winston.

Rothkopf, E.Z. (1965). Some theoretical and experimental approaches to problems in written instruction. In J.D. Krumboltz (ed.), *Learning and the Educational Process* (pp. 193-221). Chicago: Rand-McNally.

Rothkopf, E.Z. (1970). The concept of mathemagenic activities. *Review of Education Research*, 40, 325-336.

Ruediger, W.C. (1908). The indirect improvement of mental function through ideals. *Education Review*, 36, 364-371.

Skinner, B.F. (1968). *The technology of teaching*. New York: Appleton-Century-Crofts.

Thistlewaite, L. (1960). *College press and changes in study plans of talented students*. Evanston: National Merit Scholarship Corp.

Troyer, D.L. (1977). Performance objectives: Formulation and implementation. In J. Weigand (ed.), *Implementing Teacher Competencies* (pp. 98-116). Prentice-Hall.

Watts, G.H. and Anderson, R.C. (1971). Effects of three types of inserted questions on learning from prose. *Journal of Educational Psychology*, 62, 387-394.

Weinstein, C.E. and Mayer, R.E. (1986). The teaching of learning strategies. In M.C. Wittrock (ed.), *Handbook of research on teaching*, 3rd ed. (pp. 315-327). New York: MacMillan Publishing Company.

Wittrock, M.C. (1974). Learning as a generative process. *Educational Psychologist*, 11, 87-95.

Wittrock, M.C. (1978). The cognitive movement in instruction. *Educational Psychologist*, 13, 15-30.

Woodrow, H. (1927). The effect of the type of training upon transference. *Journal of Educational Psychology*, 18, 159-172.

APPENDIX 8-1

BRIEF DEFINITION AND ILLUSTRATIVE VERBS FOR SPECIFYING BEHAVIORS IN EACH CATEGORY OF BLOOM'S TAXONOMY OF THE COGNITIVE DOMAIN

Highest
Level

> *Evaluation* Ability to judge the value of material in terms of internal and external criteria.   Appraises, concludes, evaluates, judges.

↑

> *Synthesis* Ability to put parts together to form a new whole. Combines, compiles, composes, creates.

↑

> *Analysis* Ability to break down material into its component parts so that its organizational structure can be understood.   Distinguishes, separates, discriminates, illustrates.

↑

> *Applications* Ability to use learning material in new situations. Demonstrates, produces, predicts, relates.

↑

> *Comprehension* Ability to understand and explain the meaning of material.   Interprets, translates, summarizes, gives examples.

↑

Lowest
Level

> *Knowledge*   Ability to recall previously learned materials. Defines, states, identifies, matches, selects.

How to Write and Use Instructional Objectives, 5th ed., by Gronlund © 1995. Adapted by permission of Prentice-Hall, Inc., Upper Saddle River, NJ.

APPENDIX 8-2

BRIEF DEFINITION AND ILLUSTRATIVE VERBS FOR SPECIFYING BEHAVIORS IN EACH CATEGORY OF KRATHWOHL'S TAXONOMY OF THE AFFECTIVE DOMAIN

Highest
Level

Characterization by a Value or Value Complex A coherent value system controls behavior and develops a characteristic "life style." Displays, practices, demonstrates, maintains.

↑

Organization Brings together different values and begins to build an internally consistent value system. Arranges, combines, integrates, adheres.

↑

Valuing Attaches worth to a particular activity or behavior. Appreciates, initiates, joins, shows concern for.

↑

Responding Reacts to activities and assignments in some way. Answers, replies, writes, completes.

↑

Lowest
Level

Receiving Willingness to attend to classroom activities and outside assignments. Pays attention, listens, sits erect, shows awareness.

How to Write and Use Instructional Objectives, 5th ed., by Gronlund © 1995. Adapted by permission of Prentice-Hall, Inc., Upper Saddle River, NJ.

CHAPTER 9

HUMANIZING CONTENT AND PEDAGOGY IN ECONOMICS CLASSROOMS

Robin L. Bartlett
Marianne A. Ferber

To the extent that there is concern among economists that not enough students take economics courses, and that those who do, do not learn enough, it is clear that such concern is even more appropriate in the case of women and members of minorities. A substantially smaller proportion of them take introductory economics and they do not do as well as white men in the course.[1] Women are also considerably less likely to go on to take additional economics courses. Their small representation among economics majors and among practitioners of economics has been noted for some time. Thus it is not surprising that there has been much speculation and some research in an effort to determine the causes of their poorer performance in economics, although women earn higher grades overall.[2]

While in 1992–93 (U.S. Department of Education, 1995) the proportion of B.A.s earned by women was 64 percent in anthropology, 42 percent in political science, 73 percent in psychology, and 68 percent in sociology, it was only 30 percent in economics.[3] Similarly, the share of Ph.D.s earned by women in 1992–93 was 62 percent in anthropology, 61 percent in psychology, and 49 percent in sociology, and 26 percent in political science, but only 23 percent in economics. The comparisons with the other social sciences suggest that women have problems in economics that they do not encounter to the same extent in these other fields;[4] further, the fact that during the same year women earned 47 percent of B.A.s and 21 percent of Ph.D.s in mathematics, as well as 47 percent of B.A.s and 26 percent of Ph.D.s in business fields, suggests that it is neither women's inability to handle the required mathematics, nor their lack of interest in business that are the culprits. Thus it is not surprising that questions have been raised about the possibility that there may be a "chilly classroom climate" for women students in economics courses.

A good deal of earlier work has investigated whether the small representation of women among economics faculties may have contributed to this problem. The results to date have been inconclusive. Most of the studies found that having women instructors made no difference to the performance of women students (for instance, Ehrenberg, Goldhaber, and Brewer, 1995), although others found that it did (e.g., Saunders, 1994), and there is some evidence that minority students do better with instructors from the same minority group (Ehrenberg and Brewer, 1994). In addition, Watts and Bosshardt (1991) discovered that student outcomes differ depending, for instance, on the latitude in topics to be covered, as well as one-on-one time instructors spent with students. This suggests that to the extent that female instructors are more flexible in these respects there may be a gender component to the explanation. Finally, a number of researchers found that women teachers tend to have better rapport with women students (Berg and Ferber, 1983) and to evaluate the work of women students more favorably (Ehrenberg, Goldhaber, and Brewer, 1995, among others). This is all the more likely to be important because recognition and encouragement appear to be particularly important motivators for women students.

Much attention has also focused on the all too common neglect of topics related to, or of particular importance for, women and minorities (e.g., Feiner and Morgan, 1987; Ferber, 1990). While some critics have attacked efforts to reform the curriculum (e.g., D'Souza, 1991) and have claimed that charges of masculine bias are unwarranted, there is considerable evidence that a good deal of bias remains. For instance, Sheffrin (1992) scoffs at the notion that any text would fail to mention the omission of the value of unpaid work in calculating GDP. In fact, however, a 1993 survey of nine widely used introductory textbooks showed that several of them fail to do so; among the remaining ones, one mentions household production under the heading of "leisure," and none discusses ways for estimating its value, or why it would be useful to have such estimates (Ferber, forthcoming). Also, for the most part, households and families as institutions receive virtually no attention; about half of these books discuss income distribution without mentioning the disproportionate representation of minorities, women, and children among the poor; and women, as well as minorities, continue to be stereotyped, both because they tend to be portrayed in traditional occupations, and because workers and managers are almost invariably "he," while consumers are referred to as "she." Although no research has been done to determine whether and to what extent such matters influence the motivation and performance of students, it appears entirely plausible that such omissions and stereotyping might adversely effect students.

More recently feminists have been in the forefront of those who suggested that, in addition to the issues mentioned above, it is more fundamentally the traditional definition of economics and the narrow methods employed by mainstream economists to the virtual exclusion of other definitions and methods that are responsible for the alienation of so many students in economics courses, women, and members of minorities foremost among them. One does not, however, need to be a feminist in order to find fault with mainstream dogmas that range from the central persona of rational economic man, who springs to life like a mushroom, fully independent, with no need for care from others either in childhood or old age, with tastes and values fully formed and isolated from any influence of society, to the notion that it is the model of individual choice in markets that distinguishes economics from other disciplines (Becker, 1976, p. 5), the emphasis on value free and "context free" analysis,[5] and the privileging of theoretical modeling over empirical work. We shall turn to this subject next before going on to consider the role of improved pedagogy in the last section of this chapter.

Humanizing the Dismal Science

Feminist critics today continue to incorporate earlier recommendations to hire more instructors who could be role models for women and minority students, and to introduce more topics that are relevant to these students, because they are still timely,[6] but they tend to go well beyond these suggestions. As Nelson (1995, p. 132) puts it "Feminist theory raises questions about the adequacy of economic practice not because economics in general is too objective, but because it is not objective enough. Various value-laden and partial—and in particular masculine gendered—perspectives on subject, model, method, and pedagogy have heretofore been mistakenly perceived as value free and impartial in economics...." Tradition-ally, male activities have taken center stage as subject matter, while models and methods have reflected a historically and psychologically masculine patterns of valuing autonomy and detachment over dependence and connection."[7] Here we shall focus on issues that are of particular importance in the introductory economics course. Rather than discussing these matters in the abstract, we provide a varied, though certainly not exhaustive, list of examples.[8] These examples not only serve to illustrate the issues raised above, but should also be helpful to instructors who want to make their courses more interesting for and more relevant to students in general, and particularly to those who are most alienated by the traditional Economics 101.

The reforms envisioned in this chapter may be expected to help to change economics, so that students will not be expected "to believe all this stuff about individuals constantly making fully informed rational choices accounting for all expected lifetime costs and benefits" (Blank, 1993, p.133). They will no longer be taught to ignore the importance of people acting in groups, whether they be families, labor unions, trade associations, communities, or a multitude of other institutions. Nor will they be presented with models that disregard the importance of power in the economy, in society, and in the family, or presented with calculations of GDP that neglect non-market production. In sum, they will not be confronted with an economics that neglects the real world because it is untidy, complex, and even messy, and because its problems can not be solved as readily as can elegant mathematical models.

"Vive la Difference!" or a Reality Check   We often learn very little when information is only available for the population as whole, or worse, only for the dominant group, as is still occasionally the case. Bartlett's (1985; 1996) examination of the Phillips curve illustrates this point very well. This work shows that the "natural rate of unemployment" is consistently far higher for blacks than whites, and during a downturn (like 1980–83) unemployment rates for blacks rise by a greater amount. Students of color are likely to find that these observations fit more closely with their own perceptions and experiences.

Many other examples can be found where an average tells us little, but two will suffice to make the point. Showing what has happened to real income for the country as a whole hides the fact that the trend has been very different for women and men, for people at different levels of education, for recipients of wages and recipients of other forms of income. Similarly, the overall trend in the poverty rate obscures the fact that the elderly are doing considerably better than in earlier days, while for children, and especially for the increasing proportion living with only one parent, precisely the opposite is true.

How Optimal is Pareto Optimality?   Mainstream economists put great emphasis on the rule that overall well-being can be improved if and only if gainers can more than compensate losers. This is the basic tenet used, for instance, to justify free trade. What is overlooked here is that in reality the gainers rarely if ever do compensate the losers, so that the result is a redistribution of income. Ironically, it is these very proponents of Pareto optimality who argue that because interpersonal comparisons of utility are impossible, a transfer of income inevitably leaves the welfare effect indeterminate. A more realistic view would be to recognize that even though utility can not be measured precisely, winning (or losing) an extra dollar will tend to mean less to people with higher incomes. To the extent that this is the case, trade which has tended to increase earnings differentials, as many experts claim has been the case in recent years, may well have decreased overall well-being, even if there was a net gain in GDP.

Equally troublesome is the implication that when there is a simple transfer so that, given some costs involved in the transaction, gainers actually receive somewhat less than the losers have to give up, it is not possible to conclude that well-being may have improved. Yet, how many people would seriously question whether the loss in utility would be less when we take $10,000 from someone whose income is $1,000,000 and give $9,000, or even just $5,000 to someone whose income is $10,000? Thus adherence to the Pareto dictum will give a great boost to those who favor the status quo and oppose redistribution, even when common sense dictates that reducing inequality, at least in extreme cases, would tend to improve overall well-being. In this context it is also worth mentioning that a very unequal distribution of income in any case favors the status quo because those who are doing well under the present system can use their wealth to make change more difficult.

Keeping Up with the Joneses, or the Importance of Context Another issue related to income distribution is almost invariably ignored by mainstream economists when they assume that the tastes of "homo economicus" are given and are independent of his/her surroundings. It is obvious that once primary needs—for food, protection against the elements, medical care, etc.—have been taken care of, how satisfied people are with what they have is greatly influenced not only by how much they have, but how that compares to what others have. Again, is there anyone who would doubt that a person living in a neat four-room bungalow would feel quite differently about this house if it were surrounded by similar bungalows, then if it were surrounded by large mansions? Similarly, mainstream economists tend to ignore that, given the emphasis in our economy on competition, and on what we own rather than what we are, we tend to waste enormous amount of resources because everyone beyond the poverty level spends a great deal in order to keep up with the Joneses, or preferably to get ahead of them. Such an aim is as useless as an arms race, because it is a zero sum game. This would be harmless, except for the deprivation of people who can not take care of their needs, and the needs of their children, and the fact that we are using up exhaustible resources.

The "Family" as an Economic Unit It is rather ironic that mainstream economists turned their attention to the family and, emphasizing the economic advantages of the division of labor within the family, to explain why women specialize in housework (see Becker 1965), just at the time when the traditional family, once the unquestioned norm, was rapidly declining. It is equally ironic that we persist in defining the family as "two or more people related by blood or marriage," when increasingly people live together who do not fit this established, but excessively narrow definition. While in 1966 only 35.4 percent of women with husbands present were in the labor force, this figure rose to 74.9 percent in 1993. True, the neoclassical model also offers some explanations for these changes, putting primary emphasis on the increase of women's earnings in the labor market. It fails, however, to adequately note other important reasons why specialization by husband and wife may not be advantageous for either one, and particularly not for the one who is the homemaker.

Reasons that are generally neglected are: (1) Although the value of home production tends to be very high when there are young children in the family, it declines rapidly as they grow up. Meanwhile, the earnings potential of the homemaker also declines, and may never fully recover. Hence it is not likely to maximize family income in the long run. (2) At the same time, because of the declining earnings potential, the homemaker becomes increasingly dependent on the wage earner. The resulting risks in the case of divorce are obvious, but as long as heads of households are not always as altruistic as the model assumes, the disadvantages of having less bargaining power in an ongoing marriage should not be underestimated either. (3) Assuming that there is diminishing marginal utility to doing additional hours of one kind of work, as is eminently plausible, and that housework is likely to be more enjoyable—or at least less tedious—when two people do it together, there is a clear advantage from this point of view when both partners are homemakers and wage earners. Further, it should also be noted that there is considerable evidence that, in spite of the fact that homemakers often tend to have more autonomy in determining their own working conditions than many employees do, most people, women as well as men, generally prefer market work (see Bird, 1993). (4) Finally, to the extent that women specialize in housework, and men in market work, because those are the spheres in which they each have a relative advantage, and they have that relative advantage because of this specialization, there is clearly circular reasoning involved in this explanation.[9]

A Value Free Economics? Most introductory textbooks begin by making a distinction between objective economics, which is merely analytic, and entirely value free, and normative economics, which introduces value judgments and tends to be prescriptive. Needless to say, the former is the only true, scientific economics, while the latter is to be avoided at all costs. On closer examination, however, there is very little in any text that is truly free of values, albeit they are generally not recognized as such because they tend to be taken for granted. At a minimum, as Blau (1981) pointed out, ideology influences what problems are selected for investigation, how research is operationalized, and how findings are interpreted. But there is more than that. One of the fundamental premises of economics is that having more goods is better than having fewer. Yet there have been widely respected religious prophets and philosophers with very different views, perhaps best summarized by the New Testament claim that it is as difficult for a rich man to enter heaven as for a camel to go through the eye of a needle. The most ardent advocates of reducing the size and power of government take it for granted that government must not only provide security, but also must protect private property, guarantee contracts, and negotiate trade agreements with other countries. Most of them, however, see protecting the environment, and safeguarding the health of workers as unwarranted government interference.

An excellent illustration of the role of values in interpreting acknowledged facts is the ongoing dispute about the causes of the existing gender pay gap. Two major points of disagreement emerge. First, there is a good deal of dissension about the variables that should be used to explain the earnings differentials between women and men. For instance, in the extensive literature concerning academic salaries, many researchers have used rank as an independent variable. They point out that rank tends to influence how much faculty are paid. On the other hand, it has been noted that, to the extent that there may be discrimination, it is as likely to influence rank as it is to influence salary itself. Second, there is no dispute about the fact that, regardless of the explanatory variables used, in the great majority of studies they fail to explain all of the disparity between the earnings of women and men. There is, however, a great deal of disagreement whether this disparity is likely to be caused by variables that are very real, but can not be measured, or are likely to be caused by discrimination.

Economics with a Human Face Humanizing the dismal science means putting a human face on the content of the introductory economics course. The content of the course should reflect the economic realities of our students. Neo-classical models, as well as other models, should be presented with their strengths and weaknesses; the context of economic ideas and concepts should not be ignored; and finally, the basic units of analysis should be carefully considered. Instructors of introductory economics need to establish a better balance between the abstract, parsimonious models of economic theory and the cluttered, multidimensional nature of economic reality.

Humanizing the Classroom

Just as humanizing economics requires changes in the discipline more profound than the superficial approach often characterized as "add women and minorities and stir," (McIntosh 1990) so humanizing the classroom also requires changes that are more substantial than talking about famous female and African-American economists, recruiting a few students from non traditional applicant pools, and hiring a few female economists and economists of color to teach introductory economics courses. For one, integrating gender into the introductory course is only the beginning of changing the process of teaching economics by using less individualistic and passive learning models, and more collaborative and active ones that bring students from different cultural backgrounds together in a positive learning environment. The teaching strategies that are suggested here are based upon an understanding of learning styles, how learning styles may be culturally determined, and how classroom actions and interactions have different interpretations. Interestingly, however, a consensus is emerging that the teaching strategies that are most effective in a socially and culturally diverse college classroom are the very same strategies that are characteristic of teaching excellence for traditional students. (Anderson and Adams, 1992, p. 30).

Integrating gender into the introductory economics class means change. While it by no means requires dismantling all of the traditional ways of teaching, it does mean venturing into new teaching territories. First, teachers must recognize that gender is but one of the many cultural identities each student has when entering the classroom. Ethnic heritage, religious training, national origin, sexual orientation, and socio-economic status are examples of others. In any one student some of these identities are more dominant than others. Integrating gender into the course is often the first step toward exploring, accepting, and affirming cultural commonalties and differences. Second, it is equally important to be aware that students' cultural identities shape their learning styles and preferred modes of expression. Therefore, the development of a broader range of teaching and testing strategies is crucial. Third, the instructor's cultural identity interacts with that of the students to produce a unique classroom dynamic for each student. The actions and interactions of the instructor with the students, as well as between students (Fassinger, 1995), can produce a positive supportive environment or a negative hostile atmosphere not only for learning, but for interaction on a personal level.

Three important classroom strategies emerge from a recognition of these realities. Inclusive teaching requires that instructors make opportunities for three kinds of connections to occur. First, a series of initial "ice-breaking" and "up-close-and-personal" exercises. These exercises will help to reveal the cultural make up of the class and to provide some information about student interests and sensitivities, and make it easier for the instructor to develop examples and tests that are likely to be relevant to their students. Examining economic notions in ways that makes sense to students and heightens their interest in the subject, increases their motivation to learn. Second, cooperative, collaborative, and team learning activities help students to make positive connections with each other. These activities provide stronger students with the opportunity to offer weaker students the support they need, and the interaction appears to be beneficial for both. Third, instructors need to develop a sense of community, a sense of common purpose, and of responsibility among students. As feminists often point out, an effective classroom is one where the talents, abilities, and knowledge of the students are integral resources for the course. As a result, the instructor moves from the sage on the stage to a coach. Students and instructors alike engage in the learning process. Instructors who facilitate such interactions create a classroom dynamic in which students from diverse backgrounds will feel welcome, and thus contribute to the learning process.

How Students Learn   In contrast to the uniformity in teaching, an extensive educational, psychological, and sociological literature (Fiol-Matta and Chamberlain, 1994; Johnson, Johnson, and Smith, 1991; Light, 1990; Maher and Tetreault, 1994; and Schoem, 1993) suggests that students learn in very different ways. These experts conclude that instructors should develop ways for introducing more cooperation, openness, and community, and should be sensitive to how race, gender, and other cultural identities affect the classroom.

In general, women tend to prefer more concrete and experimental activities than men do, although the difference is not categorical, but rather one of degree. According to Smith and Kolb (1985) only 41 percent of all women students were abstract learners, so that only 41 percent could be assimilators, matching the learning style most suited to the field of economics. There are, however, differences between racial and ethnic groups as well. Asians and Euro-Americans tend to be abstract reflective learners, while Hispanics, and African-Americans tend to be concrete, active experimenters. In a study of 135 women from various socioeconomic classes, Belenky et al. (1986) found that women tended to prefer more "connected knowing," which is more subjective, has more involvement, and relies to some extent on intuition, over more detached objective "separate knowing."

Similarly, Chasteen (1987) noted that the balance between the cognitive and affective domain is particularly important for African-American students, and that Mexican Americans and Hispanics also have a more contextualized way of knowing.[10]

Saunders (in the preceding chapter) points out one more important aspect of learning styles, namely that students tend to learn in both cognitive and affective ways. The former involves knowledge, understanding, and thinking skills; the latter encompasses interests, attitudes, and appreciation. Therefore, he argues, the usual one-sided focus in economics classrooms on cognitive ways, and their tendency to ignore the more affective ways of learning, may well be detrimental because motivation usually plays an important part in students' willingness to acquire, retain, and use cognitive skills.

How Students Should be Taught In view of this diversity, a repertoire of teaching techniques consistent with different learning styles is preferable to using a single one, as is often done in economics. For instance, teaching strategies that give students the opportunity to collect data and to make observations would appeal to the concrete learners; reflective learners would be comfortable interpreting the data; model-building would be the forte of the abstract conceptualizers; and empirical testing would be the preferred mode of those students who like hands-on experimentation. Claxton and Murrell (1987, p. 293) cite a study which shows that student performance improved as much as 90% when the teaching techniques used matched all four learning styles noted above. Thus, instructors who wonder why their students do not comprehend a particular economic concept, and do not work hard to learn more, may not so much be doing a bad job of teaching, as they are doing a good job of teaching, but only for a subset of students.

Just as it would be preferable if a variety of teaching styles were used, so it would also be better if students were given the opportunity to demonstrate their understanding of the subject in a variety of ways. Oral as well as written exams, open-ended as well as multiple choice questions, and even opportunities for practical applications could be employed. For example, open-ended questions appear to fit the learning style of divergers; "contrast and compare" questions are likely to appeal to assimilators; practical application tests are generally helpful to accommodators; and questions with specific answers, including multiple choice questions, are a good fit for convergers. In addition, independent of the kind of questions asked, some students prefer written examinations, while others prefer to be asked questions orally.

Erickson and Strommer (1991) also point out that there are important issues involved concerning the grading of examinations. A frequently used standard, one which emphasizes competition, is that students whose performance is two standard deviations above the mean grade earn "A's," those students whose performance is one standard deviation above the mean receive "B's," and so forth. This means that students compete against each other because their grades depend not only on their own performance, but also on the performance of the other students. A frequently used alternative is a predetermined standard, where students who satisfactorily complete 90 percent of an educational task (test, paper, or presentation) earn "A's," and the levels for other grades are similarly determined. A number of experts believe that such a standard is preferable. First, students have a better understanding of what is expected of them. There is some evidence that minority students, particularly, perform better if the tasks and goals are clearly defined. Second, students are more likely to be motivated if their fate is in their own hands. Third, unlike the competitive standard, it does not inhibit cooperation. Students are more likely to help each other, giving women and students of color, who often enter the class less prepared than traditional economics majors, a better chance.[11] Finally, this approach is more likely to be a measure of effective, or ineffective teaching, while competitive standards are necessarily useless for this purpose.

Classroom Connections

Paying attention to the classroom connections is just as important as being cognizant of the different learning styles in the classroom. Many intelligent young people fail to become interested in the introductory economics course for the same reasons that they are not enthusiastic about introductory physics and chemistry courses. Tobias (1990) found that otherwise bright students were turned off by these introductory courses not because the subject matter was difficult, but because the pedagogy used made it more difficult than it needed to be. Tobias concluded that women and other nontraditional students often left such courses because they were disappointed in the lack of connection with both the subject and with their fellow students. Some of those who left were at the top of their class in other fields. Chasteen (1987), Moses (1991), Nieves-Squires (1991), and Treisman (1992) point out that African-American, Mexican American, and Hispanic students also have a more contextualized way of knowing.

Students with more affective orientations and connected ways of knowing also benefit greatly when they have a group of peers with whom they can discuss their work. Such groups are useful because they build a sense of community and students often learn better from one another and enjoy collaborative group exercises. Making connections can be encouraged by choosing the right teaching techniques (Adams, 1992), and a variety of teaching strategies that facilitate this have been developed and tested. The following is a composite list of useful suggestions that have been made by experienced educators: (1) Have the same expectations for all students. (2) Respond to students in similar ways. (3) Learn your students names and use them. (4) Attribute a comment or answer to a student by name. (5) Increase the wait time for answers. (6) Look for non verbal cues of interest and peruse them. (7) Avoid the generic use of "he." (8) Introduce the work of women and people of color. (9) Use more than one approach. (10) Stress relationship to their lives and career expectations. (11) Use small groups. (12) Develop hands-on activities.[12]

Cooperative learning groups have been used successfully at elementary and secondary levels of education and can be transferred to the undergraduate level. For example, before the end of every class, allow students to go over their notes with others sitting around them, so that they can make sure their notes are complete and correct. If there is disagreement among the students, they are more likely to ask questions than they would be if they were merely uncertain whether they understood the material. Alternatively, students can be put into more formal cooperative learning groups to work together on a presentation or to study for a test. Each member of the group may receive an individual grade, and additional bonus points if other members of the group perform well. Such cooperative learning techniques are especially preferred by women and students of color. The free-rider problem is a serious drawback of cooperative learning groups. Bartlett (1995), however, suggests a number of ways of substantially mitigating the problem. One solution is that students who will take the test for the entire team may be chosen at random. In a number of introductory and advanced classes at Denison University, over 90 percent of all students who have been placed in cooperative groups said they would choose to participate in them again if given a chance.

A laboratory curriculum, such as the one suggested by Bartlett and King (1990), is another way to provide a cooperative learning environment, and it offers students the opportunity for hands-on learning as well. One class a week may be set aside for working with data and computers, doing surveys, developing case studies, etc. The students in large classes can be assigned to smaller lab sections, supervised by teaching assistants who will help students with their assignments. Lab rooms also provide a place where students may gather at other times to collaborate on their work and, when located near faculty offices, may be expected to encourage interaction with faculty outside of the classroom.

A Chilly Classroom Climate and How to Combat It Hall and Sandler's (1982) original work on the classroom climate for women found that there were small, subtle ways of behavior even in classrooms with seasoned instructors, that affected students in adverse ways. Women (and quite possibly students of color) were interrupted more, and were called on to answer questions less frequently. They were given less eye contact that would have encouraged them to develop their answers. They were often asked factual as opposed to analytical questions. Often, their answers were not followed up on. At times instructors addressed the class as if no women were present. Such conduct takes its toll—undermining confidence and interest, and affecting performance. Thus the classroom climate is frequently not hospitable for women and minorities, but this could be changed if instructors would make the effort to avoid such subtle forms of discrimination.

Others have focused on the classroom climate for minorities. Tatum (1992), for instance, points out that students have different cultural backgrounds and experiences, and are raised into different racial or ethnic tradition. Many students may be from working class backgrounds. Some come from the dominant culture, and others from minority cultures. As a result, students tend to hear ideas differently depending upon who is saying them. Therefore it is important that instructors discover what the backgrounds of students are, and learn to connect with their students in spite of these obstacles.

One ice-breaking technique is to help students learn more about the backgrounds of their classmates by making introductions less perfunctory than they usually are when students are simply asked to give their own "name, rank, and serial number." Such a procedure is usually of little benefit in a small classroom, and even less useful in a large classroom. Far better results are obtained when students are asked to pair up and to find out something about each other that will help everyone remember them, and report the results to the class, if it is small, or to the 10 or 12 people around them if it is a large one. The kinds of questions asked could be about the student's greatest dream, worst fear, proudest moment, or special talent. The advantage of this procedure is that students end to find it much easier to introduce someone else than to introduce themselves, for that way they share the spotlight, and are likely to feel less pressure. Another exercise that has been found to work is to give students a sheet of paper with one large circle, surrounded with four smaller circles, and instruct them to put their primary cultural identity in the middle circle, while writing down their secondary cultural identities in the other four circles. When using this approach, it is helpful to give students examples of identities, such as, say, male as the primary identity, and athlete, economics major, Catholic, and Republican as secondary ones. The next step is to ask everyone to tell the class what their answers were, and for the instructor to write the various identities on the board or on an overhead. Identifying all the main cultural identities is important, so that no student will feel marginalized or overlooked. Finally, students are asked to stand when their primary cultural identity corresponds with the one called out from the list.

These exercisers provide instructors with a great deal of information about the students in their classes; they also make students feel more welcome, make them see that they are an important part of the class, and help them to make connections with each other. This is especially important for students who would otherwise find it difficult to establish connections, and hence remain, whether because of gender, race, ethnicity, class, or perhaps because of being handicapped at the margin. While some instructors may argue that this is a waste of valuable class time, to the extent that getting to know each other improves student performance, as the literature suggests is likely to be the case, the time spent on this would be well worth it.

Summary and Conclusions

The proportion of economics majors who are women increased very slowly especially at the advanced level, during more than four decades after World War II; the same appears to be true of minorities. Even more ominously, the representation of women at the undergraduate level has been declining in recent years.

Further, evidence continues to accumulate that women students do not do as well in economics courses as their male peers. In view of the of the general concern with the need to improve the level of economic literacy, this poor performance is of substantial importance.

There is considerable evidence that women are at a disadvantage in the classroom because of the perpetuation of gender stereotypes and unequal treatment of students which continue even today. Authors of introductory textbooks and teachers, particularly, can help to change this situation by devoting more attention to topics of special relevance to these students. In addition, instructors could make students in general, but particularly those who tend to feel like outsiders in the classroom, feel more comfortable by adopting improved pedagogical techniques developed by specialists concerned with these issues. Some changes have already been made in all these respects. The primary purpose of this chapter is to facilitate further progress. It is hoped that the suggestions provided here will help to do that.

NOTES

1. In fact, a number of researchers found that the male-female gap narrowed or disappeared when essay questions were used.

2. The particular focus of this chapter is on women, but we know that many of the issues raised are equally applicable for racial and ethnic minorities (Saunders, 1995). It is to be hoped that one day some research will also be done on the extent to which they may be applicable to students who are not middle class, as the great majority of those who go on to become economists are.

3. According to a report in the Winter 1996 Newsletter of the Committee of the Status of Women in the Economics Profession the figure was 29 percent in 1994.

4. Ironically, in both psychology and sociology there is now concern about women becoming too numerous in these disciplines. The American Psychological Association went so far as to convene a special panel to consider the implications of the feminization of their field (Reskin, 1995).

5. This term was used by Krueger et al. (1991).

6. Magolda (1993, p. iv) found that students were most likely to learn when they could relate the material presented to their own lives.

7. Those interested in exploring these ideas further, may want to look at Ferber and Nelson (1993) as well as the remainder of Nelson (1995) both of which provide a broader overview of feminist economics.

8. Among the many other illustrations that might have been included we mention only a few of those that are of particular relevance to current policy debates: the impact of unequal bargaining power in the labor market on the well-being of women and children; the damage done to programs that would improve opportunities for women because we fail to distinguish between government outlays that are truly current expenditures and those that constitute investment, including investment in human capital; the serious shortcomings of GDP as presently calculated, particularly as a measure of quality of life; the importance of the distribution as opposed to merely the level of income in determining well-being; and the role of women in economic development.

9. These arguments were first offered by Ferber and Birnbaum, (1977) and Sawhill (1977). See also Bergmann (1987) who notes that "To say that the 'new home economists' are not feminist in their orientation would be as much of an understatement as to say that Bengal tigers are not vegetarians" (p. 133).

10 In spite of such generalizations, it is important not to stereotype all females, or members of any other group. Obviously, some women are field-independent, among them probably those who are currently teaching economics.

11. Treisman (1992) observed a high failure rate among African-American students taking calculus, although they appeared to be fully qualified for the course. He also found that Chinese-American students who did well had formed study groups. When African-American students, after some encouragement, did so as well, their performance became more than satisfactory.

12. Johnson, Johnson, and Smith (1991); Meyers and Jones (1993); Aliaga (1993), Cones, Noonan, and Janha (1983); Ginorio (1995); Kleinsmith (1993), Rosser (1990; 1994); Sandler and Hoffman (1992).

REFERENCES

Adams, M. (1992). Cultural inclusion in the American college curriculum. In L.L.B. Border and N. Van Note Chism (eds.), *Teaching for diversity*, No. 49 (pp. 5-17). San Francisco: Jossey-Bass Publishers.

Aliaga, M. (1993). How to teach mathematics to minorities. In D. Schoem, et al. (eds.), *Multicultural teaching in the university* (pp. 172-179). Westport, CT: Praeger.

Anderson, J.A. and Adams, M. (1992). Acknowledging the learning styles of diverse student populations: Implications for instructional design. In L.L.B. Border and N. Van Note Chism (eds.), *Teaching for diversity*, No. 49 (pp. 19-33). San Francisco: Jossey-Bass Publishers.

Bartlett, R.L. (1985). *Macroeconomics: An introductory lecture integrating the new scholarship on women*. Presentation at Meetings of the American Economic Association. New York.

Bartlett, R.L. (1995). A flip of the coin—A roll of the dice: An answer to the free-rider problem. *Journal of Economic Education*, 26(2), 131-139.

Bartlett, R.L. (1996). Discovering diversity in introductory economics. *Journal of Economic Perspectives*, 10(2), 141-153.

Bartlett, R.L. and King, P.G. (1990). Teaching economics as a lab science. *Journal of Economic Education*, 21(2), 181-193.

Becker, G.S. (1965). A theory of the allocation of time. *Economic Journal*, 75(299), 493-517.

Becker, G.S. (1976). *The economic approach to human behavior*. Chicago: University of Chicago Press.

Belenky, M.F., et al. (1986). Women's ways of knowing: The development of self, voice, and mind. New York: Basic Books, Inc.

Berg, H.M. and Ferber, M.A. (1983). Men and women graduate students: Who succeeds and why? *Journal of Higher Education*, 54(4), 629-648.

Bergmann, B.R. (1987). Women's roles in the economy: Teaching the issues. *Journal of Economic Education*, 18(4), 393-407.

Bird, C. and Ross, C. (1993). Houseworkers and paid workers: Qualities of the work and effects on personal control. *Journal of Marriage and Family*, 55, 913-925.

Blank, R.M. (1993). What should mainstream economists learn from feminist theory? In M.A. Ferber and J.A. Nelson (eds.), *Beyond economic man. feminist theory and economics* (pp. 133-143). Chicago: University of Chicago Press.

Blau, F.D. (1981). On the role of values in feminist scholarship. *Signs, Journal of Women in Culture and Society*, 6(3), 538-540.

Chasteen, E. (1987). Balancing the cognitive and the affective in teaching race relations. *Teaching Sociology*, 15, 80-81.

Claxton, C.S. and Murrell, P.H. (1987). *Learning styles: Implications for improving educational practices*. ASHE-ERIC Higher Education Report No. 4. Washington, DC: Association for the Study of Higher Education.

Cones, J.H. III, Noonan, J.F., and Janha, D. (Eds.). (1983). *Teaching minority students. New directions for teaching and learning*, No. 16. San Francisco: Jossey-Bass Publishers.

D'Souza, D. (1991). The Visigoths in tweed. *Forbes* (April 1), 81-86.

Ehrenberg, R.G. and Brewer, D.J. (1994). Do school and teacher characteristics matter? Evidence from high school and beyond. *Economics of Education Review*, 13(1), 1-17.

Ehrenberg, R.G., Goldhaber, D.D., and Brewer, D.J. (1995). Do teachers' race, gender, and ethnicity matter? Evidence from the National Educational Longitudinal Study of 1988. *Industrial and Labor Relations Review*, 48(3), 547-561.

Erickson, B.L. and Strommer, D.W. (1991). *Teaching college freshmen*. San Francisco: Jossey-Bass Publishers.

Fassinger, P.A. (1995). Understanding classroom interaction: Students' and professors' contributions to students' silence. *Journal of Higher Education*, 86(1), 82-96.

Feiner, S.F. and Morgan, B.A. (1987). Women and minorities in introductory economics textbooks: 1974–1984. *Journal of Economic Education*, 18(4), 376-392.

Ferber, M.A. (1990). Gender and the study of economics. In P. Saunders and W.B. Walstad (eds.), *The principles of economics course: A handbook for instructors* (pp. 44-60). McGraw-Hill Publishing Company.

Ferber, M.A. (forthcoming). Gender and the study of economics: A feminist critique. In R.L. Bartlett (ed.), *Introducing race and gender into economics* (chapter 13). New York: Routledge.

Ferber, M.A. and Birnbaum, B.G. (1977). The new home economics: Retrospect and prospects. *Journal of Consumer Economics*, 4(1), 19-28.

Ferber, M.A. and Nelson, J.A. (1993). *Beyond economic man. Feminist theory and economics*. Chicago: University of Chicago Press.

Fiol-Matta, L. and Chamberlain, M.K. (1994). Women of color and the multicultural curriculum: Transforming the college classroom. New York: The Feminist Press.

Ginorio, A.B. (1995). *Warming the climate for women in academic science*. Washington, DC: Project for the Status and Education of Women, Association of American Colleges.

Hall, R.M. and Sandler, B.R. (1982). The classroom climate: A chilly one for women? Washington, DC.: Project for the Status and Education of Women, Association of American Colleges.

Johnson, D.W., Johnson, R.T., and Smith, K.A. (1991). Cooperative learning: Increased college faculty instructional productivity. ASHE-ERIC Higher Education Report No. 4. Washington, DC: George Washington University, School of Education and Human Development.

Kleinsmith, L.J. (1993). Racial bias in science education. In David Schoem et al. (eds.), *Multicultural teaching in the university* (pp. 180-190). Westport, Connecticut: Praeger.

Krueger, A.O., et al. (1991). Report of the Committee on Graduate Education in Economics. *Journal of Economic Literature*, 29(3), 1035-1053.

Light, R.J. (1990). *Explorations with students and faculty about teaching, learning, and student life*, First Report 1990. Cambridge, Massachusetts: Harvard University.

Magolda, M.B.B. (1992). Knowing and reasoning in college: Gender-related patterns in students' intellectual development. San Francisco: Jossey-Bass Publishers.

Maher, F.A. and Tetreault, M.K.T. (1994). The feminist classroom: An inside look at how professors are transforming higher education for a diverse society. New York: Basic Books.

McIntosh, P. (1990). *Interactive phases of curricular and personal re-vision with regard to race*, Working Paper No. 219. Wellesley, MA: Wellesley College, Center for Research on Women.

Meyers, C. and Jones, T.B. (1993). Promoting active learning strategies for the classroom. San Francisco: Jossey-Bass Publishers.

Moses, Y.T. (1991). Black women in academe: Issues and strategies. Washington, DC: Project for the Status and Education of Women, Association of American Colleges.

Nelson, J.A. (1995). Feminism and economics. *Journal of Economic Perspectives*, 9(2), 131-148.

Nieves-Squires, S. (1991). *Hispanic women: Making their presence on campus less tenuous*. Washington, DC: Project for the Status and Education of Women, Association of American Colleges.

Reskin, B.F. (1995). *Women in social and behavioral sciences*. Paper presented at the National Science Foundation's Conference on Women in Science, Washington, DC, December 14.

Rosser, S.V. (1990). *Female-friendly science: Applying women's studies methods and theories to attract students*. New York: Pergamon Press, The Athene Series.

Sandler, B.R. and Hoffman, E. (1992). Teaching faculty members to be better teachers: A guide to equitable and effective classroom techniques. Washington, DC: Association of American Colleges.

Saunders, L. (1995). *Introductory economics textbooks: A perspective*. Paper presented at the third NSF Workshop on Race and Gender in Introductory Economics Courses, Wellesley College.

Saunders, P. (1994). The influence of gender, nationality, experience, and 'warm-up' on beginning instruction performance. Paper presented at the Midwest Economic Association meetings, Chicago, March.

Sawhill. I.V. (1977). Economic perspectives on the family. *Daedalus*, 106, 115-125.

Schoem, D., et al. (Eds.). (1994). *Multicultural teaching in the university*. Westport, CT: Praeger.

Sheffrin, S.M. (1992). Economists, newest target of thought police. *The Wall Street Journal* Editorial Page, October 8.

Smith, D. and Kolb, D.A. (1985). *User guide for the learning-style inventory*. Boston: McBer and Company.

Tatum, B.D. (1992). Talking about race, learning about racism: The application of racial identity development theory in the classroom. *Harvard Educational Review*, 62, 1-24.

Tobias, S. (1990). *They're not dumb, they're different: Stalking the second tier*. Tucson, AZ: Research Corporation.

Treisman, U. (1992). Studying students studying calculus: A look at the lives of minority mathematics students in college. *The College Mathematics Journal*, 23, 362-372.

U.S. Department of Education, Center for Education Statistics: (1995). *Digest of Education Statistics*.

Watts, M. and Bosshardt, W. (1991). How instructors make a difference: Panel data estimates from principles of economics courses. *Review of Economics and Statistics*, 72(2), 336-340.

CHAPTER 10

THE USE OF MATHEMATICS AND STATISTICS IN THE TEACHING AND LEARNING OF ECONOMICS

William E. Becker

The aim of language is to say something—and not merely about the language itself. Mathematical social science is, first and foremost, social science. If it is bad social science (i.e., empirically false), the fact that it is good mathematics (i.e., logically consistent) should provide little comfort. (Herbert A. Simon, 1954)

Communication between the student and teacher requires a language familiar to both. In the United States that language is English. Mathematics is a shorthand form of communication between parties who already know what is being said. In the teaching of economics, even when it may be appropriate to use the shorthand of mathematics (because students have fulfilled an algebra, calculus or statistics prerequisite, for example), student learning is impaired because the mathematical shorthand used in economics is inconsistent with the conventions students use in other courses. I provide examples of abuses of mathematics in the teaching of economics and suggest ways to correct these problems.

Mathematics and Economics

I doubt that anyone will question the premise that the study of economics requires some knowledge of mathematics and statistics. Few will disagree with the idea that the mathematical skills of differential and integral calculus, difference equations, and the like are appropriate requirements to pass certain qualifying exams for a Ph.D. in economics. Requiring such skills of graduate students does not imply that they are necessary for an understanding of economics. That the American Economic Association has found it necessary to introduce two journals to convey and review ideas in a nontechnical manner suggests that its elected executive committee recognizes that most of the AEA membership prefer to learn without the excess baggage of specialized mathematics. As McCloskey (1985, 188), said:

> Economics depends much more on the mastery of speaking and writing than on the mastery of engineering mathematics and biological statistics usually touted as the master skills of the trade. Most of the economist's skills are verbal.[1]

How can an instructor of economics justify the use of a mathematical treatment to teach undergraduates when colleagues are relying on *The Journal of Economic Perspectives* and *The Journal of Economic Literature* to stay current in areas in which they may not specialize? *The Wall Street Journal, Business Week, The Economist* and other well known periodicals of economic news do not use mathematics for exposition; yet, instructors of economics read them faithfully. To expect that students who enter or complete an introductory or even intermediate courses will have quantitative skills beyond those required to read these publications is hypocritical and inefficient.

In thinking about how people learn economics we need to look at what economists do rather than what they say they do. The majority of economists appear to be buying and reading less mathematical writing even though many are attempting to produce more. As teachers of undergraduates we may be wise to respond to the majority of our students and rely on only those mathematical concepts that are absolutely essential for the task at hand. To identify those concepts look at the periodicals economists regularly read. If the concept is not used in those periodicals, think twice about including it in your teaching.

In what follows I identify a few mathematical and statistical concepts that have become part of the language of economics, as reflected in current periodicals. I discuss how the use of mathematical shorthand may impair the learning of even these concepts. I also make suggestions on how to improve our use of mathematics in the teaching of economics.

Algebra and Function Notation

The idea that one event or variable affects the outcome of another is necessary for an understanding of economics. The concept of causality is not difficult to grasp, as seen in the writings of numerous journalists. Students become confused, however, when functional notation is introduced as a shorthand for the relationship between two variables. This confusion has nothing to do with the idea of a relationship between variables. Rather, it is the consequence of the notation used.

From algebra classes students are acquainted with writing the relationship between two variables as

$$y = f(x)$$

where y is the (dependent) variable, which is plotted on the vertical axis of a two-dimensional diagram, and x is the (independent) variable, plotted on the horizontal axis. They have been taught that this relationship implies that for every value of x (in the domain) there is one and only one value of y (in the range). They most likely have done many exercises aimed at reinforcing the idea that only relations that assign to each element in the domain a single element in the range are functions (e.g., M.P. Dolciani, R.G. Brown, and W.L. Cole, 1986, 404).

In macroeconomics, we confuse the student by introducing consumption c as a function of income y. Consumption is typically ill-defined as either planned or expected and is written in functional notation as

$$c = f(y)$$

Typically shown in a two-dimensional graph, income y is measured along the horizontal axis (the domain), while in algebra this letter represented the vertical axis (the range). Even within macroeconomics textbooks the confusion over the axes on which the domain and range reside is magnified by having a chapter on graphs, where the vertical axis is labeled y (range) and the horizontal is labeled x (domain), while in the chapter on consumption the independent variable income is on the horizontal axis while the dependent variable consumption is on the vertical. To make matters worse, the hypothetical consumption-income relationship is typically demonstrated with a made-up example in which more than one value of consumption is associated with the same level of income. (One person making $2,500 dollars per month is observed spending $2,300, while another person with identical income is observed spending $2,450.)

In microeconomics, students must be confused when the direction of functional mapping (causality) appears to be reversed. We write the demand relationship as

$$q_d = f(p)$$

but we place the price p on the vertical axis (the range) and the quantity q on the horizontal axis (the domain).

Making algebraic relationships explicit does not necessarily help the student. It may just add to the confusion. For example, we typically write the consumption function as the straight line

$$c = a + by$$

where the letter b represents the slope of the consumption line. Algebra books, however, define a straight line in "slope-intercept form" to be

$$y = mx + b$$

where the letter b is the y-intercept (e.g., Dolciani, et al., 397). When an instructor of economics defines the marginal propensity to consume to be the letter b, is it the concept of a marginal propensity to consume or the notation that causes difficulty in learning?

Students are not perplexed by the idea of a function. Working with a straight line relationship between two variables is not overwhelming. It is the economist's shorthand notation that is confusing. This notation may appear to contradict what the student learned in algebra classes. Student learning of algebra is not reinforced when students are left to discern on their own that "b" is the intercept of a line in algebra but it is the slope of a line in economics. Seeing functions graphed one way in algebra and another way in economics is not conducive to learning or retaining learning in either algebra or economics.

Using observational techniques to assess how introductory economics students approach problems, Strober and her colleagues (1992, 1997) provide evidence to support my hypothesis that the symbolic logic used in economics hinders students with good backgrounds in high school mathematics because the conventions used in algebra and geometry appear contrary to those in economics. They also report that students have difficulty with the same quantitative issues that stymied economists from the early days of economic thought. Thus, they argue that if we want to learn how to teach economics we should look to the learning processes followed by the masters, where mathematics was not the engine of inquiry.

The fact that algebraic and economic functional notation differs is not a sufficient reason for its exclusion from any undergraduate courses in economics. The use of functional notation is so widespread in economics that a student must be familiar with it. Instructors, however, must be cognizant of the manner in which students are taught about functions in algebra classes. At a minimum, instructors should call attention to the differences in notation.

Graphs in Economics

Basemann (1992) argues that we should reallocate student time away from memorization of mathematical or formal literary derivations of theorems to practice in generative causal thinking about economics. He is concerned, however, about misleading students about the relationship between economic theory and real-world data. He uses the standard two-dimensional textbook diagram of observed consumption and income as shown in Figure 10-1 as his example. He correctly states that this scatter diagram does not represent the theoretical consumption function and that students presented with this data will get the wrong impression of regularity were none may exist. Basemann's criticism of the use of Figure 10-1 is based on estimation problems that are well known to students of econometrics but not others. His point, as with other problems of estimation, can be made by emphasizing the definition of variables. The theoretical consumption function, for example, is defined in terms of expected or planned consumption. Figure 10-1 presents observed or actual quantities. Students can understand these distinctions even if they have not had a course in econometrics and do not understand simultaneity, measurement error, and serial correlation.

Figure 10-1: **Per capita real personal consumption expenditures (*PC*) versus per capita real personal disposable income (*Y*) in the United States, 1947–87**

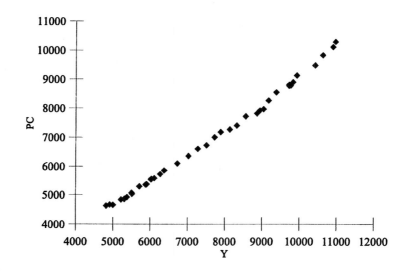

Source: *Economic Report of the President*, February, 1990.

Curiously, Basemann never addresses the errors in constructing Figure 10-1, which shows real personal consumption of 4,000 and real personal disposable income of 4,000 as the origin with no units of measurement provided. In mathematics classes students learn that the number line origin is zero. To be consistent with what students have or are learning in their mathematics classes, Basemann should have provided the units of measurement and broken the vertical and horizontal lines as shown in Figure 10-2.

In addition to labeling the axes, providing the units of measurement, and maintaining consistent interval lengths, diagrams and graphs cannot be overly cluttered. It is difficult to imagine any one diagram requiring more than five lines to demonstrate something in economics. More lines just complicate diagrams and obfuscate what should be made clear by the diagram. The business and financial press do not use complicated diagrams so why should teachers of economics?

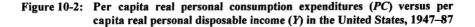

Figure 10-2: Per capita real personal consumption expenditures (*PC*) versus per capita real personal disposable income (*Y*) in the United States, 1947–87

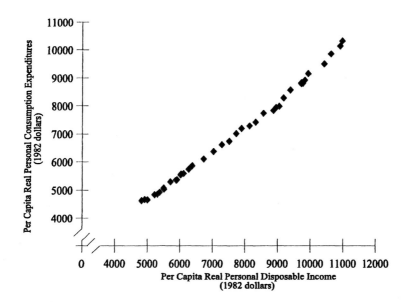

Source: *Economic Report of the President*, February, 1990.

In preparing graphs, diagrams, and other illustrations of quantitative information for use on boards, overhead projection, or handouts, six "*DO's*" and "DO NOT's" will prove helpful:

1 *DO* predraw all graphs to scale (with specific numbers rather than abstract symbols). *DO NOT* draw graphs freehand on the spot.

2 *DO* work through numerical examples or algebraic manipulations before class. *DO NOT* make up numbers for an example or attempt algebraic manipulations spontaneously in class.

3 *DO* write out definitions of all variables, parameters, and estimators when they are first introduced, or reintroduced after a while. *DO NOT* use symbols or abbreviations that have not been defined in written form.

4 *DO* label all axes, lines, and points of a graph. *DO NOT* put more than a few lines or curves on a graph; a maximum of five lines per graph is the goal. (In some cases transparency overlays or computer graphics can be used to simplify complex graphics).

5 *DO* show every step in arithmetic or algebraic sequence. *DO NOT* use expressions such as "it can be shown easily that ..."

6 *DO* work from left to right on boards and top to bottom on overheads; avoid scrolling back and forth through many pages on computer driven presentation packages. *DO NOT* jump around in the use of any medium set up for presentation in sequential form.

Whether instructors should hand out prepared graphs for use by students in class or have students draw their own graphs is debatable. Cohn and Cohn (1994), in a controlled experiment with volunteers who were given credit toward a course grade, found that instructor-supplied graphs were beneficial for students who could not draw graphs accurately in their notebooks. On the other hand, students who accurately drew graphs performed considerably better on the end-of-period economics exam than those who did not. Cohn and Cohn speculate that those better at drawing who did their own graphs had an advantage because they listened, drew graphs, and reviewed their own work, whereas the others only listened and reviewed the instructor's work. In the absence of knowing beforehand who will benefit from prepared graphs, instructors are left to their own judgment as to what is better. Regardless of whether diagrams are handed out or not, they must be accurate and consistent with what students have been taught in their mathematics and engineering courses.

Measurement and Quantitative Skills

To understand economics, students must be familiar with some measurement concepts such as ratios and index numbers. They must be able to make calculations with these concepts. At the intermediate level they need to move beyond these measurement concepts to analysis, but first and foremost they must understand the basics.

In teaching freshmen and sophomores I am no longer shocked to find students who cannot convert ratios into decimals, percentages, and equivalent fractional forms. As a matter of routine I now show every step in the formation of a ratio and alternative representations as a decimal and percentage. Students are expected to have these skills by the time they reach high school. By the time they reach college it seems that a large number of students have unfortunately forgotten arithmetic.

I find that remedial work with arithmetic and algebra is essential. For this reinforcement to be effective, however, instructors of economics cannot be sloppy with notation. As an example of sloppiness, consider the form of a consumption function that I have seen in workbooks

$$c = 2 + 8/9y$$

where c and y are measured in hundreds of dollars. The fraction 8/9 is defined to be the marginal propensity to consume; a rise in income from $900 to $1,800 is said to result in expected consumption rising from $1,000 to $1,800. But how many students calculate a fall in consumption from $209.88 to $204.94, when income rises from $900 to $1,800? Those students are correct; the term "8/9y" states that 8 is divided by the product of 9 and y. If 8/9 is the marginal propensity to consume, then the consumption function must be written as

$$c = 2 + (8/9)y$$

A working knowledge of ratios, decimals, and percentages is essential to understanding elasticities, discounting, relative prices, index numbers, and other measurement concepts that are specific to economics. Of these measurement concepts I believe that index numbers are the least appreciated by college students, even though they are among the most frequently cited statistics in economics. This may be because our emphasis in teaching has been on the calculation of index numbers as opposed to their use. To work with the consumer price index or any other index one does not need to know the intricacies of their construction. What is important to know, at least for reading articles in the popular press, is that a movement from 240 to 264 is a 24 base point change and a ten percent rise in whatever the index represents—not a 24% increase, as unfortunately, many people interpret such a movement.

Concepts From Probability and Statistics

Students need to be able to use information on averages and expected values. With articles appearing in *Business Week* on rational expectations, and discussions of the efficient wage hypothesis on the front page of *The Wall Street Journal*, the concept of an expected value cannot be ignored. Although some might argue that the introduction of the concept of an expected value, and a distribution around that value, is in conflict with the call for less mathematics in the teaching of the principles of economics, these concepts are part of the vocabulary of economics and public policy debate, as seen in the popular press. They are concepts that are used in everyday discussions of decision making. They also are not difficult to understand if the complexities of probability are circumvented. Their use can aid in the teaching of other economic concepts (such as the consumption function).

By the end of the first term every college freshman knows how to calculate his or her grade point average, or is in the process of flunking out. An extension of the concept of an average to an expected value as an average calculated over an extremely (infinitely) large number of courses (trials) follows easily. This discussion can show that because the magnitude of future measurements is unknown, there is no unique way to formulate expectations about the future.

Complex equations are not needed for a discussion of an expected value. Students have no problem grasping the idea that chance factors make the actual outcome of any future event uncertain. A shorthand notation to differentiate the expected value of a variable from any other occurrence of the variables may be helpful; this notation need not go beyond E( ). Students, however, do not need to learn about density functions or see an integral sign. They only need to be able to visualize a distribution around an expected value.

The idea that there is a distribution of course grades around the mean grade for a specific term is understood by students. Similarly, the notion of a distribution of values around the expected value of consumption for a specific level of income can be understood. A consumption function, in which there is only one value of expected consumption associated with an income level although there are many values that can be observed by chance, is made consistent with high school algebra books by reference to the distribution of consumption about an expected level. It also lends itself to a discussion of parameter estimation using real-world data.

For those instructors who wish to make consumption functions explicit, any value of consumption can be written as

$$c = \beta_0 + \beta_1 x + \epsilon$$

and the expected value of consumption can be written as

$$E(c|x) = \beta_0 + \beta_1 x$$

where ϵ is the chance factor, $E(c|x)$ is expected consumption at income level x, and the βs are, respectively, the intercept and the slope. One might think that it would be easier for the student if this consumption function were written as

$$E(c) = \beta_0 + \beta_1 x$$

but such notation is contrary to what they will be or have been exposed to in an introductory econometrics or statistics course. The expected value of consumption notation $E(c)$ is the mean calculated for the entire distribution of consumption regardless of the value of income.

In presenting this mathematical structure for the consumption function I am not arguing that it should be presented in principles classes. I am sympathetic to the notion that the consumption-income relationship (as well as other relationships in economics) can be taught without ever writing down an equation. I am arguing that this mathematical notation is preferred to the consumption function notation that is employed currently in principles texts. The use of the βs is not in conflict with the notation used in high school algebra classes and it is consistent with the regression notation used in statistics and econometrics courses. Similarly, the use of x to represent income does not conflict with the use of x in algebra books. The difference between expected consumption and realized consumption, at given income levels, is explicit in the notation.

Consumption and its expected value can be graphed in a three dimensional diagram such as that in Figure 10-3. In Figure 10-3 note that all lines are labeled and points of interest are marked. For instance, at an income level of $2,700 per month, where $x = 27$, expected consumption is $2,600, $E(c|x = 27) = 26$. The bell-shaped curve (density function) centered at this expected consumption level shows the dispersion or distribution around a consumption level of $2,600 that is possible when income is $2,700. Students can see how more than one value of consumption

Figure 10-3:   Consumption Function: $c = \beta_\phi + \beta_1 x + \epsilon$

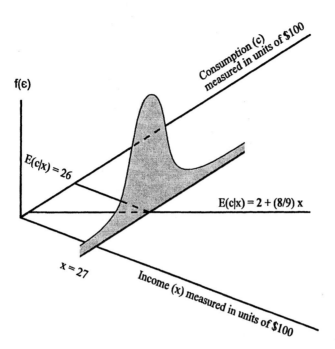

can be associated with a given level of income when the random disturbance ϵ is introduced. (The use of $100 units is deliberate. As discussed below students must be able to make unit of measurement conversions to understand tables published in business and economics periodicals. Similarly, an ability to read three dimensional diagrams is a requirement for reading these periodicals.)

The concept of a distribution also is essential to an understanding of risk and uncertainty. Modern day microeconomics requires some consideration of the role of uncertainty in decision making. As a starting point I do not advocate the introduction of formulas for the variance, standard deviation, or any other weighted measures of dispersion. The absolute difference between the highest (or the lowest) value in a data set and the expected value can be defined to be a measure of risk. For example, if the expected return on an investment A is 9 percent and the lowest return ever recorded is 3 percent, then a measure of the downside risk for investment A is 6 percent. If another investment B has an expected return of 10 percent, with downside risk of 8 percent, then which investment is preferred depends on the decision maker's attitude toward risk.[2]

Magnitudes

To work with economic concepts students need some idea of what is "big," "small," and a "reasonable" value; as Ann Landers (March 25, 1988) put it: "Figuring in the trillions is confusing to most folks." The difference in the number of individuals unemployed for a 6 percent versus a 7 percent rate of unemployment is not apparent to students. Without seeing the values they could not be expected to associate a one percentage point change with approximately one million more people unemployed. Similarly, the consequence of compounding at a 5 percent versus 6 percent rate of interest cannot be appreciated until the calculations are made.

At a minimum students should be made aware of the tables in the back of the *Economic Report of the President*, as transmitted to the Congress in February of each year. They should learn how to order documents from the Superintendent of Documents, U. S. Government Printing Office. Ideally they will experience surfing the Internet for alternative sources of data. All major media services, government agencies, and businesses now maintain home pages on the World Wide Web. For instance, the large data bases maintained by the Bureau of the Census can be accessed at *http://www.census.gov*. This Census site enables users to download data following self-explanatory menus and FTP transfers. A starting point to search for financial data is the site of the Wall Street News, at *http://wall-street-news.com/forecast*. This and other news media sites provide links to such resources as the Chicago Mercantile Exchange's information on commodity trading as well as university and research lab sites like the financial economics server at the University of Texas.

Getting students started in data analysis can be as simple as having them compare current interest rates, unemployment rates, and other economic measures that appear in newspapers with the historical values in the *Economic Report of the President*. Such comparisons will give students a sense of magnitudes. Without this historical perspective there is no way for them to know whether current values are in or out of line with past occurrences.

Concluding Comments

As with theories of learning, messiness in economics occurs when models are applied to observable phenomena. This does not mean that theoretical relationships should not be considered in the principles course or when considered that they should not be applied to actual situations. It does suggest that emphasis on mathematical detail could mask disagreement among competing schools, impair discussion, and retard the learning of economics. My former teacher, Martin Bronfenbrenner, made this point when a classmate of mine asked what to study for the Ph.D. qualifying exams. Bronfenbrenner responded that Samuelson's principles textbook should be known from cover to cover. This response was disturbing since at that time (early 1970s) I was trying to learn from the mathematics in Samuelson's foundations; Samuelson's principles textbook relied on English.

I have come to learn that Bronfenbrenner's advice is grounded in the history of economic thought. In trying to decide how much mathematics to include in our teaching of economics, we may be wise to remember what Marshall wrote to Bowley,

> But I know I had a growing feeling in the later years of my work at the subject that a good mathematical theorem dealing with economic hypotheses was very unlikely to be good economics; and I went more and more on the rules—(1) Use mathematics as a shorthand language; rather than as an engine of inquiry. (2) Keep to them till you have done. (3) Translate into English. (4) Then illustrate by examples that are important in real life. (5) Burn the mathematics. (6) If you can't succeed in 4, burn 3.[3]

Any economist can think of measurement concepts and quantitative skills that are essential to an understanding of economics. The question to be asked is at what point do we draw the line and say that additional concepts from arithmetic, algebra, geometry, statistics or other areas of mathematics are not needed for a basic understanding of economics? To use Marshall's words, what mathematics do we burn and not show the students? What quantitative skills are important in real life?

I have argued that answers to those questions can be found in the current periodicals economists read. If articles in *The Wall Street Journal, Business Week, Forbes, Barrons*, and the like do not require readers to have specialized mathematical knowledge and skill, then students in an introductory economics course should not be expected to know or to learn such things.

Many of the articles in current periodicals that deal with economic issues and policy rely on a knowledge of percentages, indices, expected values, and distributions. Some articles require a knowledge of elasticities, standard deviations, functions, and even the marginal propensity to consume. An ability to read charts and tables is taken for granted. Clearly these are quantitative concepts and skills students of economics should know on completion of a few college level economics courses.

NOTES

The author is Professor of Economics, Indiana University, Bloomington, Adjunct Professor of Economics, University of South Australia, and Editor, *Journal of Economic Education*. Parts of this draft were prepared through the support of the Universities of Adelaide, Melbourne, and South Australia, provided while Becker was on leave from Indiana University during the fall 1995. The author is indebted to Bjorn Frank (University of Hohenheim) and Scott Gordon (Indiana University) for calling his attention to Simon's writings on the use of mathematics in the social sciences and Marshall's letters on the topic.

1. For a debate on this point see the comment by High (1987) and the reply by McCloskey (1987).

2. There is no need for an instructor to introduce the variance or standard deviation as a measure of risk in a principles course but in subsequent courses this is appropriate. In a statistics course, for example, the variance is defined as the average squared deviation of observations around their mean value. In accordance with this definition, the variance can serve as a measure of risk. Because the variance is measured in squared units, the standard deviation (positive square root of the variance) typically is used as a measure of riskiness. The standard deviation is in the original units of measurement. To appreciate the definition of the variance and the calculation of a standard deviation, students will have to calculate a finite population variance from the formula

$$\sigma^2 = \Sigma(f_i/N)(x_i - \mu)^2$$

and in probability form from the formula

$$\sigma^2 = \Sigma P(x)(x - \mu)^2$$

These procedures are best left to statistics courses.

3. From Marshall's February 27, 1906, letter to Bowley as it appeared in Pigou (1956, 427).

REFERENCES

Basemann, R. (1992). The professional responsibility of the econometrician for truthfulness in the teaching of economics. In D. Colander and R. Brenner (eds.), *Educating economists* (pp. 61-79). Ann Arbor: The University of Michigan Press.

Cohn, E. and Cohn, S. (1994). Graphs and learning in principles of economics. *American Economic Review Proceedings*, 84(2), (May), 197-200.

Dolciani, M.P., Brown, R.G., and Cole, W.L. (1986). *Algebra structure and methods*. Boston: Houghton Mifflin Company.

High, J. (1987). The costs of economical writing. *Economic Inquiry*, 25(3), 543-547.

Landers, A. (1988). Figuring in the trillions is confusing to most folks. Los Angeles Time Syndicate and Creators Syndicate (March 25).

McCloskey, D. (1985). Economical writing. *Economic Inquiry*, 23(2), 187-221.

McCloskey, D. (1987). Reply to Jack High. *Economic Inquiry*, 25(3), 547-548.

Pigou, A.C. (Ed.). (1956). *Memorials of Alfred Marshall*. New York: Kelley & Millman, Inc.

Simon, H.A. (1954). Some strategic considerations in the construction of social science models. In P. Lazarsfeld (ed.), *Mathematical thinking in the social sciences* (p. 388). Glencoe, IL: The Free Press. Reprinted in H.A. Simon, *Models of bounded rationality, volume 2: Behavioral economics and business organization* (p. 209). Cambridge, MA and London: MIT Press. 1982.

Strober, M. and Cook, A. (1992). Economics, lies and videotapes. *Jourrnal of Economic Education*, 23(2), (Spring), 125-151.

Strober, M., Cook, A., and Fuller, K. (forthcoming, 1997). Making and correcting errors in economic analyses: An examination of videotapes. *Journal of Economic Education*.

CHAPTER 11

RESEARCH ON TEACHING
COLLEGE ECONOMICS

John J. Siegfried

William B. Walstad

Research on economics instruction that has implications for the effective teaching of undergraduate economics courses is the subject of this chapter. The purpose is not to provide a laborious review of the literature in economics education but rather to provide a brief guide to research results that may improve teaching effectiveness and student learning of undergraduate economics. This presentation of the main research conclusions that have emerged over the past 35 years should also be of value to department chairs or faculty committees who are responsible for making decisions about how the course is taught, and thus may use the research results in more effectively organizing economics instruction for students.

The chapter is organized into four sections. First, we review the history of research on teaching college economics to acquaint instructors with the major developments and sources of information on the subject since its origin in the 1960s. The majority of the chapter is devoted to the next two parts in which we examine the relationship between student characteristics and economics teaching, and then turn attention to the influence of course format on student learning. Here we identify key findings from the research that we hope will be of use to economics instructors and administrators. In the final section, we discuss research on the economics major.

A Historical Overview

In a 1968 Presidential address to the Southern Economic Association, *Hard Research on a Soft Subject: Hypothesis-Testing in Economic Education*, Rendig Fels (1969) described economics education as a new and exciting challenge for hard research. In Fels' view, hard research in economics education uses quantitative methods and, at times, economic theory to address questions about the teaching and learning of economics. He recommends this type of research over "soft research," or the casual empiricism that so many economists use when they discuss economics instruction with colleagues while they would demand hard findings in other areas of economics. He then reviews the eight studies that had been conducted by that time that provide hard evidence about effective economics instruction.

Research on economics education has progressed in the decades since Fels devoted his Presidential address to it. A key contribution to this development was the publication, in 1968, of the *Test of Understanding of College Economics* (TUCE). The original test was prepared by a distinguished committee of economists that included George Stigler, Paul Samuelson, and G. L. Bach. In 1991, the third edition of TUCE was published (Saunders, 1991). Over a hundred studies of teaching effectiveness in a variety of settings have used the original and revised TUCE exams as a nationally normed and standardized measure of cognitive achievement. The creation of this examination was crucial to the expansion of research on effective teaching in economics, for without a reliable and valid test measure it is difficult to conduct quality empirical studies across classrooms and campuses.

Another factor spurring the growth of economics education research was the establishment of two major outlets for reporting research findings. First, since the 1950s an annual session at the American Economic Association convention has been devoted to economics education. The results of these annual sessions, which often focus on research studies, are published in the May *Papers and Proceedings* issue of the *American Economic Review*. Second, the establishment of the *Journal of Economic Education* in 1969 gave economists and educators a specialty journal for presenting research findings. In the 25 years since its inaugural, the *Journal* has gained considerable respect, with a recent citation study ranking it in the top quartile of 130 economics journals (Laband and Piette, 1994), up from the median a decade earlier (Liebowitz and Palmer, 1984). There is little doubt that these two publications helped economists interested in research in economics education obtain credit for their work when they were reviewed for promotion and tenure. They remain the primary source of quality research and scholarship on the teaching of college economics, but other economics journals, such as the *Journal of Economic Perspectives* and *Economic Inquiry*, now regularly publish articles on economics education.

By 1979 there was sufficient published research to construct a survey of research on teaching college economics that appeared in the *Journal of Economic Literature* (Siegfried and Fels, 1979). Most of the 179 articles and books cited in that review came from the *Journal of Economic Education* or from proceedings issues of the *American Economic Review*. About half of the studies used the TUCE as the measure of cognitive achievement. That survey exposed more professional economists to the work of those conducting economics education research, reported substantive conclusions from the research, and evaluated the methodological foundation of the research.

Since the 1979 *JEL* survey, research issues in economics education received additional treatment in a three-part essay that covered theoretical model building and sound statistical methodology (Becker, 1983a, 1983b, 1983c). Subsequent publications discussed the use of econometric techniques, especially those involving qualitative and limited dependent variables, or outlined a new agenda for research on teaching college economics (Becker and Walstad, 1987; Becker, et al., 1991). The most recent step in this history is the preparation of a new *JEL* article (Becker, forthcoming). It discusses evidence on the teaching of economics to undergraduates, describes what economists do in the classroom, and makes a case for greater attention by faculty to economics instruction in colleges and universities.

The purpose of the present essay is to identify substantive conclusions about teaching and learning economics that can be drawn from the research literature, and to communicate findings in a way that a conscientious college economics teacher or administrator might find useful. We think that some of the research conclusions can be used to make changes in teaching or administrative practices that should lead to improvements in undergraduate economics instruction. We also, from time to time, identify important questions for future study.[1]

Student Characteristics and Economics Teaching

The student is the target of classroom instruction for the economics teacher and accordingly has been the main subject of research in economics education. The relationship between student characteristics and economics teaching is complex and difficult to decipher, but we see worthwhile conclusions from the research on students emerging in eight areas: (1) evaluation of teaching; (2) attitudes and achievement; (3) effort, study time, and attendance; (4) learning and teaching styles; (5) gender; (6) maturity; (7) aptitude; and (8) high school economics.

Evaluation of Teaching It is now accepted practice to use students' ratings of instruction as one factor in the evaluation of teaching at most colleges, in spite of the controversies that continue to surround such evaluations (Siegfried and Fels, 1979, 930-934). Systematic determinants of effective teaching may be difficult to discern because equally effective teachers may adopt different teaching styles due to different endowments of skills, differing perceptions of what constitutes good teaching, and different search paths to ascertain which of the available styles works best for them (Lima, 1981). Indeed, Lima may be correct in his prediction that "individuals doing research into the empirical determinants of teaching effectiveness are doomed to be searching through a haystack which simply contains no needle." (1981, 1059)

The same conclusion might be applied to weather prediction or interest rate forecasting but, nevertheless, empirical work continues on these topics; and it will likely continue on the question of what specific characteristics constitute effective teaching. If student evaluations (SETs) are an acceptable measure of some dimensions of teaching effectiveness, then it is important to know what can be done to improve those ratings.

Research has enhanced our understanding of what generates more favorable student attitudes toward economics instruction. In an early study of almost 5,000 course evaluations at the Graduate School of Business at Stanford University, Lumsden (1974) discovered that clarity of presentation, enthusiasm, and respect for students' opinions had the largest positive effect on overall course evaluations. In an analysis of over 2,500 British students at 19 universities Lumsden and Scott (1983) found clarity of presentation and imparting enthusiasm to be the most important teacher characteristics in the view of students. Of particular interest for improving evaluations was their discovery that economics instructors at the same institutions substantially underestimated the importance of these two factors and overestimated the importance of knowing the subject matter well (in the eyes of the students, who may or may not be good judges of that) and (perceived) preparation for class.

Using 1,300 SETs from the University of Southern California, Aigner and Thum (1986) found that characteristics of good teaching include clarity of presentation, organization, signaling (the use of oral statements to draw attention to an upcoming point), questioning and probing to maintain active student involvement, accepting students' ideas, and rapport with students. These instructor-specific characteristics explained more than twice the linear variation in overall course ratings than did course-specific (e.g., whether the course was required, enrollment) and student-specific (e.g., whether the student was foreign, class year) characteristics combined.

DeCanio (1986) applied multinominal logit analysis to 6,900 individual student course ratings at the University of California, Santa Barbara, and obtained results comparable to Aigner and Thum (1986). He found that organization and preparation and communication skills (e.g., value of lectures, lecture preparation, ability to explain material, and ability to answer questions) were strongly and positively associated with favorable teaching ratings.

Other more recent studies support the past findings and identify other factors. Mehdizadeh (1990) studied the evaluations of 478 students at Miami University (Ohio) who were enrolled in a principles course. The log-linear results showed that expected grade, value of supplementary materials, availability of the instructor outside of class, and student views of the course examinations had an influence on student ratings. Mason, Steagall, Fabritius (1995) collected data from 5,745 students taking principles at the University of North Florida from 1984–1991 using ETS' Student Instructional Report form as the SET measure. The results from their ordered probit analysis of three dependent variables—quality of lectures, value of the course, and quality of instruction—were positively and significantly influenced by student perceptions of: clear course objectives; good use of class time; instructor recognition when students did not understand; lectures that were not repetitive of the text; the raising of challenging questions; the use of examples; the quality of exams; the achievement of instructor goals; and, the pace of content coverage. The teacher-specific factors dominated the explanation of the dependent variables relative to other factors.

The conclusion from the research on student evaluation of teaching is that *instructors retain considerable control over the destiny of their course evaluations.* Factors such as course objectives, clarity, communication skills, enthusiasm, organization, preparation, involving and responding to students, and developing rapport with students are all ones that an instructor can directly influence or change even if the instructor has no control over course- or student-specific characteristics. The instructor can also get students to be more realistic about their expected grade by informing them of course requirements and difficulties, monitoring student performance, and giving timely feedback. Careful preparation and grading of essay or multiple choice exams can reduce student complaints about the fairness or quality of exams—a common criticism that can sink an instructor's rating. These factors are all associated with good teaching practices and the SET studies indicate that they are recognized and appreciated by students. (See also Chapter 22.)

In an early clever attempt to discern whether SET responses can identify more effective teachers, Shmanske (1988) followed the students of 17 introductory economics professors into their second economics course. Using binary variables for the different faculty he found little difference among their students in cognitive achievement in the subsequent economics course. Students' ratings of their first semester instructor also proved ineffective in separating the more successful students from the less successful students in the second course. His results, tentative though they may be, are consistent with the view that the students recognized there was actually little difference in the teaching effectiveness among the various instructors who taught them in the first semester.

Another investigation of teaching performance and SETs was conducted by Gramlich and Greenlee (1993) at the University of Michigan. They studied the relationship between final grades and SET scores for over ten thousand students enrolled in principles and intermediate micro theory courses over a two-year period. They found only a weak, although positive, correlation between SET ratings and final student course grades. They estimated that moving a teacher from the bottom quartile of the teacher rating distribution to the top quartile was associated with only a small percentage of the increase needed to move a student from a B to an A grade. There was no effect of SET on final grades in intermediate micro theory. After exploring many options, they concluded that the true relationship between SETs and final grades was "all a deep, dark mystery."

Differences in course ratings received by male and female instructors are another controversy surrounding the use of SETs. The controversy has been provoked by allegations on many campuses that students rate female instructors lower than male instructors, ceteris paribus. General surveys of research on this issue find no evidence of gender bias, however. Using a sample of SETs from over 4,000 students in 167 different introductory economics classes, Anderson and Siegfried (1997) similarly find no evidence of student bias against female instructors. They find that students in introductory microeconomics classes rate female instructors higher than male instructors while learning similar amounts from each, and in macroeconomics, students rate male and female instructors similarly in spite of learning less in the classes taught by women. Differences in the sex composition of students in classes taught by male and female instructors do not explain these results. There is some evidence that students prefer the learning environment in classes taught by women, even if they don't learn more, which may explain the results.

The most controversial aspect of SETs is their use for salary, promotion, and tenure decisions. One accusation is that instructors can "buy" better student evaluations by awarding higher grades. Aigner and Thum (1986) found evidence to support the accusation, but DeCanio (1986) and Sevier (1983) did not. Nelson and Lynch (1984) found that favorable student evaluations "seem to depend mainly on clarity of communication and instructor enthusiasm, with grades playing a secondary role" (pp. 21-22). Stratton, Myers, and King (1994) found that the introduction of mandatory SETs for faculty evaluations increased average grades given to principles students by 11 percent, but that the grade effect diminished over a nine-year period. They were not able to determine whether the increase in average grades was the result of instructors giving higher grades or instructors changing their teaching methods and becoming better teachers in response to this new incentive scheme.

Whatever is the relationship between SET ratings and grades, it may be beside the point. Dilts (1980), Blackwell (1983), Zangenehzadeh (1988), and Mason, Steagall, and Fabritius (1995) have each described a method to control for unwanted influences on SETs. If differences in grading practices (as well as other differences; for example, in class size, whether a course is required or not, or whether course enrollment is mostly Freshmen or mostly Seniors) are deemed inappropriate influences when course ratings are used for personnel decisions, they can be (more or less) excised from SETs, although few administrators may be willing to use such schemes to adjust SET ratings for faculty. The point is that SETs must be interpreted with care, in light of the purpose to which they are being applied, and in clear recognition that they measure students' opinions accurately, but may or may not measure teaching effectiveness.

Almost all economics departments use SETs in some ways to evaluate teaching. The perceived limitations of SETs have stimulated interest in measuring teaching effectiveness in other ways (White, 1995). The other methods that economics departments use to some degree include classroom visits and observations, review of teaching materials, formal follow-up surveys of students over time, and reviews for teaching awards. College administrators are also showing greater interest in the use of teaching portfolios (Seldin, 1993). With this approach an instructor collects documents and writes a report showing what the instructor is doing inside and outside of the classroom to promote good teaching. The portfolio would include course syllabi, teaching materials, an explanation of a teaching innovation or teaching methods, a videotape of classes, homework assignments, graded written work, sample exams, course grade distributions, SETs, letters from students, and a statement of teaching philosophy. The teaching portfolio provides a broader array of evidence for judging the teaching contribution of an instructor beyond what may be shown by SET scores, especially in tenure decisions. (See Chapter 22.)

Attitudes and Achievement Closely related to student attitudes towards a course or instructor, are student attitudes towards economics as a subject. The conventional belief has long been that there is a simultaneous relationship between economics achievement and attitudes towards economics. That is, if students like economics they will learn more and if they learn more, their attitude toward the subject will improve. Most of the research on this problem was originally conducted with single equation models (e.g., Karstensson and Vedder, 1974). When the simultaneous relationship is estimated with two-stage least squares, however, the results suggest that the relationship is one-way. That is, if students learn more economics, over and above what they would have known before they took the course, then they will like that subject more and are likely to take additional courses. In contrast, if they like the subject more before starting a course, that does not necessarily mean they will learn more economics during the course, or take additional courses afterwards (Walstad, 1987; Beron, 1990; Maxwell and Lopus, 1995).

The implication of these studies is that what instructors need to be most concerned about is finding ways to teach students economics so that they learn something from the course. The instructor should not be overly concerned about what students think of economics initially. If the instructor can improve economic understanding so that students have learned something meaningful from a course, then students will develop a greater appreciation (or liking) for economics, and may decide to continue to study it. In other words, attitudes towards economics are more likely a product of what students learn (and by extension, a product of teaching effectiveness or the effort of instructors) rather than a factor that predetermines learning.

Effort, Study Time, and Attendance Research on student effort generally finds that it matters, but the effects depend on the type of student and student decision-making. Leppel (1984) discovered that students who reported spending greater effort (as measured by reported study time) on a course earned higher grades. In addition, she found that students returning to campus after an absence earned higher grades than continuing students because of more hours spent studying. Borg, Mason, and Shapiro (1989) reported that the number of study hours was insignificant in explaining grades, but they attributed this overall result to a failure to disaggregate students. Further study showed that below-average students earned lower grades because they made significantly less effective use of study time than above-average students.

Studies of student effort have been examined in ways other than the number of study hours. Prince, Kipps, Wilheim and Wetzel (1981) found that student scholastic effort ([final achievement − initial achievement]/aptitude) effected achievement. Paul (1982) showed that time spent on outside employment led to lower achievement levels in principles. Raimondo, Esposito, and Gershenberg (1990) reported that part-time students had lower grades relative to full-time students taking intermediate theory courses. Schmidt (1983) observed, with empirical support, that how students allocate time spent in an economics course and the intensity with which the time is used matters for learning economics.

Absenteeism is also a serious problem affecting economics instruction. Romer (1993) estimated that roughly one-third of students in principles, intermediate, and upper-level economics courses at elite American universities were not attending. His analysis of data from a large principles of macroeconomics course showed a significant negative effect of this excessive absenteeism on course grades, dropping them by about a letter grade. Arce, Formby, and Zheng (1996) confirmed the large positive effect of attendance on learning, controlling for selection bias—the fact that more conscientious students both attend class with greater regularity and would perform better even if they didn't. The relationship between attendance and performance, however, is probably nonlinear and has a threshold before it hurts students. Durden and Ellis (1995) found that attendance mattered only after a student missed five classes, with the size of the negative effect increasing with each additional absence.

There is, unfortunately, only limited research on the effectiveness of various techniques instructors might employ to induce greater student effort. Perhaps the most common suggestions to correct the problem are actions that the instructor takes to structure time spent on the course and to give quick feedback to students. Professors might use frequent quizzes, give course exams at regular intervals, or assign numerous homework problem sets to encourage student study and participation, and to keep students focussed on the course content. In this vein, Schmidt (1983) and Marlin and Niss (1982) reported positive results for programs that required students to take weekly quizzes. To address the absenteeism problem, Romer (1993) suggests the use of exhortations to students to attend class with grade data being used to explain the cost of being absent. He also thinks that a mandatory attendance policy might be helpful in spite of the difficulties in making such a policy work.[2]

Actions that instructors take to increase student effort may not increase student learning in economics because the behavioral response of students may be unpredictable. Becker (1982), using a rigorous model of student utility maximization, confirmed that changes in instruction which permit students to convert time into learning more efficiently need not result in any change in the students' learning of economics. Benefits from more efficient pedagogical techniques that reduce student study time may be used by students to "purchase" increased learning in other subjects, or may simply be converted into more leisure. Whether instructors will find that benefits from increasing learning are worthwhile turns on the values assigned to learning different things and the value of leisure. This theory offers another explanation, in addition to group aggregation, for why studies often find that the study time variable has an insignificant or negative effect on achievement (Gleason and Walstad, 1988; Grimes, et al., 1989; Durden and Ellis, 1995).

Learning and Teaching Styles   There is growing evidence that the first conclusion from Siegfried and Fels' (1979) survey, namely that different students learn economics in different ways, is accurate and important. Wetzel, Potter and O'Toole (1982) identified three learning and teaching styles—*dependent* (a highly-structured and teacher-directed course with lectures), *independent* (students have influence over course content, structure, and assignments), or *collaborative* (extensive use of group projects and discussion). They found that matching instructors' teaching styles with students' learning styles increased learning. Whether teachers' and students' styles matched explained up to 50 percent more of the variation in student learning than traditional factors like verbal and quantitative skills. A follow-up study by Charkins, O'Toole, and Wetzel (1985) reported that the greater the divergence between learning and teaching styles, the lower the student's gain in achievement and the less positive the student's attitude toward economics.

More recently, Borg and Shapiro (1996) investigated differences in personality type on student achievement in principles of macroeconomics using the Myers-Briggs Type Indicator and a variation of it that assessed temperament. The Myers-Briggs indicator classifies people into 16 groups by using four characteristics selected from each of four opposite pairs: *E*xtrovert (E) or *I*ntrovert (I); *S*ensing (S) or *I*ntuitive (N); *T*hinking (T) or *F*eeling (F); and *J*udging (J) or *P*erceiving (P). The study found that students with three personality types (*ENTP*, *ESTP*, and *ENFP*) had significantly lower grades than the most common student type (*ISTJ*). More generally, introverts had higher grades than extroverts, and students with *SJ* temperaments performed better than students with *NT* and *NF* temperaments. The study also found that the closer the match between the temperament of the student and the instructor, the better the final grade of the student.

Although it may be impractical to type the learning styles of all students in all classes, or match teaching and learning styles, what this research suggests is that more attention needs to be given to individual differences in the classroom. Perhaps the best instructional response is to offer a variety of course assignments, use alternative teaching methods, and adopt multiple types of assessment. For administrators, the long-term implication is that economics courses, especially principles, need to be differentiated to better match teaching and learning interests. Separate sections can be offered for different prospective majors (business, education, journalism, etc.), students of different ability (honors), for instructors who want to use alternative teaching approaches (e.g., laboratories, experiments, active-learning), or on another basis of importance to students and faculty.

Gender Gender matters in economics education because at any point in time, males tend to score better than females on economics tests (Siegfried, 1979). This finding holds both in terms of simple comparisons of mean scores on the TUCE or the economics GRE, and when stock regression models are estimated that control for the effects of other variables (Hirschfeld, Moore, and Brown, 1995; Walstad and Robson, forthcoming). The significant difference in test scores is usually small, however, and whether it is of practical significance is open to debate (Ladd, 1977).[3]

Research which has used a flow regression model generally shows a different picture. With a flow model the initial stock of economic knowledge is controlled and we try to explain performance at the end of the course. In studies that have used this formulation, there is usually no difference between the performance of men and women.[4] In other words, males and females appear to learn economics at the same rate. Women may enter an economics course with less economic understanding, they seem to learn the same amount of economics as men over the course of the semester. Where the source of the initial disadvantage comes from remains a mystery.

The explanation for the gender differences on economics tests has focussed on the nature of the exam. There has been serious concern about whether the multiple choice format may put females at a disadvantage. Lumsden and Scott (1987) found that males tend to show slight superiority on multiple choice exams, but that females do substantially better on essay exams. The pattern is consistent with an earlier exploratory study by Marianne Ferber and colleagues (1983) at the University of Illinois who found a significant difference in measured understanding of economics between males and females on classroom multiple choice tests but no gender difference on essay tests.

A more recent study by Williams, Waldaver, and Duggal (1992) discovered just the opposite. In principles, economics statistics and intermediate theory courses, no significant differences were found in scores on the multiple choice components of exams. Scores on the essay components of tests were inconsistent or insignificant, with males outperforming females in principles exams, females outperforming males in statistics, and no gender difference in intermediate theory courses. Hirschfeld, Moore, and Brown (1995) reported mixed results for two standardized tests often taken at the end of an undergraduate economics program. They found no significant difference in male and female scores on the Major Field Test in Economics, but a significant difference in the male and female scores on the economics GRE. They speculated that the reasons for difference were the severe time-constraints and competitive nature of the GRE that creates a confidence gap for women in answering test questions.

What conclusion should you draw from the inconclusive research on multiple choice testing? Perhaps the best answer is that an instructor should hedge by using a variety of testing or assessments formats—multiple choice, essay, short-answer, problems, and written work. After all, past research has shown that different students learn in different ways, and test format is one of those factors that instructors can easily vary to spread the risk of negative consequences from and form of assessment.

Another gender difference that has been studied in the research literature is further study of economics. Horvath, Beaudin, and Wright (1992) found that there were gender differences in the estimated probability of continuing in economics (to the next principles course) at the University of Hartford. As grades for males and females dropped below an A, the gender gap between persistence rates for those with the same course grade widened markedly: 16 percent higher for males with grade B; 30 percent higher for males with a grade C; and 41 percent higher for males with grade D. The authors suggest that females need more validation and encouragement in the classroom than males if they are to decide to continue studying economics. Males earning Cs and Ds may also need to be given a more realistic assessment of their prospects in future economics courses. Anderson, Benjamin, and Fuss (1994) found that males had higher grades than females, ceteris paribus, and this factor permitted more males to take additional economics courses at the University of Toronto. Research by Dynan and Rouse (1997) at Harvard suggests that when women are compared to men, they received lower grades in economics courses relative to other courses, and this signaled women that they have a comparative advantage in other subjects. One way to improve the classroom climate for women is to incorporate more gender issues into principles courses (see Chapter 9). There appear to be positive benefits for student achievement in economics in such a course (Lage and Treglia, 1996). Adoption of teaching practices that promote cooperation rather than competition among students may also be beneficial (Bartlett, 1996).

Maturity Siegfried and Fels (1979) reported that measures of student maturity, such as age and year in school, usually show no relationship to cognitive performance. Other research on this subject casts some doubt on that conclusion. Miller (1982), Manahan (1983), Hodgin (1984), Reid (1983), and Cohn, Cohn, and Bradley (1995) all report that older students perform better than younger students, ceteris paribus.[5] And at least five studies report that Freshmen are at a distinct disadvantage in introductory economics, everything else the same (Bonello, Schwartz, and Davisson, 1984; Watts and Lynch, 1989; Watts and Bosshardt, 1991; and Williams, Waldaver, and Duggal, 1992). These findings have obvious implications for administrators scheduling principles courses, or faculty giving advice to Freshmen about when to take these courses. But delaying the principles course to the sophomore year may cause other scheduling complications in a sequentially structured major.

Aptitude It is well established that student aptitude as measured by college entrance examination scores is positively and significantly associated with economics test performance. Many studies have also shown that verbal, quantitative, or composite SAT (or ACT) scores have an important influence on TUCE scores or course grades in principles courses (Park and Kerr, 1990; Gramlich and

Greenlee, 1993; Brasfield, Harrison, and McCoy, 1993; Cohn, Cohn, and Bradley, 1995; Borg and Shapiro, 1996; Kennedy and Siegfried, forthcoming). Both verbal and quantitative SAT scores are important for achievement on the economics GRE taken during an undergraduate's senior year, but quantitative skills seem to be especially important in intermediate theory courses (Williams, Waldaver, and Duggal, 1992; Gramlich and Greenlee, 1993; Hirschfeld, Moore, and Brown, 1995).

Several other factors related to aptitude or overall achievement have been shown to be significant predictors of success in economic courses. The appropriate level of mathematics preparation or course work is essential for explaining grades or test scores in principles and other economics courses (Myatt and Waddell, 1990; Brasfield, Harrison, and McCoy, 1993; Raimondo, Esposito, and Gershenberg, 1990; Butler, Finegan, and Siegfried, 1994; Anderson, Benjamin, and Fuss, 1994; Lopus and Maxwell, 1995). And, overall grade point average (GPA) has been a consistently positive and significant predictor of student achievement in principles and intermediate theory courses, or as an economics major (Raimondo, Esposito, and Gershenberg, 1990; Caudill and Gropper, 1991; Gramlich and Greenlee, 1993; Cohn, Cohn, and Bradley, 1995; Hirschfeld, Moore, and Brown, 1995; and Lopus and Maxwell, 1995).

The question for economics instructors and administrators is what to do with the knowledge that aptitude, general college achievement, or prior course work makes a difference in explaining test or course performance in economics. Perhaps the best suggestion is to collect this information on students in courses whenever it is available. It is important for instructors to know something about the characteristics and composition of the students they are teaching because these data may be useful in setting the pace for the course and structuring assignments or tests. Administrators may also use this information to establish course prerequisites or to analyze the reasons for course withdrawals and changing enrollments.

High School Economics There has been a national trend for more students to study economics in high school as more states mandate the subject or more students take economics as an elective (Walstad, 1992). This development might have an effect on the content and pace of the college principles course if students arrive at the course demonstrating mastery of the basic subject matter. A national study of high school students, however, indicated that they could correctly answer only half the questions on the *Test of Economic Literacy* after taking an economics course in high school and they showed only a 7.5 percent increase in knowledge during the course (Walstad and Soper, 1988). The finding is consistent with earlier work by Saunders (1970) who concluded that having taken high school economics did not hurt students taking a college principles course, but it did not give them a significant advantage either.

Several recent studies show a more positive contribution of a high school economics course to the learning of college economics, perhaps because of improvements in the high school curriculum in the past decade. Brasfield, Harrison, and McCoy (1993) found that students in micro and macro principles who had taken high school economics had significantly higher course grades, and so did Durden and Ellis (1995). Even if students who took high school economics show no advantage in college economics, they still may be more efficient learners if they spend less time studying the course.[6]

For those high-ability students capable of learning college level principles of economics in high school, there is an Advanced Placement (AP) test in micro- and macroeconomics to measure their achievement (CEEB, 1996). These tests are reliable and valid ones for awarding college-credit in economics. A student taking the test receives a grade on a 1–5 scale, with 1=no recommendation, 2=possibly qualified, 3=qualified, 4=well-qualified, and 5=extremely well-qualified. Most colleges and universities will award college-credit for a course if the student receives a grade of at least 3 or 4. These grading standards are high: less than one percent of high school seniors take an AP economics exam; only about 60 percent of that group received a score of 3 or greater, and only about 40 percent received a score of 4 or 5.

Course Format and Student Learning

Choices made by instructors, administrators, and faculty committees often influence student learning in economics courses. Decisions involve the: (1) use of innovative teaching methods; (2) selection of textbook; (3) testing and cheating; (4) choice of class size; (5) sequence and format of courses; and (6) use of graduate instructors. Each of these considerations merits brief discussion based on recent research findings.

Innovative Pedagogies The emphasis of recent research in economics education has been on factors that matter for achievement in the context of traditional lecture and blackboard teaching. This appears to be the correct allocation of research efforts, since adoption of "innovative" teaching materials and methods has been slow in principles, intermediate and advanced courses in spite of the interest in them and demonstrated effectiveness in some cases.

Several studies have used the TUCE III norming data to investigate the use of different instructional materials and approaches in principles of economics courses (Siegfried and Kennedy, 1995; Siegfried, et al., 1996). The survey data were collected in 1989–1990 from 139 faculty members at 53 colleges and universities across the nation. The studies reported that less than 20 percent of instructors used computer exercises or television programs, and only about 40 percent assigned non-textbook readings. Aside from the textbook, instructors used homework or problem sets (55 percent in macro and 71 percent in micro), and the study guide (about 65 percent). Faculty spent 75 percent of their classroom time lecturing. The use of class time or learning aids did not vary much by type of institution or class size.

Similar findings about limited use of alternative materials and methods were reported for a wider range of courses—principles to intermediate to advanced—in a national survey conducted by Becker and Watts (1996). They discovered that the median amount of time economics instructors spent lecturing was 83 percent across different types of institution and at different levels of instruction. The chalkboard was used by 83 percent to write text and graphs, and the same percentage relied on textbooks for teaching courses. The authors concluded with a plea to faculty to adopt alternative materials and methods to improve teaching and learning in economics.

Much of the research on economics education completed in the 1970s consisted of evaluations of new (to economics) teaching methods (Siegfried and Fels, 1979). Research on alternative teaching and learning methods since 1979 has been sparse, and the past findings are now dated. This development is unfortunate because there are a number of economics faculty who are using different approaches to teaching economics. Becker and Watts (1995) describe how faculty use classroom games and simulations, experimental economics, economics laboratories, writing strategies, supplementary readings, case studies, and cooperative learning strategies in an effort to improve economics instruction. Certainly, research can be helpful in making the case for innovative methods, but in most cases faculty will have to rely on anecdotal evidence or persuasion in making a decision to use them.

One problem is that few research studies show a clear superiority of one alternative teaching method over another, or any improvement relative to the use of the traditional lecture-discussion method. There are several reasons why research often fails to show much of difference between teaching methods. Designing experiments that account for sample selection is difficult. Test instruments may not be capable of capturing the outcome effects. Implementation of the experimental procedure may vary by instructor or across institutions. Experimental methods often entail higher costs that must be weighed against uncertain benefits. Students may decide to take the efficiency gains from an innovation and spend them on other courses or on leisure. These difficulties are illustrated in a study by Cardell, et al. (1996) who found no difference in learning as measured by the TUCE when students took a principles of economics course using a laboratory versus a traditional lecture approach.

Textbook The textbook is relied on almost exclusively for reading assignments in principles courses (Siegfried, et al., 1996). Most past studies of achievement in introductory economics showed that the choice of textbook does not appear to matter (Meinkoth, 1971; Saunders, 1980). There has been no substantive research on this question in the past two decades, however. As the market shares of textbooks in economics change, it is probably desirable to reevaluate this conclusion.

The most likely reason textbook choice does not matter is the great homogeneity in content coverage among the leading principles of economics textbooks (see Chapter 13). This factor makes it difficult to capture textbook differences and separate them from instructor effects. Research shows, however, that it is possible to detect textbook effects in more extreme cases. Watts and Lynch (1989) found that using a low level intermediate theory text in a principles of economics course was associated with statistically significantly lower revised TUCE examination scores than if a standard introductory text were adopted.

Testing and Cheating Multiple choice tests are used extensively in principles of economics classes according to recent surveys. Siegfried, et al. (1996) reported that, on average, these tests accounted for almost two-thirds of course grades. Short-answer questions account for another 20 percent of course grades, and essay questions account for only about 5–9 percent of course grades. Similarly, Becker and Watts (1996) found that multiple choice testing was the predominant method of assessment in principles, with 50 percent reporting its use at least half the time. There are, of course, sound measurement reasons for using multiple choice tests instead of essay tests—less grading time, more reliability, and wider coverage of the content domain—so their widespread use by economics faculty can be justified (see Chapter 19).

Despite their positive features, multiple choice tests have been the object of severe criticism in recent years for their capacity to measure cognitive outcomes and possible negative influence on active learning. Nevertheless, the research evidence is far from convincing that fixed-response tests should be replaced with constructed-response tests, or vice versa. Walstad and Becker (1994) found that the essay component of the AP economics exam added little information about student achievement beyond that provided by the less costly and more reliable multiple choice score. Kennedy and Walstad (forthcoming) used the same test and discovered that there were students who performed significantly better on one test format than another, and that using an all-multiple choice test to measure achievement would result in a small net number of grading errors. For economics instructors, the test format decision is likely to depend on the subjective views of the relative merits of various types of questions. The research suggests that it is best to use a mixture, given individual differences and measurement issues. In fact, most principles instructors follow that practice according to the survey data.

Several research studies in the past decade have focussed on student cheating behavior in economics courses. Bunn, Caudill, and Gropper (1992) reported that cheating is inversely related to GPA, directly related to observing others cheat, and directly related to the perception of the number of students who are cheating. Kerkvliet (1994) used two different survey methods to obtain confidential data on cheating and found that the most likely cheater was a heavy drinker who was a resident member of a fraternity or sorority. Mixon (1996) separated one-time cheaters from habitual cheaters, but found little difference in factors affecting each group. In this study, the cheating behavior also was inversely related to GPA, directly related to seeing others cheat, and was directly related to associating with students who routinely cheat. The Mixon study is especially important because it suggests that instructors can reduce cheating by working on student expectations. Instructors need to clearly warn students of the swift and severe punishment that will be given to anyone caught cheating.

Another way that economics instructors try to reduce cheating on multiple choice exams is to use alternative or scrambled forms. Some concern has been raised, however, about the effect of test scrambling on student performance. There has been speculation that a scrambled test might disadvantage students compared to a test with questions that follow the order of presentation of course content. The research findings from several studies show that question order does not matter for achievement in economics, and thus instructors need not worry about the potential problem (Gohmann and Spector, 1989; and Caudill and Gropper, 1991).[7]

Class Size Average class size varies considerably in American higher education, even within a single course subject. Siegfried, et al. (1996) estimated that average class size was 44 students in introductory macro and 43 students in introductory micro. The standard deviations around the mean class sizes were 37 and 28, respectively, which indicates that class size varies substantially. Studies of introductory course class size are almost unanimous in finding no influence on standardized examination test scores as class size rises above a critical level of about 20 students (Williams, et al., 1985; Kennedy and Siegfried, 1997). This finding suggests that it might be taught cost effectively in large and small classes, if "small" exceeds 20 and test scores are the output measure. More needs to be learned about this important questions since it is one of the few determinants of learning that is easy (but not cheap) to control.

Current research on class size in economics suggests that there are at least four negative effects from taking economics in large classes beyond just test scores. First, it seems that students do not *like* large classes even if they do just as well in them (McConnell and Sosin, 1984; DeCanio, 1986). Second, large introductory classes may have an adverse effect on subsequent enrollment in economics. Maxwell and Lopus (1995) found no difference in economics learning in large or small principles classes as measured by the TUCE in twelve classes at one university, but taking economics in a large class decreased the probability of enrolling in future economics courses by 38 percent. Also, a study by Becker, Powers, and Saunders (1996) discovered that academically weaker students in large classes were more likely to drop the class than weak students in smaller sections of principles. Third, taking principles of economics in large classes may adversely affect performance in later economics courses. Raimondo, Esposito, and Gershenberg (1990) found that students who took macroeconomics in a large lecture course had lower grades in intermediate macro theory than students who took introductory macro in small class sections. The same relationship, however, did not hold for micro principles and theory courses. Fourth, large classes tend to restrict teaching strategies to lecture and the testing method to multiple choice. It is more likely and feasible for an economics instructor to use alternative teaching strategies that actively engage students (writing, discussion, games and simulations, etc.) when class sizes are small.

There is clearly an enormous variety in the size of class in which principles of economics is taught. That may be appropriate in view of research conclusions that class size does not matter for cognitive learning in the course, and that pedagogy does not vary much by class size (Siegfried and Kennedy, 1995). Universities also realize a significant monetary saving when principles of economics courses are taught in large classes (Maxwell and Lopus, 1995). Nevertheless, there do appear to be negative consequences for students and economics departments from the over reliance on large classes. Future studies also need to go beyond the simple large-small dichotomy, and evaluate the effects of class size on various outcomes (knowledge, attitudes, drops, enrollment, future learning) across a range of class sizes (10–25, 25–50, 5–75, etc.).

Course Sequence and Format Various strategies have been used in economics departments for sequencing the micro and macro principles courses—micro before macro, macro before micro, no preference, and no course splitting. Lopus and Maxwell (1995) surveyed fifty colleges and universities, half research universities and half selective liberal arts colleges. They found that 32 percent of departments teach micro first, 8 percent teach macro first, 42 percent had no order preference, and 18 percent offered a single semester course.

A legitimate research question is whether course sequence affects student learning or attitudes. An initial study of this question found that students who took a micro first and macro second sequence performed significantly better than students who took a macro first and micro second sequence, but students seem to like economics better when they took a macro-to-micro sequence (Fizel and Johnson, 1986). The study, however, was conducted at one school and used a now-dated hybrid version of the TUCE. A more comprehensive study was undertaken by Lopus and Maxwell (1995) using TUCE III data. The study used pre- and posttest TUCE scores from 2,888 students taking micro and 3,052 students taking macro principles in 53 colleges and universities in 1989–1990. The regression analysis showed that taking a prior course in macro principles had a significant positive effect on micro pretest and posttest scores, but a prior course in micro did not affect subsequent macro course performance.

This finding has important implications given that many colleges and universities require students to take micro first or have no preference. Whether these findings apply to a particular college or university is certainly worthy of further investigation at each school, whether or not it has a specific requirement. The selection of a textbook also should not be a factor determining the sequence decision because there are many two-semester principles textbooks available, about one-third of which are micro first and two-thirds of which are macro first (Lopus and Maxwell, 1995). With the availability of textbook splits, however, the appropriate course sequence is an instructional decision that should be made by an economics department after careful study.

Another research question can be raised about course format. Are intensive courses that last for three weeks as effective for student learning as a course that lasts a semester? Van Scyoc and Gleason (1993) controlled for various background factors and found students in an intensive three-week course in principles of microeconomics course scored about 11 percent higher on both the TUCE and the course tests than students in a 14-week semester course. They hypothesize that teaching and learning may be more efficient and focussed in the three-week course.

Graduate Student Instructors The one study of graduate student instructors (GSIs) in the past decade (Watts and Lynch, 1989), adds further evidence that graduate students generally are just as good teachers as regular faculty even though, other things equal, experience results in better teaching and graduate students have less experience. The empirical evidence from studies done at Princeton, Hebrew University, Carnegie-Mellon, Indiana, Florida State, Nebraska, and (now) Purdue suggests that GSIs have compensating attributes that balance their lack of experience.

Watts and Lynch (1989) did find, however, that the undergraduate students of non-native English speaking GSIs did significantly worse on a final examination than did the students of GSIs for whom English was their first language. This result is important in view of the fact that many Ph.D. students in economics in the United States now are foreign. Of obvious further interest in view of these findings, is whether the efforts of some departments and colleges to improve the pronunciation of English by non-native English speakers and to acclimate foreign students to U.S. college culture are effective.

The Economics Major

In 1980, the Committee on Economic Education of the American Economic Association co-sponsored a study of the economics major. It revealed that there was virtually unanimous agreement on a list of required courses in the major that included principles of micro and macro, intermediate micro theory, intermediate macro theory, and economic statistics, and that the remainder of the major (usually 10 courses in total) consisted of unconstrained economics electives (Siegfried and Wilkinson, 1982). The work of the past decade has involved identifying the outcomes we expect to achieve by offering an integrated "major" rather than simple access to courses. In what way and for what reasons might we expect the "economics major" to add up to more than the sum of the contributions of the individual courses? Issues of course sequencing, students' development of a critical perspective on their discipline, acquisition of sophisticated proficiencies, capacity to deal with complexity, the interconnection between disciplines, and ways to strengthen economics study are all part of the agenda.

Several contributions in the past decade have focussed more attention on the economics major and outcomes from it. First, Lee Hansen (1986) proposed a hierarchy of five proficiencies that we might reasonably expect undergraduate economics majors to acquire and demonstrate by the time they graduate. These proficiencies are: gaining access to existing knowledge; displaying command of existing knowledge; displaying ability to draw out existing knowledge; utilizing existing knowledge to explore issues; and, creating new knowledge. Second, a more comprehensive statement about the economics major came from the "study-in-depth" report for the Association of American Colleges (see Chapter 6; Siegfried, et al., 1991). The six economists who prepared this report concluded that the goal of the economics major was to get students to "think like an economist," and described what that meant in terms of the content and skills that should be taught to students. The challenge, of course, is to devise valid instruments to measure the diverse outcomes or proficiencies of the economics major. Multiple choice tests, such as the Major Field Test in Economics or the economics GRE, may not adequately capture what the students know, learn, or experience when they major in economics. The character of the outcome measure certainly influences the behavior of faculty and students. When these outcomes from the major can be measured, or assessed more accurately, more effort will be devoted to teaching those proficiencies, and there will be more research on those dimensions.

Another recent concern has been the decline in the number of economics majors. Siegfried (1995) found that the number of economics degrees fell by 20 percent between 1992 and 1994 after inching steadily upward at about one percent annually during the prior decade. This decline has stimulated new research on the economics major. Salemi and Eubanks (1996) hypothesized that the decline in economics majors was partially the result of students being discouraged from pursuing business degrees, and supported their thesis with data from one university. Willis and Pieper (1996) suggested that there was a correlation between the decrease in the demand for workers in the financial services industry, a traditional employer of economics majors, and the decline in the number of economics degrees. Brasfield, et al., (1996) identified several characteristics of economics departments that were associated with decreasing or increasing numbers of majors. Margo and Siegfried (1996), however, suggest that the current decline is not something to worry about from a historical perspective; after short-term fluctuations, the number of majors tends to return to a fixed share of undergraduate degrees.

Despite the recent studies, little is known about the factors over time that affect student decisions about the choice of major. The problem is that the decision-making process for selecting a major is a subtle and complex one that involves continuous assessment of courses, instructors, grades, alternative majors, employment prospects, and other factors during high school and college (Walstad, 1996). A past survey of economics majors found that at least 15 different factors were important in varying degrees for the major choice and that the decision was made at different points in time: 12 percent in high school; 19 percent freshman year; 46 percent sophomore year; 20 percent junior year; and 3 percent senior year (Siegfried and Raymond, 1984). It would be naive for economics departments to think that simple changes in grading standards or course requirements will reverse trends unless more is known about student decision-making and the behavioral responses of other departments. These and other issues affecting economics majors clearly merit further study.

Conclusion

Our knowledge of how to improve the effectiveness of undergraduate economics instruction has improved substantially since the 1960s. Studies have been conducted on a variety of topics, in some cases using the best research techniques available to economists. Economics instructors and administrators no longer have to be satisfied with the casual observations of colleagues as answers to questions about the teaching and learning of economics. Instead they can rely on a body of research literature that is beginning to provide answers to many questions. In this chapter, we have identified some findings from the research literature on economics education that have direct and indirect implications for the teaching of college economics. More answers will come over the years because researchers are continuing to undertake scholarly studies that advance our understanding.

NOTES

1. Further consideration of methodological issues is omitted from this review because they have been thoroughly discussed in the publications cited in the previous paragraph, or are discussed in recent research articles in the *Journal of Economic Education*.

2. For a discussion of the pros and cons of a mandatory attendance policy see the correspondence section of the Summer 1994 issue of the *Journal of Economic Perspectives*.

3. Many of the statistically significant findings in economics education research are subject to the same qualification. Much is often made of statistically significant differences in performance on the TUCE examination between an experimental and control group, when the magnitude of the difference is relatively small (e.g., under 10 percent). Whether such differences indicate a practically significant effect, however, will be known only when we can place a value on being able to answer one, two, or three additional questions on the TUCE.

4. See Watts and Lynch (1989) or Lopus and Maxwell (1995) for counter examples.

5. Other maturity characteristics may be important, although they have been given little study. For example, Leppel (1984) found evidence that married students perform better, and that students returning to school after an absence scored significantly higher than continuing students.

6. These American findings are supported by studies in other nations. In Canada, Myatt and Waddell (1990) found students with high school economics had high course grades in principles, and although the effect decayed over time, there was still some positive residual in intermediate economics courses. Also, A-level economics courses in secondary schools in the United Kingdom and Singapore contribute to higher student learning in principles courses in the United Kingdom and Singapore (Lumsden and Scott, 1987; Tay, 1994).

7. A third study by Carlson and Ostrosky (1992) found no difference in test reliability or validity in alternative forms of exams, but some minor benefit for students taking an ordered exam. The results, however, do not control the random assignment of students to exam forms over all exams given during a semester.

REFERENCES

Aigner, D.J. and Thum, F.D. (1986). On student evaluation of teaching ability. *Journal of Economic Education*, 17(3), (Fall), 243-265.

Anderson, G., Benjamin, D., and Fuss, M. (1994). The determinants of success in university economics courses. *Journal of Economic Education*, 25(2), (Spring), 99-121.

Anderson, K.H. and Siegfried, J.J. (forthcoming, 1997). Gender differences in rating the teaching of economics. *Easter Economic Journal*.

Arce, D.G., Formby, J.P., and Zheng, B. (1996). *Student performance and induced class attendance in introductory economics: Evidence from a controlled experiment.* Working Paper No. 263, Department of Economics, University of Alabama.

Bartlett, R.L. (1996). Discovering diversity in introductory economics. *Journal of Economic Perspectives*, 10(2), (Spring), 141-153.

Becker, W.E. (1982). The educational process and student achievement given uncertainty in measurement. *American Economic Review*, 72(1), (March), 229-236.

Becker, W.E. (1983a). Economic education research: Part I, Issues and questions. *Journal of Economic Education*, 14(1), (Winter), 10-17.

Becker, W.E. (1983b). Economic education research: Part II, New directions in theoretical model building. *Journal of Economic Education*, 14(2), (Spring), 4-10.

Becker, W.E. (1983c). Economic education research: Part III, Statistical estimation methods. *Journal of Economic Education*, 14(3), (Summer), 4-15.

Becker, W.E. (forthcoming). Teaching undergraduate economics: The case for more actively involved students and better outcome measurement. *Journal of Economic Literature*.

Becker, W.E., Highsmith, R.J., Kennedy, P., and Walstad, W.B. (1991). An agenda for research on economic education in colleges and universities. *American Economic Review*, 81(2), (May), 26-31.

Becker, W.E., Powers, J., and Saunders, P. (1996). *Problems of missing student data in the TUCE III data set and the importance of class size in student achievement.* Department of Economics, Indiana University, April. Working paper.

Becker, W.E. and Walstad, W.B. (1987). *Econometric modeling in economic education research.* Boston: Kluwer-Nijhoff.

Becker, W.E. and Watts, M. (1995). A review of teaching methods in undergraduate economics. *Economic Inquiry*, 33(4), (October), 692-700.

Becker, W.E. and Watts, M. (1996). Chalk and talk: A national survey on teaching undergraduate economics. *American Economic Review*, 86(2), (May), 448-453.

Beron, K.J. (1990). Joint determination of current classroom performance and additional economics classes: A binary/continuous model. *Journal of Economic Education*, 21(3), (Summer), 255-276.

Blackwell, J.L. (1983). A statistical interpretation of student evaluation feedback: A comment. *Journal of Economic Education*, 14(3), (Summer), 28-31.

Bonello, F.J., Swartz, T.R., and Davisson, W.I. (1984). Freshman-sophomore learning differentials: A comment. *Journal of Economic Education*, 15(3), (Summer), 205-210.

Borg, M.O. and Shapiro, S.L. (1996). Personality type and student performance in principles of economics. *Journal of Economic Education*, 27(1), (Winter), 3-27.

Borg, M.O., Mason, P.M., and Shapiro, S.L. (1989). The case of effort variables in student performance. *Journal of Economic Education*, 20(3), (Summer), 308-313.

Brasfield, D.W., Harrison, D.E., and McCoy, J.P. (1993). The impact of high school economics on the college principles of economics course. *Journal of Economic Education*, 24(2), (Spring), 99-112.

Brasfield, D.W., Harrison, D.E., McCoy, J., and Milkman, M. (1996). Why have some schools not experienced a decrease in the percentage of students majoring in economics. *Journal of Economic Education*, 27(4), (Fall), 362-370.

Bunn, D.N., Caudill, S.B., and Gropper, D.M. (1992). Crime in the classroom: An economic analysis of undergraduate student cheating behavior. *Journal of Economic Education*, 23(3), (Summer), 197-208.

Butler, J.S., Finegan, T.A., and Siegfried, J.J. (1994). Does more calculus improve student learning in intermediate micro and macro economic theory? *American Economic Review*, 84(2), (May), 206-210.

Cardell, N.S., et al. (1996). Laboratory-based experimental and demonstration initiatives in teaching undergraduate economics. *American Economic Review*, 86(2), (May), 454-459.

Carlson, J.L. and Ostrosky, A.L. (1992). Item sequence and student performance on multiple choice exams: Further evidence. *Journal of Economic Education*, 23(3), (Summer), 232-235.

Caudill, S.B. and Gropper, D.M. (1991). Test structure, human capital, and student performance on economics exams. *Journal of Economic Education*, 22(4), (Fall), 303-306.

Charkins, R.J., O'Toole, D.M., and Wetzel, J.N. (1985). Linking teacher and student learning styles with student achievement and attitudes. *Journal of Economic Education*, 16(2), (Spring), 111-120.

Cohn, E., Cohn, S., and Bradley, J. (1995). Notetaking, working memory, and learning in principles of economics. *Journal of Economic Education*, 26(4), (Fall), 291-307.

College Entrance Examination Board (CEEB). (1996). *Advanced placement course description: Economics* (May 1997, May 1998). New York: CEEB.

DeCanio, S.J. (1986). Student evaluations of teaching—A multinomial logit approach. *Journal of Economic Education*, 17(3), (Summer), 165-175.

Dilts, D.A. (1980). A statistical interpretation of student evaluation feedback. *Journal of Economic Education*, 11(2), (Spring), 10-15.

Durden, G.C. and Ellis, L.V. (1995). The effects of attendance on student learning in principles of economics. *American Economic Review*, 85(2), (May), 343-346.

Dynan, K. and Rouse, C. (forthcoming, 1997). The underrepresentation of women in economics: A study of undergraduate students. *Journal of Economic Education*.

Fels, R. (1969). Hard research on a soft subject: Hypothesis-testing in economic education. *Southern Economic Journal*, 36(3), (July), 1-9.

Ferber, M.A., Birnbaum, B.G., and Green, C.A. (1983). Gender differences in economic knowledge: A reevaluation of the evidence. *Journal of Economic Education*, 14(2), (Spring), 24-37.

Fizel, J.L. and Johnson, J.D. (1986). The effect of macro/micro course sequencing on learning and attitudes in principles of economics. *Journal of Economic Education*, 17(2), (Spring), 87-98.

Gleason, J.P. and Walstad, W.B. (1988). An empirical test of an inventory model of student study time. *Journal of Economic Education*, 19(4), (Fall), 315-321.

Gohmann, S.F. and Spector, L.C. (1989). Test scrambling and student performance. *Journal of Economic Education*, 20(2), (Summer), 235-238.

Gramlich, E.M. and Greenlee, G.A. (1993). Measuring teaching performance. *Journal of Economic Education*, 24(1), (Winter), 3-13.

Grimes, P., Krehbeil, T.L., Nielsen, J.E., and Niss, J.F. (1989). The effectiveness of *Economics U$A* on learning and attitudes. *Journal of Economic Education*, 20(2), (Spring), 139-152.

Hansen, W.L. (1986). What knowledge is most worth knowing—For economics majors. *American Economic Review*, 76(2), (May), 149-152.

Hirschfeld, M., Moore, R.L., and Brown, E. (1995). Exploring the gender gap on the GRE subject test in economics. *Journal of Economic Education*, 26(1), (Winter), 3-16.

Hodgin, R.F. (1984). Information theory and attitude formation in economic education. *Journal of Economic Education*, 15(3), (Summer), 191-196.

Horvath, J., Beaudin, B., and Wright, S. (1992). Persisting in the introductory economics course: An exploration of gender differences. *Journal of Economic Education*, 23(2), (Spring), 101-108.

Karstensson, L. and Vedder, R.K. (1974). A note on attitude as a factor in learning economics. *Journal of Economic Education*, 5(2), (Spring), 109-111.

Kennedy, P. and Siegfried, J. (forthcoming, 1997). Class size and achievement in introductory economics: Evidence from the TUCE III data. *Economics of Education Review*.

Kennedy, P. and Walstad, W.B. (forthcoming). Combining multiple-choice and constructed response test scores: An economist's view. *Applied Measurement in Education*.

Kerkvliet, J. (1994). Cheating by economics students: A comparison of survey results. *Journal of Economic Education*, 25(2), (Spring), 121-134.

Laband, D. and Piette, M. (1994). The relative impacts of economics journals: 1970–1990. *Journal of Economic Literature*, 32(2), (June), 640-666.

Ladd, H.F. (1977). Male-female differences in precollege economic education. In D.R. Wentworth, et al., (eds.), *Perspectives on economic education*. New York: Joint Council on Economic Education.

Lage, M.J. and Treglia, M. (1996). The impact of integrating scholarship on women into introductory economics: Evidence from one institution. *Journal of Economic Education*, 27(1), (Winter), 26-36.

Leppel, K. (1984). The academic performance of returning and continuing college students: An economic analysis. *Journal of Economic Education*, 15(1), (Winter), 46-54.

Liebowitz, S.J. and Palmer, J.P. (1984). Assessing the relative impacts of economics journals. *Journal of Economic Literature*, 22(1), (March), 77-88.

Lima, A.K. (1981). An economic model of teaching effectiveness. *American Economic Review*, 71(5), (December), 1056-1059.

Lopus, J.S. and Maxwell, N.L. (1995). Should we teach microeconomics principles before macroeconomic principles? *Economic Inquiry*, 38(2), (April), 336-350.

Lumsden, K. (1974). The information content of student evaluation of faculty and courses. In K. Lumsden, (ed.), *Efficiency in universities: The LaPaz papers* (pp. 175-204). Amsterdam and New York: Elsevier Scientific.

Lumsden, K.G. and Scott, A. (1983). The efficacy of innovative teaching techniques in economics: The U.K. experience. *American Economic Review*, 73(2), (May), 13-17.

Lumsden, K.G. and Scott, A. (1987). The economics student reexamined: Male-female differences in comprehension. *Journal of Economic Education*, 18(4), (Fall), 365-375.

Manahan, J. (1983). An educational production function for principles of economics. *Journal of Economic Education*, 14(2), (Spring), 11-16.

Margo, R.A. and Siegfried, J.J. (1996). Long-run trends in economics bachelor's degrees. *Journal of Economic Education*, 27(4), (Fall), 326-336.

Marlin, J.W. and Niss, J.F. (1982). The advanced learning system, a computer-managed, self-paced system of instruction: An application in principles of economics. *Journal of Economic Education*, 13(3), (Summer), 26-39.

Mason, P., Steagall, J.W., and Fabritius, M.M. (1995). Student evaluations of faculty: A new procedure for using aggregate measure of performance. *Economics of Education Review*, 14(4), 403-416.

Maxwell, N.L. and Lopus, J.S. (1995). A cost effectiveness analysis of large and small classes in the university. *Educational Evaluation and Policy Analysis*, 17(2), 167-178.

McConnell, C.R. and Sosin, K. (1984). Some determinants of student attitudes toward large classes. *Journal of Economic Education*, 15(3), (Summer), 181-190.

Mehdizadeh, M. (1990). Loglinear models and student course evaluations. *Journal of Economic Education*, 21(1), (Winter), 7-21.

Meinkoth, M.R. (1971). Textbooks and the teaching of economic principles. *Journal of Economic Education*, 2(2), (Spring), 127-130.

Miller, J.C. (1982). Technical efficiency in the production of economic knowledge. *Journal of Economic Education*, 13(3), (Summer), 3-13.

Mixon, F.G. (1996). Crime in the classroom: An extension. *Journal of Economic Education*, 27(3), (Summer), 195-200.

Myatt, A. and Waddell, C. (1990). An approach to testing the effectiveness of teaching and learning of economics in high school. *Journal of Economic Education*, 21(3), (Summer), 355-363.

Nelson, T.P. and Lynch, K.A. (1984). Grade inflation, real income, simultaneity, and teaching evaluations. *Journal of Economic Education*, 15(1), (Winter), 21-37.

Park, K.H. and Kerr, P.M. (1990). Determinants of academic performance: A multinominal logit approach. *Journal of Economic Education*, 21(2), (Spring), 101-112.

Paul, H. (1982). The impact of outside employment on student achievement in macroeconomic principles. *Journal of Economic Education*, 13(3), (Summer), 51-56.

Prince, R., Kipps, P.H., Wilhelm, H.M., and Wetzel, J.N. (1981). Scholastic effort: An empirical test of student choice models. *Journal of Economic Education*, 12(2), (Summer), 15-25.

Raimondo, H.J., Esposito, L., and Gershenberg, I. (1990). Introductory class size and student performance in intermediate theory courses. *Journal of Economic Education*, 21(4), (Fall), 369-381.

Reid, R. (1983). A note on the environment as a factor affecting student performance in principles of economics. *Journal of Economic Education*, 14(4), (Fall), 18-22.

Romer, D. (1993). Do students go to class? Should they? *Journal of Economic Perspectives*, 7(3), (Summer), 167-174.

Salemi, M. and Eubanks, C. (1996). Accounting for the rise and fall in the number of economics majors with the discouraged-business-major hypothesis. *Journal of Economic Education*, 27(4), (Fall), 350-361.

Saunders, P. (1970). Does high school economics have a lasting impact? *Journal of Economic Education*, 1(1), (Fall), 39-55.

Saunders, P. (1980). *The lasting effectiveness of introductory economics courses. Journal of Economic Education*, 12(1), (Winter), 1-14.

Saunders, P. (1991). The third edition of the test of economics in college economics (TUCE III). *American Economic Review*, 81(2), (May), 32-37.

Schmidt, R. (1983). Who maximizes what? A study in student time allocation. *American Economic Review*, (73), (May), 23-28.

Seldin, P. (1993). *Successful use of teaching portfolios*. Bolton, MA: Anker Publishing.

Sevier, D.A. (1983). Evaluations and grades: A simultaneous framework. *Journal of Economic Education*, 14(3), (Summer), 32-38.

Shmanske, S. (1988). On the measurement of teacher effectiveness. *Journal of Economic Education*, 19(4), (Fall), 307-314.

Siegfried, J. (1979). Male-female differences in economic education: A survey. *Journal of Economic Education*, 10(2), (Spring), 1-11.

Siegfried, J. (1995). Trends in undergraduate economics degrees: A 1994–95 update. *Journal of Economic Education*, 26(3), (Summer), 282-287.

Siegfried, J., Bartlett, R., Hansen, W.L., Kelley, A.C., McCloskey, D., and Tietenberg, T. (1991). The B- economics major: Can and should we do better? *Journal of Economic Education*, 22(3), (Summer), 197-224.

Siegfried, J. and Fels, R. (1979). Research on teaching college economics: A survey. *Journal of Economic Literature*, 17(3), (September), 923-969.

Siegfried, J. and Kennedy, P.E. (1995). Does pedagogy vary with class size in introductory economics? *American Economic Review*, 85(2), (May), 347-351.

Siegfried, J. and Raymond, J. (1984). A profile of senior economics majors in the United States. *American Economic Review: Proceedings*, 74(2), (May), 19-25.

Siegfried, J., Saunders, P., Stinar, E., and Zhang, H. (1996). How is introductory economics taught in America? *Economic Inquiry*, 34(1), (January), 1182-1192.

Siegfried, J. and Wilkinson, J.T. (1982). The economics curriculum in the United States: 1980. *American Economic Review: Proceedings*, 72(2), (May), 125-142.

Stratton, R.W., Myers, S.C., and King, R.H. (1994). Faculty behavior, grades, and student evaluations. *Journal of Economic Education*, 25(1), (Winter), 5-16.

Tay, R.S. (1994). Students' performance in economics: Does the norm hold across cultural and institutional settings? *Journal of Economic Education*, 25(4), (Fall), 291-302.

Van Scyoc, L.J. and Gleason, J. (1993). Traditional or intensive course lengths? A comparison of outcomes in economics learning. *Journal of Economic Education*, 24(1), (Winter), 15-22.

Walstad, W.B. (1987). Applying two stage least squares. In W.E. Becker and W.B. Walstad (eds.), *Econometric modeling in economic education research* (pp. 111-134). Boston: Kluwer-Nijhoff.

Walstad, W.B. (1992). Economics instruction in high schools. *Journal of Economic Literature*, 30(4), (December), 2019-2051.

Walstad, W.B. (1996). Recent research on the economics major: Comment. *Journal of Economic Education*, 27(4), (Fall), 371-375.

Walstad, W.B. and Becker, W.E. (1994). Achievement difference on multiple choice tests in economics. *American Economic Review*, 84(2), (May), 193-197.

Walstad, W.B. and Robson, D. (forthcoming). Differential item functioning and male-female differences on multiple choice tests in economics. *Journal of Economic Education*.

Walstad, W.B. and Soper, J.C. (1988). A report card on the economic literacy of U.S. high school students. *American Economic Review: Proceedings*, 78(2), (May), 251-256.

Watts, M. and Bosshardt, W. (1991). How instructors make a difference: Panel data estimates from principles of economics courses. *The Review of Economics and Statistics*, 73(2), (May), 336-340.

Watts, M. and Lynch, G.J. (1989). The principles courses revisited. *American Economic Review*, 79(2), (May), 236-241.

Wetzel, J.N., Potter, W.J., and O'Toole, D.M. (1982). The influence of learning and teaching styles on student attitudes and achievement in the introductory economics course: A case study. *Journal of Economic Education*, 13(1), (Winter), 33-39.

White, L.J. (1995). Efforts by departments of economics to assess teaching effectiveness: Results of an informal survey. *Journal of Economic Education*, 26(1), (Winter), 81-85.

Williams, D.D., Cook, P., Quinn, B., and Jensen, R. (1985). University class size? Is small better? *Research in Higher Education*, 23(3), 307-317.

Williams, M.L., Waldaver, C., and Duggal, V. (1992). Gender differences in economic knowledge: An extension of the analysis. *Journal of Economic Education*, 23(3), (Summer), 219-231.

Willis, R.A. and Pieper, P.J. (1996). The economics major: A cross-sectional view. *Journal of Economic Education*, 27(4), (Fall), 337-349.

Zangenehzadeh, H. (1983). Grade inflation: A way out. *Journal of Economic Education*, 19(3), (Summer), 217-226.

CHAPTER 12

LECTURES AS AN INSTRUCTIONAL METHOD

Phillip Saunders

Arthur L. Welsh

All instructors, at one time or another, find themselves in situations where a good lecture (one way talk) is the most effective means of achieving their particular instructional objectives. Since good lectures are a necessary part of an effective instructor's repertoire, particularly in large enrollments principles of economic courses, the goal of this chapter is to provide information, ideas, and suggestions that might help you, with the aid of additional effort and practice, to become a more effective lecturer. We begin by making four main points about lectures. We then discuss two common criticisms of the lecture method of instruction and what might be done to mitigate these criticisms. The heart of the chapter examines each of the four main parts of a good lecture. We conclude with a check list that we hope will be helpful to economics instructors in planning, organizing, presenting, and evaluating their lectures.

Four Main Points

The four main points about lectures that we want to make at the outset are:

1 There is no "one best way" to lecture.
2 Lectures are more useful for some purposes than others.

3 A lecture does not have to last the whole class period.

4 The actual presentation is only one part of good lecturing—much more is involved than simply talking at students.

We will discuss each of these points briefly.

There is no "one-best-way" to lecture The person who seeks a single "true" magic formula that will solve all of his or her problems in lecturing searches in vain. Effective lecturing is compatible with a variety of personality types and styles of presentation. Each person must develop the techniques that best meet lecture objectives, given their own personality, tastes, talents, and predilections. This is not easy, and instructors must be prepared for a certain amount of hard work and disappointment as they experiment and develop a lecture style that is best for them. We can be influenced by others, and we can often get good ideas and techniques from others, but attempts to "copy" another person's lecture style often don't work unless this style is genuinely compatible with our own basic identity.

Lectures are more useful for some purposes than others Bligh (1971) has argued convincingly that the lecture method's comparative advantages lie in *transmitting information* and *setting up a framework for analysis*. Lectures are often less effective than other teaching methods in promoting independent thought, developing critical thinking skills in students, and in changing student attitudes. If one wants to achieve these latter objectives, he or she should be aware of the limitations of one-way talk (and chalk), and modify lectures accordingly and/or supplement them with other modes of teaching.

A lecture need not last the whole class period The necessity of achieving objectives for which the straight lecture is well suited, while at the same time trying to achieve objectives for which the lecture method is not well suited, often leaves instructors torn. This potential anguish diminishes considerably, however, once we recognize the simple point that more than one thing can go on during the same class period. Lectures can be combined with other modes of instruction, and a single class period can contain more than one lecture. We will have more to say about this later when we deal with one of the major objections to the straight lecture method.

The actual presentation is only one part of good lecturing The presentation of a lecture is much like the tip of an iceberg; there is more there than meets the eye. A lecture presentation must be firmly anchored on a foundation of planning, organization, and evaluation. Since all four of these tasks are important, we will return shortly to a separate discussion of planning, organization, presentation, and evaluation.

Two Criticisms of the Lecture Method

Two of the most common criticisms of the lecture method are that "books are better," and that "active participation on the part of the learner is more effective than passive listening." These criticisms are not to be taken lightly. Once recognized, however, their seriousness can be minimized. The rest of this section will discuss and partially rebut each of these criticisms. We will end up noting that the lecture, with appropriate modifications, still has an important place in college teaching. To be sure, bad lectures deserve all the criticism they get; but a good lecture, used under the right conditions, is a tremendously efficient vehicle for transmitting information and setting up a framework for analysis.

Books are better Boswell reported that Samuel Johnson criticized lectures as far back as 1766 on the general grounds that "I can not see that lectures do as much good as reading the books from which the lectures are taken." Johnson also noted "If your attention fails, and you miss a point of the lecture, it is lost; you cannot go back as you do upon a book."

Ignoring the facts that lectures and books can be complementary goods as well as substitute goods, and that many students do not and will not read the assignments in the text until they have been to class to "find out what's important," (and maybe not even then), there are three other points to be made in rebuttal to this criticism.

First, listening to a lecture can be a very different experience from reading a transcript of the same material. Hawkins, Davies, and Majer (1973, p. 23) have noted that "The content may be the same, but the process is different." "Social facilitation" may occur during a lecture when students can see others simultaneously concerning themselves with the same ideas, and each member of the class may be stimulated by the awareness that other students are responding to the lecturer at the same moment.

Second, a lecture can be more flexible than a written presentation. A good lecturer can organize his or her presentation to allow for the "attention failures" noted by Johnson (we call them "micro sleeps" now), and in college classrooms the opportunity to ask clarifying questions and review unclear points should be much greater than in the type of public lecture to which Johnson may have been referring. Also, no book ever got any instant feedback from a reader. All but the most obtuse lecturers, however, can get clues from their students about how well things are or are not going over, and they can modify their presentation accordingly.

Third, and most important, the one thing that a lecture can do much better than a book is to provide a *live model of a person thinking*. An enthusiastic lecturer setting up a problem and thinking it through can provide a memorable experience for students that is hard to duplicate in any other way. Facial expressions, body language, and changes in pace and inflection all give clues to aid comprehension and understanding that are not available from a printed page.

Active participation is better than passive listening The reasons most people object to passive listening as opposed to active participation are usually based on learning theory and experiments that emphasize the importance of verbalization, reinforcement, and feedback to the student. It is true that most conventional lectures do not provide a great deal of opportunity for student verbalization, reinforcement, or feedback. But, once this weakness is recognized, it can be dealt with by encouraging students to question you, by asking your students questions, by combining lecture demonstrations with problem solving assignments given as homework, and/or by breaking up the lecture at certain key points. We should also note here that simply because a student's body is sitting still during a lecture does not necessarily mean that his or her mind is passive. Indeed, the student's mind is often highly active—many times with the wrong activity—during the lecture. The trick is to get the student's mental activity working in the right direction.

In the last chapter of his 1972 book, *The Summer Game*, Roger Angell uses the fascinating term, "The Interior Stadium" and refers to the "interior game—baseball in the mind."[1] Later David Bergman used the term "internal dialogue" to explain why students in his lecture courses commented that he brought the class out in discussion even though there were no formal class discussions. He hypothesized that they had the "illusion of a discussion" and stated:

> Somewhere between the lecture and their notebooks a dialogue had quietly taken place. This internal dialogue is often as stimulating as, and more open than, any classroom discussion. Moreover, the internal dialogue always focuses on just those issues that interest us. . . .It always concerns itself with what bothers us most (Bergman, 1983, p. 49).

In lecturing we want to try to make sure that it is our game, and not some other, that is being played in the student's interior stadium. We can use rhetorical questions and other techniques to initiate an internal dialogue in the student's mind. In this way active participation, learning from listening, and even reinforcement can occur during a lecture if the student tries to anticipate and implicitly predict the outcome of the speaker's discourse or argument. The student is reinforced if the speaker's next idea confirms the prediction.

Returning to our third main point that a lecture need not last a whole class period, or that one class period can be broken into different parts, it is often a good idea to stop lecturing and solicit some form of response by students.[2] A general "are there any questions?" is not likely to be as effective as asking some particular question of your own in a non-threatening manner. Rather than singling out a particular student, you might put a question on the board or the overhead projector and have the whole class meditate on the answer for a minute or so before discussing it in detail. Or you might give your students a problem and let them break into small "buzz" groups to discuss it for 3 or 4 minutes before reporting their answers and/or their confusion about what the problem or question means. If it is feasible, the small group technique has the advantage of promoting social interaction among classmates and giving vent to any latent needs for self expression. Students are more likely to ask questions of each other in such situations than they are to ask the instructor. Fear of asking "dumb" or "obvious" questions is also lessened when students find out they are not the only ones who don't have a clear notion of what is going on. And when questions from the group are discussed in front to the whole class, it is possible to cloak some individual problems in the guise that "some members of the group aren't clear on. . ." or "one or two of us wonder why. . . .?"

The first time such a "break" to discuss a new question or problem is used, it is important to put the class at ease with a statement not the effect that "This is a tough point, and I want to make sure you understand it before going on to the next one. I'm going to put a question on the screen (board) so you can see if you really grasp the idea. Don't get nervous; this is not a pop quiz or anything like that. Just study the question for a few minutes, and think out an answer. Then we will discuss any ambiguity in the question or any problem you might have in arriving at the answer."

If a lecture-demonstration is coupled with going over homework problems, it's important that the instructor does *not* do all the work, show off his or her superior knowledge, and make the answers appear to be self-evident. If the answers are self-evident, why go to the bother of assigning homework problems? If the answers are not self-evident, let the students know that you appreciate the effort they have expended. Give them some guidance at first, and then gradually allow them to take over and present their own solutions. Studies have shown that in teaching students to solve problems, knowledge of how to go about them is more important than the knowledge of the principle involved (Bligh, p. 136). A live demonstration of setting up a problem and working it through can be useful for students at first, and it is probably important for the instructor to point out the answer or the conclusion if it appears that many students have not arrived at it by themselves. But there is a lot of evidence that the discovery of a conclusion by oneself can have considerable motivational value for a student, and Beard (1970, p. 38) reports that "teachers who solve all the problems, displaying their own superior skills, tend to depress interest in all but their most able students."

The Main Parts of a Good Lecture

Let us now turn to the four main parts of a good lecture: Planning, Organization, Presentation, and Evaluation. We will discuss each of these parts separately.

Lecture planning Lecture planning should start with a consideration of your students' "learning set" and how they are most likely to "encode" and process information (see Chapter 8). In principles of economics courses, and even in many upper division courses for economics majors, the background and prior experiences of most students are likely to be quite different from those of the instructor. This is often particularly difficult for young, beginning economics instructors to appreciate. The fact that they have recently been students themselves often misleads them. The problem is that most new instructors have recently been successful, strongly motivated students, with a deep interest in the subject who have gone on to graduate work in economics. This is not likely to be typical of the students entering his or her large (usually "required") principles economics classes. Only about 3% of principles students decide to major in economics, and less than 3% of economics majors go on to enroll in Ph.D. programs in economics. Some planning effort must be directed to motivating students, and you should plan to open each lecture with some indication to students of why the topic is of importance to them. You should also try to work out specific examples that will be meaningful to them.

Even experienced instructors sometimes fall into the trap of trying to jam too much material into a single lecture. An important step in lecture planning, therefore, is deciding what material to leave out. Instructors who have just won professional status and are full of their subject must *strongly* resist the temptation to try to cover too much material and to go into too great detail. As emphasized in Chapter 8, the human mind has a limited capacity to process information, and adding too many elements to an intellectual task causes confusion and inefficiency. Wilbert J. McKeachie, a psychologist who has devoted his professional career to analyzing learning and teaching, has emphasized this problem and offered a suggestion to deal with it. McKeachie (1980, pp. 32-33) states:

> Probably one of the greatest barriers to effective lecturing is the feeling that one must cover the material at all costs. While it may seem irrational to cover material when students are not learning from it, one should not underestimate the compulsion one feels to get through one's lecture notes. A remedy for this compulsion is to put into the lecture notes reminders to oneself to check the students' understanding—both by looking for nonverbal cues of bewilderment or of lack of attention and by raising specific questions that will test the students' understanding.

Instructors vary considerably in the type of notes they prepare in planning a lecture. Ruth S. Day discusses several different formats ranging from verbatim transcripts to pictorial and tree diagram formats, and she notes: "The process of devising the notes may become more important that its product" (Day, 1980, p. 111). In general, you should not plan to cover more than three to five major points in a 50-minute lecture, and you should carefully work out elaborating examples and the transitions from one major point to another.

Too little detail is to be preferred to too much, and the following "rules" of sequencing should be used in planning lectures and other instructional activities. These rules appear in Davies (1981, p. 91), who attributes them to Herbert Spencer.

- proceed from the know to the unknown;
- proceed from the simple to the complex;
- proceed from the concrete to the abstract;
- proceed from the particular to the general;
- proceed from observation to reasoning;
- proceed from a whole view to a more detailed view to a whole view.

All of these sequences attempt to make new material more meaningful in terms of the student's existing learning set. And, as indicated in Chapter 8, material encoded in a meaningful learning set is more easily transferred to new situations than is material encoded by rote. Instead of talking about equilibrium prices in general, for example, it helps to start by focusing on a particular price that has some meaning for the student, such as tuition or movies. Initial examples dealing with diagrams should have specific numbers attached, and it is wise to work them out in advance on an overhead transparency, rather than relying on blackboard work where it is difficult to get things drawn exactly to scale. Overlays are useful in ways that conventional blackboard diagrams are not. They are especially useful for building up complex diagrams piece by piece. Moreover, they have the added advantage that they can be reversed or "peeled" back for clarification. A transparency is also available for later reference, whereas limited space often forces lecturers to erase the board.

If you plan to make frequent use of diagrams in your presentations, it is a good idea to work out one or two homework problems that require the students themselves to draw and interpret diagrams. This way you can be sure that they are aware of what variables are on what axes, and it helps them get a "feel" for the data through their fingers as they connect the points on a demand curve, an indifference curve, or an iso product curve, for example. Once students have worked out an example involving a specific set of numbers, it is easier to move to a more general form where exact numbers need not be specified and we can simply refer to diagrams where "P_1 is greater than P_2," "Q_1 is less than Q_2," etc., etc.

Since it usually involves a considerable amount of effort, forcing yourself to work out specific numerical examples and homework problems in the planning stage is one good way to insure that you keep your learning objectives limited and avoid the common error of trying to cover too much material. If you can't, or don't, take time to work out examples and problems, how can you expect the typical student to get deeply involved in what you're trying to teach?

Another important point to consider in planning your lectures is that your students' learning set will probably change as the semester progresses. As they become more familiar with the techniques and procedures of economics, and as they become more familiar with your lecturing style, they should be able to process larger and more complex "chunks" of information later in the course than at the beginning. The amount of detail and elaboration you plan to devote to a topic or a concept, therefore, should be related to where it will appear in the course sequence. Topics and concepts which require knowledge of prerequisite concepts and understanding should be covered toward the end of the course rather than at the beginning. But in cases where there is some flexibility in the sequence of topics, consideration must be given to what topics have preceded the lecture you are planning. A well planned lecture at one point in the course might not be a well planned lecture at another. A lecture on derived demand in factor markets, for example, would have to be planned differently if it preceded your lectures on non-competitive product market structures than if it did not.

Lecture organization   Everything we know about learning emphasizes the importance of organization or "structure." Some structure or framework for analysis is necessary to make a subject comprehensible, and unless ideas and facts can be placed in a structured pattern in the student's mind they are easily forgotten. A knowledge of how things are related is also the easiest way to facilitate the transfer of ideas to new situations. What may seem like a well organized set of ideas to the lecturer may not appear to be nearly as clear or so well organized to the listener, who typically has far less familiarity with and sophistication in the subject matter. Students may not know where the material fits in with other ideas, how it will be used, or why it is important. The lecturer must help students forge these links. Therefore, it is important to state the organization at the beginning of the lecture, to outline or itemize the main points to be covered, and to summarize and pull things together at the end.

1 *State the organization at the beginning.* The classic dictum "First tell 'em what you're going to tell 'em. Then tell 'em. And, finally, tell 'em what you've told 'em" has much to be said for it. Many lecturers feel there may be too much repetition using this format. But experience indicates that repetition which may seem "redundant" to the speaker is actually "reinforcing" to the listener.

Several different organizational patterns are possible for various lectures in economics, and each has its uses for particular purposes. If one wants to cover a lot of ground dealing with an overall framework or a series of definitions, a *classification hierarchy* may be the most appropriate organization. The notions of total cost, fixed cost, variable cost, and marginal cost, for example, might best be structured in this way. For other purposes, a *problem centered* organization may be most appropriate. In introducing the notion of price elasticity of demand, for example, one might pose the question: Why is it that raising the price of some products (gasoline or alcohol) seems to bring in more revenue while raising the price of other products (a specific brand of gasoline) may bring in less revenue?[3] The organizational principle of *comparison and contrast* might be the most appropriate one for dealing with an issue such as the national debt where problems of false analogies abound. Other organizational patterns to consider are *concept to application* and *familiar to unfamiliar*.

Regardless of which organizational principle is being used in any particular lecture, it is important that the students know what it is, so they know what to listen for and so they can set up some of the implicit anticipations and predictions mentioned above. (Letting students lay out the bases in their interior stadium is a great aid in helping them to deal with Abbott and Costello's immortal question "Who's on first?") The introduction to the lecture should also indicate to students why it is important that they understand the material to be covered.

2 *Itemize the main points.* Itemizing the main points of a lecture on the blackboard, the overhead, or a class handout has several advantages for both lecturer and student. The items provide "memory pegs" on which details and

examples can be hung, and they help to make it clear when the lecturer is moving from one point to another. If points are itemized, the student who daydreams or has a "micro sleep" finds it easier to realize that he has missed something, and can ask a fellow student or the lecturer to fill him in later. Itemizing also aids memory when we can say "there are three points on this topic" or "there are two items in this category and three in the other." In itemizing, it helps to keep lists relatively short. If you have more than four or five points, try to break the list into parts or subgroups.

3 *Summarize at the end.* In summarizing the lecture it may be more helpful to pose significant questions than to simply repeat statements of fact. McKeachie (1986, p. 222) notes that experiments by D.E. Berlyne "found that asking students questions, rather than presenting statements of fact, not only improved learning but also increased interest in learning more about the topic." And Hawkins, Davies, and Majer (1973, p. 26) state that questions "remind students of material they should have gained and what implications they should consider. Questions help the student structure what he has learned on the topic, in that particular lecture and cumulatively." And they continue "At the end, it is also useful to review concepts, noting how they relate to each other and to previous ones."

Lecture presentation The beginning is by far the most important part of the lecture presentation.[4] At the beginning of each lecture the day's topic(s) should be tied in with familiar material, perhaps by reviewing the main points of the preceding lecture or by citing some current event that relates to the day's lecture. As indicated above, you should indicate why the topic(s) is (are) important for the students to understand and try to motivate them to want to pay attention. Beyond the other points already discussed above under "organization," much of what remains to be said about good lecture presentations appears to be simple common sense: lectures should be delivered in a clear and confident voice that does not go too fast and varies in emphasis and intonation; they should be aptly illustrated with a variety of stimuli and specific examples, accompanied by abundant eye contact with the listeners; time should be allowed for students to absorb difficult points and take notes; etc., etc. Yet is it often saddening to sit in a college lecture room and witness the extent to which such obvious maxims of common sense are ignored, disregarded, or simply overlooked.

Seven specific things that lecturers should keep in mind in thinking about their presentations are: enthusiasm is important; nonverbal behavior or "body-language" is important; silence, as well as voice inflection, can be golden; some apparently mundane considerations can be crucial; a sense of humor, a stock of catchy examples, and/or a few special "tricks" can be valuable aids; variety in *stimuli* is the spice of living through a lecture; yet it helps to develop a more-or-less standard *procedure* in dealing with major points in your presentation.

Let us elaborate briefly on each of these items before turning to evaluating lecture presentations.

1 *Enthusiasm is important.* There is a lot of evidence that the lecturer's own enthusiasm is an important variable in arousing student interest and motivation, and experimental studies show significantly higher exam performance by students who have been exposed to enthusiastic as opposed to passive lecturers. If lecturers do not convey some sense of intellectual excitement in the topics they are presenting, it is very difficult to arouse student interest or attention.

2 *Nonverbal behavior is important.* If you don't think that "body-language," such as facial expressions, posture, and gestures are important communicators, compare a transcript or a radio tape with a TV tape of the same presentation.

Much of an instructor's enthusiasm or lack of enthusiasm is communicated non-verbally rather than with the actual words spoken.[5] If you *really* want to encourage students to ask questions, greet questions with a smile, an approving nod, and preface your answer with a "good question" or "I'm glad you asked that." If you appear irritated, or appear to resent an interruption of your beautiful spiel, it doesn't make much difference what you say; students will get the "cue" not to ask questions.

3 *Silence can be golden.* Closely related to non-verbal behavior and voice inflection is the use of silence. A pregnant pause can be useful in encouraging student response. One must be sure to allow sufficient time for them to digest, meditate, and react to questions. What may seem like a long time to you standing in front of the room may not really seem very long to the students. Develop patience in resisting the temptation to "plug" silent "gaps." How do you do this? Recall the person who stopped a man on New York's Lower East side and asked "How do you get to Carnegie Hall?" The reply was, "Practice, practice, practice."[6]

4 *Some mundane things can be crucial.* If your classroom is hot and stuffy, if the "black" board is a "grey" board thick with fine white chalk dust, if the window blinds are not drawn to shield the board from glare, if a light bulb is missing, if you don't have chalk or markers for more recent dry erase boards, if your handouts aren't duplicated on time, or if your reserve readings are not available in the library when the students need them, then it is foolish to ignore these problems and blunder about on the grounds that such "mundane" details are beneath your professional dignity. Modesty compels us to recognize that on some days opening a window, getting a wet paper towel, drawing a blind, arranging to have a bulb or a broken chair replaced, or moving the class outside may be our most significant contribution to student understanding. Your concentration may make you oblivious to your surroundings, but not many students have the powers of concentration or the desire to overcome bad physical conditions. Cultivate janitors, secretaries, and librarians if you want to be sure that you have enough chalk or markers, your handouts are ready on time, and your reserve readings are available. Bobby Burns noted that "The best laid schemes o' mice an' men gang aft a-gely." Don't get tripped up by "mundane" details. Allow lead time, and *PLAN AHEAD.*

5 *Humor, catchy examples, and special tricks.* Robert M. Kaplan and Gregory C. Pascoe (1977) conducted a study with 508 university students that found that humorous examples were recalled better than non-humorous ones, and most lecturers have one or two favorite "tricks," ploys, especially dramatic examples, or jokes that they like to employ. If some way could be devised to pool and access this accumulated "wisdom" of the thousands of economics instructors, we would probably all be better off—although what works for one person might not work for another.

Prolonged silence, flipping an overhead projector on and off, or letting a permanently mounted screen roll up with a bang have their value as attention getters at certain key points if they are not overworked. Developing one or two ploys of continuing "in-humor" can be useful in establishing rapport with large classes. Try to keep them limited in number and reserved for key points. One that we have used, for example, deals with a repeated harping (at our expense) on the point that the price where "the amount bought equals the amount sold" is not the same thing as an equilibrium, or a market clearing price. This is akin to the instructor who is worried about the audibility of his voice and asks all students who cannot hear him to please raise their hands. Or the instructor who takes attendance by asking all students who are not present to please stand up. These ploys usually go over with most of our principles students, but we don't know if other instructors could use them effectively or not, and we use fewer of them in our smaller upper division classes than in our large principles classes.

Another device we use when we think that principles students are not getting the material but are afraid to ask questions is to set up a dialogue with ourselves in which we play the part of both the instructor and the prudent student ("prude") or the casual observer ("cas") who just happens to wander in and start asking questions. The simulated dialogue can also be used to dramatize other points such as the independence of the Fed if one wants to play the part of both Harry Truman and Marriner Eccles or George Bush and Alan Greenspan. You don't have to be a professional actor to pull this one off, but a certain amount of ham (or corn) helps.

In working out numerical examples in class, we sometimes make simple errors in addition, subtraction or multiplication, and then use these occasions to dramatize our human frailties and let students know that we appreciate some of the agonies they have gone through by exclaiming "Hell, that's only the 12th mistake I've made so far today" or a exaggerated "Heavens, that's the first mistake I've ever made in my entire life" accompanied by an elaborate show of anguish accompanied with a wink.

A confident instructor is not afraid to admit mistakes, or that s/he doesn't know the answer to a question, and humor is far more effective when it is at the instructor's, not the student's, expense. In talking about the importance of the items selected for measurement in dealing with price indexes, for example, we sometimes dramatize the notion of a "market basket" of goods by drawing a ludicrous picture of a market basket on the board. Our artistic "talent" then becomes a source of amusement as well as a focus for understanding. Evoking mental images of Alfred

Marshall basking on a roof top in Palermo or Indians tieing a cowboy to two horses headed in the opposite directions can be useful in arousing student interest in the price elasticity of demand, and so on.

A stock of "tricks" and vivid examples can be a real aid in lecturing. They best serve a devices to stimulate interest and attention. Like fertilizer, they can be useful in encouraging growth—in this case, student understanding of economics—if they are not overdone and are used in the proper amount.

6 *Variety of stimuli.* In addition to voice inflection and avoiding the common error of letting sentences trail off at the end, presentations can be varied by using a combination of overhead projector, board work, and in class handouts. In listing main points or key definitions, the board or the overhead is sometimes preferable, since students may pay more attention to things they have copied themselves. (An overhead promotes more eye contact and student feedback than the board, and as mentioned above, flipping the on/off switch gets attention.) But, if a series of related points is to be covered in a cumulative sequence over several periods, an outline handout, with space for a student's marginal notes, may be preferable. Outlines can provide the students with an opportunity to concentrate on the big ideas unhindered by the necessity of taking detailed notes. They are also very useful to students who miss classes, but students should be encouraged to keep them and bring them to class.

If the board or overhead is used, be sure the print is large and legible to all, and try not to stand in front of what is written or projected. William Becker's list of six Do's and Do Not's in Chapter 10 is worth reviewing at this point, and Hawkins, Davies, and Majer (1973, p. 26) have also suggested two helpful techniques of board work:

a Write down complete statements (or words) not just symbols. Students tend to copy down just what you write and later wonder what you meant. Your notes should help recollection, not hinder it.

b Start at the top of one panel, move down and then go up to the next. Do not skip around, and do not erase a panel until all available ones are used.

7 *Standard procedure in making major points.* It may help your students understand your lectures and take better notes if you use a standard procedure in making major points. Such a procedure might be to first make a concise statement of the point and write it on the board or an overhead transparency; then restate the point in more detail with illustrations and examples that relate this point to others that students already understand; then solicit some student response to indicate if they understand the point before offering a final, brief recapitulation and restatement (See Bligh, 1971, pp. 79-88).

Evaluating lectures In the most fundamental sense, your lectures are a success if the students learn what you want them to learn. (For an alternative definition of a successful lecture, see Kenneth Elzinga's Chapter 7.) If your appropriately established objectives are met, other forms of evaluation are secondary. Yet most lecturers don't have to wait until the test results are in to see how their presentations are going over—just watch the students! Do they come on time or straggle in? Do they sit upright and appear to be interested in what's going on or are they slouched over and extending their "micro sleeps" into "macro sleeps"? Is there sparkle or haze in their eyes? Are they taking notes on the right things? Do they ask the right questions? If you are getting preliminary warning signs from these observations, there are better reactions than sulking and nursing your bruised ego in silence, or boiling up with indignant rage. And, even if you are not getting preliminary warning signs, you may want to pass out an anonymous questionnaire occasionally as a visible sign to the students that you're trying to do a good job, and are interested in improving. The questionnaire need not be elaborate, but it might include some questions on the classroom environment (such as light, noise, temperature) and the student's usual condition during your class (fatigue, hunger) as well as comments on the audibility of your voice, amount of material covered, speed of delivery, and clarity of board work or overhead transparencies.[7] Whatever questionnaire you use, don't wait too long to use it. If students are asked to take questionnaires seriously, they want their comments to benefit them *before* the course is over. They, legitimately, are more concerned with their own experiences than the experiences of students who follow them.

In addition to obtaining student feedback, you might want to ask a trusted colleague to sit in on some of your lectures and make suggestions for improvement. This type of feedback usually works best if it is focused on a limited number of specific points. Without some form of checklist focusing on classroom atmosphere and lecturing techniques, conversations with colleagues often become excessively dominated by discussions of content rather than lecturing skills. Appendix 12-1 shows a "Classroom Observer Checklist" that we have found useful to help avoid this problem. Rather than trying to cover all of the points on this checklist, it often helps to have the observer concentrate on only the four or five points you are most interested in.

Although comments from your students and colleagues can be helpful, the best critic of all may very well be yourself. Remember another of Bobbie Burns' gems:

> O wad some power the giftie gie us
> To see ourselves as ithers see us!
> It wad frae mony a blunder free us
> And folish notion.

The advent of videotape now makes it possible "To see ourselves as ithers see us." It takes courage, but it can be done in private, and reviewing videotapes of one or two of your lectures offers a powerful tool for self-study and self-evaluation. Many of us have unconscious, annoying or distracting personal mannerisms that even our best friends, let alone semi-dependent students, are reluctant to tell us about. Often, they have to be seen to be believed—and corrected. Chapter 21 covers videotaping in more detail.

Conclusions

Good lecturing, far from being an artistic talent with which people are born, is a skill which can be developed and improved with thoughtful consideration and practice.

If we may be permitted on final example from the world of baseball, consider the case of George Shuba, an outfielder from the Brooklyn Dodgers in the early 1950s, who Roger Kahn (1972, p. 224) notes was called "The Shotgun" because of his ability to spray line drives to all fields "with a swing so compact and so fluid that it appeared as natural as a smile." In compiling his wonderful book *The Boys of Summer*, Kahn visited Shuba at his home some years after his retirement from baseball and had occasion to comment on his "natural" swing. Shuba, then in his basement, reached up to a beam in the ceiling and lowered a rope with a clump of knots that hung waist high. Then he showed Kahn a bat which had been drilled and filled with lead, and went to a file and pulled out a whole ream of charts marked with X's. Kahn notes:

> "In the winters," he said, "for fifteen years after loading potatoes or anything else, even when I was in the majors, I'd swing at the clump six hundred times. Every night, after sixty I'd make an X. Ten X's and I had my six hundred swings. Then I could go to bed. You call that natural? I swung a 44 ounce bat 600 times a night, 4,200 times a week, 47,200 swings every winter. Wrists. The fast ball's by you. You gotta wrist it out. Forty-seven thousand two hundred times."

Fortunately, it doesn't take this much practice to become a "natural" lecturer.

NOTES

1. Angell (1972, pp. 308-310) notes: "At first, it is a game of recollections, recapturing, and visions. Figures and occasions return, enormous sounds rise and swell, and the interior stadium fills with light ... Any fan, as I say, can play this private game, extending it to extraordinary varieties and possibilities in his mind. Ruth bats against Sandy Koufax .. Hubbell pitches to Ted Williams ... By thinking about baseball like this—by playing it over, keeping it warm in a cold season—we begin to make discoveries. With luck, we may even penetrate some of its mysteries."

2. Peter Frederick (1986) suggests several ways in which the degree of student-faculty interaction can be increased in lecture situations.

3. One of our favorite ploys on the topic of price elasticity of demand is to project a picture of farmers dumping milk from a truck or Brazilian coffee fields burning and ask "why would they do this?" When students say, "to drive up the price," we ask, "but won't they have less to sell at the higher price?" "What good is a high price if you don't have as much to sell?" Thus, we are off and running.

4. McKeachie (1994, p. 56) notes: "Studies of the attention of students during lectures find that, typically, attention increases from the beginning of the lecture to ten minutes into

the lecture and decreases after that point. One evidence of this was that after the lecture students recalled 70 percent of the material covered in the first ten minutes, and only 20 percent of the material covered in the last 10 minutes."

If attention starts to wane after ten minutes, pause and ask questions or, as indicated above, "break" the lecture with some activity so that when you start again it seems like the first ten minutes of a new lecture.

5. Ivor Davies (1981, p 152) has noted: "Albert Mehrabian has estimated that only about 7 percent of the emotional impact of a person's message comes from words. Vocal elements contribute something like 38 percent of the message. Facial expressions, on the other hand, contribute 55 percent. Thus non-verbal communication is an important part of instructional technique."

6. Patricia Andrews (1989, p. 4) has noted: "Research has shown that if an instructor asks a question and then counts to 10 (slowly and silently) he is likely to elicit some student response. One study showed that the number of student responses increased by 80% when instructors used this technique."

7. A questionnaire form developed to evaluate lectures at London University is reproduced in Beard (1972, p. 123-124). One thing we like about the London form is that it solicits the students' perceptions of some of the "mundane" factors such as light, visibility, and temperature mentioned above, and it also obtains information on the students' own condition in terms of fatigue and hunger. Not all of the problems in maintaining interest or attention are the instructor's fault, and if it turns out that a large number of students are always tired or hungry at the time your class meets, you want to be aware of this problem and try to deal with it, perhaps by allowing students to bring snacks or by trying to schedule your class at a different hour in the next semester.

REFERENCES

Andrews, P.H. (1989). Improving lecturing skills: Some insights from speech communica-tions. *Teaching and Learning at Indiana University*, February.

Angell, R. (1972). *The summer game*. New York: Poplar Library.

Beard, R. (1972). *Teaching and learning in higher education*, 2nd ed. Baltimore: Penguin Books.

Bergman, D. (1983). In defense of lecturing. *Association of Departments of English (ADE) Bulletin*, (76), (Winter), 49-51.

Bligh, D.A. (1971). *What's the use of lecturers*. London: University Teaching Methods Unit.

Davies, I.K. (1981). *Instructional techniques*. New York: McGraw-Hill.

Day, R.S. (1980). Teaching from notes: Some cognitive consequences. In W.J. McKeachie (ed.), *Learning, cognition, and college teaching: New directions for teaching and learning* (2) (pp. 95-112). San Francisco: Jossey-Bass.

Frederick, P.J. (1986). The lively lecture—8 variations. *College Teaching*, 34(2), 43-50.

Hawkins, S., Davies, I., and Majer, K. (1973). *Getting started*. Mimeographed guide for beginning instructors. Bloomington, Indiana: Indiana University.

Kahn, R. (1972). *The boys of summer*. New York: Harper and Row.

Kaplan, R.M. and Pascoe, G.C. (1977). Humorous lectures and humorous examples: Some effects upon comprehension and retention. *Journal of Educational Psychology*, 69(6), 1-65.

McKeachie, W.J. (1980). Improving lectures by understanding students' information processing. In W.J. McKeachie (ed.), *Learning, cognition, and college teaching: New directions for teaching and learning* (2) (pp. 95-112). San Francisco: Jossey-Bass.

McKeachie, W.J. (1994). *Teaching tips: Strategies, research, and theory for college and university teachers*, 9th ed. Lexington, Massachusetts: D.C. Heath.

APPENDIX 12-1

Classroom Observer Checklist

Numerical scale for rating each item: (1) improvement is needed; (2) adequate, but could be improved; and, (3) little room for improvement.

Make written comments for any item that is particularly strong or particularly weak, and try to identify the one strongest and the one weakest aspect of the lecture presentation.

Overall Classroom Atmosphere

    _____   1 Instructor appears enthusiastic.

    _____   2 Students appear alert and attentive.

Organization

    _____   3 Initial outline of content clearly stated.

    _____   4 Initial statement of why this content is important for students to understand.

    _____   5 Main points organized in logical sequence.

    _____   6 Use of examples and elaboration to emphasize and clarify main points.

    _____   7 Clarity of transition between main points.

    _____   8 Effectiveness of summaries of main points.

Presentation

    _____   9 Voice is audible and understandable.

    _____   10 Makes effective use of voice inflection.

    _____   11 Maintains eye contact with students.

    _____   12 Makes effective use of blackboard or overhead projector.

    _____   13 Makes effective use of non-verbal behavior.

    _____   14 Allows adequate time for students to think and organize material presented.

    _____   15 Provides adequate time for student questions and responses.

    _____   16 Responds to students' questions in a helpful manner.

    _____   17 Instructor is free of distracting mannerisms.

CHAPTER 13

THE PRINCIPLES OF ECONOMICS TEXTBOOK: HISTORY, CONTENT, AND USE

William B. Walstad

Michael Watts

William Bosshardt

The principles of economics textbook is a major, and in many cases, the only source of information for students taking their introductory courses in the discipline. Today, a wide range of ancillary materials for the textbook reinforce its influence over the character of the course. Test banks are used to create exams and extensive instructor's manuals provide classroom ideas for presenting the text content. Study guides take students through out-of-class reviews of the course material. Microcomputer software and CD-Rom programs animate graphical analysis, review basic concepts and sometimes simulate "the real world." Despite this pervasive influence, few new instructors know much about the history of principles textbooks, the textbooks market or, in a comparative sense, the specific content of many different textbooks. This chapter offers insights into each of these areas plus suggestions for how to select and use a principles textbook.

The tradition of textbook writing is a long one in the economics profession, perhaps beginning with the *Wealth of Nations*. This history is briefly described in the first section of the chapter. The next two sections describe the structure of the textbook market and several specific complaints frequently aimed at the current textbooks. The fourth and fifth sections of the chapter examine the content of seven leading textbooks. The analysis can be used to describe a "consensus" text, which provides a benchmark for reviewing both the content and pedagogical features of other leading principles textbooks. The final section of the chapter presents some considerations about selecting a textbook and using it with students.

A Short History of Principles Textbooks

As Paul Samuelson notes in the foreword to this volume, there is a long tradition of textbook writing in the economics profession that has attracted the interest and efforts of many different kinds of economists. Among the principles books currently in print, we find some authors at leading research institutions, some at urban commuter campuses, and others at small liberal arts colleges. Some are Nobel laureates or prominent candidates for this award; most are not.

This research versus teaching orientation has existed among textbook authors since shortly after the publication of *The Wealth of Nations*, which was certainly more than a basic textbook, but did serve that role too for many decades, and through several editions. Malthus, Ricardo, and especially Mill and Marshall wrote principles books that are still in print today, and are seen by many contemporary economists as the leading texts of the 19th and early 20th centuries. But in fact these books, written by the intellectual giants among the classical and neoclassical economists, were often not the leading textbooks of the previous century, at least in terms of their market share. Many of the best sellers were written by less familiar figures. For example, Jane Marcet's *Conversations on Political Economy* (first published in 1816) ran through many editions, and Harriet Martineau's monthly issues of *Illustrations of Political Economy* (published from 1832–34) sometimes sold 10,000 copies per issue, and counted the Czar of Russia and Princess Victoria on its list of dedicated readers (Shackleton, 1988).

Marshall expressed a strongly negative opinion of Marcet and Martineau's work, but Ricardo and Mill were more favorably impressed and supportive of these "popularizing" efforts for the new discipline. Around the same time, works by Robert Owen and William Cobbett dealing with political economy and a wide range of other topics were popular with workers and tradesmen, including those organized by the fledgling trade unions. Because of this partisan support, and the authors' generally populist and often idiosyncratic approaches to this material, these works have usually been treated as somewhat suspect by academic economists.

From 1870–1914, Millicent Fawcett's *Political Economy for Beginners* ran through nine editions, and in this same period of time the early American and Austrian textbooks began to appear. But Marshall's *Principles* held strong and prevailed into the 1920s, particularly in terms of prestige within the discipline and in maintaining the neoclassical approach as economic orthodoxy despite challenges from the German historical school and institutionalists like Veblen and John R. Commons. Then things became more unsettled, especially in the United States.

From 1920–1930, college enrollments in the United States approximately doubled. Between the 1910–11 and the 1925–26 academic years, credit hours of economics offered in American institutions of higher education increased about 500 percent. That meant that by the mid-1920s there were not enough qualified instructors to staff these courses in traditional (i.e., small) class formats. This also appears to be the time when a large number of the most prominent economists in the country first moved out of the principles classrooms to specialize in coursework designed for economics majors, and eventually in courses for graduate students.[1]

Fairchild, Furniss and Buck adapted Irving Fisher's textbook to take the "best seller" position in the U.S. market during this period of flux. Their book remained dominant until Paul Samuelson re-focused the textbook market, and our introductory courses, with the publication of his *Economics* in 1948. Samuelson's book is now seen as the first of the "modern" textbooks. In one sense his text continued the direct line from the classical and neoclassical schools, since he added Keynesian macroeconomics to basically neoclassical microeconomics—and recall that Keynes himself was strongly influenced by his one-time teacher, Alfred Marshall.[2] It may not have been the first to attempt to introduce Keynesian macroeconomic theory at the principles level, but it was the first successful book to offer this new dimension.

Samuelson's text captured a large market share, and was a dominant sales leader in the industry for a number of years. Over time, other books appeared with similar formats, but offering different features which were received as improvements in the marketplace, at least for some groups of students. The "improvements" included easier reading levels and other differences in writing style, increased used of purely pedagogical aids, and some variation in content. As the industry became even more competitive, more new textbooks offered slightly different products to pursue different "niches" in the market. But in retrospect it is clear that during this century no other textbook has fit the role of the revolutionary or innovative leader on anything like the order of magnitude achieved by Samuelson's book (Elzinga, 1992). This brings us to a discussion of the current textbooks and the market structure in the principles textbook industry.

Monopolistic Competition or Oligopoly?

In many respects, the market for principles of economics textbooks can be characterized as monopolistically competitive. Certainly there is a high degree of differentiation and nonprice competition in the market. We now have one and two semester textbooks, books for high and low-ability students, books with differing emphases on economic theory and ideology, some books with extensive ancillary packages and others with minimal packages, etc. The competition has also produced a wide range of pedagogical aids, such as two- and four-color printing, the use of cartoons, "boxed features," and learning objectives, all designed to make the product more attractive and useful for students and instructors. Among ancillary materials, study guides, instructor's manuals, test banks, computer tutorial and simulation programs, books of readings on current issues, and even anthologies of teaching tips offer students and instructors additional help. When these new content or pedagogical features prove attractive to text adopters, they are quickly incorporated into future editions of many old and new textbooks.

The perception of the principles textbook market as monopolistically competitive is also compatible with several well known and widespread complaints about the textbooks. Stiglitz (1988) notes that there may be "too many similar products at the center of the market and too few products at the fringes" (p. 172). He predicts a pattern of "subtle" innovations, and quick imitation of successful improvements and gimmicks by the competition. While some books will cater to special needs and serve special markets, they still can not represent a radical departure from the "standard" text. Most publishers and textbook authors believe that only a small degree of innovation is acceptable if a book is to have a chance in the main part of the market.

Stiglitz also argues that effective barriers to entry into the market tend to limit the degree of innovation. The standard books tend to be of high quality in terms of appearance and content presentation and there are many supplements that are now expected to be available from major textbook publishers. Whether or not all of these features are effective pedagogically—and we have no major research on that question for the economics discipline—the extensive support packages clearly represent both product differentiation and barriers to entry.

The standardization in the textbook market also contributes to standardization in the curriculum, and vice versa. Given this situation, most professors are not likely to bear the cost of changing their courses given the prospect of limited and uncertain benefits, including minimal financial incentives for doing this work. Therefore, so little impetus for change in the textbooks comes from that direction. Thus, the textbook market may be in an inefficient Nash equilibrium, which may explain some of the dissatisfaction with principles textbooks and courses.

The alternative to a monopolistic competition model is oligopoly. This perspective is discussed by Werner Sichel (1988) in a comment on Stiglitz's paper. He observed that although there are many principles textbooks there are few textbook publishers, and noted that the top ten firms probably account for 90 percent of textbook sales. Sichel also thinks that in this concentrated industry the practice of price leadership prevails, with dominant firms' price increases soon followed by other firms in the industry. On a day-to-day basis, the firms compete on the basis of the textbook (and ancillary) products, not prices.

Sichel argues that a new textbook "clone" has less chance of capturing significant market share in an oligopoly than in a monopolistically competitive market, because of the barriers to entry by established textbooks and their publishers. Truly innovative books, if successful, may capture a significant market share and reap the great rewards, but only after a high degree of risk is faced by the textbook author and large investments are made by the publisher. The advantage of being established also gives incumbent authors and publishers ample time (editions) to adopt any new features which appeal to buyers, even when those features come from competing textbooks (including new entrants). Sichel claims that the monopolistically competitive model suggests that the allowable time lag for imitation would be shorter. For these reasons, he believes that oligopoly is a better way to describe the textbook market. This position is also consistent with complaints about the widespread homogeneity among texts, and a lack of radically new approaches.

Criticisms of Textbooks

Regardless of which of these general models of the textbook market seems most convincing and comprehensive, both claim to explain why there will be a prevailing standard for features, format, and content in the principles textbooks. Innovations in the existing textbooks will tend to be minor, and imitation of the successful minor innovations will occur quickly. Still, there may be lags before there is widespread adoption of these changes as the industry standard. This general background provides some perspective for examining particular criticisms of the principles texts.

Textbook Size The average size of the leading texts has grown from about 600 pages to about 800–900 pages in the past 35 years.[3] This development has raised the criticism that textbooks are too encyclopedic and that there is simply too much material presented for an instructor to cover in a principles course. No one, neither textbook users nor authors, seems particularly happy about the size of the textbook. The size problem is probably the result of a combination of the rapid advancement of knowledge in economics over the past three decades and market forces rather than a conspiracy among publishers. The knowledge advances in economics have been substantial and have resulted in additional coverage on public choice, the economics of information, alternative macro models (monetarism and new classical economics), and many other new topics. The problem for principles textbooks and instructors is that few topics have been cut to make room for the new content and new pedagogical features. (See also Chapter 4.)

Nor is there much incentive for textbook writers to cut. When instructors or textbook adoption committees evaluate a text, they rarely eliminate it because it contains too much material. The reason for not choosing a text is because it does not cover some current topics or issue of interest to the adopter. Ryan Amacher (1988) concludes that "authors and editors therefore find themselves in a position where it is better to include than to exclude" (p. 155). Thus, product competition leads to more material being included in the text than can be reasonably covered in the course. And there is a pedagogical defense of the encyclopedic approach, consistent with the idea of letting instructors tailor the books to better fit their own classes.

Current Topics Textbooks are also continually criticized for lack of coverage of selected topics or inadequate emphasis. A recent example of this is the call for the inclusion of more international economics in principles textbooks that began in the 1980s. The perception among many economists was that the principles textbooks were giving limited attention to international economics, both in terms of the quantity of the coverage provided and the degree to which it was integrated throughout the texts. Many books relegated their international material to two or three chapters at the end of the book. These past practices were not due to the ignorance of textbook writers or their lack of appreciation of the significance of the world economy. Rather, several pedagogical and practical issues are at stake. A substantive discussion of international economics and finance is predicated on some understanding of micro and macro theory; as a consequence, international chapters were often placed at the end of a textbook.

In some ways, the textbook writers have responded to this criticism, although it is still difficult to tell if the response is cosmetic or substantive. A survey of principles textbooks with a 1988–1990 copyright found that there were visible efforts by textbook writers to include more coverage of international economics, but concluded that more work was need to integrate the material and give it coherence so that the changes lived up to the authors' claims (Lee, 1992). So, it is difficult to tell if concern for more international economics has proven to just be part of the "fad and fashion" pattern in the revision of principles textbook that focuses on the most current issues. Passing fancies do occur, but seem to shape textbook content at the edges to meet current concerns without fundamentally altering the core material. These additions are dropped in later editions after the attention fades—witness the significant attention given to radical or Marxian economics, urban economics, labor unions, and input-output models in past editions and their omission or brief coverage in today's texts.

Micro, Macro and Other Concerns For many years principles instructors have debated whether microeconomics should be presented before macroeconomics. The original (i.e., Samuelson) position was that macro should be taught first because it more powerfully develops or exploits a student's initial interest in the subject. After all, macroeconomics covers the "big" issues of unemployment, inflation and economic growth, that are found in daily media reports and affect all of us to some degree. When taught well, a first course in macroeconomics helps sustain student interest even when they go on to learn microeconomics.

But the micro-first proponents gained ground in recent years for several reasons. Most important, perhaps, is that such courses provide the necessary micro foundations for macro theory, and avoid the need to repeat material on supply, demand, elasticity, etc. And following the lead of Gary Becker, microeconomists have demonstrated that economic principles can be applied to a wider range of topics than might have been imagined in 1948, with results even principles students find interesting. Most principles textbooks have yet to change to a micro-then-macro format, perhaps because textbook writers are royalty maximizers, as noted by Edwin Dolan (1988). He believes that the textbook format will change when a large percentage of economics departments change to a micro-first *course* sequence. The issue, however, may no longer be important because of the responses of publishers to market changes. The advent of split volumes for micro and macro has made such changes both easier to make and less important for adopters. With splits, few books are eliminated from adoption decisions on the basis of micro or macro sequence, even if both halves of the same textbook are to be used. Students may also find a split volume less intimidating and easier to use.

Many other criticisms have been leveled against principles textbooks, too numerous to discuss in detail here. Some of these include the textbook neglect of "real world" data, the need for better explanations of basic economic measures and statistics in textbooks, publication lags in textbook production, and alternative ways to present material in textbooks. Principles instructors can probably find many more candidates for the list, especially when the textbooks are examined from a narrow content or ideological perspective.[4] What is also unknown is how new developments in technology (e.g., CD-rom, the Internet) will affect textbook production and classroom use in the future. What is fairly certain is that economics instructors will continue to criticize textbooks for sins of omission and commission as they have since they were first used for instruction. Although current textbook publishers and writers do respond to market forces, the market structure in the industry tends to slow content and pedagogical innovations—a situation that is likely to continue in the future.

Evaluating Texts Over the years there have been numerous attempts to use new pedagogical approaches in the principles course, such as television, computers, and programmed learning. As these innovations were introduced, there were usually a number of research studies that investigated the effectiveness of the new approaches (Siegfried and Fels, 1979). Few showed significant, let alone cost-effective improvements in student learning. So the textbook-lecture approach remains as the dominant type of pedagogy, perhaps in a more secure position than ever. Yet solid research on the use of textbooks in the principles course is almost nonexistent.[5] We know very little about how they are or might be used, or if some texts can serve students (or certain types of students) better than others.

Key reasons why textbook evaluations have not been undertaken on a systematic basis are that the costs to do so are high, and the benefits uncertain, limited, and subject to free-rider problems. Results suggesting a negative effect from the use of a particular textbook are likely to initiate strident rebuttals, while the product differentiation discussed earlier makes it more difficult to compare books, and the periodic but non-standard revision dates across books limit the useful "shelf-life" of both individual and comparative reviews. Finally, many evaluation systems might well favor established textbooks. These books have already met the market test, whereas innovative new entrants are particularly susceptible to first-edition "bugs" which make them more vulnerable in direct comparisons. Of course, many economists would claim that the market test is the only evaluation worth passing in these lucrative fields. Despite these problems, we decided to conduct a limited content analysis on a small sample of textbooks. Those results are presented in the following section.

A Content Analysis of Some Leading Textbooks

Table 13-1 reports various measures of content coverage and pedagogical features in current editions of seven leading textbooks: Baumol and Blinder (1994), Byrns and Stone (1995), Gwartney and Stroup (1995), Lipsey and Courant (1996), McConnell and Brue (1996), Parkin (1996), and Samuelson and Nordhaus (1995). These particular textbooks were surveyed for a variety of reasons: the textbooks by McConnell and Brue and by Byrns and Stone are long-time favorites in a middle of the road position, both in terms of the level of analytical rigor and any liberal/conservative sentiment. Samuelson and Nordhaus is here by virtue of this book' s unique role as an innovator in the modern textbook market and because, with Lipsey and Courant, it caters more to the upper end of the market in terms of rigor in both content coverage and presentation. The books by Baumol and Blinder and by Parkin are perhaps a bit upper level in orientation, but primarily they are major competitors in the middle part of the market. Furthermore, Baumol and Blinder are prominent economists known for liberal/Keynesian viewpoints, while Parkin is a prominent scholar with a more conservative outlook, particularly in terms of monetary policies. Gwartney and Stroup was one of the first textbooks to stress public choice theory and a conservative viewpoint at the principles level. All of the books are in at least a third edition, and sold by major publishing houses.

A series of broad content categories with an extensive list of subtopics under each of these general headings was prepared for our content analysis of the textbooks, adapted from a similar table in an earlier version of this chapter (Walstad and Watts, 1990), which covered six of these same seven textbooks.[6] The categories in that study were originally developed from a page-by-page review of one of the more rigorous textbooks that covered more topics than most, and then expanded as other books were reviewed, as necessary, to list all of the concepts presented in the books. A similar list of basic pedagogical features in the books (e.g., numbers of graphs and tables) was also prepared. For this updated survey, we started with the final version of the 1990 table, and added or deleted a few concept or pedagogical categories based on the review of the seven different textbooks.

The same list of counting rules was used as in the earlier study. In particular, a concept was considered to be covered on a page of text if at least three complete sentences of text or a table or a graph was devoted to the explication of the concept. This counting system obviously results in many pages being counted in more than one concept category, and in some overstatement of how much coverage is allocated to some topics (compare total pages occurring to the actual number of pages for each book in Table 13-1.) However, the concepts developed earlier in the text that are used to develop another concept are not counted as occurring again (e.g., supply and demand is not counted again when the supply and demand for

Table 13-1: Textbook Page Content Allocated by Categories

Broad Categories	(1) #	(1) %	(1) S/N-E	(2) #	(2) %	(2) S/N-E	(3) #	(3) %	(3) S/N-E
Fundamental Concepts	52	5.1	41	45	4.9	39	56	5.3	42
Micro Theory	312	30.6	244	279	30.7	240	308	29.0	232
Micro Topics	168	16.5	131	164	18.0	141	166	15.6	125
Macro Theory	214	21.0	167	220	24.2	189	222	20.9	167
Macro Topics	112	11.0	88	117	12.9	101	81	7.6	61
International Theory	32	3.1	25	34	3.7	29	31	2.9	23
International Topics	49	4.8	38	22	2.4	19	39	3.7	29
Comparative Systems	32	3.1	25	18	2.0	15	35	3.3	26
Pedagogical Features	323	31.7	252	226	24.8	194	358	33.7	270
Biographies	3	0.3	2	20	2.2	17	13	1.2	10
Blank Pages	14	1.4	11	11	1.2	9	38	3.6	29
Total Pages	1311			1156			1347		
Actual # of Pages	1020		797	910		782	1062		801

Note: The texts are: (1) Baumol/Binder (1994); (2) Byrns/Stone (1995); and (3) Gwartney/Stroup (1995).

Table 13-1: Textbook Page Content Allocated by Categories (Continued)

Broad Categories	(4) #	(4) %	(4) S/N-E	(5) #	(5) %	(5) S/N-E	(6) #	(6) %	(6) S/N-E
Fundamental Concepts	52	6.1	53	53	5.9	55	52	5.2	58
Micro Theory	261	30.5	268	258	28.8	268	315	31.4	349
Micro Topics	102	11.9	105	158	17.7	164	100	10.0	111
Macro Theory	178	20.8	183	198	22.1	205	199	19.8	220
Macro Topics	124	14.5	127	91	10.2	94	106	10.6	117
International Theory	47	5.5	48	33	3.7	34	30	3.0	33
International Topics	57	6.7	58	70	7.8	73	26	2.6	29
Comparative Systems	20	2.3	21	34	3.8	35	21	2.1	23
Pedagogical Features	350	40.9	359	468	52.3	485	481	48.0	532
Biographies	0	0.0	0	2	0.2	2	28	2.8	31
Blank Pages	24	2.8	25	3	0.3	3	3	0.3	3
Total Pages	1215			1368			1361		
Actual # of Pages	856		878	895		928	1003		1110

Note: The texts are: (4) Lipsey/Courant (1996); (5) McConnell and Brue (1996); and (6) Parkin (1996).

Table 13-1: Textbook Page Content Allocated by Categories (Continued)

Broad Categories	(7) #	%	S/N-E	(8) %	S/N-E	Min. %	Max. %
Fundamental Concepts	31	3.9	31	5.2	41	3.9	6.1
Micro Theory	231	29.3	231	30.0	237	28.8	31.4
Micro Topics	129	16.3	129	15.1	119	10.0	18.0
Macro Theory	177	22.4	177	21.6	170	19.8	24.2
Macro Topics	98	12.4	98	11.3	89	7.6	14.5
International Theory	24	3.0	24	3.6	28	2.9	5.5
International Topics	47	6.0	47	4.8	38	2.4	7.8
Comparative Systems	19	2.4	19	2.7	21	2.0	3.8
Pedagogical Features	267	33.8	267	37.9	299	24.8	52.3
Biographies	14	1.8	14	1.2	10	0.0	2.8
Blank Pages	20	2.5	20	1.7	14	0.3	3.6
Total Pages	1057				1067		
Actual # of Pages	789		789		869		

Note: The text is (7) Samuelson/Nordhaus (1995). Columns under (8) are the average percentages and average S/N-E across the seven books. Min. % is the minimum percentage and Max. % is the maximum percentage for that category.

money are introduced). All concepts and features counted as being treated on a page of text under those rules were recorded on a pages occurring list, which was later converted into the summary classification table presented above.

One other review feature was adopted to facilitate comparisons across books. Because the texts vary in terms of page size, and column width and format on a page, we established a Samuelson/Nordhaus-equivalent (S/N-E) page standard. In each book, we counted the words on three pages of pure text—pages with no graphs, no major section breaks employing large typefaces, no long quotations with small or indented typesetting, and no extensive white-space areas. From these values, we determined the percentage of words per page in each of the books relative to the 1995 edition of Samuelson and Nordhaus, and used that index to convert the raw page counts shown in the table to the values shown in the S/N-E column.[7] This is our best comparative measure of the total amount of coverage on a given topic in each of the books, subject to the limitations of our basic counting system.

Size Changes Perhaps the first thing to note about our sample of textbooks is that, on average, the books are shorter now than they were in 1990. For the six continuing books in our sample, looking at S/N-E total pages using the 1989 edition of Samuelson-Nordhaus as the basis for standardizing pages in all of the other volumes, the average fell from 886 pages in 1990 to 810 pages here.[8] In 1990, there was also much greater variance in length among the six books than there is now—the standard deviation of 110 pages then was 12.4 percent of the mean page length; the current standard deviation of 58.4 pages is down to 7.2 percent of the mean 1989 S/N-E page length.

The overall decrease in page length explains some of the drops in page count coverage here, and some of the drop in percentage coverages too, since listing more than one concept per page in our pages occurring table allows coverage for all sections to total more than 100 percent. We suspect this trend is related to an interest in shorter and easier textbooks, as departments scrambled to maintain student enrollments against the national trend of falling enrollments in economics over this period (see Siegfried, 1995). Not all of the books got shorter, however. In 1989 S/N-E pages, the change was + 9 for Baumol and Blinder, -102 for Byrns and Stone, +36 for Gwartney and Stroup, -86 for Lipsey and Courant, -67 for McConnell and Brue, and -242 for Samuelson and Nordhaus. Some of these changes appear to be publisher based, because the two books published by McGraw-Hill and the two published by Harper Collins all got shorter, while the two books published by Harcourt Brace Jovanavich both got longer.

More fundamentally, however, most of the books seemed to be trying to get closer to the average length in coverage—the two books that added pages were both more than 100 pages below the average text length in 1990, and three of the four that cut pages were above the average length then. The pattern looks very much like the Hotelling model of spatial competition in models of imperfect competition. It also demonstrates the principle of consumer sovereignty, because in the preface to the 1989 Samuelson-Nordhaus textbook, those eminent authors had stated that "Above all, we want this book to be authoritative, comprehensive, and clear... A *comprehensive* survey of modern economics needs 950 pages" (p. x, emphasis in the original). Two editions later, this book appeared with 242 fewer pages.

The "Consensus" Text   As found in the 1990 review, there continues to be more homogeneity among the books in considering the broad subject headings among the review categories than among the individual topics that are classified under those different headings. As shown in Table 13-1, the fundamental concepts group is covered on 4 to 6 percent of the pages in all of the books, with an average coverage of 5 percent representing 41 S/N-E pages. The micro theory sections comprise 29 to 31 percent of the books with an average of 30 percent and 237 S/N-E pages. Micro topics and institutions were covered on a minimum of 10 percent (in Parkin) to a maximum of 18 percent (in Byrns and Stone) of pages. The average coverage was 15 percent and 119 S/N-E pages. There was minimal changes in the average percentages devoted to these areas from the 1990 study.

Macro theory receives 20 to 24 percent of the page coverage, with the average of 22 percent representing 170 S/N-E pages. The lowest percentage coverage in this area is in Parkin and the highest is in Byrns and Stone. The average coverage in this area is a substantial drop from the 1990 average of 29 percent and 243 standardized pages. We believe that one of the reasons for that drop is that less attention is being given to the Keynesian cross model relative to the aggregate supply and aggregate demand model. There is also an across-the-board drop in the number of times basic macro theory concepts are being covered in the courses and books, which may instead reflect the interest in somewhat thinner, easier, and more concise coverage in most of the areas presented in the principles courses.

The range of coverage for macro topics is from 8 percent (Gwartney and Stroup) to 15 percent (Lipsey and Courant). The average coverage is 11 percent, or 89 S/N-E pages. That is down about one percentage point and 20 S/N-E pages from the 1990 survey. Most of the drop comes from two books, Baumol and Blinder (down from 15 to 11 percent), which fell to the average level of coverage for all seven books, and McConnell (17 to 10 percent), which also moved closer to the average coverage of this material after having the highest percentage of coverage in the 1990 study.

Coverage of international theory averaged 4 percent and 28 S/N-E pages, and ranged from 3 to 6 percent. These figures are little changed from 1990 and suggest that the trend to internationalize textbooks may be over. Attention to comparative systems ran from 2 to 4 percent, averaging 3 percent and 21 S/N-E pages. Not surprisingly, given the events of recent years, the figures for comparative systems are sharply lower than they were in 1990, when average coverage was 5 percent and 38 pages. The collapse of the former Soviet Union has made it harder to hold up the traditional idea of a centrally planned economy for principles students to see and care much about. And while the transitional economies are certainly not yet full fledged market economies, things are changing so rapidly and erratically in most of those nations today that it is difficult for textbook authors to present information to students that will not be out of date by the time students see it.

The pedagogical features other than graphs, tables, and charts (which are counted under the various topic areas they are used to illustrate or discuss) appear on between 25 percent (in Byrns and Stone) to 52 percent (in McConnell and Brue) of the pages in these textbooks. The average is 38 percent, or 299 S/N-E pages. In 1990, the comparable averages were 33 percent, and 282 pages. These features increased their share of space even while total page coverage was falling. Principles textbooks are getting increasingly more colorful, with more space devoted not only to the standard glossaries, indexes, end-of-chapter discussion questions, and graphing review/primers, but also to a wider array of boxed features—sometimes built around one or more general themes carried throughout a book, but sometimes related only to the particular topic of a chapter or specific page. These boxed features and other "hooks" for student interest are more and more built directly into the textbooks, not only in ancillary materials such as computer software and audio visual supplements.

Nevertheless, there are also differences across the books in these areas. Graphs are used more heavily in some books than in others, appearing on between 22 percent (in Gwartney and Stroup) to 37 percent (in Byrns and Stone) of the textbooks' non-index pages. And as in 1990, only some of the books include learning objectives, (Parkin; Gwartney and Stroup), math notes or extensions (Lipsey and Courant), and cartoons (Gwartney and Stroup; Parkin; and, Baumol and

Blinder). All of the books feature pages with other kinds of illustrations and pictures, but these are especially prevalent in Parkin, Gwartney and Stroup, and Baumol and Blinder. Interviews with noted economists, or more standard biographies of past and present economists, appear on a high of 3 percent of pages in the Parkin textbook, but not at all in Lipsey and Courant. And generally, the biographies don't get as much attention as short, colorful examples and real-world applications in boxed inserts of one form or another. Overall, it is hard to avoid the conclusion that if the MTV generation of students is not here yet, it appears we expect them to arrive soon. It is ironic for that to be happening when evidence indicates that economics teachers are reluctant to adopt innovative teaching methods (see Becker and Watts, 1996).

The average coverage for each broad category, in terms of the percentage and S/N-E page measures, is shown in the last four columns of Table 13-1. While no single textbook exactly meets this consensus specification, none of the books is very far from it, either, as shown by the last two columns in the table that show the minimum and maximum percentage for each category. On several measures the books seem to be more alike now than they were in the 1990 survey—shorter, with more pedagogical features, and somewhat less coverage of concepts. Some will view this as reflecting a high degree of consensus in the discipline itself, others as an indication of effective barriers to entry into the textbook market, and perhaps a few as an outright conspiracy among publishers and authors. Whatever the reason, the data indicate that the content coverage in principles textbooks is fairly standard, and that there is consensus.

Comparisons within Categories

Within the major content blocks, the differences across coverage of individual concepts is more pronounced, both in terms of identifying what materials have not been accepted as universally important by the authors, and in identifying how authors target particular market levels, segments, or niches by expanding, contracting, or even deleting coverage on certain topics.[9] As we review these differences below, all of the page comparisons are in S/N-E pages.

Fundamental Concepts The least amount of difference in topic treatment within categories is found in this introductory section of the textbooks, and all of the books cover all of the fundamental topics, except that Baumol and Blinder do not explicitly define the terms positive and normative. Some of the books devote many more S/N-E pages to this material than others, however: the page counts for Lipsey and Courant, McConnell and Brue, and Parkin are over 50, while the page counts for Samuelson and Nordhaus and Byrns and Stone are in the 30s. Parkin has more than twice as many page counts for opportunity cost than any of the other books, and Gwartney and Stroup can say the same about gains from voluntary exchange. Lipsey and Courant treat production possibilities frontiers much more briefly than the other books, while McConnell and Brue do much more with the circular flow model.

Micro Theory Some similarities in coverage are as important as any differences in the micro theory category. For example, basic supply and demand models are covered on over 20 S/N-E pages in four of the seven books, on 17 or 18 pages in two others, but only on 14 in Baumol and Blinder. But Baumol and Blinder offset that difference by having nearly twice as much coverage (9 pages) on price controls than almost all of the books except Parkin (who has 8 pages on this topic), and Baumol and Blinder are also the only book to break out a long (15 pages) separate block of material on marginal analysis per se. Elasticity is covered on 13 to 19 pages in four books, and on 7 to 10 pages in Gwartney and Stroup, Samuelson and Nordhaus, and Byrns and Stone. Production schedules get 7 to 11 pages in all of the books except McConnell and Brue and Gwartney and Stroup, where they receive only 4 pages. Cost curves are dealt with in 10 to 12 pages in all of the books except Baumol and Blinder, where they get 20 pages. Perfect competition is covered on 13 to 22 pages in all of the books, monopoly models get 11 to 16 pages in most of the books, but only 7 pages in Samuelson and Nordhaus and 9 in Lipsey and Courant. All of the books devote extensive coverage (15 to 27 pages, but most around 20) to competitive labor/factor markets, and 9 to 22 pages to the idea of measures of economic and market efficiencies. Public goods get 2 to 6 pages of coverage everywhere except Parkin, where they get 10. Externalities are treated more extensively by Parkin (13 pages) and McConnell and Brue (10 pages) than in other books (5 to 8 pages). Public choice material is mainstream now, receiving 7 to 15 pages of coverage in all of the books except Gwartney and Stroup (23 pages) and Baumol and Blinder (2 pages). Consumer surplus is covered for 2 to 4 pages in all of the books except McConnell and Brue; producer surplus, however, is only developed as such in two books—Parkin and Lipsey and Courant. Indifference curves are covered in all of the books for 5 to 9 pages, except Parkin where they receive 15, but this and related topics (isoquants and isocosts) are usually found in a book's appendices.

Some areas of differences related to newer topics in microeconomics are starting to show up in the micro theory sections, although the total pages involved on these topics are usually small. For example, Samuelson and Nordhaus don't mention principal-agent issues, while all of the other books do, but only on 1 to 3 pages. Four of the books now discuss risk and uncertainty, three for 7 to 9 pages, three for one or two pages, and Gwartney and Stroup not at all. Property rights are discussed in all of the books, but only very briefly except in Gwartney and Stroup, who give the topic 11 pages. Transactions costs aren't mentioned by three books—McConnell and Brue, Samuelson and Nordhaus, and Baumol and Blinder—but are, though only briefly (1 to 3 pages), in the other books. Input-output analysis is now covered only in the Baumol and Blinder text. General equilibrium is covered at some depth only in Samuelson and Nordhaus, briefly mentioned in Byrns and Stone, and not covered at all in the other books.

An obvious question still remains about books that only briefly treat relatively new and/or advanced concepts for principles students: Does such coverage really serve to teach these concepts in a meaningful way, or is it a case of marketing books to instructors/adopters who plan to teach these topics at considerably greater length than the textual coverage implies, without offending those who plan to skip the material and may believe that their colleagues should skip it too? Certainly not all principles classes should be trying to teach all of these concepts.

Micro Topics and Institutions The universally covered micro topics and institutions have basically not changed since the 1990 textbook survey: public finance topics (11 to 23 pages), government regulation (10 to 17 pages, including regulation of natural monopolies), mergers and antitrust policies (8 to 15 pages), types of firms and securities (3 to 9 pages), unions (very briefly in Lipsey and Courant and Samuelson and Nordhaus, but for 8 to 17 pages in the other books), income distribution and redistribution policies (9 to 31 pages), and at shorter lengths minimum wage laws, poverty (except in Lipsey and Courant, where it is covered on 11 pages), discrimination, tax incidence, and health care and medical economics. Obviously the books differentiate themselves by the amount of coverage they allocate to these topics, but there seems to be a market imperative to cover these topics in some fashion. Many other topics appear to be optional—e.g., some books cover and some don't cover such topics as comparable worth, OPEC and energy issues, and immigration. And there are a number of topics covered only in one or two books, sometimes due to special interests or research reputations of the authors. To list a few examples, only Baumol and Blinder discuss Baumol's disease, and only Parkin discusses the economics of crime. Almost always, the coverage of these topics is limited to at most only a few pages. Once again, this seems to be marketing forces at work, or in some cases perhaps just a reflection of brief favorite teaching examples from the different authors.

Macroeconomics As was true in the 1990 survey, in both the macro theory and macro topics sections, where professional disagreement is so widely publicized in both the policy and research arenas, we found a surprising degree of consensus among the textbook authors. That really isn't surprising, however, given the imperative in the macro principles class to cover all of the standard measurement issues; the key problems of inflation (7 to 13 pages in four books, but much more in Lipsey and Courant, and moderately more in Parkin and Samuelson and Nordhaus), and unemployment (8 to 24 pages); money, banking, and central banking issues (13-29 pages); and economic growth (7 to 13 pages in Gwartney and Stroup, McConnell and Brue, and Baumol and Blinder, 39 pages in Parkin, and 19 to 27 pages in the other books). And as we noted earlier, there seems to be considerable consensus forming around the aggregate supply and aggregate demand models of analysis, which now receive substantial coverage in all of the books. The Keynesian framework of aggregate expenditure categories and spending and tax multipliers still appears on more pages than the AS-AD models in five of the seven books (the two exceptions are Byrns and Stone and Gwartney and Stroup), but as noted earlier, the use of the Keynesian cross model as the basic framework for macroeconomic analysis has faded as the page coverage devoted to the AS-AD models has increased. Other standard topics in these sections include the national debt (9 to 21 pages), money creation (4 to 8 pages), monetary policy (which gets 19 to 22 pages of coverage in four of the books, but only 8 pages in Byrns and Stone, 9 pages in Baumol and Blinder, and 27 pages in Gwartney and Stroup), fiscal policy (13 to 19 pages in five books, but only 10 pages in Lipsey and Courant, and 7 pages in Samuelson and Nordhaus), competing schools of macroeconomic thought (12 to 20 pages in five books, and 28 and 32 pages in Byrns and Stone, and McConnell and Brue, respectively), money supply and demand (4 to 7 pages), interest rates (1 to 4 pages in all of the books except Parkin, who has 11 pages), rational and adaptive expectations (2 to 4 pages, except for Parkin's 7), the underground economy (1 to 2 pages), and the Great Depression (1 to 4 pages). The optional macro topics are actually smaller in number than for micro, and include such things as incomes policies (covered in three of the books), industrial policy (present in two books), limits to economic growth (in four books), indexing (four books), and the Laffer curve (in four books). As in micro, these optional topics rarely receive more than a few pages of coverage even in the books that present them.

International Categories In international theory, all of the books have 9 to 16 pages on comparative advantage and the gains from trade, 5 to 14 pages on exchange rates, a few pages on balance of payments (except for McConnell and Brue, Parkin, and Lipsey and Courant, who have 7 to 11 pages), and 9 to 22 pages on free trade versus protectionism. Terms of trade are discussed very briefly by four books, and the J curve gets 2 pages in two books. Recent exchange rate histories and events are discussed in all of the books except Lipsey and Courant, and all of the books except Gwartney and Stroup briefly cover the gold standard and the Bretton Woods agreement. The LDC debt crisis is briefly mentioned in three books.

The above content analysis gives an instructor an indication of the relative amount of content coverage that can be expected to be found in a principles textbook. The analysis does not select a textbook for an instructor or show how best to use it with students, two final issues to which we now turn.

Textbook Selection and Use

One of the most important instructional decisions that an instructor makes is the selection of a principles textbook. The text is the primary means of conveying content information, and in many ways is more valuable for the student than lectures or discussion because it is not constrained by time limits and offers a broader and deeper coverage of many topics. The textbook can also offset poor teaching practices and help reduce confusion for students. This is not to say that the textbook is a substitute for the instructor; it is more likely a complement. Some professors, however, fall into the trap of attributing all student learning to their teaching skills and forget about the contribution of the textbook.

Selection So, how does a professor select a good textbook to enhance student learning? There are no hard rules here, only guidelines. Each professor has different instructional goals, and some may have no choice in the adoption decision when a common textbook must be selected. The first bit of advice for those who do have a choice is to do some homework. Don't rely on the book representative to make the decision for you or select the textbook based on one factor, such as the glossy graphics. Get copies of several principles books that you want to consider, or ones that other professors recommend to you, and give them careful study.

The fact that most textbooks are fairly standardized, as shown in the previous analysis, make the evaluation job somewhat easier for you. Even if you can't read each textbook cover to cover (who would want to?), or *do a detailed content analysis*, you can select four or five content topics you think are essential for the course and then make comparisons among texts on those topics. Ask yourself if the content is accurate and current. You also need to judge whether the content is too difficult or easy for the type of students that you teach. You need to determine if the writing is clear and if the material is well-organized. Some instructors make the mistake of picking a text solely based on their interest in a particular issue, forgetting the fact that most of the time spent by you and your students will be on basic principles of micro or macroeconomics, not a pet issue. You should be sure to assess how well the textbook treats the core concepts because you can more easily correct problems or omissions related to your pet topic issue.

After your content and coverage evaluation, *turn to the pedagogical features*. As shown in the content analysis, most principles of economics textbooks contain numerous instructional aids that are supposed to help students. These aids include such items as advanced organizers, boxed examples or applications, sample test questions, section summaries, and end-of-chapter problems with or without answers. Again, the best evaluative strategy is to sample the chapter content material you know well and determine if you think the pedagogical features you think are important will help students learn the material. Fancy artwork and graphics or too much artwork and graphics, for example, can distract the student and breakup the reading, thus making it more difficult for them to sort out the main ideas from all the other details.

The final part of the evaluation is to *examine the ancillary materials*. Your students may use the study guide, so you should determine if it gives them enough practice or application of the textbook material in each chapter. The more comprehensive the study guide, the more likely that the student will have sufficient opportunity to master the material. The instructor's manual should also be reviewed for whether it does a good job of giving you tips for teaching concepts and extra questions to use for class discussion. And you should especially review the test bank if you plan to make use of multiple choice tests. Many inexperienced instructors have adopted a text only to find that the multiple choice questions in the accompanying testbank are of poor quality (see Chapter 19). Using a poor quality test bank causes headaches for the instructor and frustration among students.

There are, of course, more ancillaries than just the study guide, instructor's manual, or test banks. Some textbooks have microcomputer programs, CD-ROMs, videotapes, and other technological complements. It would be a mistake to make the textbook selection solely on the basis of these options. In most cases, instructors will not use the technological supplements in class and they are not likely to be used by most students out of class. They receive much more attention from instructors than they deserve, and are developed by publishers to sell more textbooks. The best advice is to judge the textbook content and coverage first, next the text's pedagogical features, and then the print ancillaries (study guide, instructor's manual, and test bank). Only then should you consider the technological ancillaries, and only if you or your students will make full use of them.

Textbook Use Most instructors assume that students know how to read and use a principles textbook, but this is not often the case. You should devote some time at the beginning of the semester or quarter to *showing students how to make most effective use* of an 900-page textbook that seems overwhelming at first glance. You should give the students an overview of the major features of the textbook and indicate how they can be used to enhance learning. In the syllabus, break down the textbook content, organize it into major sections, and identify what chapters *will* and *will not* be covered in the course. The message that you want to give students is that the textbook is an integral part of the course and that it can be a useful guide to direct learning.

The most valuable suggestion that you can give students involves how they should read each chapter. Some instructors find it is helpful to *tell students to read for the main ideas the first time, read for understanding the second time, and read to check yourself the third time.* Most students make it through the first two steps, but miss the third. Here you can really help. Near the beginning of the course, show students how the textbook material gets translated into test questions (essay and/or multiple choice). You can highlight this point by assigning students a passage of the text to read before class and then give them a set of sample test questions on that assigned reading at the next class session. Students will be more motivated to read the textbook if you show them why they need to read the textbook, how it affects their learning, and what the connection is with the class tests.

Of course, no textbook meets the needs of every instructor. Sometimes what the textbook says and what the instructor teaches can diverge. In this situation it is best to *explain to students why you and the textbook differ* on this point and state the reasons for your position. Ignoring the discontinuity between what you say and what the textbook says only causes confusion in the minds of students. Some instructors also like to use supplementary readings (newspaper or magazine articles, books). Although these readings offer different perspectives on issues or present newer material, the instructor needs to remember to show the connections between these supplements and the textbook, if they are to be effective additions to the classroom presentations and textbook material.

One of the major psychological criticisms of textbooks is that they promote memorization and factual learning at the expense of higher forms of thinking. The best way to counter this tendency is to *make the textbook an active resource in and out of the classroom.* You can do that by assigning end-of-chapter questions for homework that require critical thinking or use these questions for class discussion. Students can write a short summary of pros and cons of an issue based on a section they read in the textbook. To check for student understanding of a graph, you might ask them to draw a key graph and explain it, then compare their response to that found in the text. Another idea is to have students read a passage from the textbook and explain what it means. The use of active teaching methods in combination with the textbook can make it a more valuable resource and motivate students to use it. (See Chapters 15–16 for additional ideas.)

Conclusion

The selection of a textbook is a major instructional decision that influences what the student learns in the classroom and beyond. That decision is more complicated today than in past eras, because of the far greater number of textbooks on the market.

But that variety and the critical nature of the text adoption decision is somewhat illusory, given the high degree of standardization in the textbooks. At least over the broad content categories and pedagogical features of texts, there appears to be a high degree of consensus about what material should be included and how it should be presented. In fact, most differences in textbooks for the principles course come at the smallest of margins: some books include a page or two on a subject not covered in other books, or devote a few more pages to a topic than other books.

Alternative reasons for this pattern were discussed earlier in this chapter. Apart from the possible existence of a professional consensus on core concepts, which is not admitted in the deeply felt and widely expressed criticisms of principles textbooks, the main explanation focuses on the market structure of the industry producing the books and packages of ancillary materials. Monopolistic competition or oligopoly, with both product differentiation and extensive nonprice competition, is probably the best way to characterize the market. Although the basic content and format of the leading principles textbooks are fairly standard, most product differentiation in the books comes from the slight variations produced by topic emphasis or omission. Most of the other nonprice competition occurs in the range of ancillary products offered for a textbook, and other components of the marketing effort including the size of a company's sales force. The structure of this market may well contribute to the many criticisms instructors have voiced concerning principles texts.

NOTES

1. This paragraph is based on Leamer (1950).
2. On this, see the memoir of Marshall in Keynes' *Essays on Biography*.
3. For a study on the increasing number of pages in eight principles books and other changes since their first edition, see Carvellas, Kessel, and Ramazani (1996). Although there has been a leveling off or reduction in the size of textbooks in recent editions, they are still large and encyclopedic by any standard.
4. For an example of a free-market critique of some textbooks, see Taylor (1982). Kent (1989) criticizes textbooks for neglecting entrepreneurship. Feiner (1993) find flaws with textbooks in coverage of issues relating to women and minorities. (See also Chapter 9.) An edited book by Aslanbeigui and Naples (1996) offers several critical perspectives on particular topics and methods in principles textbooks.
5. See Meinkoth (1971) and Watts and Lynch (1989) for two of the few quantitative studies of the effects textbooks can have on student performance.
6. We dropped the Heilbroner and Galbraith book from the analysis because it was not revised, and replaced it with the Parkin textbook. That book now meets our third edition or higher criterion and has made major gains in sales.
7. The index numbers used for the S/N-E equivalents were: Baumol and Blinder (.782); Byrns and Stone (.859); Gwartney and Stroup (.754); Lipsey and Courant (1.026); McConnell and Brue (1.037); Parkin (1.106); and Samuelson and Nordhaus (1.000).
8. Since one S/N-E page in 1989 equals 1.023 S/N-E pages in the 1995 edition, we adjusted the page counts to the same base page year in comparing the length of coverage across two editions of the same textbook in reporting the page counts for entire volumes. We did not make this adjustment for much shorter sections on subtopics.
9. The table data on topic coverage within categories is extensive, covering some 150 topics. For brevity, that table is not reproduced here and only a summary of the major highlights is provided. A copy of the previous table can be found in Walstad and Watts (1990).

REFERENCES

Amacher, R. (1988). A comment. *Journal of Economic Education*, 19, (Spring), 152-156.

Aslanbeigui, N. and Naples, M.I. (1996). *Rethinking economic principles: Critical essays on introductory textbooks*. Chicago: Irwin.

Baumol, W.J. and Blinder, A.S. (1994). *Economics: Principles and policy*. San Diego, California: Harcourt Brace Jovanovich.

Becker, W.E. and Watts, M. (1996). Chalk and talk: A national survey on teaching undergraduate economics. *American Economic Review*, 86, (May), 448-453.

Byrns, R.T. and Stone, G.W. (1995). *Economics*. New York: Harper Collins.

Carvellas, J., Kessel, H., and Ramazani, R. (1996). Counting pages: The evolution of the economic principles text. In N. Aslanbeigui and M.I. Naples (eds.), *Rethinking economic principles* (pp. 225-242). Chicago: Irwin.

Dolan, E.G. (1988). A comment. *Journal of Economic Education*, 19, (Spring), 169-170.

Elzinga, K.G. (1992). The eleven principles of economics. *Southern Economic Journal*, 58(4), 861-879.

Feiner, S.F. (1993). Introductory economics textbooks and the treatment of issues relating to women and minorities, 1984 and 1991. *Journal of Economic Education*, 24, (Spring), 145-162.

Gwartney, J.D. and Stroup, R.L. (1995). *Economics: Private and public choice*. San Diego, California: Harcourt Brace Jovanovich.

Heilbroner, R.L. and Galbraith, J.K. (1987). *The economic problem*. Englewood Cliffs, New Jersey: Prentice Hall.

Kent, C. (1989). The treatment of entrepreneurship in collegiate principles of economics texts. *Journal of Economic Education*, 20, (Spring), 153-164.

Leamer, L.E. (1950). A brief history of economics in general education. *American Economic Review*, 40, (December), 18-33.

Lee, D.Y. (1992). Internationalizing the principles of economics course: A survey of textbooks. *Journal of Economic Education*, 23, (Winter), 79-88.

Lipsey, R.G. and Courant, P.N. (1996). *Economics*. New York: Harper Collins.

McConnell, C.R. and Brue, S.L. (1996). *Economics*. New York: McGraw-Hill.

Meinkoth, M.R. (1971). Textbooks and the teaching of economic principles. *Journal of Economic Education*, 2, (Spring), 127-130.

Parkin, M. (1996). *Economics*. Reading, Massachusetts: Addison-Wesley.

Samuelson, P.A. and Nordhaus, W.D. (1995). *Economics*. New York: McGraw-Hill.

Shackleton, J.R. (1988). Why don't women feature in the history of economics? *Economics*, 24, (Autumn), 123-126.

Sichel, W. (1988). A response. *Journal of Economic Education*, 19, (Spring), 178-182.

Siegfried, J.J. (1995). Trends in undergraduate economics degrees: A 1993-94 update. *Journal of Economic Education*, 26, (Summer), 282-287.

Siegfried, J.J. and Fels, R. (1979). Research on teaching college economics: A survey. *Journal of Economic Literature*, 17(3), (September), 923-969.

Stiglitz, J.E. (1988). On the market for principles of economics textbooks: Innovation and product differentiation. *Journal of Economic Education*, 19, (Spring), 171-177.

Taylor, J.B. (1982). *American economics texts: A free market critique*. Reston, Virginia: Young America's Foundation.

Watts, M. and Lynch, G.J. (1989). The principles courses revisited. *American Economic Review*, 79, (May), 236-241.

Walstad, W.B. and Watts, M. (1990). Principles of economics textbook: History and content. In P. Saunders and W.B. Walstad (eds.), *The principles of economics course: A handbook for instructors* (pp. 141-160). New York: McGraw-Hill.

CHAPTER 14

IMPROVING CLASSROOM DISCUSSION IN ECONOMICS COURSES

W. Lee Hansen
Michael K. Salemi

"My discussion section never really had much discussion. The instructor asked a few questions but we never got into any meaty issues."

"The instructor in this course (a small upper division course) spent almost 100 percent of the time lecturing. The few times he tried to get a discussion going, it failed completely. I thought small classes were intended to permit discussion that can't occur in large principles courses."

"Our discussion in this course have been boring and a waste of time. Neither the instructor nor the students know much about how to have good discussions."

Responses from student course evaluations

"The purpose of a college education is to teach students how to think."
"Students perceive that economics courses are hard because we expect them to show that they can think like economists...not just repeat material they have memorized."

Anonymous

When asked what they hope students will take away from their courses, most economics faculty mention higher order cognitive skills. They talk about the ability to evaluate an argument, to analyze some situation, to apply what is learned. Most of all, they want their students to be able to think and, in appropriate contexts, to think like economists.

Exactly what thinking like an economist means is rarely specified fully enough for students to grasp, largely because the concept's meaning is elusive even to economists. Students soon realize that whatever thinking like an economist means, they must learn how to do it by listening to lectures and subsequently relaying this material back to the instructor in their exams.

We believe that instructors devote too little class time to helping students learn to think like economists. They often fail to recognize that classroom discussion is effective both for developing critical thinking skills and in revealing whether students are actually acquiring them. But even when they realize the value of discussion, instructors are often unable to capitalize on their knowledge because they do not know how to organize and lead a discussion.

The purpose of this chapter is to convince and to teach: to convince instructors that discussion (or some form of two-way talk) should be part of every teaching plan; and to teach instructors how to organize and lead fruitful discussions. Both beginning and experienced teachers should find this chapter useful because both are likely to have some initial difficulty with discussion. The technology set out in what follows really works! With careful preparation and some practice, almost any instructor can lead discussions that will help students acquire and develop the thinking skills we, as economics instructors, want them to have.

The Importance of Using Two-Way Talk in the Classroom

We first set out a hierarchy of non-lecture teaching techniques that we call two-way talk. *Two-way talk* is talk between the teacher and a student or talk between students themselves. Lectures are one-way talk—students listen and try to understand what is said but do not formulate "talk" or responses of their own.

Several types of two-way talk can be part of a teaching plan. During the course of a lecture, the instructor can initiate questions and field responses. This technique is recommended as a way of checking student understanding of the lecture content and of breaking long lectures into smaller chunks. (See Chapter 12.) A second two-way talk strategy is pausing during a lecture to answer student questions about the lecture. While the initiative lies with the students, the instructor controls the amount of time devoted to questions and answers. Alteratively, instructors can have students engage in recitation or "drill" activities such as reporting on homework exercises. Drill is useful for checking on what students know, but the focus is on providing "correct" responses rather than on developing critical thinking skills.

A more venturesome approach calls for students to work on a question or problem as part of a small group and then report the group's results or conclusions to the class as a whole. In a still more venturesome approach, the instructor and students can participate in a formal discussion of a reading assignment for the purpose of gaining a deeper understanding of what the author—not the lecturer or the textbook writer—is saying.

A discussion-centered course differs fundamentally from a lecture course by requiring a different instructional approach and course reading materials that are at the opposite end of the spectrum from traditional textbooks. The demands of our curriculum, while limiting the possibilities for discussion-centered courses, do not preclude a role for group discussion. This form of instruction can be practiced in the once-a-week discussion sections of large lecture courses and in smaller, advanced courses where more complex and unsettled topics are considered.

Our list of techniques orders two-way talk activities from initiating questions, where the instructor retains almost complete control over the flow of information, to group discussion, where the instructor gives up that control. The list orders the activities in another way, from those that provide students a minimal opportunity to acquire thinking skills to those that afford substantial opportunities to develop these skills by giving students practice in formulating answers and questions of their own.

Using two-way talk techniques thus involves important tradeoffs. There is a tradeoff between course breadth and depth—more material can be covered with lectures but discussion facilitates a deeper understanding of the material. Also, in lectures the instructor can guarantee that concepts are presented clearly and accurately. In two-way talk sessions, students listen to one another and must process a more extensive but lower quality stream of information. With discussion it may be more difficult for students to obtain precise concept definitions and take down a well-organized set of class notes. Yet, in the process of discussion they gain facility in applying those definitions when they use them to frame their questions and answers.

Two-way talk may leave some students confused, but, in our view, this is necessary for real learning to occur. Some students may not understand their colleagues' questions or responses. Others may be swayed by weak or even incorrect arguments. But along the way, students learn to judge the merits of an argument and to take responsibility for their own understanding. They become active learners and real learning occurs.

Why use two-way talk in the classroom? Two-way talk techniques give students practice doing in class what we say we want them to be able to do in life. These techniques require students and faculty members alike to think in class, to frame their own answers to questions, and to interpret written material using the discipline embodied in the course's content.

Discussion is a special type of two-way talk. With other two-way talk activities, students aim at providing the "correct" answer. Typically, a correct answer does exist, and the instructor usually takes pains to make that abundantly clear. Such activities are beneficial because they require students to switch from passive to active mode and to apply course concepts themselves rather than simply recognizing a correct application when it is presented. But these activities do not train students to think independently.

A successful discussion, on the other hand, requires ambiguity and is designed to force each student to struggle with resolving that ambiguity. Discussion requires background reading material rich enough so that many potential interpretations and many answers exist to questions that can be asked about the material. In the course of discussion students aim at producing their own answers and interpretations and at understanding and evaluating the interpretations and opinions of their colleagues.

Good discussion is exciting. The material is interesting and relevant to the class, and students are stimulated by the realization that they alone will interpret and evaluate the material. The instructor will not provide the "right answers" at the end of class. The only answers available are those produced by the students through their interaction with the material and with the comments and observations of other students as the discussion unfolds. Thus, discussion offers a means for instructors to promote an appreciation for the relevance and vitality of economics while at the same time sharpening the higher order thinking skills of their students.

Most of what follows is devoted to explaining the five elements that underlie effective discussion. The next five sections treat each element in turn. The last section offers some additional tips on other types of two-way talk teaching strategies.

Element 1: Integrating Discussion into the Course Plan

The first element underlying effective discussion is development of a suitable course plan. Because discussion is appropriate only when course goals go beyond memorization of terms and manipulation of equations, the instructor should begin by identifying course concepts that students are to master at higher cognitive levels. Discussion takes a lot of time and it makes sense to allocate it to help students master important economic concepts.

The course syllabus should state that students are expected to develop higher level thinking skills and an appreciation for the importance and relevance of the course material. It should also explain that discussion is an important part of the strategy for accomplishing these goals. Students should know that discussions "count" in the computation of grades. This does not mean the instructor must grade a student's discussion participation. In our view, grading participation is a bad idea because it is hard to do fairly and because it may make some students reticent to contribute. Instead, instructors should explain that widespread participation is essential to the class's understanding of the material. They can also use five-minute quizzes to reward students who have prepared for discussion and include discussion questions among their examination essay questions.

To sum up, students must be led to understand from the beginning that discussion is an essential part of the teaching plan of the course and that they have an obligation to participate in discussion.

Element 2: Selection of Discussion Material

Effective discussion requires instructors to select material that is appropriate for classroom discussion. A test of appropriateness is whether an instructor can answer "yes" to the following four questions.

Does the material contain a sufficient number of ideas to warrant discussion? To test whether a particular piece is sufficiently rich and hence worth discussing, the instructor should try to write several interpretive questions about it. What constitutes an interpretive question is taken up later in this chapter. For now, suffice it to say that these questions should be interesting, should require the students to interpret what the author has written, and should support more than one reasonable answer.

Is the material self-contained? The selection should be able to stand on its own, so that there is no need to look up key terms or obtain supplementary information. Everyone should be able to come to the discussion equally well prepared, and the only reference necessary during the discussion is the selection itself. This does not mean, of course, that the selection cannot build on knowledge acquired from the course textbooks, lectures, and other reading selections already covered in the course.

Is the material reasonably well written? Material that is poorly written and organized will cause the discussion to get bogged down in efforts to determine exactly what the author said. Material that is well written permits the discussion to focus on the deeper issues of interpretation. To qualify, the material need not apply economic logic faultlessly. Straightening out a confused or incorrect presentation of economic ideas is a good discussion outcome, but discussion should focus on intellectual rather than stylistic confusion.

Is the material interesting to both the instructor and the students? It is essential that the instructor find the material interesting because instructor enthusiasm for course material is an important source of motivation for students. A helpful check for an instructor on whether students are also likely to find the material interesting is to ask whether they will think it takes up important issues, offers new insights, or helps resolve some puzzle.

Where can the instructor find material suitable for discussions? Generally, such material will not be found in textbooks because the authors have taken pains to provide "the answer" to any and all questions the textbooks consider. One source of material is a book of readings. Some are published as free-standing collections and others as text-book supplements although fewer principles texts offer them now than in the past. The selections in these books are usually well written and interesting, but whether they contain sufficient ideas to support discussion may not be fully clear. The test, as always, is whether the instructor can write good interpretive questions about the reading.

Another source of material is those business and economic periodicals oriented to the interested lay person rather than to the professional economist. *Challenge, The Public Interest, Business Week, Fortune* and *The Economist* regularly publish articles suitable for discussion. *The Journal of Economic Education* and the *Journal of Economic Perspectives* also offer useful articles.

Most regional Federal Reserve Banks publish periodic reviews which include many articles on issues of current interest; frequently these articles are suitable for discussion in upper division courses and occasionally they are suitable for discussion in a principles course. A good example is Paul Krugman's article "Past and Prospective Causes of High Unemployment" (*Economic Review* of the Federal Reserve Bank of Kansas City, 79,4, 1994, 23-43) which is suitable for discussion in intermediate macroeconomics courses. Another is the selection of essays "The Government's Role in Deposit Insurance" (*Review* of the Federal Reserve Bank of St. Louis, January/February, 1993, 3-34) which is appropriate for the regulation section of a money and banking course.

A third source of discussion material is the financial press, particularly *The Wall Street Journal*. The *Journal* regularly includes feature articles on various aspects of the U.S. and world economies and also editorials on economic policy. Many of these pieces are rich enough to support discussion. The *Journal* annually publishes an Educational Edition, a guide to reading the *Journal*, which it provides free of charge to students. (It also publishes a monthly Classroom Edition which reprints recent articles and an accompanying Teacher Guide, intended for K–12 teachers, to show how the articles can be used in the classroom.) One particularly good discussion article is "The Meaning of Inequality" by Herb Stein which appeared in the *Journal* on May 1, 1996, and concerns the recent controversy about whether income inequality is increasing. Another is Alan S. Blinder's "The $5.15 Question" which appeared as an op-ed piece in *The New York Times* on Thursday, May 23, 1996. The Stein and Blinder articles are worth discussing, to show how they move from presenting evidence to taking normative positions on the issues of inequality and the minimum wage, respectively.

A final source of discussion material is the body of classic economic writings or what might be known as the Great Books of economics. Adam Smith's seventh chapter of *The Wealth of Nations*, "On the Natural and Market Price of Commodities," is in many respects a far more interesting and challenging treatment of prices and markets than that provided by modern textbooks. John Stuart Mill's twelfth chapter from *Principles of Political Economy*, "Of Popular Remedies for Low Wages," gives useful insights pertinent to recent debates and research on the impact of minimum wage laws. John Maynard Keynes's twenty-fourth chapter from *The General Theory of Employment, Interest, and Money*, "Concluding Notes on the Social Philosophy Toward which The General Theory Might Lead," discusses the proper role of government in a market economy. Chapters four through six of

Irving Fisher's *The Theory of Interest* provide an excellent opportunity for students to discuss the determinants of equilibrium interest rates.

Of more recent but not current vintage, R. A. Radford's article, "The Economic Organization of a P.O.W. Camp" in *Economica* (1945) offers a fascinating description of how markets evolved within German prisoner of war camps during World War II. Arthur M. Okun's *Equality and Efficiency: The Big Tradeoff* (1975) offers four provocative chapters on different dimensions of the tradeoff. And, finally, Robert Heilbroner's "Reflections: The Triumph of Capitalism" in *The New Yorker*, January 23, 1989, presents a richly textured discussion of the decline of command economies, placed in the context of Smith, Marx, Keynes, Schumpeter, and other great economists. All of these readings provide first rate material for classroom discussion.

Element 3: Preparing Discussion Questions

Good questions are the necessary starting point of successful discussions. But what is a good discussion question? To answer that question it is useful to classify discussion questions in two ways: by the type of answer the question seeks to elicit, and by the role of the question in advancing the progress of the discussion. The two-way classification and some of our recommendations are summarized in Figure 14-1.

We first elaborate on Figure 14-1. We next present some guidelines for writing interpretive questions and for using follow-up questions during discussions. We conclude this section by introducing the concept of a question cluster. Examples of question types, question roles, and question clusters are given in Figures 14-2 through 14-5.

Figure 14-1: A Two-Way Classification of Discussion Questions

Question Types

		Interpre-tive	Factual	Evaluative
	Basic	Yes	No	No
Question Roles	**Supporting**	Yes	Yes	No
	Follow Up	Yes	Yes	No
	Concluding	Possibly	No	Yes

Question Types Across the top of the matrix are listed the three question types: interpretive, factual, and evaluative. Question type describes the type of answer the question seeks to elicit.

A *factual question* asks for specific information that can be found in the reading assigned for discussion. The "facts" of the reading are the words used by the author. Sometimes these "facts" may differ from the facts as they are understood by the participants. In discussion, however, it is necessary to focus on the facts as the author presents them. In effect, factual questions all are versions of the question "What did the author say about... ?" Sometimes factual questions simply seek to clarify the meaning of a word or phrase used by the author. Whatever the case, the response helps establish for everyone exactly what the author said. As mentioned before, the reading must be self-contained. In the present context, this means that the article omits no important facts and that its key facts are not controversial.

FIGURE 14-2   **Cluster of Questions for:**
R.A. Radford, "The Economic Organization of a P.O.W. Camp," *Economica*, 1945, 189-201.

Basic Question
What, according to Radford, accounts for the development of an exchange system in the POW camp?

Supporting Questions
Can the development of the system be explained by the equality or lack of equality in the distribution of supplies?

Were prisoners generally unhappy with their particular allotment of supplies and thereby motivated to develop an exchange system?

Which force does Radford think was most important in accounting for the evolution of the exchange system?

Does Radford believe that differences in preferences gave rise to exchange?

Does Radford believe that prisoners might have developed an exchange system because they were used to living in an exchange economy?

Concluding Question
What weights would you assign to the various forces Radford notes as having contributed to the development of the exchange system?

```
FIGURE 14-3    Cluster of Questions for
               Arthur M. Okun,
               Equality and Efficiency: The Big Tradeoff, 1975.


               Basic Question
               What is the relationship between Okun's concept of the "leaky
               bucket" in Chapter 4 and the goals of income equality and
               equality of opportunity discussed in Chapter 3?


               Supporting Questions
               What does Okun mean by the "leaky bucket"? Why does he use
               the bucket metaphor? What does he mean by the leaks in the
               bucket? Why do these leaks occur? Why haven't they been
               plugged?

               How does Okun distinguish between income equality and equality
               of opportunity? When he speaks of income equality, what does
               he mean? What does he mean by equality of opportunity?
               What are the similarities and differences between the two terms?

               According to Okun, what does the existence of the leaky bucket
               mean for the achievement of income equality? What does the
               existence of the leaky bucket mean for the achievement of
               income? What does Okun say about the relative impact of the
               leaky bucket on these two goals?


               Concluding Question
               How do you evaluate the tradeoff between income equality and
               equality of opportunity in light of the leaky bucket?
```

An *interpretive question* asks discussion participants for an interpretation; it asks them to explore what the author meant by what s(he) said. In contrast to a factual question, an interpretive question requires the participant to use higher order cognitive skills together with the evidence, or facts, reported in the reading to arrive at an answer. Interpretive questions are the backbone of successful discussions precisely because they require students to practice using these higher order skills. We explain how to write a good interpretive question below.

An *evaluative question* asks participants for a judgment. It invites them to consider the material in terms of their own experience and to determine whether they agree or disagree with the author's point of view. While an evaluative question requires the participant to relate the material to his or her own experience, participants should base their answers on the reading and discussion of the reading.

An evaluative question is not an invitation to provide unsupported opinions. It is, however, an invitation to use one's own values in answering.

FIGURE 14-4   **Cluster of Questions for**
                    Paul Krugman, "Past and Prospective Causes of High
                    Unemployment, *Economic Review*, Federal Reserve Bank of
                    Kansas City, January/February, 1993, 3-34.

Basic Question
According to Krugman, what economic forces explain why the natural rate of unemployment has risen in Europe but not in the United States?

Supporting Questions
How does Krugman use figures 1 and 2 to explain rising unemployment?

How can one compute the unemployment rate from these figures?

What economic forces determine the position of the reservation wage line?

What does Krugman mean when he says that "...a likely explanation for this rise is the collision between welfare state policies that attempt to equalize economic outcomes and market forces that are pushing toward great inequality."?

Why does Krugman believe that there is a connection between rising inequality in the United States and rising unemployment in Europe?

What does Krugman mean by inequality?

What market forces are pushing toward greater inequality?

How, according to Krugman, can technological change work against unskilled workers?

Concluding Question
What, if anything, can be done about the problem of rising inequality in the United States and rising unemployment in Europe?

Question Roles Along the side of the matrix in Figure 14-1 we list the four roles that questions play in discussion: basic, supportive, follow-up, and concluding. Each role identifies how the discussion leader intends to use the question in the discussion.

A *basic question* is used to begin a discussion. It should concern a very important issue in the reading and should stimulate participant responses. Participants should find a basic question interesting and should not perceive it to be rhetorical. Basic questions are what the discussion is about.

A *supporting question* is used by the leader to organize discussion of the basic question. How the leader organizes discussion and what supporting questions s(he) prepares will depend on the basic question and ultimately on the reading itself. For example, if the basic question addresses a complex issue in the reading, the leader might use supporting questions to break the basic question into smaller parts. If the basic question hinges on a particular concept used by the author, the leader might use a supporting question to ask participants what the author means by that concept. If some facts bear on the basic question in an important way, the leader might use supporting questions to bring those facts forward. The leader uses supporting questions to move the discussion toward an answer to the basic question. S(he) prepares these questions in advance.

A *follow-up question* probes the response that a student has made to an earlier question. The leader uses follow-up questions to prompt participants to make additional contributions to the discussion. S(he) also uses them to direct "traffic" during a discussion. A good leader listens actively, looking for connections between the responses offered by participants. S(he) uses follow-up questions to make those connections apparent to the participants and to explore their meaning. (Peter, how does your notion of fairness differ from Sue's?) It is not possible to prepare follow-up questions in advance; the leader creates them "on the fly."

A *concluding question* is used by the leader to draw a line of discussion to a close.   There comes a time in the discussion when the leader perceives that participants have done as much as they can to address the issues raised by a basic question. At that point, the leader uses concluding questions to move on to another basic question or to end the entire discussion. One kind of concluding question asks participants to provide a summary answer to the basic question. Another asks participants directly whether the issues are sufficiently resolved. A third asks them to make judgments about the arguments that have been raised. In all cases, the students rather than the leader wrap things up.

FIGURE 14-5   Cluster of Questions for
                 Irving Fisher, *The Theory of Interest*, Augustus M. Kelley,
                 Clifton, New Jersey, 1974, Chapters 4-5.

                 Basic Question
                 What, according to Irving Fisher, is the relationship between
                 human impatience and the rate of interest?

                 Supporting Questions
                 What does Fisher mean by human impatience?

                 Why, according to Fisher, is there a relationship between the time
                 shape of the income stream and human impatience?

                 What effect would an increase in human patience have on the real
                 rate of interest? ...on the money rate of interest?

                 If all humans are impatient, could the money rate of interest ever
                 be negative? Why or why not?

                 Concluding Question
                 Do you believe that human impatience is an important force in
                 determining the rate of interest in the United States today?

Writing Good Interpretive Questions Good interpretive questions are the linch pin of effective discussions. By asking good interpretive questions, the discussion leader transfers responsibility for critical thinking to the students and makes the discussion challenging. The challenge comes not only in sifting through the evidence to come up with a response but also in evaluating the responses provided by other participants.

A good interpretive question satisfies four criteria. First, it asks students to explain the author's meaning. It asks for more than a quotation stating the author's conclusions. If the author states her views clearly, as is often the case in scientific writing, a better interpretive question would ask students how the author reached her view or how she supported it.

Second, a good interpretive question is interesting. The leader is curious about the answer and thinks that the students will be too. Curiosity is a powerful motivator. Third, a good interpretive question can be answered with evidence from the reading. The instructor should check to make sure that sufficient evidence is available. While students should be encouraged to cite the evidence, the leader should take care not to "lock onto" a single answer. The leader must remain open to the possibility that participants will come up with interpretations that are new.

Fourth, a good interpretive question appears to permit more than one answer. Literature is inherently ambiguous; scientific writing is not. Scientific authors try hard to make their arguments clear. Nevertheless, it is often unclear to students how detailed arguments fit together and how they are supported by evidence. This lack of clarity tends to make students willing to contribute their own interpretations and to demand explanations of their colleagues.

In order to remind participants that they are to answer using evidence from the reading, it is useful to begin an interpretive questions with the words "Why, according to the author . . . . ?" or "What does the author mean by . . . .?" A good interpretive question about the Radford article is: "What leads Radford to believe that the exchange system in the P.O.W. camp operated effectively?" Some students will cite "unity of the market and the prevalence of a single price" as evidence. Others will ask how monopoly profits fit in. Still others will mention the ascendence of cigarettes as a numeraire. The emergence of multiple responses challenges participants to understand and evaluate the responses; it challenges the leader to ask follow-up questions that help participants do so.

Using Follow-Up Questions   The use of follow-up questions is the most effective strategy a leader has to ensure that responsibility for advancing and evaluating arguments in the discussion remains with the students. Because they prefer clear answers, students often try to transfer that responsibility back to the discussion leader by asking him or her a direct question. The leader uses follow-up questions to deflect that responsibility back to the participants.

The following scenario illustrates how a leader might use a follow-up question. The leader has started with the basic question (What makes Radford believe that the exchange system in the P.O.W. camp operated effectively?). One student responds that the system was not effective because it was not fair. At this point, the leader has several follow-up options. S(he) might ask the student what he or she means by fair or what evidence indicates the system was not fair. Or s(he) might ask other students whether they agree that the system was not fair. If students demand the "right" definition of fair, the leader might ask them what Radford means by "fair."

Whether or not to ask a follow-up question and what kind of follow-up question to ask are decisions the leader must make spontaneously. A flow chart outlining the purpose of follow-up questioning and specific questions that the leader can use to accomplish those purposes is given in Figure 14-6.

Question Clusters   A question cluster is a collection of questions prepared by the discussion leader to address a main idea or ideas in a reading selection. In our experience, writing question clusters is the best way, first, to decide whether a reading is suitable for discussion and, second, to prepare to lead that discussion. A good question cluster satisfies three criteria. First, it addresses an important and interesting idea in the reading. Second, it includes basic, supportive, follow-up, and concluding questions. Third, it uses the right type of question for each question role.

FIGURE 14-6   A FLOW CHART FOR FOLLOW-UP QUESTIONS

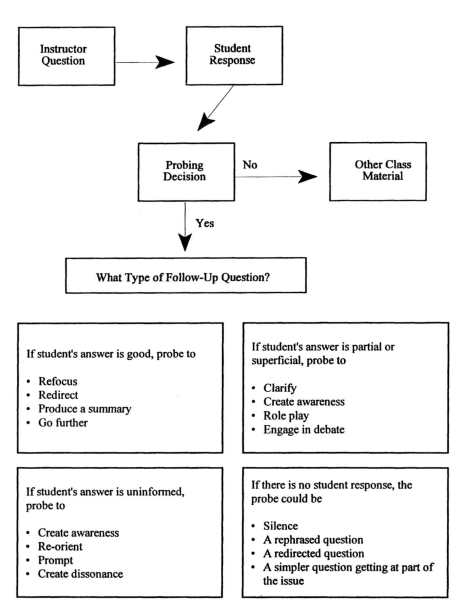

A good question cluster has: interpretive questions for basic questions; interpretive and often factual questions for supportive questions; and at least one evaluative question as a concluding question. A good cluster lies along the principal diagonal of Figure 14-1. Examples of good question clusters are given in Figures 14-2 through 14-5. The Radford and Okun articles and their clusters are suitable for discussion in an economics principles course. The Krugman article and its cluster could be used in an intermediate macroeconomics course. The Irving Fisher reading and its cluster are suitable for either an intermediate macro or financial markets course.

The principle used to choose the right question type for each question role is that participants earn the right to evaluate a reading by first interpreting it. Both interpretive and evaluative questions play important roles in a discussion. By interpreting a reading, participants develop the higher order cognitive skills we want them to have. They develop a deeper understanding of the reading that forms a basis for addressing the non-native issues raised by it. Having an opportunity to evaluate a reading is an important source of motivation and helps bring closure or resolution to the discussion. Evaluative questions also signal to the participants that their informed opinions are important.

Instructors should generally write out their question clusters and hand them out to students in advance of discussion. In our experience, students find it helpful to know what questions will be asked as they prepare. Discussion itself is often more lively when students have had an opportunity to prepare their first answers in advance.

Element 4: Creating a Contract for Effective Discussion

Discussion can be exciting and rewarding for both the leader and the participants provided that all agree to fulfill their responsibilities. Figure 14-7 lists the responsibilities of discussion leaders and participants. It is helpful if the discussion leader distributes this information and makes an explicit contract with participants to abide by "rules" of effective discussion.

For the leader, three responsibilities stand out above the rest. First, it is essential that the leader prepare question clusters in advance. It takes some work to identify those ideas in a reading that are suitable for discussion. It requires still more work to write a good interpretive question that can function as the basic question for the discussion and to write supportive questions that will break the discussion down into "bite sized" parts. Only after the leader has prepared question clusters will it be fully clear that an article is suitable for discussion.

Second, the leader must listen intently to the participants. The leader is responsible for helping the participants develop critical skills and identify the connections among the answers they contribute. To do this, the leader must first hear what each participant is saying.

Third, the leader should confine himself or herself to asking questions. Many times in the course of a discussion the participants will "invite" the leader to provide "the right answer" or to take charge in some other way. The leader must not succumb to these temptations. Instead, the leader should ask questions that help the participants arrive at their own answers.

For the participants, three responsibilities stand out above the rest. First, participants should read the material carefully before the discussion. They should read actively rather than passively. This means underlining key words or phrases. It means highlighting ideas that are repeated. It means making notes on points that are important or cannot be understood. It means jotting down questions in the margins of the pages. Students who have not read the material should still be expected to participate. This may require them to do a quick reading while the discussion proceeds, entering in later if they are capable of doing so.

Second, participants should strive to back up their interpretations and judgements with evidence from the reading, being able to refer to the writers own words so that other participants can see the basis for the response. A well-supported view is more valuable both to the participant who contributed it and to other participants. Participants should strive always to be ready to answer the follow-up question "Why?" and often its corollary "Where does the author say that?"

Third, participants should listen carefully to what their colleagues are saying. It is as important to understand and evaluate the arguments of others as it is to frame one's own contributions. Discussion is a dialogue that requires both talking and listening.

Element 5: Leading Discussions Effectively

To this point, we have focused on how to prepare for a discussion. We now turn our attention to the mechanics of leading a discussion effectively. What follows is a list of tips we have found to work; the list is not exhaustive. The reader should keep in mind that there are many effective discussion leading styles and that each leader should seek to develop a style that suits their own teaching personality.

Seating Arrangements and Seating Charts The same principle applies in the choice of a seating arrangement and the use of a seating chart: the role of the leader should be de-emphasized and the role of participants enhanced. The ideal seating arrangement is a circle because it de-emphasizes the importance of the leader and because it permits each participant to face the others. If a circle is impossible, a U-shaped seating arrangement with the leader at the mouth of the U is a good substitute. This means that classes which feature discussion should, whenever possible, be scheduled in rooms with movable chairs and tables.

The leader should use a seating chart which should be made up by the instructor as students arrive or when the class begins. The chart facilitates calling participants by name, a practice that increases their motivation. It also assists participants in learning one another's name which, in turn, helps create a feeling of community. The chart permits the leader to keep a brief record of who has participated and what contributions they have made. This helps the leader to involve everyone and to develop connections among the contributions of different participants. This can be done be asking: Allen, how does your idea bear on the point that Ted made earlier?

Directing Questions to Participants It is a controversial issue whether the leader should call on volunteers or feel free to direct questions to participants. Our view is that directing questions is both acceptable and desirable. By directing questions the leader is able to break through the extended silence that sometimes occurs in discussions and to reinforce the responsibility of the participants to be prepared for discussion. This practice helps the leader keep the discussion focused rather than drifting off to unrelated matters.

Direct questioning may make some students uncomfortable. A good way to remedy this problem is to give students the right to pass whenever they wish and to ensure them that they are not being graded on their contributions. When students pass, the leader should come back to them later to give them a new opportunity to contribute.

Encouraging Participation Ultimately, interesting readings and good questions will stimulate participation. But the style of the discussion leader can encourage as well. The leader should not appear to judge participants' contributions. Rather, the leader should ask follow-up questions when the meaning of a contribution is not clear. This is not to say that "anything goes." But the objectives of discussion are far better accomplished when criticism of a contribution originates with the participants rather than with the leader.

The leader should thus appear receptive and interested in what participants have to say. The leader can encourage participation by referring to insightful contributions made earlier by participants. (Sue, Joe's point seems to fit in with what you were saying earlier. Have you any reaction?) To the extent that it is comfortable to do so, the leader can also employ "warmer" body language.

Involving All Participants One of the hardest tasks for the leader is to involve everyone in the discussion. Some participants are natural volunteers and there is a tendency for them to dominate the discussion. While the leader need not attempt to divide discussion equally among the participants, it is important that everyone who is prepared to do so contribute something. In our experience, valuable ideas often come from students who are naturally quiet. Directing questions to students helps ensure widespread participation.

FIGURE 14-7   **RESPONSIBILITIES OF DISCUSSION LEADERS AND PARTICIPANTS**

This sheet could be included as a part of the syllabus if extensive use is to be made of classroom discussion. If discussions are held only occasionally, this list could be given out when the reading assignment for the discussion is made.

Discussion Leader
1. Read the material carefully.
2. Prepare clusters of questions carefully and in advance.
3. Pose questions carefully.
4. Develop the discussion in depth.
5. Strive for answers.
6. Avoid difficult or technical terms.
7. Listen intently.
8. Involve each participant.
9. Confine yourself to asking questions.
10. Evaluate your leadership with a formal critique sheet.

Participants

1. Read the material carefully.
2. Offer evidence from the reading to support your answers.
3. Don't base your answers on outside material unless everyone has read it.
4. Listen carefully.
5. Ask for clarification of any point that you don't understand.
6. Challenge answers that you do not agree with.
7. Be willing to change your mind if someone shows you to be in error.
8. Answer the questions posed by the leader before making additional points.
9. Stick to the subject.
10. Do not interrupt when someone else is speaking. If someone else makes the point you wanted to make, don't repeat it.
11. Be as brief as possible. Do not continue to talk after you have made your point.

Note: For additional details, see W. Lee Hansen, "Improving Classroom Discussion in Economics,' *Resource Manual for Teacher Training Programs in Economics* (New York: Joint Council on Economic Education, 1978), Chapter 6.

Improving Students' Preparation for Discussion   One way of ensuring effective student preparation, as well as stronger and more successful participation. is to link group discussion to other course objectives, such as increasing students' ability to develop good discussion questions or enhancing their writing skills. For example, students can be asked to bring with them to class three previously-prepared discussion questions: one factual, one interpretative, and one evaluative. The discussion can be started by asking students to pose their interpretative questions. As the discussion proceeds, students will bring up factual questions that may impede their ability to understand an interpretative question. ·When the interpretative questions have been resolved, students can be asked to present their evaluative questions. This approach ensures closer reading of the selection, places responsibility directly on students, and shows students that their questions are important for everyone in gaining a better understanding of the reading.   Another effective device is to ask students to bring to class a written precis of the selection to be discussed. A precis, which might range from 100 or 300 words, offers a tight abridgement of the selection, trying to retain as much as possible of the author's own words. This is an excellent exercise in reading, thinking, and writing. To find out how well students are doing in developing these two skills, their papers can be collected, commented on, and later returned.

Tips for Other Types of Two-Way Talk

Much of our advice about discussion organization and leading carries over to other two-way talk teaching strategies as well. Here we explain which parts of our discussion framework transfer more readily to other settings.

Using follow-up or probing questions is a technique that teachers can use in almost any setting. The purpose of these questions is always the same—to transfer the responsibility for producing a further answer back to the students.

Asking interpretive questions is also a technique that works in other settings. An interpretive question asks for a disciplined response; it requires the student to use higher order cognitive skills to arrive at an answer. Even in the midst of a lecture, it is useful to ask students to explain (to themselves if not to the class) why some particular part of the lecture makes sense. (In your own words, Joe, explain why in the example we just considered it makes sense that price should fall.)

Finally, using a seating chart, calling students by name, and directing questions to students are all practices that can be used effectively in a variety of settings. They are good ways to raise the level of student interest in classroom activities.

A Concluding Comment

To some the approach presented here may seem overly structured and rigid. Yet this structure produces freedom—the freedom to pursue collectively and systematically the meaning of the readings we choose to have our students read. The approach is based heavily on that of the Great Books Foundation. Our own experience and that of others indicate that it can and does work. Considerable effort is required to master this approach. But its benefits have lasting value by sharpening students' reading and thinking skills, deepening their understanding of economics, and contributing to the goals of a liberal education.

NOTES

This chapter draws upon Chapter 6 of the *Resource Manual for Teacher Training Program in Economics,* by Phillip Saunders. Arthur R. Welsh, and W. Lee Hansen (New York: Joint Council on Economic Education, 1978). That chapter, in turn, draws heavily on the training and discussion methods developed by the Great Books Foundation (Chicago, Illinois) which are reflected in the books it prepares for use by participants in its Great Books discussion groups.

CHAPTER 15

STUDENT WRITING AS A
GUIDE TO STUDENT THINKING

Jerry L. Petr

Maybe...it's time to redefine the 'three R's'—they should be reading, 'riting and reasoning. Together they add up to learning. It's by writing about a subject we're trying to learn that we reason our way to what it means.

Zinsser, 1988, p. 22

This chapter is grounded on the knowledge that there is a close relationship between writing and thinking. Clear writing reflects clear thinking. Because one of our goals in teaching economics is precisely student "clear thinking" about our subject, this chapter addresses the use of writing to attain that goal.

Resting on that foundation, this chapter is built upon several related corollary ideas. First, student writing, often seen primarily as an evaluation tool in the form of essay tests, term papers and the like, is better viewed as a learning-facilitator. The vigorous contemporary "writing across the curriculum" movement emphasizes that the first purpose of student writing is to *create* learning, rather than to evaluate it. Understanding writing as a productive learning tool, rather than primarily as a grading aid, permits a refreshing reconsideration of types and timing of useful writing activities.[1]

Second, "writing to learn" recognizes clearer thinking as a joint product with clearer writing, placing higher priority on an instructor's contribution to a student's thinking than to more technical editorial skills. To most economics professors this is a liberating notion as it encourages a focus on understanding and expression rather than on spelling and grammar. And it is certainly a more efficient notion as it maximizes time spent on areas in which we have a comparative advantage.

Third, even when we use student writing in its more traditional role as an instrument of "evaluation," we should quickly ask "evaluation of what"? It should be much more than evaluation of student knowledge of subject matter, although that is a valid and valuable objective. But writing can be even more effectively used for evaluation of the mental processes by which the student generates and manipulates economic ideas. Used in that way, it becomes a diagnostic tool in the hands of a skilled professor, who can then try to direct those processes more toward greater facility with "the economic way of thinking." (See Chapter 22.)

A fourth benefit of a writing-oriented pedagogy is the potential for writing to assist with student "self-evaluation" of economic understanding. "We write to find out what we know..." asserts William Zinsser (1988). If that is true, and I share Zinsser's conviction on that point, writing is a direct and immediate way for the student to assess his or her progress in our discipline. In many cases, "I don't know what to write" really means "I don't know what I think." As a student recognizes that fact, "teachable moments" will occur. If we keep uppermost in our minds that the primary function of evaluation is assessment of learning, not determination of grades, we understand that the primary evaluator should be the student him/herself. Writing opportunities aid the student in that process.

Viewing assessment/evaluation in that way also enriches our understanding of the "revision" process in writing. If we insist that what is being revised is student understanding of the concepts of our discipline, revision is a more valued process for student and teacher than if revision is only a mechanism for editorial corrections. "Writing to learn" is not the same thing as "writing to publish." The first wants the process of cognitive growth; the second wants the polish of product perfection.

A fifth virtue of student writing is its contribution to "participatory" learning. Educators may not agree on the many particulars of pedagogical tactics, but few can be found who would deny the superiority of "active" over "passive" learning modes. (See Chapter 16.) "Passive learning" may even be an oxymoron, like "lucid economist." To write is to engage one's mental talents with the task at hand. Such active engagement leads to the construction of knowledge—to learning. From my own teaching experience, I am willing to assert that a day without writing is a day without learning.

Finally, while the previous points have focussed on the merits of "writing to learn," the obverse activity, "learning to write" is a welcome joint outcome. While economic knowledge is a wonderful thing, particularly to its purveyors, the knowledge is considerably devalued if not accompanied by the ability to communicate. Because effective writing depends upon having something to write about, and a vocabulary to draw upon, by providing writing assignments in our subject matter we may have better opportunity to enhance useful student writing skills than the professors of English composition. Particularly in a College of Business

Administration, which is where I teach, asking students to confront, master, and use the rhetoric of economics and business should contribute significantly to their talent at professional communication. Such professional discourse skills are educational assets not likely to be achieved in a basic composition course.[2]

Each of the attributes described above is implicitly acknowledged by the resurgent General Education movement on U.S. college campuses. General Education programs invariably have a significant writing component, often spread across disciplines, stimulating faculty in many areas to become more skilled at incorporating student writing in course planning. Attention to student writing, therefore, is not only sound pedagogy; it is increasingly an institutional expectation.[3]

This chapter, then, is designed to present some ideas, and to stimulate others, about using a variety of forms of writing to initiate, facilitate and evaluate student learning in economics. Yes, we will consider the most common classroom writing form, the essay exam (but only briefly), focussing instead on diverse other opportunities for students to explore their ideas by presenting and examining them on paper. Economic writing may include journals, in-class commentaries, news analyses, essays, research papers, group project reports, data interpretations, lecture summaries, presentation outlines, and more. It can be beneficial whether graded or not, or even whether seen by the professor or not. Students of economics can write to query, to clarify, to explore, to understand, and to learn. In the process, not only their economics but their writing will benefit.

Writing to Learn

Fundamentally, any teaching strategy or method rests upon an epistemology, explicit or implicit. Our assumptions, beliefs and understandings about learning and the learning process must, at least subconsciously, shape our classroom activities.

I like Zinsser's description of learning, quoted at the beginning of this chapter, because it is consistent with my epistemological ideas. It emphasizes learning as an action, a process, and not as the accumulation of information. To learn is to build.

What is built is an always tentative understanding of the way the world works. How it is built is through repeated, reinforcing engagement by the learner with that world, its events, its ideas, its people, its diversity, its challenges. Knowledge is not built, I think, through absorption, adhesion, or osmosis. Writing is one method of accomplishing the requisite interaction of student with world.[4]

And—as our English department colleagues have been trying to tell us for years—because "writing is a form of thinking" (Zinsser, 1988, p. viii), to write economics requires the ability to "think economics." Good academic writing is discipline-specific, relying on a unique blend of vocabulary, concept, method, precedent and history, typifying that discipline and reflecting its thought-patterns (its metaphors, if you will). That may be especially true in economics, where, for decades, our textbook writers have emphasized precisely that "economics is a way of thinking."

Every economics instructor soon realizes that student ability to string words together grammatically does not constitute good economic writing. Lacking an understanding of the differences between "gross" and "net," ignoring divergence between "real" and "nominal," using "purchases" and "transfers" synonymously, students illustrate the importance of vocabulary, concept and a "disciplinary rhetoric" to effective communication in our subject matter. For that reason, a generalized freshman course in "English composition" does not automatically create competent writers of economics; however, developing competent writers of economics in our classrooms will lead to more competent economics being done there. It is, therefore, my hope that by linking the "writing-in-the-discipline" movement with the "writing-to-learn" movement (Kirsht, Levine and Reiff, 1994), we can progress toward a more informed and substantive dialogue with our students.

Asking those students visibly to reason their way into our discipline via written exercises obviously allows us one means of evaluating how well they're doing. But the "doing" we are able to focus on here is the reasoning process itself, the footprints of the mind at work, rather than the final product of learning, the answer, which is conventionally the subject of our evaluation. It is exactly this aspect of course writing assignments that provides the biggest payoff for my teaching efforts.

Surely every educator has painfully sharp experiences of the adage "there's many a slip 'twixt cup and lip" as s/he recalls the mystifying and discouraging differences between the insightful wisdom we dispense and the tortured miscomprehensions we encounter on the subsequent examination. Where have they (or we, depending on your generosity) failed?

Evaluating student writing allows us to answer precisely that question. By tracking that errant mind through the thickets of misunderstood concepts, misapplied jargon and faulty relationships, we can locate the misapprehension and retrieve the misdirected thought. The evidence, provided by student writing, of how and why my carefully prepared instruction comes unraveled as it passes through their thought processes is my single greatest asset as I seek to improve student learning. The "aha" experience occurs regularly as I trail the student intellect into the quagmire and follow the footprints to the edge of the quicksand. Prior to the next learning adventure, I can place a warning sign or guidepost at each such trouble spot. I am not alone in reporting that student writing makes it "easier to observe what they are learning" (Hansen, 1993, p. 217). Being a good "tracker" of learning is an exhilarating experience.

Writing, therefore, is both a means to learning and a diagnostic tool for assessment of strengths and weaknesses in the teaching-learning process. To accomplish each of those ends, writing tasks can be varied in form and in audience. But, in one form or other, writing can be a valuable component in any economics course.

Types of Classroom Writing

Many different educational objectives can be achieved through diverse types of writing assignments. Several of these will be discussed in the paragraphs that follow. Let's work from the more imaginative to the more traditional, starting with interesting processes of student-faculty written dialogue, and moving through a variety of less or more familiar writing assignments.

Economic Issues Notebooks One of the most successful writing exercises I've used in a Principles of Economics class works on several levels of writing and thinking—and, as a by-product, in its implementation creates raw material for still more writing activity. The project involves student preparation of an annotated economic issues notebook or journal. Throughout the academic term the student is required to maintain a notebook of news clippings relevant to a topic the student has selected at the beginning of the term. In a macro-principles course, topics have included inflation, unemployment, budget deficit, trade deficit, and more.

One form of student writing generated by this project is simply student "annotations" required to accompany each clipping. Annotations are not summaries of the clippings, but are to be the students' intellectual interaction with the news and opinions they contain. Annotations can express bewilderment, reinforcement, extensions, comparisons with other news items or with class or textbook interpretations, or may raise questions for further discussion. Each requires student interaction with economic ideas, and each provides, for the instructor, a window on the student mind.

Thus, in my reviews of the notebooks, I can ask students to extend or integrate concepts they mention, or I can simply push them a bit farther than they have gone by asking "why?". I don't try to "grade" these notebooks, but prefer to use them as a form of extended dialogue with students about the topics at hand. In maintaining my part in the conversation, I try to alleviate the bewilderment, acknowledge the reinforcement, evaluate the extensions, react to the comparisons, and answer the questions. In this way, each student and I have a unique written "chat" about issues on the student's mind. Part of the responsibility I accept in these conversations is to keep the dialogue fresh by requiring frequent student entries (3–4 times per week), and by offering regular responses (once every 3–4 weeks). Collecting a few at a time and returning them promptly maintains vitality in the interaction, spreads out the burden, and avoids ever having the entire set weighting down my desk or my conscience.

As the notebook grows, it becomes the informal raw material from which a more structured and organized writing product can grow. A natural conclusion to the project is student preparation of a summary paper on the selected topic which assembles the notebook's wisdom in a concise document. Drawing upon self-generated resources allows the student to appreciate the growth of his/her understanding as the term has evolved. What had been, for example, a rather concrete lamentation about the impact of job loss on family well-being has become a more analytical awareness of economy-wide repercussions of unemployment, or unemployment compensation. Unreflective hand-wringing at the horror of deficit spending becomes modestly reflective consideration of trade-offs involved in deficit reduction. The activity generates a tangible written product; but, more importantly, it enhances the student's sense of intellectual growth and accomplishment.

And, surprisingly, students like this project. I introduced this activity with enthusiasm for its learning potential and apprehension about its potential for student hostility. I was right on the first count and wrong on the second. It requires effort; it takes time; but apparently the sense of learning accomplished outweighs those costs and leads to strong student support. The notebook project seems to give them a welcome (and unusual?) sense of *quid pro quo*.

Obviously, as we discuss student preparation of a significant paper as a possible outcome of the annotated notebook project, we have entered the realm of paper-writing as a component of "writing to learn."

Small Group Writing As my teaching has evolved, my writing assignments have evolved as well. I have moved from what were, a generation ago, the typical "term paper" assignments, through assignment of a series of short "reflective essays" on topics of immediate importance to the class, and on to my current emphasis on sequenced small group writing projects. Of course each form of student writing has its own advantages and disadvantages, but I have been satisfied that the educational benefit-cost analysis attendant to this evolution has been positive.[5]

In a recent article, Davidson and Gumnior (1993) describe a "Writing Consultant Program" in the Indiana University School of Business. The Indiana program involved hiring professional writing instructors to work collaboratively with Business faculty to develop and implement effective discipline-related writing activities.

I have been a utilizer and beneficiary of a similar project in the University of Nebraska College of Business Administration. Supported initially by external funding, the College was able to employ two Ph.D. composition specialists to staff a "Writing Lab" that has emphasized small group writing projects in diverse business and economics courses. Both at Nebraska and at Indiana the collaborative projects emphasize writing as a vehicle to facilitate learning both the concepts and the rhetoric of the subject matter disciplines. Both programs stress the "construc-tion" of knowledge via writing and re-writing. And both programs utilize group work (Nebraska exclusively, Indiana occasionally) to develop team skills and to reduce the number of written assignments any instructor will receive.

While the details of the group work vary from class to class and from discipline to discipline, I have typically formed four-person groups each charged with preparing four short (3–4 page) project reports during a semester. This structure allows each person to be a "lead author" once, allows sufficient time for a significant process of writing-editing-rewriting to take place on each project, and, we always hope, can result in a rather polished finished product as the result of each assignment. (Honesty compels me to acknowledge that each of these desired outcomes is not always completely achieved.)

This format allows for a varied set of assignments, and, consequently, instruction in diverse types of writing activities. Most recently, the four assignments in my Comparative Economic Systems class included a comparative assessment of two alternative text materials used in class (advisory to me as class instructor), an "op-ed" essay on the relative impact of government involvement in various OECD countries (to be submitted to a newspaper or other periodical), an advisory letter on 21st century economic issues to be sent to a presidential candidate during the 1996 election campaign, and a mini-lecture on the Russian economic transition suitable for delivery to a Principles of Economics class.

Some of these involved a bit of library research; others only required thoughtful consideration of material the students had seen in regular classroom activities. Each of the assignments had a "real" audience for whom the material was being prepared. And in preparing each, the groups had weekly consultation with a composition expert who could raise questions, focus thinking, challenge assumptions, and focus attention on the quality of argument used by students.[6]

Additionally, as suggested by composition theorists and by our Writing Lab consultants, such diverse assignments can be calibrated to move students through different rhetorical styles starting with the more conventional and informal and progressing through "successive approximations" of more discipline-specific discourse (Bartholomae, 1984).

Other positive by-products of this group-writing focus have included formation of mini learning communities that then also function as study groups for exams, and the integration of otherwise isolated individuals (international students, for example) into the mainstream of classroom activity.

Anyone who has ever participated in or organized group efforts understands that no such process ever is flawless or seamless. Some groups work better than others; individual conflicts or uneven effort can mar group satisfaction. Nevertheless, there are sufficient remedies available to justify group writing programs as constructive components of most courses in economics. And the collaboration of composition specialists with discipline experts has proven valuable to both, and beneficial to students who observe professionals working together to address educational tasks.

Data Interpretation and Manipulation I include discussion of data interpretation and manipulation in this chapter because such tasks may present interesting puzzles about which students can write. They can be yet one more source of intellectual footprints thereby giving them value beyond their obvious contribution to quantitative economic analysis or mastery of model manipulation. And, while such assignments were also featured in the first edition of this *Handbook*, I now am impelled to emphasize, underline and reinforce the importance I place on this dimension of my instruction and of student expression.

And, while I acknowledge the value of traditional problem sets as checks on student mastery of economic models and utilization of quantitative concepts, and I applaud the "active learning" that they demand, it is not the text-based problem sets that are my primary data-based teaching tool or pedagogical concern. The end-of-chapter (or study guide) "canned" problems, useful though they may be for concept clarification or reinforcement, are perceived by student and teacher alike as artificial and "make-believe." Experienced educators recognize that students have no trouble separating the game of academic "let's pretend" from the real world of their interests and activities in ways which effectively erase the classroom material from their consciousness.

Therefore, I am more intrigued and challenged by the implications and possibilities involved in a somewhat different use of data and data manipulation for the purposes of learning economics and evaluating that learning. Suppose we assume, as I have for three decades, that a major purpose of each of my economics class is to foster, or extend, the students' "economic literacy." Suppose further that we define "economic literacy" to mean comprehension of day-to-day journalistic presentation of business and economic information, particularly that relevant to course topics. What happens if we ask our students to "explain" a chart, graph, table or diagram from the front page of a daily newspaper, a copy of a corporate report, or the latest edition of the *Economic Report of the President*?

I can answer that question with confidence and with dismay, because I have performed the exercise over and over again. The answer, over and over again, is that many students exhibit a discouraging amount of functional illiteracy in data interpretation. The charts and tables in texts are ignored, the data displays and graphs in periodicals are slipped over because our students don't know what to make of them. As instructors, we overlook that illiteracy because the prose in the text tells the student what the table shows (provides an interpretation). But ask the student to provide the explanation for a data display for which the accompanying interpretation is lacking, and the results are stunning. Many (most?) students can not draw useful inferences by correctly integrating title, headings, data, footnotes and structure of the display into a meaningful statement.

Ignorance revealed is opportunity presented. If learning takes place through interaction of student with environment, we can place students in circumstances where data interpretation is necessary for success. Asking students to write about data taken from current and significant source materials is one avenue toward achieving an interpretive literacy which, I'm afraid, most of us have simply, and wrongly, taken for granted.

My response has been to include data interpretation as a significant aspect of at least one-half of the assigned course activities. In a typical course, two out of four group paper or semester essay assignments will be data based or have a significant data component. "Using data from the World Bank, United Nations, the OECD, and the U.S. Government, prepare an Op-Ed essay in which you compare the domestic economic role and influence of the U.S. Government with the impact of the public sector in other major OECD countries." Every exam, in every course, will contain tables or graphs or charts from the text, or a periodical article, or a newspaper, which illustrate key points of our study. In those cases, I minimally want the student to correctly explain the contents of the display.

The real success occurs if the student can then explain the importance or relevance of those data to our conceptual learning. If the student can read a table of Russian economic performance indicators for 1990–1995 and relate them to contemporary Russian economic policy, we have made the grade. However, in half the cases, students are likely to interpret the fact that the rate of change in GDP was −15% in 1993 and −12% in 1994 as illustrative of Russian GDP "growth" in 1994. Such analysis would not be acceptable for most future employers of our students.

My attempt to involve students with "real" rather than "make-believe" economics of course is not unique. Lee Hansen has argued persuasively that students need to read more "real" economics and less "textbook" economics because it is "real" books that "reveal economists doing what economists do" (Hansen, 1988, p. 272).

Adil Abdalla describes an international data gathering activity, and reinforces the importance of teaching such skills by commenting on problems such as "Inconsistency of data reported," "Disregard for current information," "Nonrecognition of world events," and "Noncollegiate level" (Abdalla, 1993, pp. 234-235). Joyce Jacobsen reports on imaginative data-creation and reporting exercises, (Jacobsen, 1994) and also cites other research corroborating the beneficial effects of student writing on student learning (Langer and Applebee, 1987).

Data interpretation is one aspect of our educational task in which we can reinforce learning as a collaborative activity. To ask small groups of students to solve data arrays cooperatively is to encourage students to learn from one another and actively to build on knowledge already existing in the classroom. Group tasks, including preparation of written reports, achieve many of the learning objectives we value while allowing student interaction and exploration to take the place of some of the one-directional communication that normally fills our classrooms. And, as one of my English department colleagues observes, it also dignifies and encourages the most regular form of informal learning in which we all participate.

A somewhat more sophisticated use of data interpretation as a learning activity is to request students to affirm or refute an argument or position through the use of a table, or chart, or graph, that is provided for them. (Almost any supposedly empirically-based political assertion will serve very well.) Such a request may require students to consider aspects of the information or interpretation that are more subtle or complex than they might voluntarily explore on their own.. You may be amazed to discover, as I was, that students are often willing to affirm almost any marginally plausible inference supplied for a data array.

Students have, in rather large numbers, been willing to use comparison of 1995 data with 1990 data to illustrate the impact of Communist central planning in Russia (although Gorbachev's "perestroika" was initiated in 1987 and the Soviet planning system had effectively collapsed by 1990.) When asked to make international comparisons of countries' expenditures on health care, they are typically willing to ignore definitional distinctions between public or government spending and total (public plus private) spending from one economy to another. "Millions" and "billions" become interchangeable. Per capita and aggregate data are indiscriminately compared. Critical distinctions are not overabundant in our students' intellectual tool kit. They may become more abundant if they are more frequently needed and if we devote much more attention, skill and instruction to their mastery.

Student writing about data is some of the most productive diagnostic raw material which educators can obtain. By observing the visible grappling, on paper, of the student mind with quantitative information, we, as teachers, can learn amazing amounts about student assumptions, powers of observation, ability to relate concepts, fundamental grounding in basic mathematical principles and more. Armed with such knowledge, we are much better prepared to aim our educational fire at the most appropriate targets. I believe you'll find that we've been overshooting.

Cartoon Analysis   Although political/economic cartooning (editorial page variety) seems related to data arrays only to the extent that both are visual representations of information or ideas, I think there is a more fundamental tie that merits a brief discussion of cartoon analysis at this point. Drawing appropriate inferences from data, and discerning figurative insight from a fanciful cartoon both require high-level cognitive skills. For me, the two tasks are closely related because asking students to perform them and to write about that performance has revealed closely related problems and has provided similar insights into student learning difficulties in our discipline. I also group the activities together because interpreting charts, graphs, and tables and interpreting political/economic cartoon messages are both skills requisite to the economic literacy we seek as an educational objective.

Asking students to interpret economically-targeted editorial cartoons, like asking them to interpret media-presented data displays, often reveals shockingly concrete (mis)understandings of subtly witty allusions intended by the cartoonists. One English department colleague of mine suggests that both cartoon and display interpretation "assumes symbol literacy in the special dialects of economics." The fact that political cartooning is frequently metaphorical or representational seems lost on many students who struggle to understand at the literal or concrete level, or who don't possess the requisite "symbol literacy." On the one hand, I've come to feel sorry for the cartoonists' profession whose work so regularly goes unappreciated; on the other hand, I see these revealed misunderstandings as fertile raw material with which we should be able to craft helpful learning experiences. The "bottom line" is that it is difficult to understand or appreciate any of these by-ways of the student mind unless one asks students to map them for us via their written reactions to a variety of intellectual stimuli.

Essay Exams   For the most part, the writing activities discussed to this point are primarily learning activities and only secondarily evaluation activities. They do, as we have emphasized, facilitate self-evaluation by the student; and they most emphatically are of diagnostic help to the instructor.

But when we look at writing activities in which the emphasis most clearly shifts over to the evaluative function, our eyes must finally fall upon the essay exam. The essay question or the essay exam is undoubtedly the most common use of writing for evaluation purposes, and it is frequently the only type of writing asked of students in an undergraduate course. Since the construction and grading of essay examinations is discussed in detail in Chapter 20 in this *Handbook*, I will simply emphasize the point that exams serve pedagogical as well as evaluative purposes. They can promote learning by encouraging reflection, integration, synthesis, and by creating yet one more building block in the edifice of the course.

In keeping with my emphasis on viewing student writing as a type of intellectual footprinting, my focus in creating essay questions is to help me assess and to help students develop more sophisticated cognitive skills. That is, I want to sample student ability in areas of application, synthesis and evaluation rather than simple recall or association. An essay question that asks students to evaluate the likely macroeconomic consequences of alternative fiscal policy proposals of Democratic and Republican politicians is more likely to promote learning and reveal understanding than an essay question that asks students to define and explain Federal Reserve monetary policy tools. Likewise, an essay question which requires student analytical thinking certainly provides more interesting intellectual tracks for the instructor to follow than one which only reveals memory.

Essay exams, paper writing, problem solving, notebook preparation provide varied opportunities for student writing. These types of writing activities include those most often used in economics courses. But they do not exhaust the list of productive writing exercises that can promote learning economics.[7]

Other Writing Activities   Although I am not (yet) quite to the point of unfailingly following such a precept, I would be willing to defend the argument that, for many of my students, "a day without writing is a day without learning." As one who is committed to the "constructivist" epistemological argument that we must actively "build" our knowledge of the world (rather than passively "receiving" it), I try to put my students in the "building" mode, using pencil as hammer, as often as possible. Some of the additional activities take place out of class, some are accomplished in class, but each reinforces the idea that we learn economics by doing economics. We learn reflective analysis by doing reflective analysis. And I want my students to do it with pencil in hand so that I can watch. Such activities need not be long and they need not be graded

Convinced that student engagement with subject matter is essential to student learning, I have, in an old-fashioned way, traveled "back to the future" by assigning frequent, often daily, written homework assignments. These assignments take many forms, ranging from explanation of text ideas, to analysis of text-related newspaper articles, to clarification and critique of graphs or tables associated with the concepts being taught. In every case, my objectives are student involvement with the subject matter, student practice with the kinds of analysis I value, and student intellectual footprints that I can follow before they grow cold. In this way students are encouraged to stay "on task" regularly, and I am a daily recipient of evidence on student understanding. And, these regular assignments can be designed as useful preparation for exams and group projects. In-class writing activities also have a constructive role to play in a "participatory" learning environment. It can be useful, for example, to ask students to write for one another—the instructor need not always be audience—as they work through the understanding and implications of an economic concept. Students can be asked to devote five minutes of class time to writing a paragraph explaining or applying a specific economic concept under discussion. Then, allowing small groups (four or five students) to distill from their collected paragraphs a single preferred explanation can lead to highly constructive learning activity. While each group's final product may not have the polish and subtlety of a professor's well-honed lecture notes on the same topic, the student work has the advantage of direct involvement and internalization. I am convinced that more learning takes place as student "A" and student "C" compare their interpretative paragraphs than when their colleague, student "B," transfers the professor's lecture into sketchy notes.

Another useful form of in-class writing can be student preparation of "summaries." These can either be brief summaries of reading assignments or, often more revealingly, summaries of a class session which is drawing to a close. Such immediate feedback on student perception of class material can be a wonderfully helpful indicator of teaching effectiveness. Why wait until the periodic hour exams to find out how woefully misinterpreted our instruction has been? Finding out the same thing earlier and regularly allows more immediate and effective corrective steps to be taken.

When such summarization focuses on what has taken place in the immediately preceding class time, it will rely upon the most common form of in-class writing, student notetaking. Education research has consistently shown notetaking to be a positive component of the education experience (Carrier, 1983) but, among economic educators, it is surely one of the most neglected variables of effective learning. If it is true that students can "write to learn," presumably we can usefully pay some attention to the writing they do daily, in their class notes.

Deliberate involvement of the instructor with student notes and notetaking skills can pay dividends for both teacher and learner. Notetaking incorporates some degree of active student involvement with our student matter. If, with help, students can regularly move beyond simply using notetaking as a "recording" activity and instead use it as a "processing" activity, it becomes increasingly valuable. Such "processing" could involve *relating* a lecture idea to prior class or text material, *questioning* the meaning or applicability of a lecture concept, or *suggesting* a follow-up line of investigation, for example.

But even when notetaking serves only the recording purpose, it can be an opportunity for strengthening specific student skills. One very inadequately developed student skill is the ability to discern the "big idea," to tap the "key concept," to separate major points from minor filler. An instructor who occasionally examines student notebooks, or thumbs through textbooks which have been "highlighted" by students, will quickly encounter this inadequacy. Deliberately planning brief activities which improve those notetaking skills may pay significant learning dividends.

Simply interrupting a normal lecture session after the first twenty minutes to discuss what a "good" set of notes on those twenty minutes should contain would make a significant contribution to most students. Asking them to share and discuss their notes with each other will allow them to learn from their peers. Brief class discussion of why specific elements are included and others are excluded will generate notetaking patterns that can be replicated. Providing an instructor-prepared set of notes on that twenty-minute segment (fairly representing the amount and sophistication of notes which could have been taken by an astute student) will show a student what developing such as skill can add to his/her educational benefits.

This whole process and practice of discerning degrees of importance, developing logical chains of argument, and consciously placing ideas in proper relation to one another is also contributory to much more effective essay writing when exam time rolls around. That soon becomes apparent to students and provides substantial motivation to understand and master these specific writing skills.

The various forms of writing activities discussed in these pages often can be combined in educationally useful ways. As is indicated above, small group analysis of a significant body of economic data is frequently included in the series of paper assignments I make in any class. Essay examination questions can incorporate thought-provoking elements from other class writing assignments. (For example, after asking students to write a short paper on the "trade offs" involved in various deficit-reduction plans, I would consider following up with an exam question which required students to offer macroeconomic policy advice to an incoming President.) The primary objective is to provide opportunities for students to grapple with the subject matter in ways which cause them to expand their understanding and to provide, to their instructor, evidence of how well that is happening.

The creation of writing assignments which involve students intellectually, generate learning opportunities, and provide insight on student progress is limited only by faculty imagination. And, in some cases, perhaps it's true that "the more imaginative, the better."

Consider a playful, and effective, writing assignment used by a faculty colleague of mine who, probably not coincidentally, is a wonderful writer. [8] A biologist who is also committed to the concept of writing to learn, he requires each of his many students to submit 40 lines of original poetry about a biological organism of their choice. This becomes writing the students want to do, that requires them to learn something about the organism, that sends them to appropriate source material, and that stimulates their expressive imagination. What more could we as educators want?

Writing poetry as a method of learning economics? Try it. Or better yet, develop your own equally creative collection of assignments which target the same objectives. Writing is an immensely flexible activity which can assist us in seemingly limitless ways.

Conclusion

Writing facilitates learning, and vice versa.

More specifically, this chapter has argued that active student involvement in the processing of ideas is an essential element of learning, in economics as in any other academic area. Further, a written record of that idea-processing is crucial to instructor assessment of what is happening in the students' minds as a result of classroom instruction. Such assessment should go beyond *what* the student thinks is correct to *why* the student comes to that conclusion. A variety of carefully considered writing forms and assignments can contribute to the teaching process, the learning process and the assessment process thereby better grounding the entire educational endeavor.

As the economics educator considers the use of writing in his/her teaching activities, the following appear to be salient points for consideration and reflection.

1 Learning occurs as student minds interact with our subject matter and thereby construct meaning and understanding. Listening is not learning. Writing is one possible method of generating the desired student intellectual engagement.

2 Writing allows each of us to find out what we know. The plaintive student lament, "I knew the answer, but I just couldn't write it down" is false. If we know it, we can write it; if we can write it, we know it. Even more amazingly, we are often surprised, after writing it down, that we know as much as we do. All this is true of students, as of ourselves.

3 More important, I think, than showing us what students know, writing shows us why they think they know it. Student writing reveals student thought processing and provides a "snapshot" of that process. Such a snapshot allows processes to be compared, and defended, and amended. It is immeasurably more helpful to a classroom instructor to know *why* students are misunderstanding our discipline rather than simply once again to find out that they are.

4 Although writing as an evaluation tool is a common educational notion, we too often ignore the self-assessment dimension of the writing process. It is not only the instructor who benefits from the diagnostic insights offered by student writing. The student him/herself often arrives at even more helpful insights and understandings via the process of organizing and explicating latent notions.

5 Multiple and creative types of writing can each contribute to a learning environment. Annotated issues notebooks, economic journals, small group projects, data interpretation, homework assignments, in-class writing, concept paragraphs, summaries of class activities, poetry writing are but a few of the

possible written forms which can contribute to learning. Many of these forms of writing can serve their purpose without being read and evaluated by the instructor.

6 Assignment of frequent, short, analytical essays which require reflection on the applications and implications of class material are typically more effective learning-generators than are the commonly assigned "research" or term papers. They are so primarily as a result of the regularized student interaction with subject matter which they require. Such repeated interchange allows (perhaps requires) the growth and refinement of ideas and the continually closer approximation of the language and thought, the dialect, of our discipline. If it can be possible for students, or student groups, to edit and rewrite these brief assignments, not only their economic understanding but also their writing ability will be further enhanced.

7 An overlooked area of student economic illiteracy is inability to interpret and analyze data presentations with precision and accuracy. Such illiteracy can be reduced by using writing assignments that require and develop those interpretive skills. Again, the student writing reveals the problem areas and allows instructional assistance to be applied efficiently.

8 If developed carefully, essay examinations can be one effective aid in the assessment of student understanding. To help with that process, essay questions should probe high-level cognitive skills and should require careful explication of thought.

9 Writing to learn in the college classroom fosters instructor awareness of student individuality and enhances student ownership of the educational process. Being reminded of student individuality improves our educational function as we respond more directly to the diverse needs and problems reflected in our students. Student ownership of learning removes the teacher or the text from the center of the educational process and puts the student there instead. The student whose individual educational needs are being addressed, and who accepts his/her role as active agent in the academic environment, is much more likely to attain academic success.

10 Writing activities, although often individual, can also be used to stimulate group interaction which leads to formation of shared understandings, focus discussion, generate stronger arguments, encourage revision, and lead to new and sharper re-examinations of material and concepts.

11 Finally, writing to learn also contributes to learning to write. Good writing is mostly about the cogent presentation of ideas. The processes and activities discussed in this chapter produce that cogency about economics, which enhances the students' ability to communicate in our subject matter. Once the substance is present, the editorial aspects of spelling, grammar, and other technical details can be addressed as needed. But that's another chapter.

All in all, then, "writing to learn" can be a significant part of a successful economics classroom. "Writing across the curriculum" is an important pedagogical emphasis, as vital to our segment of the curriculum as it is to any other. Economic educators who increase their awareness of developments in this currently energized educational area should find that enhanced student interaction with material, and improved instructor diagnostic ability combine to increase instructional effectiveness and student satisfaction dramatically.

NOTES

In preparing this revised chapter, the author wishes to acknowledge good advice and helpful bibliographic suggestions from colleagues Rick Evans, Tom O'Connor and William Walstad.

1. A valuable resource on the Writing Across the Curriculum movement is Bazerman and Russell (1994.) Cohen and Spencer (1993) bring the WAC movement to economics instruction.

2. My Writing Lab colleagues point out to me that composition theorists draw a distinction between "writing-to-learn" and "writing-in-the-disciplines" programs that may not be sufficiently clear in this chapter. (This distinction is discussed in Kirsht, Levine & Reiff (1994).) My intention is to put highest priority on "writing-to-learn" assuming that more effective writing-in-the-discipline will contribute to that end.

3. A stimulating look at both General Education and Writing Across the Curriculum is provided by Cohen and Spencer (1993).

4. These points are also made with power and clarity in Knoblauch and Brannon (1983).

5. Composition authority Kenneth Bruffee (1983, 1993) is particularly forceful in emphasizing the collaborative nature of effective writing.

6. Cohen and Spencer (1993) also stress the importance of this development of argument.

7. The several *Journal of Economic Education* articles in the "References" to this chapter provide additional suggestions for economics-related writing options.

8. I refer to John Janovy, author of many and varied works including the highly acclaimed naturalist essays in *Keith County Journal*, New York: St. Martin's Press, 1978.

REFERENCES

Abdalla, A.E.A. (1993). A country report project for an international economics class. *Journal of Economic Education*, 24, (Summer), 231-236.

Bartholomae, D. (1984). Inventing the university. In M. Rose (ed.), *When a writer can't write* (pp. 134-165). New York: Guilford Press.

Bazerman, C. and Russell, D.R. (Eds.). (1994). *Landmark essays on writing across the curriculum*. Davis, CA: Hermagoras Press.

Bruffee, K.A. (1983). Writing and reading as collaborative or social acts. In J. Hays et al. (eds.), *The writer's mind* (pp. 159-169). Urbana, IL: National Council of Teachers of English.

Bruffee, K.A. (1993). Writing and collaboration. In K.A. Bruffee, *Collaborative learning: Higher education, interdependence, and the authority of knowledge* (pp. 52-62). Baltimore, MD: The Johns Hopkins University Press.

Carrier, C.A. (1983). Notetaking research: Implications for the classroom. *Journal of Instructional Development*, 6, 19-25.

Cohen, A.J. and Spencer, J. (1993). Using writing across the curriculum in economics: Is taking the plunge worth it? *Journal of Economic Education*, 24, (Summer), 219-230.

Crowe, D. and Youga, J. (1986). Using writing as a tool for learning economics. *Journal of Economic Education*, 17, (Summer), 218-222.

Davidson, L.S. and Gumnior, E.C. (1993). Writing to learn in a business economics class. *Journal of Economic Education*, 24, (Summer), 237-243.

Hansen, W.L. (1988). 'Real' books and textbooks. *Journal of Economic Education*, 19, (Summer), 271-274.

Hansen, W.L. (1993). Teaching a writing intensive course in economics. *Journal of Economic Education*, 24, (Summer), 213-218.

Jacobsen, J.P. (1994). Incorporating data collection and written reports in microeconomics. *Journal of Economic Education*, 25, (Winter), 31-43.

Kirsht, J., Levine, R., and Reiff, J. (1994). Evolving paradigms: WAC and the rhetoric of inquiry. *College Composition and Communication*, 45, (October), 369-380.

Knoblauch, C.H. and Brannon, L. (1983). Writing as learning through the curriculum. *College English*, 45, (September), 465-474.

Langer, J.A. and Appleby, A.N. (1987). *How writing shapes thinking: A study of teaching and learning*. Urbana, IL: National Council of Teachers of English.

Zinsser, W. (1988). *Writing to Learn*. New York: Harper & Row.

CHAPTER 16

ACTIVE AND COOPERATIVE LEARNING STRATEGIES FOR THE ECONOMICS CLASSROOM

Beverly Cameron

Most undergraduate economics courses involve passive instruction, most notably the lecture (Becker and Watts, 1996). Few courses spend a significant amount of class time on small group work, discussions, case studies, simulations, or cooperative work (Siegfried, et al., 1996). Asking students to write papers or solve problems on assignments and tests is as much active learning as many courses require. By not including active and cooperative learning techniques in economics courses we limit learning opportunities for our students. Active learning and cooperative learning increase the interaction between students, encourage the use of economic tools and theories, and provide additional opportunities for the instructor to model effective thinking in an economics context.

Active learning comprises many ideas, but basically it requires that students *participate* in the learning process. It requires that students *use* content knowledge, not just acquire it. Cooperative learning is a technique that requires students to work together in small fixed groups on a structured learning task. This chapter further defines and give examples of a variety of active and cooperative learning strategies that can be used in undergraduate economics courses. A menu of ideas is offered so instructors can select the strategies that best fit their teaching styles, personalities, and courses.

Suggestions for Active Learning

Active learning "involves providing opportunities for students to meaningfully *talk and listen, write, read,* and *reflect* on the content, ideas, issues, and concerns of an academic subject" (Meyers and Jones, 1993, p. xi). "Learning is not a spectator sport. Students do not learn much just sitting in class listening to teachers, memorizing prepackaged assignments, and spitting out answers. They must talk about what they are learning, write about it, relate it to past experiences, apply it to their daily lives. They must make what they learn part of themselves" (Bonwell, 1992, p. 1).

Active learning techniques shift class activity from a teacher-centered process to a student-centered process. This can make instructors nervous because they feel they are losing the control they had in lecture classes. To lessen these concerns instructors can progress along a continuum of active learning techniques, introducing the least risky activities first. The following suggestions can be used in any size class including large lecture-based classes (Bligh, 1972; Weimer, 1987; Bonwell, 1992). The list, starting with the least risky, are as follows:

1 *One-minute paper or quiz*—With this technique the lecture is interrupted for one or two minutes to ask students to write their ideas or solve a problem posed by the lecturer. *(The depreciation of the Mexican peso in 1995 increased the price of imported goods in Mexico. How did this price increase affect Mexico's consumer price index?)* The instructor can then model the thinking process an economist would use to analyze situations of currency depreciation to answer the question. The one-minute paper introduces active student involvement into the lecture, provides an opportunity to use effective thinking skills, and is a source of feedback on learning for both students and the instructor.

2 *"Buzz groups"*—With buzz groups the lecture is occasionally interrupted to ask small groups (two to three individuals) of students to discuss a concept or problem suggested by the lecturer. *(Using marginal utility theory explain why rational people often buy things at garage sales that they wouldn't buy in a store.)* The informal groupings can be made by asking students to turn to the person(s) next to them. Then a few groups are asked to share their ideas with the entire class. Buzz groups change the pace of the lecture and allow active participation in the learning process. The buzz group also helps to break the lecture into more easily absorbed sections. The objectives of using buzz groups within lectures vary, but can be to: (a) allow students to clarify unclear points for each other, (b) give the lecturer feedback on students' understanding of a topic, (c) give students time to consolidate and clarify learning and understanding that has taken place earlier in the lecture, (d) provide an opportunity for analytical thinking, (e) allow an opportunity for lecture material to be applied to a situation or problem that is particularly relevant to students, (f) encourage reticent students to put their ideas into words, and (g) foster a cohesive class spirit through the exchange of ideas.

3 *Establish a "question box" to use as a springboard for class discussions*—Ask students to drop questions that arise from the class, readings, or assignments into a box that can be placed on the lecture room desk, at the classroom door, on your office door, or in the departmental office. Regularly answer *all* questions during class time and use the questions as a starting point for class discussions, one-minute papers or buzz groups. The question box gives students who might be shy about speaking in class an opportunity to ask questions, as well as providing the instructor with feedback and a starting point for class discussions.

4 *Starting from student input*—The instructor asks the class for key points from the assigned reading and writes the responses on the board. He/she then elaborates on the students' points, gives technical restatements of terms, adds necessary detail, and applies the concepts or theories to student's experiences. *(Explain how students can use the concepts of producer and consumer surplus in job interviews to maximize their wages.)* This lecture modification provides an opportunity to make students think, forces them to relate the course content to their personal experiences and background knowledge, gives the instructor feedback on how much of the material students understand, encourages the instructor to proceed at the pace of the class, and actively involves students in the class.

5 *Controlled class discussion*—Students raise questions in class or respond to the instructor's questions and discussion follows. The objectives of this method of teaching are "clarification on matters of fact and the development of lines of thought and interest that have been stimulated" (Bligh, 1972, p. 199). The instructor can start a discussion with closed questions that require a one or two word answer *(Britain ran large export surpluses during most of the 19th century. Does it follow that Britain as a whole must have been enormously wealthy by the time Queen Victoria died in 1901?)* and progress on to questions which require more analysis *(What economic and political circumstances must exist for a nation to run large export surpluses over many years?)*. When instructors don't get responses from students after asking a question(s) they don't have to wait for students to raise their hands. Rather, they can look toward a section of the room and take any answer that is offered.

6 *Simulations*—Many simulations have been suggested in the economics literature For instance: (a) allowing a free market to come to an equilibrium by assigning students roles as buyers with limited funds or sellers with production costs, (b) assigning students roles as oligopoly producers and buyers to illustrate problems faced by cartel pricing agreements when members have an incentive to sell independently, and (c) multiple expansion of bank deposits where students are assigned roles as bankers, borrowers, and businesses. (See Chapter 17.) At the end of a simulation the instructor should ask students to summarize the over all concept or theory the exercise illustrated, or provide the summary themselves. Summaries ensure that students see the "big picture" as well as the interesting details. (See Breen and Boyd (1976), Halstead (1989), Sinden and O'Hanlon (1981), Williams (1993), and Starr (1994) for examples of classroom simulations.)

7 *Role playing*—Students can be asked to argue or defend the position of prominent economists in history of thought classes *(Malthus, Marx, Keynes)*, or to take the role of various interest groups in environmental or public finance courses *(those who suffer negative externalities as a result of a production process versus the producer).* The research and commitment required as students prepare to present and defend a position or view, especially when it is not one that they agree with, can motivate analysis and synthesis of course content to a greater extent than written assignments or examinations. In large classes, students can be divided into several smaller groups to allow more than one student to play each role. Students who may not have been assigned roles can be asked to critique, summarize, or judge the debate between role players.

8 *Combination lecture and small group discussion class format*—The combination of small discussion groups separate from, but in conjunction with, lectures is likely the most popular modification of the lecture method. Discussion classes often focus on application of lecture and text book theories that explain current economic events, more detailed expansions of lecture topics, working through selected problems and cases, and questions from students. Separating lectures and classes that require a great deal of active participation helps clarify expectations for students and makes it easier for the instructor to allocate marks for class participation. This combination format ranges from one lecture period per week and three or four discussion classes to three lectures and one discussion period. The combination allows instructors to transmit a great deal of factual material to students during lecture periods while allowing time for active student involvement in discussion classes. (See also Chapters 12 and 14.)

Although no significant differences in academic achievement appear to result from the formal combination methods, research shows that many students favor combinations of lectures and discussion sessions as opposed to all lectures or all discussions. Studies are not conclusive on the optimal combination of lectures and discussion groups per week or semester, but research results lead McKeachie (1994) to conclude that when instructors must give information and also develop concepts, the use of both lectures and discussions is a logical and popular choice."

Four other variations that can be used with a lecture class when students are asked to sit in pre-assigned work groups are outlined below in the section of this chapter dealing with cooperative learning.

Cooperative Learning: What Is It and Why Is It Valuable?

Cooperative learning differs from informal small group work or discussion by requiring students "to practice, at a higher level, positive interaction and individual accountability, as well as more sophisticated group-processing skills . . . groups work together over a longer period, such as several weeks or an entire semester, toward a shared goal" (Meyers and Jones, 1993, p. 75). Cooperative learning groups allow students to work on problems or cases that would be too difficult or time consuming for an individual to complete. Groups discuss, solve, or analyze problems or case situations presented by the instructor. Successful cooperative learning experiences depend on the instructor's ability to pose interesting and challenging problems.[1]

A strength of cooperative small group work is peer tutoring. Research shows that peer help or tutoring can enhance student academic achievement and that small group work tends to benefit all students, particularly the poorer students, without disadvantaging the better students (McKeachie, et al., 1986). The work of Cooper, et al. (1990) also concludes that student retention of class material is often enhanced by small group work.

Four of the least demanding forms of cooperative learning that can be used with a lecture class are (Cooper, et al., 1990):

1 *Titles and topics*—Give student groups titles or topic sentences for forthcoming lectures and ask them to integrate prior knowledge with these topics by generating questions or predictions and verifying them when the lecture occurs. *(Before lecturing on factor markets, topic sentences can help students see the parallels between factor and—previously covered—product markets.)*

2 *Discussion of lecture points*—Ask student groups to discuss lecture material during or after a lecture. This can include group work on problem sets or assignments. *(After a discussion of central bank interest rate targeting policies ask groups to discuss the positives and negatives of this policy for business.)*

3 *Mini-lectures and thinking practice*—Give small groups the opportunity to discuss or practice using effective thinking skills after fifteen minutes or less of a lecture. The lecture then becomes a series of "mini" talks interspersed with cooperative learning. *(Lecture on the formula for income elasticity of demand and then let groups calculate one or two coefficients from data you provide. Groups can also be asked to suggest goods that are likely to have positive or negative income elasticity coefficients.)*

4 *Group summaries*—Use small group discussion to provide closure or a summary at the end of a lecture. If done in written form, this technique can provide valuable feedback to the instructor. *(Ask groups to list or paraphrase the three or four main points or concepts in your lecture, and then show students your list of key points for that class. If the points and concepts generated by groups don't match those you think you covered in the lecture, suggest that students review their notes to identify your key points and concepts.)*

Other More Challenging Cooperative Learning Assignments

Macroeconomics Ask students to calculate a reasonably accurate twelve month consumer price index for undergraduate students at your institution. Students should be directed to national, state, and urban consumer price indices that might be applicable, and then be asked to examine the market-basket items and weights to determine if they match the spending patterns of the "typical" student. If students determine that the official indices do not accurately reflect their spending patterns and cost of living increases, they should create a "student cost of living index" for the past year or two. Items such as tuition bills, room and board fees, the cost of books, transportation home, campus entertainment, phone bills, and so on are likely to be prominent items in the student indices.

Comparison of the groups' student cost of living indices and market baskets at the completion of the assignment could also lead to interesting discussions. The discussions are likely to be lively since the topic is relevant to all members of the class.

Introductory supply and demand Provide students with price and quantity changes for a selected group of products. (These price and quantity changes could be produced in class using auction games to sell imaginary goods or by assigning some students roles as buyers with differing amounts of money and assigning others roles as sellers with differing costs.) Ask groups to specify whether the changes could be attributed to demand or supply shifts or to movements on the curves. Then use the supply and demand model from the text or lecture to predict changes in the equilibrium price and quantity under a variety of other specified circumstances.

No paper is required for this assignment, and the results can be easily specified in a table(s) with short explanations indicating the reason(s) for the changes. When selecting markets to simulate or use as examples it is best to select those that are of interest or relevance to student's lives (e.g., the market for new and used textbooks, student parking passes on campus, apartment rents near campus, the black-market for tickets to important football or basketball games). The more relevant the selected markets are to students the more lively the group discussions.

Macro or labor economics Provide students with a variety of national, regional, state, and/or city-specific price indices (e.g., CPI, wholesale price index) or direct them to sources for this data. Then select a group of individuals in an area not specifically covered or represented by a price index (e.g., a rural area or region, workers in a particular factory or industry, retired individuals, single mothers) and ask students to determine if the wages, benefits, and so on for this group are likely to have kept up with the cost of living over a specified period. Social security benefits, union negotiated wage settlements for one or more firms, and/or welfare benefits can be used to estimate the income changes the group in question received over the time period.

This assignment would be difficult to complete individually, it has the benefit of using actual data, and the conclusion can be presented in one or two pages accompanied by separate sheets for calculations. In a policy-oriented class students might also be asked to suggest federal, state or local policies which could be used to ensure that specified segments of society did not experience reductions in their real incomes over time.

Money, banking and finance Give groups an imaginary amount of money to "invest" in one or more of the stock, bond, futures, foreign currency, options, and commodities markets. Each investment decision must be justified by some economic analysis of current or predicted monetary or fiscal policies in the United States or its major trading partners, sector growth, and so on. The market price of each investment in a group's portfolio should be monitored weekly.

This cooperative learning project motivates students to keep track of current events and the financial news. It can also prompt numerous questions and discussions as students try to apply course theory and tools to the real world. End of course marks can be assigned to each group given their portfolio's performance relative to that of other groups, or bonus points can be given for above average portfolio performance.

Tips for Using Cooperative Groups

Rooms and furniture Group work is easier when room furniture can be arranged to allow group members to face each. However, it is also possible in fixed-seat rooms if students are willing to sit on steps, the floor, desks, or turn in their seats.

Group size The optimal group size is usually between four and six. This is large enough for responsibilities to be shared and divisions within the group to be balanced; yet it is small enough that everyone has a chance to share ideas, and out-of-class meetings aren't too difficult to arrange. When groups are larger than six the dynamics can shift so that some students don't participate, and it is harder to arrange meetings if these must be held outside of class time. In smaller groups, three for example, two students can dominate or leave the third out of the group process. Less than four in a group can also make it difficult for complicated projects or assignments to be completed and still do a good job.

Forming groups It is best to have the instructor assign individuals to groups rather than let students select their own groups. This avoids problems with sub-groups caused when friends, roommates, or boyfriends and girlfriends cause others in the group to feel excluded. Instructor-formed groups also lessens the possibility that academically weak or strong students end up together causing uneven performance between groups.

The criteria the instructor uses for forming groups should be random or at least follow a visible pattern. Some instructors ask individuals to give themselves points for certain characteristics that may effect groups and then stand in order of their total and number off in to groups (e.g., 1 point for each year spent in the labor force, 4 points for being a senior, 3 points for juniors, and so on, 2 points for being an economics major, 1 point for being a non-major, 4 points for those with a 4.0 GPA, 3 points for a 3.0 GPA, and so on, 1 point for each decade in which they have lived, and so on). Numbering off by alphabetical order on the class list is another possibility, as is asking students to line up by height and number off, but these methods don't help to balance group composition by ability.

Individual and group accountability When grades are assigned for group work, it is advisable to provide for both individual and group accountability. This helps solve the "free rider" problem where a few students do most of the work and others make few contributions but benefit from a group grade.

One marking scheme is to ask each group to hand in a mark-consensus sheet signed by each group member. For example, if a group has five members, 5 marks are allocated by group consensus; if six members, 6 marks, and so on. Groups may allocate marks equally or in accordance with an individual's contribution to the group. If one group member does more work than others, he or she may be allocated more than one mark; if one person does less than others, he or she may be allocated less than one mark, and so on. For instance, if the group project receives an 85%, a person with 1.2 group-consensus marks receives 102% (= .85 X 1.2), and a person with 0.8 group-consensus marks receives 68% (= .85 X .8). It is important that the mark consensus sheet be handed in *before* the students know the project grade or in-group pressure may ensue to push an individual's mark allocation over certain grade thresholds rather than reflecting contributions to the group effort.

With this scheme a student may receive more marks than the assignment is worth, and therefore more than 100 marks (out of 100) for the course. If this is a concern, a limit can be set on the maximum number of marks an individual may receive for a group project. (e.g., an individual could be limited to 120% on any assignment.)

Another accountability scheme involves asking students to evaluate other group member's contributions at the end of the course. Then the group's entire project or assignment marks are allocated to individuals according to the average of the points given to him or her by other group members. An alternative is to ask group members to rate their own contribution to the group effort as well as the efforts of other group members. The individual then receives points depending on how close his or her self-evaluation is to other's evaluation of his or her contribution to the group.

Letting groups decide assignment weights When course grades are composed of individual and group efforts, groups can be allowed to decide, within some limits, how much of the course grade should depend on individual effort and how much on group effort. This method allows students to take more control for their marks and it often empowers and motivates learning and group effort (Michaelsen, Cragin and Watson, 1981).

Writing tests and exams for classes that emphasize active and cooperative learning When the course goal is teaching students to use economic tools to become effective thinkers and problem solvers, and a great deal of class time is devoted to helping students develop and practice these skills, tests and examinations must reflect and evaluate the accomplishment of this goal. Multiple choice tests that only ask for definitions, recall of information, and basic comprehension or short answer questions that require regurgitation of text or lecture material will not measure the more complex use of effective thinking skills. Therefore, tests and examinations, although they may include multiple choice questions, should be composed of questions that evaluate a student's effective thinking and problem solving skills. This means that well designed multiple choice, short answer, or essay questions which call for analysis and application skills are needed to ensure that students have met the course goal. (See Chapters 19–20.)

Projects and Assignment Do's and Don'ts

All assignments and projects are not suitable for group work (Michaelsen, 1992 and 1993). When designing and evaluating an assignment or project for small group work ask yourself the following four key questions:

1. Will this assignment promote *individual accountability*?
2. Will this assignment facilitate *learning of course concepts*?
3. Will this assignment *build group cohesiveness*?
4. Will this assignment facilitate *learning about the positive potential of group problem-solving and decision-making*?

Group assignments promote *individual accountability* if they:

- Make the level of individual members' preparation and participation visible to the instructor and/or their peers.
- Have a significant impact on the course grade.

Group assignments *facilitate learning the course concepts* if they:

- Require students to produce a *visible* product (preferably one that could be graded).
- Are challenging enough that they can *not* be successfully completed by any of the group members working alone.

- Cause students to engage in group discussions that are specifically focused on using course concepts.
- Allow students to practice using concepts to solve problems which are similar to those they will face *after* the class (or unit of instruction) has been completed.

Group assignments *build group cohesiveness* if they:

- Require input from a broad cross section of group members.
- Ensure that opportunities, efforts, and rewards are equitably distributed among group members.

Group assignments *facilitate learning about the positive potential of group problem-solving and decision-making* if they:

- Involve activities that groups do well (e.g., process information).
- Avoid activities that groups do poorly (e.g., create a polished document of any substantial length).

Examples of assignments that groups do well include one-minute position papers or other short writing projects, individual and group mini-tests with immediate scoring, and group projects or presentations where students are required to coordinate tasks and arrange to integrate individual contributions long before the project is due. Projects that allow comparisons with the work of other groups also add to motivation. Assignments that are not suited to effective group work include group projects or presentations that are not coordinated early and often end up being thrown together for a deadline, and lengthy papers where sections are written by individuals and the paper ends up being "collated by stapler" at the last minute.

Making the Change to Active and Cooperative Learning in Economics Courses

If you've been using the lecture as your main teaching tool, introducing active learning in your classes may seem at first like a loss of control or an abdication of your role as instructor, but a large number of instructors suggest it will help you teach students to become effective thinkers and problem solvers. And, after a few successes with active and cooperative learning strategies you'll likely wonder why you didn't use these strategies earlier. Many instructors find that their class attendance increases, students become more interested in the course material, and assignment and exam performance shows that more students develop effective application and analytical skills. Instructors also report that teaching becomes more interesting and exciting as they share the responsibility for learning with their students.

NOTES

1. Two course designs where cooperative learning is the dominant feature are guided design (Wales, et al., 1986 and 1987) and team learning (Michaelsen and Black, 1994). Both methods allow for lectures to be integrated with group work, but the group feature dominates. Guided design involves a series of tools and a strategy for their successful use. Students are explicitly guided through steps to solve problems and reach logical conclusions or decisions. *(Students can be given actual problems faced by firms, regulatory agencies, or state and local governments, and have their problem-solving processes and solutions compared with those produced by professional economists.)* Team learning features are: (1) permanent small heterogeneous student work groups, (2) grading that is based on a combination of individual performance, group performance, and peer evaluation, (3) the majority of class time is devoted to small group activities, (4) a six-step instructional activity sequence that focuses the majority of class time on helping students use course concepts and tools rather than just learn about them. An occasional lecture can be given to clarify problem areas or supplement material in the assigned readings. However, the majority of class time is spent with students actively involved in the learning process or watching the instructor explicitly model an effective thinking and problem solving process.

REFERENCES

Becker, W.E. and Watts, M. (1996). Chalk and talk: A national survey on teaching undergraduate economics. *American Economic Review Papers and Proceedings*, (May), 448-453.

Bligh, D.A. (1972). *What's the use of lectures?* Harmondsworth, Middlesex, England: Penguin Books.

Bonwell, C.C. (1992). Risky business: Making active learning a reality. *Teaching Excellence, POD Network in Higher Education*, 1992/93 Essay Series, 1–3.

Breen, W. and Boyd, J.H. (1976). Classroom simulation as a pedagogical device in teaching money and banking. *Journal of Financial and Quantitative Analysis*, 11(4), 595-606.

Cameron, N.E. (forthcoming, 1997). Classroom simulation of money supply expansion. *Economic Inquiry.*

Cooper, J., Prescott, S., Cook, L., Smith, L., Mueck, R., and Cuseo, J. (1990). *Cooperative learning and college instruction.* Long Beach, CA: California State University Institute for Teaching and Learning.

Halstead, J. (1989). SOVPLAN: An in-class simulation of central planning. *Economic Inquiry*, 27(2), 357-361.

McKeachie, W.J. (1994). *Teaching tips*, 9th ed. Lexington, MA: D. C. Heath.

McKeachie, W.J., Pintrich, P.R., Lin, Y., and Smith, D. (1986). *Teaching and learning in the college classroom: A review of the literature.* University of Michigan, Ann Arbor, MI: National Center for Research to Improve Postsecondary Teaching and Learning (NCRIPTAL).

Meyers, C. and Jones, T.B. (1993). *Promoting active learning: Strategies for the college classroom.* San Francisco, CA: Jossey Bass.

Michaelsen, L.K. (1992). Team learning: A comprehensive approach for harnessing the power of small groups in higher education. *To Improve The Academy*, 11(1), 107- 122.

Michaelsen, L.K. (1993). Do's and don'ts for small group assignments. In B. Cameron (ed.), *Teaching at the University of Manitoba: A handbook* (pp. 22-24). Winnipeg, Manitoba: University Teaching Services, University of Manitoba.

Michaelsen, L.K. and Black, R.H. (1994). Building learning teams: The key to harnessing the power of small groups in higher education. *Collaborative learning: A sourcebook for higher education*, 2. State College, PA: National Center for Teaching, Learning and Assessment.

Michaelsen, L.K., Cragin, J.P. and Watson, W.E. (1981). Grading and anxiety: A strategy for coping. *Exchange: The Organizational Behavior Reaching Journal*, 6, 8-14.

Siegfried, J.J., Saunders, P., Stinar, E., and Zhang, H. (1996). Teaching tools: How is introductory economics taught in America? *Economic Inquiry*, 34(1), 182-192.

Sinden, J.A. and O'Hanlon, P.W. (1981). A market simulation game to value unpriced goods and services. *Regional Science and Urban Economics*, 11(1), 101-119.

Starr, P. (1994). Seductions of Sim: Policy simulation game. *American Prospect*, 0(17), 19-29.

Wales, C.E., Nardi, A.H., and Stager, R.A. (1986). *Professional decision-making*. Morgantown, WV: West Virginia Center for Guided Design.

Wales, C.E., Nardi, A.H., and Stager, R.A. (1987). *Thinking skills: Making a choice*. Morgantown, WV: West Virginia Center for Guided Design.

Weimer, M.G. (1987). *Teaching large classes well: New directions for teaching and learning*, 32. San Francisco: Jossey-Bass.

Williams, R.B. (1993). Market exchange and wealth distribution: A classroom simulation. *Journal of Economic Education*, 24(4), 325-334.

CHAPTER 17

EXPERIMENTAL ECONOMICS
IN THE CLASSROOM

Charles A. Holt
Tanga McDaniel

If you are frustrated with how little students seem to retain from your standard lecture classes, you may wish to mix some classroom experiments into the schedule. Although the idea of using experiments in class has been around since the time of Chamberlin (1948), most applications are the product of recent research in experimental economics. This research is not intended to facilitate teaching, but the spinoffs include easy-to-explain setups in which the students are placed into the market or economic decision-making situation being studied. Even non-experimentalists have realized that these laboratory exercises can be effective teaching devices.

Classroom experiments are short, interactive exercises designed to facilitate understanding of key economic ideas. For example, students can be allowed to negotiate trades in a market where it is possible to compare their behavior with equilibrium predictions. In this manner, their first exposure to a particular economic concept is experiencing the economic incentives and forces first hand. In effect, they are producing the data that (with luck and carefully structured discussion) can allow them to discover relevant economic principles for themselves. We have found that this "bottom-up" participatory approach to learning can raise student interest and motivation. We believe that effective experiments can induce learning at a deeper level that results from being convinced about the usefulness of an otherwise abstract economic theory.

This chapter describes how to design and run teaching experiments, with simple props (no computers necessary). We begin with examples of basic market and game setups. Then we provide some hints about how to make such experiments more effective. Finally, we survey the various types of experiments that have been developed and the admittedly limited research on the effectiveness of this approach.

Some Examples

The two most popular types of classroom experiments are competitive markets and games. We begin with an example of each. These examples will get you started and will provide a context for the specific hints and suggestions in the subsequent section.

A Market Experiment The supply-and-demand model is the central concept of any introductory microeconomics course and the starting point of most macroeconomics courses. Students are often lulled into a false sense of understanding as they draw the smooth intersecting curves. This overconfidence may be mixed with skepticism when they go through the list of assumptions needed for "perfect competition." We have found that a market experiment is a useful way to begin the class, even before the presentation of the supply-and-demand model.[1] Playing cards can be used to eliminate the need for a lot of advance paper work. For example, the instructions in Holt (1996) begin:

> We are going to set up a market in which the people on my right will be buyers, and the people on my left will be sellers. Several assistants have been selected to help record prices. I will now give each buyer and seller a numbered playing card. Some cards have been removed from the deck(s), and all remaining cards have a number. Please hold your card so that others do not see the number. The buyers' cards are red (hearts or diamonds), and the sellers' cards are black (clubs or spades). Each card represents one "unit" of an unspecified commodity that can be bought by buyers or sold by sellers.

If the seller can arrange to sell the unit at a price above this cost, then the seller "earns" a profit that equals the difference between the price and the cost. Similarly, the number on a buyer's card is the monetary value of a "unit" to the buyer, and a buyer earns profit by arranging a purchase at a price that is below this value. A buyer with a 10 of diamonds, for example, would be willing to purchase a unit of the commodity at any price below $10, the lower the better.

Earnings in an experiment like this are not necessarily paid, and you can say this in advance, but to maintain interest it helps to pass out forms on which the students can keep track of their hypothetical earnings. A single page of instructions, with an earnings record form on the back, can be made up in advance, using the materials presented in Holt (1996), which also contains instructions for the assistants who record and verify prices. One advantage of these instructions is that the only advanced planning required is selecting the cards and copying the instruction sheets; the instructor does not have to write value and cost numbers for each period on these sheets.

After the cards are distributed and the instructions are read, the buyers and sellers are brought together in a trading "pit" where they can negotiate prices, as instructed:

> Buyers and sellers will meet in the center of the room (or other designated area) and negotiate during a 5-minute trading period. Prices must be multiples of 50 cents. When a buyer and a seller agree on a price, they will come together to the front of the room to report the price, which will be announced to all. Then the buyer and seller will turn in their cards, return to their original seats, and wait for the trading period to end. There will be several market periods.

Some of the high-cost sellers and low-value buyers may not be able to arrange mutually profitable trades, but the others form buyer-seller pairs. Prices are reported to an assistant who checks to be sure that the price for a buyer-seller pair is "legal," i.e., is above the seller's cost and below the buyer's value. Legal prices are announced aloud so the other traders can find out about the going prices. After the trading stops, the remaining cards are collected. While students return to their desks to calculate their earnings, the cards are counted, shuffled, and dealt again to traders prior to the start of the subsequent period. Prices typically stabilize around some general average after several periods of trade.

The numbers on the black cards given to sellers are the marginal costs that determine market supply (although this fact is not explained prior to the trading). Similarly, the numbers on the red cards given to buyers are marginal valuations that determine the market demand. Equilibrium prices are those for which the number of units demanded equals the number supplied, and this can be illustrated by drawing the (step-function) supply and demand curves or by counting up supply and demand directly. For example, consider the following configuration:

Black (spades or clubs):	2, 2, 3, 3, 4, 4, 4, 5, 5, 5, 7, 7, 7, 8, 8, 8
Red (hearts or diamonds):	10, 10, 9, 9, 8, 8, 8, 7, 7, 7, 5, 5, 5, 4, 4, 4

At a price of $6, there should be ten sellers who are willing to sell (those with costs of 2, 3, 4, and 5). Similarly, the ten buyers with values above $6 should be willing to purchase, so $6 is an equilibrium price.

The best procedure here is to lead the students into discovering the supply-and-demand model for themselves (whether or not they have previously seen general textbook presentations). One way is to reveal the card numbers *ex post* and focus discussion on what would (or did) happen out of equilibrium. A sequence of questions might be: if the initial prices were too low, say at $3, would there be more interested buyers than sellers, how would sellers respond to this buyer enthusiasm, and how high would prices rise in response? If you need to be convinced of the inadequacy of standard teaching methods, just reveal the card numbers (out of sequence), calculate price averages, and ask for a theory that explains the observed outcomes.

The result of this discussion will be a supply-and-demand array similar to the one shown in Figure 17-1. The price sequences are shown on the right side of the figure for four periods of trading; each dot represents a negotiated price in the order in which it was reported.[2] Period 1 began with three trades at $8, but all subsequent trades were in the equilibrium range. These data show a clear convergence to the competitive price and quantity predictions.

FIGURE 17-1   Data From a Classroom Market

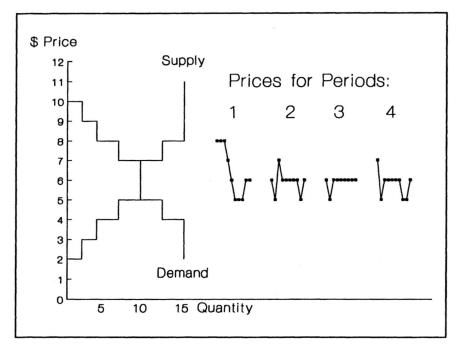

Students often want to find out about relative earnings, but it is useful to focus their attention on the total earnings of the group as a whole and on whether it is possible to reconfigure the trades to increase this total. This leads naturally to a discussion of surplus maximization and the efficiency of market allocations. There is a lot of public information about the going price; this information tends to keep low-value buyers and high-cost sellers out of the action. The result is that the market achieves 90-100% of the possible gains from trade for most supply-and-demand arrays, without the help of a perfectly informed and all-powerful planner. In fact, the contrast between the clarity of the competitive, surplus-maximizing outcomes and the complexity of the underlying theoretical assumptions could not be greater. If we had only one lecture to give to non-majors, it would be a classroom trading exercise designed to show how a decentralized market allocates resources efficiently.

Economic Games   It is also straightforward to use playing cards to implement many economic games. To get some feel for how students might perceive such a game, without knowing the context or purpose, please read the following instructions taken from Holt and Laury (forthcoming, 1997):

> This is a simple card game. Each of you will be given 4 cards, two of which are red (hearts or diamonds), and two of which are black (clubs or spades). The exercise will consist of a number of rounds. When a round begins, I will come around to each of you in order, and you will play two of your four cards by placing these two cards face down on your desk. I will pick up the cards you play and put them on top of the stack in my hand. Your earnings in dollars are determined by what you do with your red cards. For each red card that you keep, you earn two dollars for the period, and for each black card that you keep you will earn nothing. Red cards that are placed on the stack will affect everybody's earnings in the following manner. I will count up the number of red cards, and everyone will earn this number of dollars. Black cards placed on the stack have no effect on the count. When the cards are counted, I will not reveal who made which decisions, but I will return your cards to you at the end of the round (by returning to each of you in reverse order and giving you the top two cards off of the stack in my hand). To summarize, your earnings for the period will depend only on what people do with their red cards:
>
> your earnings = $2 times the # of red cards you kept +
> $1 times the total # of red cards that I collect from everyone, including yourself.

Are there any questions?

Each person has a *unilateral* incentive to keep the red card, worth $2 instead of playing it for a private gain of $1. However, as long as there are more than two people in the class, the aggregate earnings of the class as a whole go up when the red card is played. This is just a stylized public goods game where everyone has an incentive to free ride and not contribute (not play red). Notice that the black cards are used so that students cannot see and react to what the others ahead of them are doing.

The most convenient way to prepare the experiment is to print the instructions above a record form to be used by students to record their decisions and earnings. This form would have a row for each period (1-5) and 4 columns labeled: "period," "# red cards kept," "total # red cards played," and "cumulative earnings." Any change in treatment, like altering the payoffs, can be explained above the row for the period in which the change goes into effect. This experiment is less interesting for the subjects than the market experiment discussed previously, so it is a good idea to pick one person at random *ex post* and pay them some fraction of their earnings, in cash.[3]

The discussion can focus on the fact that we typically see a lot of free riding in this experiment, just as one would expect in economic situations where the cost of cooperating is high and the benefits are widely dispersed over a large group of others. Here you can offer an example (e.g., what if it were up to each individual to clear the snow in front of his own house) and ask the class for others. The discussion can also touch on whether there would be more selfish behavior in large groups (an anonymity effect) or whether there would be more cooperation in large groups (since there are more people who might benefit from an individual's generosity).

This public goods game is a type of prisoner's dilemma in which individual and social incentives differ. Indeed, the importance of the prisoner's dilemma paradigm is indicated by its inclusion in many principals books. Another simple prisoner's dilemma game can be set up by giving each student two numbered cards, say a 4 and a 6 (which correspond to dollar amounts). Students are paired, and each person decides which card to play. This decision is a choice between "pulling" $4 to oneself or "pushing" $6 to the other person.[4] Here, the cooperative outcome is for each person to "push" a 6, but the individually rational outcome is for each person to "pull" a 4. The discussion can focus on how cooperation may be affected by payoffs and repetition, and on what the results mean in terms of economic applications. For example, the point of modern bankruptcy law is to get investors in an insolvent firm out of a prisoner's dilemma in which each has a private incentive to demand loan repayment, but the firm would be worth more if it were allowed to continue after renegotiation of the debts.[5]

Practical Suggestions

This section discusses a number of factors you should keep in mind if you are planning to use experiments as a teaching aid: class size, the amount of time available, the subject and level, student motivation, and the nature of your current lectures.

Experiments which require many steps or props are obviously more difficult with large lecture classes. Many problems can be mitigated by advanced planning, however. Specifically, the design and procedures should be well planned, and it usually helps to have brief instructions, one page if possible, to hand out and to facilitate recording of decisions and outcomes. If you teach very large classes, you may consider using only a subset of the class as participants in the experiment.

In some cases it is necessary to devote an entire class period in order to allow for discussion of the results. To make the best use of time, it will be helpful to plan your discussion in advance. Specifically, think about what types of questions should be asked, and the clearest way to present the data. One way to begin a discussion is by asking leading questions such as those suggested in the market experiment described above. However, too many questions will give the answers away and may create boredom. Having students participate in recording data can be helpful, e.g., a student observer can plot transactions prices on a transparency with the same scale as the figure used to show supply and demand, as in figure 1.[6]

Because more issues in microeconomics lend themselves to experimental study, you will likely find more opportunities to use experiments in microeconomics courses.[7] As noted above, supply and demand and market efficiency are central concepts of all introductory economics courses; therefore, one of the best opportunities for using experiments may be in the very beginning of your principals classes (micro or macro) before these concepts are formally introduced. Classes that involve applications of game theory are also a good place to try simple experiments. This can be done easily by having students play the games themselves before the underlying theory is discussed.

Experiments can be useful in graduate classes as well, but on a more limited basis because of time constraints and subject matter. Some students from non-capitalist economies may be skeptical about the effectiveness of markets. By having them participate in market experiments they can observe for themselves how prices and quantities adjust in response to supply and demand.

Even if you teach non-economics majors you may find it beneficial to incorporate experiments. For instance, in general business classes one of the core concepts studied is bargaining. Many types of experiments have been designed to study various types of bargaining behavior, e.g., ultimatum and multilateral bargaining (see description below). In fact, several universities offer Practical Bargaining classes with significant amounts of in-class negotiations.

To maintain students' interest, try using experiments that are imaginative and rich in detail. As a research tool, experiments are often formatted in context-free language so as not to bias subject responses, but this is less of a concern for classroom experiments where the goal is to illustrate as opposed to test ideas. In fact, it is sometimes best in a classroom setting to actually tie the experiment to real economic applications. There is no fixed rule here, and the amount of richness depends on the context and the time available. Suppose that you ran the previous section's voluntary contribution experiment, but with playing a red card being associated with "working an hour on the church flower bed," and keeping a red card being associated with "watching football on TV." Here the context might dominate the admittedly minor economic incentives and divert discussion to issues of social morality. Similarly, the playing card version of the prisoner's dilemma game discussed above is quick and simple, and appropriate for generating a discussion of behavioral determinates of cooperation (e.g., repetition) in a game theory class. On the other hand, putting this game into a more complex, multi-person setting, as in the bankruptcy application discussed above, may be more appropriate for a class like Law and Economics where the focus is on the applications. For an international trade class, the prisoner's dilemma setup could be formulated and explained in terms of two countries in trade dispute. That is, although each country involved in 2-way tariff war would be better off if both countries would abolish all tariffs, each country may have a unilateral incentive to impose protectionist policies in order to secure political support from blocks of swing voters.[8]

Another way to encourage students to take the exercise seriously is to provide incentives. For example, tell students that one of them will be randomly chosen at the end of class and paid some fraction of his cumulative earnings. Incentives do not have to be monetary, however; non-monetary motivations can be just as effective in promoting serious participation in market experiments where student interest is likely to be high. In a somewhat less interesting prisoner's dilemma card game, we prefer to pay a randomly selected person, *ex post*. This practice also deflects questions about "What am I supposed to be trying to do?" Sometimes a simple solution can be effective and entertaining. One of us was giving a lecture on forecasting at Louis Pasteur University in Strasbourg on Valentine's Day. Correct forecasts were rewarded by passing out small red hearts (from a graffiti pack), and this seemed to stimulate a lot of interest in using past information efficiently.

Some people prefer to use extra credit as an incentive, e.g., Williams and Walker (1993). This no doubt raises student interest and motivation, but we see several potential problems.[9] First, extra credit raises anxieties, reduces the fun, and increases the burden on the instructor to allocate earnings opportunities in a fair manner. For example, a seller with high costs in a market experiment would be justifiably upset about losing extra credit as a result of low earnings. Second, to the extent that an implicit grade distribution is used, extra credit turns the situation into a zero-sum game, which gives students an incentive to be more rivalistic. Similarly, basing payments on points or competition between groups of students can misrepresent the relevant economic incentives in a subtle but harmful manner. For instance, all of your efforts to convince students that international trade is not a zero-sum game may be wasted if you have a trade experiment in which the reward goes to the group with the best economic performance relative to the others.

Kinds of Experiments

To make the best use of experiments in the classroom you should carefully consider which types of issues to address. We believe that the best use of classroom experiments is to illustrate important fundamental ideas that require a deep understanding (e.g., market efficiency), or abstract theoretical concepts (e.g., backward induction). It is especially true with abstract concepts that students may welcome discussions and demonstrations that make the ideas tangible and more concrete. In this section we list the various types of experiments that can be done easily in the classroom.[10]

Individual Decisions: Many policy issues are closely tied to measuring contingent valuations of non-traded goods, like environmental quality. In practice, these valuations are obtained with hypothetical questions about what one would be willing to pay for a specific good. It is interesting to compare the valuation numbers obtained form hypothetical questions with the numbers obtained from procedures designed to elicit true values (based on real economic commitments). For example, one can ask students what they are willing to pay for ball point pens, and then auction them off in a manner that elicits their maximum willingness to pay.[11] One way to do this is to show the students ten ball point pens and ask them to write their name and bid on a scrap of paper with the understanding that the bids will be collected and ordered, and the ten pens will be sold to the ten highest bidders at a price that equals the highest rejected bid (the eleventh highest bid). Other individual decision experiments can involve forecasting and Bayes' rule (Holt and Anderson, 1996) and information cascades (Anderson and Holt, 1996).

Auctions: These include first price, English, Dutch, and second price (Vickrey) auctions. In first price auctions, the person with the highest bid receives the auctioned good and pays the price he bids. The most exciting of these to run is a Dutch auction, with the price lowered sequentially until the first person calls out "mine" and purchases at that price. Here, the purpose can be to point out the wide variety of auction institutions that can be and are used around the world. In second price auctions the person with the highest bid receives the auctioned good but pays the second highest bid. The auction of ball point pens described in the previous paragraph is the n-prize analogue of a second price auction.

Bargaining: These include ultimatum and multilateral bargaining experiments. In an ultimatum game, a single player makes a take-it-or-leave-it offer to another player. In multilateral bargaining experiments, two players alternate making proposed divisions of a sum of money the total of which decreases after each rejected offer. It is also possible to let students bargain in an unstructured context with neither knowing the other's valuations or costs. Some discussion issues include: when are stalemates more likely, what are effective negotiation strategies, etc.?

Games: In addition to the Prisoner's Dilemma and Public Goods games described above, it is easy to use cards to implement other games. Of particular interest are games with multiple equilibria, such as the Battle of the Sexes and Chicken (this is a game useful for modeling defense strategies between counties). Also, Davis and Holt (1993, Chapter 2 appendix) describe how to use trays and coins to demonstrate the failure of backward induction in a Centipede game.

Markets: Students seem to enjoy interacting in market situations. These experiments can be used to illustrate the effects of monopoly power, price controls, and quality deterioration in "lemons" markets. Be warned, monopolists are not always successful at raising prices in a pit-market encounter with a group of buyers who negotiate prices sequentially. The monopolist has a stronger position if you require him to sell all units at a single price posted in advance (Davis and Holt, 1993, chapters 3 and 4).

Macroeconomics: The multi-market nature of macro models makes these exercises harder to implement, and the attempts that we know of often involve major commitments where the students interact repeatedly a number of times during the semester (Gremmen and Potters, 1996). It is possible instead to set up simpler situations that illustrate particularly difficult concepts, like costly search for a high wage or the inverse relationship between interest rates and bond prices.[12]

As you gain experience using various types of experiments and evaluate their usefulness for your own classes, you can stay updated on new approaches using the following sources: (i) The *Journal of Economic Education* contains articles about economic experiments in general; (ii) the "teaching tips" section of *Economic Inquiry* periodically contains notes on classroom experiments; (iii) The *Journal of Economic Perspectives* contains an ongoing column featuring short descriptions of various classroom exercises; and (iv) *Classroom Expernomics* is a newsletter put together by participants of a series of conferences at the University of Arizona on classroom experiments.[13] In addition, the Southern Economic Association and the Western Economic Association annual conferences now have sessions focused on experiments in the classroom. Also, classroom experiments are becoming increasingly available as part of the axillary material provided by textbook publishers (e.g., Delemeester and Neral, 1995).

Evidence on Effectiveness

Fels (1993, p. 69) is careful to point out that the extent to which experiments can be useful teaching tools depends on their quality, "Whether several experiments can make a real difference probably depends on how well they reinforce other material in the course." In assessing whether a particular series of experiments promotes learning and interest, it will be necessary to evaluate the overall quality of the program. To date, statistical evidence is hard to find. Gremmen and Potters (1996) conclude that experimental techniques can be effective in raising exam scores in a controlled comparison. In contrast, Cardell et al. (1996) report that standardized tests were not raised by an experimental treatment that included active learning, data analysis and classroom experiments. Most comments on the effectiveness of classroom experiments are admittedly subjective and anecdotal, e.g., DeYoung (1993) and Joyce (1996). Although the evidence on learning effectiveness from controlled comparisons is limited, we are confident that classroom experiments are useful in maintaining student interest and in promoting understanding of basic concepts. Classroom experiments require additional time to reinforce points that are covered in the regular lectures, so there is a tradeoff between depth and breadth of coverage. We believe that it is important to drive home the basic lessons about how and when markets allocate resources efficiently. Joseph (1965, p.565) concluded his discussion of classroom experiments by remarking: "It may well be that if we taught less, the students would learn more."

NOTES

1. Some early examples of classroom market experiments are found in Chamberlin (1948), Smith (1962), and Joseph (1965).

2. This price sequence is from a classroom experiment conducted in Tsukuba, Japan, with the instructions translated into Japanese by Steve Turnbull.

3. Random payment can be explained: "All earnings are hypothetical, except as noted below. You can use the space below to record your decisions, your earnings and your cumulative earnings. After we finish all periods, I will pick one person with a random throw of dice and pay that person 5% of his or her total earnings, in cash. All earnings for everyone else are hypothetical. To make this easier, please write your name: _____ and the identification number that I will now give each of you: _____. Afterwards, I will throw a 10-sided die twice, with the first throw determining the "tens" digit, until I obtain the ID number of one of you, who will then be paid 5% of his or her total earnings in cash."

4. Hal Varian has written a computer program that implements the playing card version of a prisoner's dilemma game.

5. Scott Bohannon developed a bankruptcy game as one of a series of experiments for a very popular Law and Economics class at the University of Virginia. The popularity of this class is indicated by the fact that about 200 students enrolled during the year (in a program with about 200 majors who graduate each year).

6. See DeYoung (1993) for some useful advice on presenting results in a market experiment. In particular, he suggests plotting a trader's price directly above the cost step if the person is a seller and directly below the value step if the person is a buyer. This allows students to visualize the split of the trading surplus and to spot inefficient trades of units to the right of the intersection of supply and demand.

7. Joyce (1996) suggests a number of classroom experiments for an intermediate microeconomics class.

8. Of course, the unilateral imposition of tariffs may reduce surplus-based welfare measures.

9. Some of these issues are discussed in Williams and Walker (1993).

10. Fels (1993) provides a list of published accounts of various experiments that have been used in classes, along with other information such as class sizes, the type of class (micro or macro), the type of reward used, and whether or not the experiment was computerized.

11. Davis and Holt (1993, chapter 8) discuss such elicitation procedures.

12. A sequential search computer program is available from the authors on request by email: holt@virginia.edu.

13. Past issues of *Classroom Expernomics* are available on the World Wide Web at http://www.marietta.edu/~delemeeg/expernom.html.

REFERENCES

Anderson, L.R. and Holt, C.A. (1996). Classroom games: Information cascades. *Journal of Economic Perspectives*.

Cardell, N.S., Fort, R., Joerding, W., Inaba, F., Lamoreaux, D., Rosenman, R., Stromsdorfer, E., and Bartlett, R. (1996). Laboratory-based experimental and demonstration initiatives in teaching undergraduate economics. *American Economic Review*, 86(2), 454-459.

Chamberlin, E.H. (1948). An experimental imperfect market. *Journal of Political Economy*, 56, 95-108.

Davis, D.D. and Holt, C.A. (1993). *Experimental economics*. Princeton: Princeton University Press.

Delemeester, G. and Neral, J. (1995). *Classroom experiments to accompany Taylor's economics: A user guide*. Boston: Houghton Mifflin Company.

DeYoung, R. (1993). Market experiments: The laboratory versus the classroom. *Journal of Economic Education*, 24, 335-351.

Fels, R. (1993). This is what I do, and I like it. *Journal of Economic Education*, 24, 365-370.

Gremmen, H. and Potters, J. (1996). Assessing the efficacy of gaming in economics education. *Journal of Economic Education*.

Holt, C.A. (1996). Classroom games: Trading in a pit market. *Journal of Economic Perspectives*, 10(1), 193-203.

Holt, C.A. and Laury, S.K. (forthcoming, 1997). Classroom games: Voluntary contributions to a public good. *Journal of Economic Perspectives*.

Holt, C.A. and Anderson, L.R. (1996). Classroom games: Understanding Bayes' rule. *Journal of Economic Perspectives*, 10(2), 179-187.

Joyce, B.P. (1996). Experiments and the intermediate micro class. *Classroom Expernomics*, 5(1), 1-3.

Joseph, M.L. (1965). Role playing in teaching economics. *American Economic Review*, 50(2), 556-565.

Smith, V.L. (1962). An experimental study of competitive market behavior. *Journal of Political Economy*, 70, 111-137.

Williams, A.W. and Walker, J.M. (1993). Computerized laboratory exercises for microeconomics education: Three applications motivated by the methodology of experimental economics. *Journal of Economic Education*, 24, 291-315.

CHAPTER 18

USING TECHNOLOGY FOR
TEACHING ECONOMICS

William B. Walstad

Ann Harper Fender

Jean Fletcher

Wayne Edwards

The opportunity to use technology for the teaching and learning of economics has never been greater. Instructors now have at their disposal sophisticated equipment, software programs, and computer networks for teaching. Instructors can bring in the world to class through the use of television and videocassette players. Microcomputers and the software programs permit students to learn economics at their own pace. The Internet lets students make connections between what they learn in class and resources throughout the nation and the world.

The problem for the economics instructor is to figure out how to make the best use of technology to enhance student learning. This task is a challenging one. The instructor must first spend time understanding how to use the technology. Then time must be spent deciding how it can best help students learn. The instructor must also be willing to accept the ever-present risk that teaching technology may not be very effective or live up to the expectations we have for it. For some, the time cost and risk may simply outweigh any benefits. For others, the benefits can be substantial and will far outweigh the costs as the technology opens up new possibilities for learning and makes teaching more interesting and exciting. The chapter seeks to increase the pool of instructors that fall into the latter group—those enjoying net benefits from an instructional investment in technology. To do so, the chapter first offers a historical perspective and then gives some practical suggestions for using technology to teach economics.

A Historical Perspective

Many instructors thought that the microcomputer would herald a new era for the teaching of economics. The reason that it would become an indispensable tool was because it could be used for problem solving, graphing, and quantitative analysis—skills which are given strong emphasis by economics instructors. Before this "new era" conclusion is accepted, the idea needs to be put in a historical perspective because the microcomputer is just one of many educational "innovations" over the years that was expected to revolutionize economics instruction.

In the 1960s, some thought television was going to dramatically improve economics instruction in the college classroom (Coleman, 1963). It did not have a profound effect because it is very difficult to replace labor with this technological capital in an effective and cost-efficient way. Television became another supplement for instruction—a complement to rather than a substitute for the teacher. The addition of videocassette players in the 1970s and 1980s gave economics instructors more flexibility over the use of television programs in the classroom, but it made the video technology no more effective as an instructional device. The same conclusion applies to the more recent introduction of videodisc players.

In the 1970s, computer instruction on the mainframe took center stage as the new educational innovation for teaching economics. Extensive research was conducted on computer-assisted instruction in economics, but the positive results were limited (Siegfried and Fels, 1979, pp. 940-42).[1] Computer-assisted instruction was found to generate no more (and no less) economic understanding than more conventional methods. The problem was the cost. This innovation cost instructor time to set it up, cost students time to use, and cost institutions the expense for equipment and maintenance. Computer-assisted instruction on the mainframe did not make sweeping changes in the economics curriculum because there were few cognitive benefits relative to the costs. The acceptance among economics faculty was limited to a few "dedicated" ones for whom the "psychic" benefits outweighed the costs.

What about the influence of the microcomputer as it rose to prominence in the 1980s? Microcomputer instruction in economics is certainly better than the mainframe use of the computer because it offers more flexibility for the instructor and students. Students also learn skills from a personal computer that can be easily taken with them once they leave the campus, which was not the case with mainframe instruction. Pre-college and college education in the use of microcomputers means that more students are trained to use this technology and may be more willing to accept its use for instruction.

In spite of the advances, little is known today about how much microcomputers get used for teaching economics courses. The evidence from software developers and surveys suggests that the instructor demand is low and classroom use is slight for microcomputer programs for teaching economics (Porter and Riley, 1992; Becker and Watts, 1996). Those instructors who like personal computers and economics software programs will find them effective for use in instruction, but it is doubtful that microcomputer use will be widespread across economics courses. Most courses are too "packed" to include microcomputer programs as anything more than a supplement to lectures and the texts, unless the instructor finds innovative ways to use the programs. There are also continual hardware upgrade and software compatibility problems at many campuses that limit instructor and student use. Sumansky (1986) noted over a decade ago that instructors see the programs as "appendages to a curriculum or a course in economics—optional but not integral, interesting but not important" (p. 486).

In the 1990s, the Internet gave new life to the microcomputers for economics instruction and opened up new possibilities for teaching. Computer networks permit students and instructors to improve communication via E-mail. They also facilitate searches for information and obtaining data for research projects. Instructors can establish homepages that contain assignments and course information. It is doubtful, however, that the Internet will completely alter economics instruction given the past history of technological innovation in the subject. The effects will be positive, but more modest than expected in spite of what the truly committed claim can be done.

With this perspective in mind, we can now turn to three different types of technology and offer suggestions on how instructors might go about achieving above average returns on this investment for classroom instruction. We begin with a brief look at television and videotapes, then turn to spreadsheets and microcomputer tutorials, and finally discuss teaching applications for the Internet.

Television and Videotapes

Televisions and videocassette players are now relatively inexpensive and widely available in many college classrooms. The instructor who wants to use television can show an economics program from a prepared videotape series or a video clip from a commercial broadcast of economics news and reports.

The most recent example of a new videotape series and textbook for the principles course is *Economics USA* (Mansfield and Behravesh, 1995). These programs use events from American economic history to present macro- or microeconomic principles to students and to acquaint students with the economic decisions that policy-makers faced with those events. When used on a selective basis, the 30-minute programs offer variety and can be used to supplement lectures and the textbook materials. Television programs such as this one give instructors a distinct alternative to the traditional lecture.[2]

Instructors can also videotape current television programs and show them to students to illustrate an economic concept or apply economic principles to current economic events. The sources for programs vary greatly, but several provide a reliable stream of economic reports that can be used for instruction. Economics segments can be videotaped from nightly news broadcasts by *ABC*, *CBS*, *NBC* or *CNN*. For example, the unemployment rate is announced monthly. When there is an economic report associated with the unemployment rate announcement it can be shown to students to make the connection between what is presented in the textbook and real events. More extensive economic reports and stories can be obtained from such programs as *Moneyline*, the *Nightly Business Report*, or *Adam Smith's Money World*. The views of economic experts are often found in *C-Span* broadcasts of speeches, panel discussions, and hearings before Congressional committees. Regular news reports from other nations (e.g., *NHK* from Japan) are often shown on educational channels, and can offer students a different national perspective on economic issues and events.

Some Suggestions The real challenge with the use of television in the classroom is not finding economics programs to show, but making it an active rather than a passive learning experience. Just showing the videotape and hoping that students will learn something from it will not be very effective. Students have grown up watching so many television programs that it is difficult for them to think critically when they view a videotape and extract the key ideas. Students consider videos a way to pass time or be entertained. The instructor, therefore, needs to make a clear connection between what is discussed in class, or presented in the textbook, and what students see on the tube. What follows are a few suggestions to make the use of television more effective for instruction.

First, know what economic concept or set of concepts you want the videotape segment to illustrate. A television program or video clip can cover a great deal of material, some central to the course and others completely extraneous. Pick the key points and build instruction around them. *C-Span*, for example, annually shows the lengthy Congressional testimony of the Federal Reserve Chairman on the goals of monetary policy. It is neither interesting nor instructive for students to watch the whole testimony. A portion of it, however, that focuses on a few concepts you presented in class can add relevance to the topic of monetary policy that might otherwise seem quite abstract when simply read about in a textbook.

Second, prepare your students to see the videotape. You should tell students why you are using valuable class time to show a videotape segment. Help them make the connection between what you discussed in class and what they will see. Giving students a few questions to answer when viewing the videotape will focus their attention on the central ideas.

Third, make the post-viewing experience as active as possible. Follow-up with a class discussion of the questions you asked students to answer. You might also have students turn in written answers to your questions. Indicate how the videotape content might be used on quizzes and exams. The key idea is to design active learning activities to engage student thinking about what they have seen and counteract the passivity of just watching a sequence of images.

Fourth, when possible use shorter rather than longer videotape segments. Student attention wanes considerably as a video program is shown. If a video program is long (more than ten minutes), it is best to stop it at different points and check that students understand what they saw and preview what they will soon see. A better alternative than to have students view a full class program is to show them just part of a program or a short video clip. This approach can be used to highlight key points without putting students into a passive viewing mode.

Microcomputer Software

The possibilities for using microcomputer software for teaching economics has improved dramatically in the past decade (Boyd, 1993). There are now spreadsheet programs that can be used by the instructor to create problem solving exercises and simulations/games for students. Publishers have produced an array of tutorials, simulations/games, graphics packages, and testing software to accompany their economics textbooks, especially for principles of economics. There are many instructional computer programs developed by professors for use in particular courses. We turn now to a brief description of the major types of instructional software, and assess their advantages and disadvantages.

Spreadsheet Exercises Simple economic experiments have been shown to be very effective in fostering understanding of the functioning of markets (see Chapter 17). Student learning can be reinforced during the experiment by using spreadsheet programs, such as *Excel*, *Quattro Pro*, or *Lotus*, to produce tables and graphs using the data on which the experiment is based.

In a micro principles course, for example, students can participate in a double oral auction. In such an experiment, students designated as buyers are each given a maximum value to pay for the product, while sellers are each given an amount that is the minimum they are to accept. Buyers and sellers try to maximize their surplus through their bargaining skills, and negotiated prices are posted at the conclusion of each trading period. At the conclusion of several rounds (prices usually converge after only 2 or 3 trading sessions), students are given the underlying data and asked to construct a graph of supply and demand functions, determine the equilibrium price, and compare it to the convergence price for the experiment.

The following table shows the typical information about the buyers and sellers in a market that students might be given:

Buyer ID #	Maximum will pay	Seller ID #	Minimum will accept
1	4	1	4
2	6	2	6
3	8	3	9
4	11	4	13
5	14	5	17
6	19	6	22
7	24	7	28
8	30	8	35
9	36	9	43

Having already graphed problems from the text, students know they must have "price" and "quantity demanded" columns to graph demand and "price" and "quantity supplied" columns to graph supply. It is interesting to observe how frequently students who seem to understand the theory from the text initially have trouble constructing demand functions from the information provided by the double oral auction experiment. The two most common errors are assuming only one buyer at each price and using buyer ID numbers as quantities demanded. Either results in graphs students quickly recognize as nonsensical. Realizing they have to add up the number of consumers willing to buy at each price reinforces the concept of demand more effectively than reading or hearing about it.

Spreadsheet applications can be advantageous in supporting many other ideas from the principles courses. Income effects, substitutes, and complements are clearer if students use equations to represent demand functions and graph them. The ease of data transformation and the visual examples so readily available on the computer screen make it easier for students to understand the difference between intercept and slope adjustments. The students are also less reluctant to practice these skills than is typically the case when assigned exercises require graphing and tabular manipulation by hand. In fact, many end-of-chapter problems or exercises are easily adapted as computing projects for lab sessions or course assignments.

Spreadsheets can also be effectively used at the intermediate level to make abstract concepts more concrete. One of the goals of intermediate theory courses is to give students an appreciation for the mathematical basis of microeconomic theory. Using spreadsheet or graphics software reinforces students' understanding of economic concepts as mathematical functions. In intermediate theory, students are asked to use graphical representations to illustrate mathematical solutions. Also, computer projects that were developed to teach principles of economics can be revised for use at the intermediate level by increasing the complexity of the assignments and by using more sophisticated mathematical functions.

For example, students can be given a set of production functions (or utility functions) and asked to determine whether the isoquants (or indifference curves) are strictly convex. After testing mathematically for convexity, they must confirm the finding graphically. This requires students to understand that an isoquant (or indifference curve) is obtained by arbitrarily choosing a production level, solving for capital input as a function of labor input and graphing the function. Similarly, graphs can be used to confirm solutions to other questions, such as whether production functions exhibit diminishing returns. When giving assignments like these, it is probably best to provide minimal guidelines and allow the students to figure things out. A typical assignment would be a list of three production functions with instructions to give both mathematical and graphical evidence on whether they exhibit: (1) diminishing returns, (2) convex isoquants, and (3) increasing, constant, or diminishing returns to scale.

A primary advantage of using spreadsheet exercises is that they force the student to apply what they see in the textbook graphs to the computer screen. The process of drawing a supply or demand curve or solving an equation and seeing the results on the computer screen can actively reinforce through another medium what the student reads about in the textbook. A possible disadvantage is that spreadsheet exercises may not be very interesting or exciting for the students, and they may not be any more effective than traditional paper and pencil graphing or problems. The spreadsheet exercises also take time for the instructor to develop, which may explain why some instructors turn to prepared tutorials.

Tutorials Publishers of textbooks have concentrated their development of software on drill and practice exercises, tutorials, and problem sets to complement the textbook used by the instructor.[3] The main justification for tutorial software lies in the complexity of the material. As most instructors know from years of teaching, economics is difficult for students to master. A tutorial provides a way of reinforcing the text and classroom presentations without spending additional instructor or class time on a topic. They can be an exciting alternative to a traditional study guide or workbook.

One example of a comprehensive tutorial program is *DiscoverEcon*. It is designed for use with the McConnell and Brue *Economics* principles text (13th edition). In this tutorial, there are modules for all chapters of the textbook. In each module, a narrative introduction is provided, and several multiple choice questions appear to test the user's understanding of the material as he or she progresses. In most cases, at least one exercise (which is a group of related questions) is included, as well as one or more essay question. The exercises are set up so that the questions and the user's responses can be printed out and turned in for homework. This is especially useful for the essay questions where little feedback is available from the program. For the exercises and multiple choice questions, the program provides correct responses for any questions the user answered incorrectly.

A companion program to *DiscoverEcon* is *Interactive Key Graphs Tutorial*. The orientation of this program, as its title indicates, is graphical analysis. Establishing a separate program for graphical examples is worthwhile, given that it is a primary instructional tool employed in principles classes and that many students find graphs particularly challenging. Twenty-one modules are included in this program. Most allow the user to request changes be made, such as shifts in the curves, to demonstrate the impact of these changes. Using *Interactive Key Graphs Tutorial* together with *DiscoverEcon* gives students an independent means of studying the course material. These programs also make it easier to use the computer with traditional methods because of the ability to print out exercises as homework.

Tutorial software is not without problems. They may cover the content, but often not in the most imaginative way. Students need to be sufficiently motivated and interested to learn economic content from a drill-and-practice exercise. It can be tempting for students to just press the return key to find the correct answer without really thinking about the problem and solving it. The software is also "captive" in the sense it is tied to the textbook and is usually not a free-standing commodity. The quality of the software also varies because textbook companies may not have a great deal of incentive to produce software that is another ancillary for a textbook (Porter and Riley, 1992).

Simulations/Games   While the primary microcomputer contribution of text publishers to economics courses has been tutorial software, the primary contribution from instructors and private developers has been simulations/games (Post, 1985).[4] Instructors may prefer them because they have more potential for getting students involved in the course content than do drill-and-practice tutorials or spreadsheet problems. Simulations allow students to make decisions and examine their effects on the modeled phenomena, so that they become active rather than passive learners in the decision-making process. Games use competition to excite students and give them an incentive to cover the material. A simulation/game combines the best features of each to get students to look at complex situations. A simulation/game will not guarantee student interest, but when well constructed it can generate excitement and serve as an effective instructional device.

Oligopoly models, for example, lend themselves to either experiments or simulations/games. After covering four models (Cournot, Bertrand, Stackelberg, shared monopoly) in class lectures, students can be grouped into teams (each team represents a firm). Each team, knowing only their own cost functions, must make production decisions without knowing what the industry demand function is or what the production decisions of competitors are. After each team has disclosed production amounts, the market price is revealed by the game director. Teams must calculate profit at the end of each round, and they derive the demand function from the results of sequential rounds of production decisions. Then they must decide on a strategy for future production given the behavior of competitors. This simulation/ game is successful in demonstrating demand interdependence and illustrating game theory explanations of oligopoly behavior.

Depending upon time and resources, these simulations/games can be very complex (multiple firms and nonlinear demand functions) or very simple (duopolies with linear demand and constant marginal cost). The line fitting capabilities of most spreadsheet packages allow students to easily "discover" demand equations for standard functions (e.g., linear, polynomial, logarithmic, expotential). For linear models, students only need to observe two rounds of decisions and algebraically solve for the demand equation. For more complicated functions, the instructor can provide a table of historical price and quantity results or set up a simulation so that students can generate a data sample to determine the demand function. Students can then calculate the appropriate production quantity based on one of the oligopoly models (specified by instructor or left to team discretion). Class discussion of solutions and behavior strategies devised by teams is usually lively and instructive.

The penetration of microcomputer simulations/games into economics courses is still limited. Most simulations/games do not explicitly present an economic concept and may cover many interrelated concepts. There is more teaching responsibility for the instructor and scarce class time must be used to make certain that students understand the concepts underlying the simulation/game. The programs also vary in quality and may be difficult to use or expensive to obtain from private developers or commercial vendors. Thus, the use of simulations/games in economics courses, already overcrowded with other content, requires more determination by the instructor to make it more valuable than traditional lecture and discussion.

Some Considerations The microcomputer and economics software can enhance teaching and learning, but this cannot be done without foresight and work by the instructor. Here are a few general points to consider.

First, know what concept or concepts the software will illustrate for students and assess how well you think it does the job. Following this recommendation requires that you have a good understanding of the software program and how the students will actually use it. Don't give computer assignments or conduct simulations/games with students unless you have gone through the process of doing the exercise or playing the simulation/game yourself. Be sure to know whether the computer equipment that the students will use can handle the software.[5] Spend time identifying the key concepts that students will learn from using the software.

Second, avoid using microcomputer programs to do what can be more easily accomplished with more conventional methods. Ask yourself in what ways the high-tech software will do a better job presenting these ideas than conventional low-tech alternatives such as course transparencies, graphing the problem on graph paper, or completing a print study guide or workbook exercise. Spreadsheet exercises, tutorials, and simulations/games are most beneficial when they help students to understand a concept or evaluate their mastery of it with greater ease and at more depth than can be achieved with conventional methods. Will the new technology really improve student understanding or is it just a high-tech gimmick?

Third, figure out how you will integrate the use of software in your course. If spreadsheet exercises are used, what percent of the grade will be assigned for the completion of each assignment? How will you assess the learning from a game or simulation? What incentives will students have to do a spreadsheet exercise or tutorial? These and many other questions must be answered if software use is to be meaningful. You have to make a decision about whether you want software to be an integral part of the course, requiring your time to set it up and the student's time to use it, or simply a minor supplement to the textbook and your lectures.[6]

The Internet and World Wide Web

The Internet has the potential to become a valuable new tool for teaching economics, if an instructor can figure out how to make the use of it. The task can be a real challenge because the rapid pace of technological change makes it difficult to imagine the many uses and applications of the Internet for teaching economics that will emerge over the next decade. Economics instructors are currently using the Internet for teaching in three basic ways—for communication, obtaining information and data, and course projects. Each one is discussed in the following sections to indicate the many creative ways that the Internet is being used.

Communications Electronic mail (E-mail) is perhaps the most useful feature of computer networks that can be easily used by economics instructors with students (Manning, 1996). E-mail enhances communication between the instructor and student. The electronic messages arrive in the instructor's "mailbox" at any time, and a reply can then be given at the instructor's convenience. For easily answered questions, this method is often more expedient for the student than waiting until the instructor is available during office hours. E-mail lets both the student and the instructor initiate and respond when they have a free moment or have a pressing need (such as guidance on a homework problem). In addition, students who are reluctant to speak out in class or visit an instructor are encouraged by this quasi-anonymous form of communication to participate in the course and receive feedback from the instructor. E-mail will clearly become a more important communication vehicle for economics instructors in the future because it expands the opportunity to make connections with students.

Apart from communicating directly with one student, the instructor can use E-mail to send course information to all students at the same time. Some examples of materials which could be sent the include course syllabus, lecture notes, homework assignments, and test scores. This approach can reduce paper usage since the students can store and retrieve the information electronically. It also benefits students who missed a class meeting due to illness or some other unavoidable event (and at the same time it limits the excuse of not receiving the assignment when it was handed out). Students can also "hand in" assignments, or send a draft for comments from the instructor before the final version is due.

An E-mail discussion list can also be established for a course. Students can post questions (and comments) about course content that other students can read and answer. Students communicating with one another on course material is often a very useful way to learn. The instructor can set up a course discussion list on the university computer and students would then be able to reach across sections (and instructors) to ask questions and receive possible answers.

Apart from course-specific postings, the instructor can help students subscribe to "conferences" on economic topics through newsgroups and electronic bulletin boards. These topics are accessed by interested parties all over the United States and, indeed, the world, and thus provide an interesting source of commentary.[7]

Such a vast array of input, however, can be overwhelming. Students who use these discussion lists need to learn how to scan and sort postings to limit the amount of material they read.   A valuable project is to have students write a paper that summarizes the major points of controversy on an economic issue as found on the discussion list, and then asks for their perspective.

Information and Data Most university libraries allow electronic access to their card catalogues, which is a good starting point for showing students how to access information on the Internet.   Students can search for books and articles, not only in their home library, but virtually any university in the United States and abroad. Search time for the student is minimized because a source can be pinpointed before ever going to the library. In many cases, requests for interlibrary loans or reprints of journal articles can be made electronically. Any time-saving procedure that reduces barriers to completing a project and makes access easier to resource materials should help improve the quality of a term paper or report.

Another instructional opportunity created by the Internet comes from the economic and financial information that can be quickly and conveniently found to add a "real world" dimension to a class topic. In macroeconomics courses, for example, students can be assigned to track current economics statistics such as GDP growth rates, unemployment rates, interest rates, inflation rates, or productivity so that they see the connection between what is written in the textbook and what is reported in the media. Students can also access newspapers and magazines (e.g., *New York Times, Washington Post, Business Week*, or *The Economist*) for more in-depth reporting of economic and financial news in both macro- or micro-oriented courses. During the semester, students can be assigned to find a course-related economics article, write a summary or report on it, and submit it to the instructor via E-mail along with a copy of the article. Students are more likely to participate in this information gathering and reporting because it reduces the opportunity cost associated with conventional library searches for newspapers and magazine articles.

Once the student (and instructor) moves beyond basic library and news media information, the variety of resources that can be used for teaching or research are extensive.   There are on-line data bases, such as those of the Bureau of Labor Statistics, Federal Reserve System, and other governmental or private organizations. If students are required to do any research where such data are used in a term paper or project, the Internet is often the best tool for acquiring data from these organizations.   There are also on-line journals, papers, reports, government documents, and other items that can be used for research projects. With the enormous resources available, finding the information you or students need can be especially difficult.   The best resource for reducing search costs for you or advanced students is Bill Goffe's *Resources for Economists on the Internet*, which can be easily accessed via the Internet.[8] The guide is designed for economists, but instructors can use it to design research projects and guide students to particular relevant sources of information.

Course Webpages   One instructional use of the Internet that puts together the best of its communication and information features is the development of a World Wide Web site for a course.[9] Course pages can include a syllabus, lecture or class notes, assignments, reference materials, and feedback that permit better graphics and more detail than in typical E-mail listings previously discussed. Of particular value are the "hot links" that connect to the course materials to other relevant sites on the web. The student simply clicks on the hot link and is connected to the source site and whatever information it contains. These links have the potential to encourage students to choose which information avenues to pursue, and get them more actively involved in the course materials or assignments.

Creation of a website for a course requires use of a web browser and software such as *Netscape*. Many books are available on how to create homepages and computer magazines feature frequent articles about using the web and creating a homepage. Most campuses have workshops on creating a homepage that enable the instructor to create one within a few hours of finishing the training. Economics faculty are building course web sites at an impressive rate as the time cost of creating one is becoming smaller with new software and as more instructors develop and share their expertise. Many course sites can be found on the homepages of economics departments and can be located using a web search engine, such as *Yahoo*.[10]

A more active learning use of the web is to have students create individual parts of a course page. To do so, the instructor creates the framework for the course page using hyper text markup language (html). The instructor determines the basic page design and content. It typically contains information about the course and instructor, perhaps the syllabus, a summary of links to relevant references, and a listing of student names. The student names can be organized individually, or divided into groups for collaborative work. Each student or group of students creates a file name for the work done for the course, and the instructor creates links on the course homepage to the work produced by the students.

The student file contains that student's coursework which is on-going so the file grows over the semester. It can include brief weekly response papers to questions posed in class, links to materials the student finds relevant to assigned papers, links to other students' sections of the homepage, links to work done in other courses that is on a homepage, annotated bibliographies of source material found on the web with links to the sources, and either full papers which the student has written for the course or abstracts of the full texts. In this way, the course website can be integrated with assigned papers, further emphasizing via the public nature of the web that a person writes to communicate with others. What the web adds to traditional writing assignments is the opportunity for individual assignments to be integrated with other assignments, with work in other courses, with other classmates' work, and the broader world of economic thinking and research that is accessible through the network.

Examples In an introductory micro course taught by two authors of this chapter, students are evaluated through weekly multiple choice quizzes, a final comprehensive exam, and individual and group writing assignments using the web. The writing assignments are typically four mid-length papers (4-5 pages each) on different topics listed in the course syllabus. The topics require the student to relate course material to past or present issues that involve public policy. The assignments stress evaluating the efficiency and equity implications of the economic issue and the alternative policies designed to address the issue. The individual's written work is then put on the student page of the web site for the course. In addition, students work together in groups to devise a policy to address a socioeconomic problem (e.g., poverty). The written narrative for each group project is brief and summarizes the group's proposal. This proposal is put on the course website, and each group also presents its project orally and visually to the rest of the class near the end of the semester. The instructor assigns a single grade to the project, and, all group members receive the group grade.

In this course, all students attend three hours of class and one hour of lab per week. Student associates conduct the lab under the supervision of the faculty member. In the labs, students participate in economic experiments, do group work on computational and graphical worksheets, and are given instruction in using html to create individual and group webpages. Students who know how to create web pages are often quite willing, and eager, to share their knowledge with peers and instructors. Although some might argue that the brief time devoted to creating html documents might be better spent on further content instruction, it is not certain it would add much to student learning. Instead, the web projects seem to generate student enthusiasm for the course and encourage conversation among students about economic issues that has more beneficial effects on learning.

An intermediate micro course can also use the web in a way similar to the introductory micro course that was previously described. Early in the semester, students are divided into groups to study an industry. The groups of three to four students can be self-formed or each student might be asked to list several industries of interest, with the instructor forming groups based on revealed interests. Each group develops an industry file which the instructor links to the course homepage. The industry file includes sections describing the general condition in the industry, examining industry supply and demand conditions, and analyzing microeconomic problems facing the industry and possible solutions. The industry file contains text, data, and graphs relevant to the microeconomic conditions of the industry. Group members also search the web for information relevant to the industry.

In addition to participating in the group project, each student writes critiques of two journal articles for the course. The first reviews an article related to consumer behavior and demand; the second critiques an article relating to supply conditions or market failure. Students are urged to locate articles related to the industries they are studying, thereby creating a beginning bibliography for each group's industry study. The critiques are linked to the course homepage and each group can link the critiques to its industry project. Students discover that they also can relate work of students outside the group to a particular group's industry project.[11]

Each group makes three brief presentations to the class during the course: one on demand, one on supply, and one on policy proposals relevant to the group's industry. The presentations include a demonstration of the group's developing contributions to the course homepage. Clearly this is time taken from lecture and other class activities. Limits on time allotted to each presentation reduce the time taken and also give students incentives to organize and choose words carefully. Giving students take-home rather than in-class exams also frees two to three class periods for the presentations. The presentations, followed by questions and faculty comment, can usefully complement lectures and can extend the material already covered. In classes that follow the presentations, reference to particular presentations can be used to reinforce the points being made.

Some Implications As in the past, new technology such as the Internet will not completely alter economics instruction, but there are likely to be some changes from it. *First, economics instructors need to prepare for a different role in teaching when using the Internet.* Instructors should spend less time presenting information and more time giving students a framework for processing information when using the Internet. With the Internet, the instructor serves more as a coach, a facilitator, or a reactor than as a direct conveyor of information or course controller. The use of the Internet also means that there will be more demands on the instructor to tie the course content to the "real world," and fewer excuses for why this cannot be done, especially in such a timely and rich subject as economics.

Second, group work will be facilitated and encouraged in economics courses that use the Internet. The Internet lets students easily work on small group projects outside of class. There is greater collaboration and sharing among groups and individuals than is possible in a traditional classroom. This possibility alters the group dynamics from large-group to small-group discussion. It will also change evaluation practices from grading based solely on individual achievement to grading based on a combination of individual and group performance. The ability to work with others to produce a project becomes as important as the ability to complete a project alone. Economics instructors need to figure out a way to take advantage of the many new opportunities for group work.

Third, an economics course should be more satisfying for the students when the Internet is used for teaching. The Internet lets instructors communicate more easily with students, and vice versa. This means that the instructor can use the technology to give better guidance and feedback that meets individual needs, and that students can easily seek help from the instructors. Students can also communicate more easily with each other, which can be used to reinforce learning, do group work, and strengthen course participation. In addition, the barriers to obtaining information or knowledge are lowered, thus reducing student frustration with course material. These communication and information factors, if harnessed properly, should contribute to greater student satisfaction with an economics course.

Conclusion

Instructional technology has great potential to reduce reliance on the traditional lecture method which is so embedded in the teaching of undergraduate economics. Whether instructional technology—be it television, microcomputer programs, or the Internet—significantly improves student learning is far from certain because of the number of factors involved in making the technology effective. The most important one is the willingness of the instructor to spend time learning about the technology and designing ways that it can be used to help students learn. The instructor must also be willing to take the risk of using the new technology with students. Improvements in technology and the greater availability of instructional technology on campuses are reducing the investment costs and eliminating a great deal of the risk for the individual instructor. The experiences of those who have invested the time and accepted the risk suggests that incorporating new technology in a course is worthwhile for both students and the professor. It adds variety and interest that go well beyond what is possible in traditional instruction. It rejuvenates a professor's enthusiasm for teaching and reinforces the commitment to student learning. More economics instructors should accept the challenge.

NOTES

1. Schenk and Silva (1984, p. 240) offer several explanations for the lack of positive CAI results that have to do with the poor quality of the computer materials and poor classroom use. These criticisms also apply to microcomputer programs, although software development has improved (Porter and Riley, 1992; Boyd, 1993).

2. Professor Timothy Taylor gives twenty lectures on micro- and macroeconomics which are on four videotapes as a series called *Economics: An Introduction*, (Teaching Company of Springfield Virginia) [1-800-TEACH-12].

3. Previous reviews of text-related economics software can be found in Walbert (1989) and Yoho and Walstad (1990). A review of software available from textbook publishers in economics that is partially complete can be viewed on the World Wide Web at *http://www.cba.unl.edu/eced/ncree/reviews/review.htm.*

4. Many examples of classroom computer simulations/games or experiments developed by instructors can be found in the *Journal of Economic Education* (for examples, see the Fall 1993 and Fall 1995 issues).

5. Two problems that limit the use of microcomputer software in instruction is the availability of hardware and software incompatibility across machines. These problems seem to be on-going because new programs require more sophisticated equipment and new operating software makes instructional software dated. Colleges and universities struggle to upgrade their computer stock to meet the changing demands of the computer software and new technological developments.

6. There is a need for empirical research on the effectiveness of computer software, no matter what type is used. Whether students learn more or their attitudes improve from using such programs remains a matter of some speculation. Porter and Riley (1996), report

positive results from computer exercises, but they were done in introductory statistics with only a small sample of students.

7. One of the indirect benefits of the Internet is that it lets students obtain an international perspective on an economic issue or question. Students can interact with individuals from other nations or obtain economic information from other countries.

8. The guide is available free of charge and is updated quarterly by Professor Goffe. One easy way to get a copy of this report is to send an E-mail to: *econ-wp@econwpa.wustl.edu* with a subject line that reads: *get econ.faq*. The guide can also be located on the web at *http://econwpa.wustl.edu/EconFAQ/EconFAQ.html*.

9. For examples of course webpages, visit the EconEd Web at:
   http://ecedweb.unomaha.edu.

10. By selecting the "view" option at the top of the Netscape framework and then choosing "source" under that option, one can examine the instructions which generated that course homepage. Those instructions can be copied and pasted into the editor being used to create the homepage, then adapted to the particular course being taught. The potential user can see examples by opening "file" on the Netscape menu, then opening "open location." A box will appear, in which the viewer types an URL, or universal resource locator. For an example of the URL for introductory economic classes visit:
   http://www.gettysburg.edu/~fendera/econ103s96.

11. Examples of the intermediate micro web pages can be found at:
   http://www.gettysburg.edu/~fletcher/econ245.html and at:
   http://www.gettysburg.edu/~fendera/econ245.top.html.

REFERENCES

Becker, W.E. and Watts, M. (1996). Chalk and talk: A national survey on teaching undergraduate economics. *American Economic Review*, 86(2), (May), 448-453.

Boyd, D.W. (1993). 'The new microcomputer development technology' implications for the economics instructor and software author. *Journal of Economic Education* 24(2), (Spring), 113-125.

Coleman, J.R. (1963). Economic literacy: What role for television. *American Economic Review*, 53(2), (May), 645-652.

Manning, L.M. (1996). Economics on the Internet: Electronic mail in the classroom. *Journal of Economic Education*, 27(3), (Summer), 201-204.

Mansfield, E. and Behravesh, N. (1995). *Economics USA*, 4th ed. New York: W. W. Norton.

McConnell, C.R. and Brue, S. (1996). *Economics*, 13th ed. New York: McGraw-Hill Book Company.

Porter, T.S. and Riley, T.M. (1992). CAI in economics: What happened to the revolution? *Journal of Economic Education*, 23(4), (Fall), 374-378.

Porter, T.S. and Riley, T.M. (1996). The effectiveness of computer exercises in introductory statistics. *Journal of Economic Education*, 27(4), (Fall), 291-299.

Post, G.V. (1985). Microcomputers in teaching economics. *Journal of Economic Education*, 16(4), (Fall), 309-312.

Schenk, R. and Silva, J.E. (1984). Why has CAI not been more successful in economic education: A note. *Journal of Economic Education*, 15(3), (Summer), 239-242.

Siegfried, J.J. and Fels, R. (1979). Research on teaching college economics: A survey. *Journal of Economic Literature*, 17(3), (September), 923-69.

Sumansky, J. (1986). College economics and the computer revolution. *Social Science Microcomputer Review*, 4(4), (Winter), 480-486.

Walbert, M.S. (1989). Grading software programs accompanying selected principles texts. *Economic Inquiry*, 27(1), (January), 169-178.

Yoho, D.L. and Walstad, W.B. (1990). Microcomputer software for the principles of economics course. In P. Saunders and W.B. Walstad (eds.), *The principles of economics course: A handbook for instructors*. New York: McGraw-Hill, 161-179.

CHAPTER 19

MULTIPLE CHOICE TESTS
FOR THE ECONOMICS COURSE

William B. Walstad

The evaluation of students is one of the most taxing responsibilities for economics instructors. To make that task easier, multiple choice tests are often administered. Ease of use, however, provides no guarantee of the test quality. Test constructors must have solid understanding of this fixed-response method if they are to assess student knowledge in a course with any degree of accuracy.

This chapter is designed to help economics instructors make better multiple choice tests, whether they are used in principles or intermediate economics courses.[1] The first section discusses the positive features of multiple choice tests because many instructors are not aware that this method is often superior to the essay method for evaluating students. The second section outlines procedures for constructing mid-term or final exams, and presents guidelines and examples of how questions should be prepared for multiple choice tests. The third section explains how the statistical analysis of the test data can be used to identify weaknesses in questions and to improve the quality of future tests. The final section suggests how to prepare students for multiple choice exams and use them for classroom learning.

The Case for Multiple Choice Testing

Multiple choice tests have distinct advantages over the other major alternative, the essay test, or its short-answer derivative. The most compelling advantage arises from the constraints facing teachers. When class sizes are large, it is time-consuming to grade essays and more difficult to give quick feedback to students. Spending hours reading essays means less time available for other duties—preparing lectures and materials, seeing students, serving on committees, and conducting research. The grading time for multiple choice tests is negligible—a major benefit for instructors.

Some instructors think that the economy in scoring offered by multiple choice tests cheapens the education of students. Personal preference aside, there is no established evidence to suggest that multiple choice tests are less effective ways to measure student achievement in economics. In fact, multiple choice tests provide more objective assessments of economic understanding because there is no bias in scoring. Bias in essay scoring comes from such factors as knowing the name of the student, the mood of the instructor, the order in which essays of the class are read, how many times the essays are read, and the importance given to matters of composition. None of these sources of bias enter the scoring of multiple choice tests. Fixed-format questions are also highly structured with one correct answer, and contain none of the vagueness that affects the grading of essays.

Another benefit comes from the ability to sample the content domain. A look at the content of economics textbooks shows that there are a multitude of topics covered in any text. Essay tests with three questions, or short-answer tests with five-to-seven questions, may assess only a limited portion of the content domain of the textbook chapters or the lectures for which the tests are designed. Multiple choice tests, in contrast, usually contain 30–40 questions and allow the instructors more flexibility to evaluate students on a much wider range of content. The instructor can also measure the depth of understanding by placing a series of questions about a topic on the exam.

The advantages of less bias and wider sampling of the content domain mean that multiple choice tests are more reliable indicators of student performance than essay tests. With essays, there is a much stronger element of chance influencing the test score because students may be unlucky if the instructor asks one of three essay questions on a topic that the student did not study; it is less likely that one-third of the multiple choice questions will be on material that the student did not study. The measurement error introduced from subjective nature of essay grading compounds the problem.[2]

It is sometimes argued that multiple choice questions are less desirable because they work only on recall, whereas essays tap higher-order thinking in students and allow students to express themselves. This argument really depends on the quality of each test. Multiple choice questions can be written at different cognitive levels. For example, the *Test of Understanding of College Economics* (TUCE) (Saunders, 1991) is a standardized achievement test that has multiple choice questions written at three cognitive levels: (1) recognition and understanding; (2) explicit application; and (3) implicit application.[3] The first level focuses on the identification of concepts and terms and mainly taps student recall or identification skills. An example of a recognition or understanding question is:

> Which of the following is counted as "investment" in national income accounting?
>
> *A. building a new factory.
> B. buying an existing house.
> C. purchasing corporate stocks and bonds.
> D. depositing money in a commercial bank.

Questions at the higher cognitive levels, however, require students to use economic concepts either when the concepts are directly mentioned or when they are implied in the question. An example of an implicit application question from the TUCE is:

> In an economy where there is unrestricted competition in all markets, coal is the primary source of heat for most households. Suppose a supply of natural gas which can provide heat at a much lower cost is discovered. What is the most likely effect of the natural gas discovery on the price of coal and the quantity of coal produced?
>
> | | Price | Quantity |
> |-----|-------|----------|
> | *A. | decrease | decrease |
> | B. | decrease | increase |
> | C. | increase | decrease |
> | D. | increase | no change |

This question is not necessarily more difficult than being able to identify an example of investment, but it does require that the student apply supply and demand analysis to determine the correct answer.

Essay tests may not always demonstrate that students show complex understanding. Asking students to "explain why we have a Federal Reserve System" may not reveal higher-level thinking because the students will most likely "regurgitate" the five reasons you gave in your lecture or that were listed in the textbook. Essays, moreover, can be so vague and unstructured that there might be several possibilities for student response. An essay question such as "criticize minimum wage laws" may produce several responses that are valid from an economic perspective but that do not necessarily require the student to use the supply and demand analysis that the instructor wanted students to use in explaining the problems with an increase in the minimum wage. Several well-written items in choice format could handle either the Federal Reserve topic or the minimum wage topic at several cognitive levels with more precision and in less time for the student to answer and the instructor to grade.[4]

The other consideration is the purpose of the assessment. If the purpose is to find out what students know and whether they can apply basic concepts to new situations, then multiple choice tests can handle the task quite well and even better than essays. If the purpose is to find out how well students write, then essays might have an advantage, but the time limitation for responding to essay tests certainly makes them suspect as an accurate gauge of student writing. There are also better ways to assess student writing—term papers, short papers, in-class exercises. These writing assignments make the essay test a poor substitute. (See also Chapter 15.)

Now if these arguments still raise doubts about the worth of multiple choice tests, then conduct the following experiment in your class. Give students a test with multiple choice questions for half the period and essay questions (or short-answer) for the other half. Score each half of the test and then correlate the scores. What you will find is that students who do well on the multiple choice questions are likely to do well on the essay questions, and vice versa.[5]

Constructing Classroom Tests

There are two elements to constructing a classroom test. The first element is the creation of a test plan or log for covering the content. The second element entails preparing questions for the exam. Each element is discussed in the sections that follow, but special attention is devoted to guidelines for preparing test items.

The Test Log   What do you need to do first to make a good quality test for classroom use?   The initial step is basically an iterative process that results in the development of a table outlining the content covered by the items on the test. You can begin by identifying the economic concepts for the test and then finding or writing questions that will be used to assess that content; or, you can start by selecting or writing questions, and then describe what economic content the questions cover. In the end there should a content descriptor for each item on the test. An example of a test log for a mid-term exam in a microeconomic principles course is shown in Table 19-1.

With this test log, you know how many questions are being used to cover the material in five chapters assigned for the test and some of the characteristics of the test questions.   A quick scan of this 35-item test tells you the percentage of questions that will be allocated to each chapter. For example, the largest percentage (26) of questions is devoted to the material in the chapter on pure monopoly. The listing shows you if you missed any central concepts and should add questions, or if you should delete questions that duplicate material covered by other questions. The test log also gives you a sheet to use in review sessions to give students hints about what to study.

Other information about the characteristics of the test can be obtained from the test log. You can count how many questions use tables (5) or graphs (7), and how those stimuli are distributed across the test. The source of the question is also reported in the table, with the a column indicating the test bank or department file

Table 19-1: Item Log

Chapter 22: Costs of Production (17.1% of questions)

1.	#4	when diminishing marginal returns begins
2.	#57	(graph) which graph is correct?
3.	#66	diseconomies of scale—why they occur?
4.	#67+	(table) total variable cost calculation
5.	#52	average fixed cost as output increases
6.	#26	marginal product and marginal cost relationship

Chapter 23: Pure Competition (20.0%)

7.	#23	(table) profit maximization and normal profit
8.	#32	total revenue-total cost—the shutdown condition
9.	#49+	reason for increasing cost industry
10.	#73	increase in demand in increasing cost industry
11.	**	(table) on average total cost, average variable cost
12.	#68	marginal revenue = marginal cost problem
13.	#87	(graph) on short-run and long-run equilibrium

Chapter 24: Pure Monopoly (25.7%)

14.	#1	demand curve for pure monopolist
15.	#6	(table) demand schedule and total revenue
16.	#7	marginal conditions for profit maximization problem
17.	#9	marginal revenue and price elasticity
18.	#19	(graph) setting price and output by monopolist
19.	#22+	(table) cost data and profit maximization calculation
20.	#24	when monopolist will close down from losses
21.	#33	optimal social price for monopoly
22.	#35+	economic incentives for price discrimination

Chapter 25: Monopolistic Competition (17.1%)

23.	#3	comparison to pure competition
24.	#29	efficiency and monopolistic competition
25.	#7+	(graph) long run equilibrium
26.	#24	(graph) average costs and advertising
27.	**	demand curve for monopolistic competition
28.	#42	allocation of resources

Chapter 26: Oligopoly (20%)

29.	#20	joint profit maximization for cartels
30.	#25+	price leadership
31.	#32	comparisons of structures when price > mc
32.	#33	(graph) oligopoly in long run
33.	**	concentration ratios
34.	**	kinked demand curves
35.	#39+	cost-plus pricing

number (#). A plus (+) after the number denotes that the questions have been revised and asterisks (**) in the column means that the question is new. This item information gives you a detailed record that you can use for test analysis or constructing future exams.

Finally, you might want to classify items for the test log according to a taxonomy of the cognitive level. This classification work will give you a good indication about how much of the test requires higher-level thinking. With this data, you can produce a content and cognitive level matrix for the test showing the relative distribution of questions by content categories and cognitive levels.

Test Banks and Software The availability of test banks for many economics texts means that the time to produce multiple choice tests that match the content in the textbook has been considerably reduced. It used to be the rule that essay tests take less time to prepare but more time to grade, while multiple choice tests take more time to prepare and less time to grade. Some instructors now think that all you have to do to create a multiple choice test is to make a list of the item numbers from the test bank and then let the departmental secretary produce the test. That procedure is the wrong one to follow because it assumes that all the questions in the test bank are good. Anyone who has looked at test banks knows the quality of items varies.

Fortunately, test software for textbooks gives you much greater control over test construction. The software lets you print selected questions from the test banks that come with textbooks.[6] You also have the option to create new questions or to revise the existing questions. This test software means that the instructor, and not the test bank writer, is responsible for the quality of the questions on course exams. if test bank questions meet instructor approval, fine, but, if not, the questions can be modified to correct perceived deficiencies. New questions can also be written that require higher-order thinking or that cover special applications that were only presented in the lectures.[7]

Preparing Items Selecting a multiple choice question from a test bank, revising a question, or writing a new question are tasks that require careful scrutiny of the two parts of a multiple choice question. The first part of the question is called the *stem* and it sets up the problem for the student to consider. The second part presents the *alternatives* to the student. The set of alternatives consists of a correct answer, and incorrect alternatives which are also called *distractors*. The following points highlight desirable features that should be exhibited by the stem or the alternatives before the question is included on the test. Table 19-2 provides a summary listing of these guidelines.

A Central Idea. The stem in a good test question should present one central idea and not several concepts or terms. A stem that simply states: "Trade barriers:" is vague and confusing for the students because there are a variety of "trade barriers," —tariffs, import quotas, voluntary export restraints, nontariff barriers. A better

Table 19-2: Guidelines for Writing, Revising or Selecting Multiple Choice Questions

1. The stem should present one central problem or concept and relevant qualifying phrases.
2. The stem should include all words that would otherwise appear in each alternative.
3. The stem and alternatives should be written as clearly and simply as possible with words whose meaning are clear to students.
4. Alternatives should be homogenous in form, have a consistent grammatical structure and be in logical order.
5. Alternatives should not provide irrelevant clues to the correct answer because of response length, repetition of phrases, or grammar.
6. Alternatives should not use "all of the above," "none of the above," or a type of "some of the above" as possible responses.
7. The stem should not be negatively stated with words such as not, least, incorrect, or except.
8. Each item should be independent so that answering one item does not help in answering another item.
9. The item should be only one correct or best answer, but all distractors should be plausible.

stem would be one that asks: "Which statement about tariffs is true?" and then lists the alternatives. The question clearly focuses on one concept—tariffs.

Clarity and Brevity. The question should be written as clearly and simply, and be as brief as possible. Extra words, unnecessary jargon, and confusing language make a question harder, even if students know the concepts. There is no need for the item to become a test of reading skills when it is designed to test understanding of introductory college economics.

Consider how this tariff question might be improved:

Which one of the following statements about tariffs is true?

    A. Tariffs decrease employment in domestic industries, whose products they protect.
  *B. Tariffs benefit some groups at the expense of the national standard of living.
    C. Tariffs increase the market for our exports by reducing our imports.
    D. Tariffs encourage the growth of our most efficient industries.

When this question was administered to a large group of students who had taken economics, only 29 percent could correctly answer it. When the alternatives were rewritten as follows to make them simpler and more direct, 58 percent of a similar group of students provided a correct answer:

Which one of the following statement about tariffs is true?

   A. Tariffs increase the market for exports.
   B. Tariffs decrease employment in protected industries.
*C. Tariffs benefit some groups at the expense of others.
   D. Tariffs encourage the growth of the most efficient industries.

Use the stem. Another rule to make items easier to read can be illustrated with the above question. The stem could be simplified further by stating: "Which statement about tariffs is true? Tariffs:". The rule here is that the stem should include all words that otherwise would appear in each alternative, thereby reducing the reading load for students.

Form and Grammar. Alternatives should be consistent in form and grammatical structure, and be listed in logical order. In the revision of the alternatives for the tariff question, the switching of original option C to make it revised option A, and placing original option A as revised option B was done to pair the verbs *increase* and *decrease* as the first two options. The two unrelated verbs (benefit and encourage) are paired as the final two options. This change gave the alternatives more balance.

No clues. Irrelevant clues to the correct answer provided by response length, repetition of phases, or grammar should be avoided in items. Notice that the above item is typed so that the alternative with the shortest length comes first, and then longer alternatives follow in ascending order. The alternatives could also be typed in order of descending length. By typing alternatives in ascending or descending order, you do not give any clues to the student about the right answer. When possible, the position of the correct alternatives should be randomized on a test, so that the answers do not fall into a logical pattern that can be decoded by students.

All, None, and Both Options. Another mistake made is the use of "All of the above," "None of the above", or "Some of the above" (e.g., "both A and C") alternatives. These alternatives violate the rule that responses should be independent and mutually exclusive. These options also force the student to make sure that the alternative selected is absolutely correct, rather than having the student select the most correct response. Consider the question:

The location of the product supply curve depends on:

   A. production technology.
   B. costs of required resources.
   C. the number of sellers in the market.
*D. All of the above.

For option D to be chosen, the other options must be absolutely correct. Although ambiguity does not appear to be a problem with this question, selecting the D option places extra burden on students to make sure that A, B, and C are absolutely correct rather than asking students to select the most correct answer.

The major problem, however, with this question is that you do not get independent and mutually exclusive assessment of alternatives. Once students know that two options are correct (A and B), then students can assume that D is the correct answer, without having to judge the option C. Students are also given a conflicting message when choosing A, B, or C: they would be penalized for selecting a correct response *because* there are other correct responses.

For a "None of the above" example, considering the following question drawn from a test bank:

A perfectly competitive firm might first consider exiting from an industry when:

   *A. price is less than average variable cost.
    B. price is greater than average variable cost.
    C. the price is set so that accounting profit is being made, but economic profit
         is zero.
    D. None of the above.

The correct answer is supposed to be A. When "None of the above" is included, students have to decide if A is absolutely correct. Some students could correctly think that the firm may shutdown in the short-run when price is less than average variable cost, but that does not necessarily mean that the firm begins thinking about exiting the industry at that point. Under those circumstance, option D could be correct.

Problems also are present when a combination of alternatives are used. In the above question, "None of the above" could be replaced by an option that read "A and C, but not B." This combination violates the independence and mutual exclusivity of alternatives; if the students know that C is incorrect, there is no need to consider the combination ("A and C, but not B").

Avoid Negatives. Negative items should be avoided, if possible. These items are easily identified because they include such words in the stem as *not, least, except,* and *incorrect.* There are many negatively-stated items in test banks because it is often easier to ask students to identify something that is not characteristic or incorrect rather than writing a question that asks them to identify something that is characteristic or correct.

The reason for the caution is that negative wording requires a change in mental set and tends to be more confusing for students. A test should be an accurate measure of economic understanding, not reading skills. Students are also more likely to misread the item because it is easy to skip over terms like "not" or "least," especially when they are *NOT* highlighted with italics, capitals, or underlining.

These items should be written in the positive direction to test if students know that something is correct rather than incorrect. An awkward item from one test bank that begins "Which of the following is not what an economist would call a productive resource," could be easily revised to, "Which of the following is considered a productive resource by economists."

Item Independence. Sometimes test banks have a series of questions based on a table or a graph. Care should be exercised in the selection of more than one question related to a table or graph because items should provide an independent assessment of student understanding. When the answer to the second question depends on the answer to the first question, you increase the potential for a double penalty to students who answer the first question wrong and a double credit to students who answer the first question right. For example:

The next *two* questions refer to the following consolidated balance sheet for the commercial banking system. Assume the required reserve ratio is 30 percent. All figures are in billions of dollars.

Assets	Liabilities and Net Worth
Reserves $200	Demand deposits .. $600
Loans 600	Capital stock 700
Property 500	

1. There are excess reserves in this commercial bank system of:

    A. $10 billion.
    *B. $20 billion.
    C. $30 billion.
    D. $180 billion.

2. The commercial banking system can expand the supply of money by a maximum of approximately:

    A. $23.5 billion.
    B. $36.5 billion.
    C. $51.9 billion.
    *D. $66.6 billion.

To answer question 2, students have to be able to answer question 1. Rather than putting students in a double jeopardy situation, select one question (preferably item 2 because it assesses an understanding of excess reserves, the calculation of the multiplier, and deposit expansion). Most questions that follow a table or graph in test banks are not independent. It is best to select one question to use based on a stimulus.

One Correct Answer. Finally, multiple choice items should be written so that there is only one correct alternative or one best answer. The other alternatives are to be plausible, but incorrect. You need to double check each item to make sure that there is a correct answer because distractors are sometimes too plausible. It is more embarrassing for you to have students discover a wrong answer in class or detect a problem with a question, while they are taking your test than for you to find the problem in the privacy of your office. Most errors of this type can be avoided by taking the exam first, as if a student were taking it.

Despite these precautions, there are still occasions when students find more than one correct answer. For instance, consider this test bank item:

As price increases along a linear demand curve, the price elasticity of:

    A. supply increases.
  *B. demand increases.
    C. demand decreases.
    D. demand does not change.

Response B is keyed as correct based on material in the textbook. A clever student, however, might have selected D and would be correct if an assumption was made that the linear demand curve was vertical. Since you are not told what the shape of the demand curve is in the stem, students who marked D must be given credit and their grades changed. If the question is to be used in the future, the stem needs to have the qualifying phrase "that is downward sloping" inserted after "curve" to insure that there is one correct answer.

Few instructors face public criticism over the test questions they write, but the classroom can become the courtroom when tests are returned. A major point to emphasize to students is that answering a multiple choice question involves selecting the *best* or *most* correct answer from the set of alternatives given in the question, not any others. Some students, especially the more able, also want to know why the answer they selected is not correct or the option you selected is correct. You must be prepared to defend your answers and give a good rationale for your chosen option; otherwise you must give students credit for their responses. If you don't clearly respond to students' objections, then they think that you are being "unfair," and this perception can affect their evaluation of your instruction. You should also remember that the situation need not be adversarial. The test discussion period can be used to reinforce points made during instruction: "Remember when I described the cost curves for a pure monopoly in class, well this multiple choice question...."

Test Analysis

Information is vital to effective classroom instruction. One benefit of multiple choice testing is the opportunity to analyze the test data. From the statistical analysis, you can study overall class results to determine grades, assess individual performance to spot areas of weakness, and use item data to evaluate how well questions worked with students. Most colleges and universities have an office where you can turn in the exams and have them scored within twenty-four hours. The test analysis comes back with more data than you probably need, but it can all be helpful in judging the overall test and individual items. Selected test data is shown in Table 19-3 for the test that was described in Table 19-2.

Overall Statistics Most instructors are familiar with basis statistics such as the mean, standard deviation, and range, so there is no need to discuss those in detail here. You can see from the overall data in Table 19-3 that for the 40 students taking the test the scores ranged from 18 to the maximum possible score of 35. The class average was 27.13, which means that the average percent correct on the test items was 77 percent. The large majority of students appeared to show good knowledge of the test content, which was expected because this class contained a larger proportion of high ability students than normal. When the test grades were assigned, 55 percent received an A or a B grade.

The meaning and interpretation of the coefficient *alpha* may not be so familiar and merits further attention. Alpha measures the internal consistency or reliability of a test. Internal consistency indicates whether the items in the test are assessing a common characteristic, which in this case would be student ability to understand the costs of production and the four market structures. One way to conceptualize the meaning of internal consistency is to think of splitting the test in half and correlating student scores on both halves. The alpha coefficient provides an estimate of the average of all possible split-half correlations. The formula for alpha is:

$$\alpha = \frac{n}{n-1} [1 - (\Sigma V_i / V_t)]$$

where, $\underline{n}$ is the number of items on the test, V_t is the variance of the total test; and ΣV_i is the sum of the variance of individual items.

Values for alpha can range from zero to one. When scores on individual items are uncorrelated, alpha is zero, and when there is perfect correlation, alpha is 1.00. Between the extremes, the more highly items correlate with each other, the higher the coefficient will be. There is no absolute standard for judging reliability, but the higher the coefficient, the better. The alpha for most standardized achievement tests in economics is in the range of .80–.90. Classroom tests in economics will more likely be in the range of .60–.85. For this test, the alpha of .76 suggests that it is a very reliable measure of student knowledge over the chapters covered.[8]

Item Difficulty Before you return the exam to students it is best to check the item statistics on the multiple choice question to see how the item performed with your sample of students. Item difficulty is the ratio of the number of students who answered the item correctly to the total number of students who took the item. In item data shown in Table 19-3, of the 40 students who took the item, 29 marked the

Table 19-3: Selected Test Data

A. *Overall Test Data*

Number of Subjects =	40	Number of Questions =	35
High Score =	35	Low Score =	18
Test Mean =	27.13	Test Median =	28.17
Standard deviation =	4.43	Variance =	19.66
Coefficient alpha =	0.76		

B. *Frequency Data for One Item*

		Options			
	A	B	C	D	Total
1) Number	6	2	29	3	40
2) Percent	15.0	5.0	72.5	7.5	100

3) Group Data

	A	B	C	D	Total	
High	0	0	18	1	19	94.7%
Middle	3	1	6	1	11	54.5%
Low	3	1	5	1	10	50.0%
Option Means	23.7	22.5	28.2	27.0	-----	-----

C. *Item Statistics*

1) Difficulty = 0.73
2) Correlation (r_{pbis}) = 0.38
3) Discrimination (high-low) = 0.45

correct answer, so item difficulty is .73. This ratio is sometimes referred to as a *p* value, or it can be expressed as a percentage.

There are no hard rules for determining whether an item was "too hard" or "too easy" for students. That decision will depend on such factors as the purposes of the test, the characteristics of the students in the class, or the circumstances of the testing. For nationally normed tests of achievement such as the TUCE, the *p*-values tend to range from about .30 to .70, with an average difficulty of about .50. If everyone guessed, the *p*-value would be expected to be .25, on average, so values below .25 are considered too hard. Values above .75, conversely, are thought to be relatively easy.

The .50 average *p*-value and .30–.70 range are probably too exacting for classroom tests because the students would get only half the test questions right. Unless you plan to curve the test, this .50 level will result in many low grades. Item difficulty on classroom tests are more likely to range from .50–.90. Those instructors who design classroom tests as an achievement measure will be on the lower end of the range, while those instructors who design mastery tests will probably be on the higher end. The general point is that a sound test consists of items with a range of difficulty at the level at which you think the students should be performing.

What may be more enlightening is the frequency data for each option. You should question any item where the percent marking a distractor is greater than the percent marking the correct answer. If that is the case, check the key to see that you correctly marked it. If you did not make an error, then try to determine why students selected that option. The study of the incorrect responses of students should give you some insight into why they are confused about a question and help prepare you for the class discussion when you return the examination.

You can also use the response data to improve items for future use: item difficulty can be changed by making distractors more or less plausible. In Table 19-3, data on option B indicates it is weak because only 5 percent of the sample selected it; option D is a stronger distractor because 15 percent of the sample selected it. Keep a file on test questions you would like to use again with the difficulty and option frequency data so you can make improvements in questions.

Item Discrimination The other major piece of information to be extracted from item analysis is the discrimination of the item. A discrimination index provides an estimate of how well an item does in separating students with more economic understanding from those students with less understanding. There are two types of discrimination measures that are usually reported.

Point Biserial. The point biserial correlation coefficient measures the correlation between the students' scores (a continuous variable) and their scores on a test item (a dichotomous variable). The formula is:

$$r_{pbis} = \frac{\overline{X}_R - \overline{X}_w}{S_T} \; [p(1-p)]^{1/2}$$

where: $\overline{X}_R$ is the mean test score for the students getting this item correct, $\overline{X}_w$ is the mean test score for the students getting the item incorrect, S_T is the test standard deviation, p is the proportion getting the item right, and $(1-p)$ is the proportion getting the item wrong.

With this item the r_{pbis} was .38. What does this number mean? An ordinary Pearson product-moment correlation would have a range of +1.00 to –1.00. The r_{pbis} is a special type of Pearson correlation and its range is somewhat restricted. The general rule is that items with a negative correlation are probably defective, or the key is incorrect, because this would indicate that students who got this item right had lower mean scores than students who got the item wrong.

On national achievement tests, the point biserial correlation sought is at least .20, but on classroom tests, the correlation will probably range from .10–.50. Items with higher correlations are usually preferred in making up a test (if you have data from past administrations), but you should be aware from looking at the correlation formula that higher correlations are more often found with items of average difficulty. Items with low correlations are candidates for inspection and revision because of possible problems with ambiguity or other defects.

High-Low Discrimination. A simpler, but less accurate, way to measure discrimination is to break the sample into three groups as shown in Table 19-3. The "high" and "low" headings for the box represent the students scoring in the upper and lower 25–30 percent of the class on the overall test. This method is only approximate because it is difficult to make precise percent cutoffs, especially with smaller samples. For this item, 48 percent of the sample is in the "high" group and 25 percent of the sample is in the low group.

This discrimination index is determined by subtracting the proportion correct of the group with a high score on this test from the proportion correct of the group with a low score on the test. For this item, there was a proportional difference of .45 (.947–.500). Again, there is the problem of interpreting the meaning of this "high-low" number. The index can theoretically range from +1.00 to –1.00, but a negative number is a clear indication of an poor item. A good discriminator will be .40 or greater, although any positive discrimination level indicates that the item is helping to differentiate students. As the index number moves toward zero there is more reason to suspect the discrimination power of the item.

Sample Size and Group Character Caution must be exercised in the analysis of items from class tests. Decisions about questions based on small class sizes should be very tentative. Large sample sizes are sometimes recommended before you can be confident of the item results. The difficulty and discrimination characteristics of items can also vary from one group to another. It would not be unusual to find that with one group of students a question was hard (.50) and very discriminating (.45), while with another group the question was easier (.70) and less discriminating (.20). These factors, however, should not dissuade you from having the test scored because the item data can be very useful in identifying flawed questions, how questions "worked" with students, or in revising questions for future use. Just keep in mind that the results will depend, in part, on the sample size and student characteristics.

Active Test Preparation for Students

Many students are often ill-prepared for taking multiple choice tests in economics, especially those enrolled in principles courses. Instructors sometimes hear students say that "your tests are harder than those I get in my other subjects. They really make you think." One reason for this comment is that economics lends itself to application and analysis, and other forms of higher-level thinking. In selecting questions for a multiple choice test, economics instructors like to put questions on a test that require more than simple recognition and recall of definitions, and thus prefer ones requiring application of concepts or economic analysis (e.g., using of supply and demand to explain changes in price or quantity without mentioning the terms in the question). The multiple choice tests that the student experiences in other social sciences (e.g., history, sociology) may not demand as much analytical thinking or problem solving as found in economics tests. Given this difference in test experience, economics instructors need to spend more time preparing students for the types of multiple choice questions on economics exams. Otherwise, students may become frustrated with economics or develop negative attitudes towards the subject.

Several teaching and learning strategies can be used to prepare students for taking multiple choice exams. Perhaps the easiest and most obvious course of action is to make previous exams available for inspection and review before an exam. The problem with this strategy is that it often does not actively engage the student. The student gets a copy of the exam from you or the library. The student looks over the test questions and answers, but does not have the real experience of thinking through the questions under time limits. Also, some instructors may not want past exams to be available for review because good multiple choice questions are hard to write and some of the better questions need to be kept secure for future use.

A better approach to test preparation are strategies that actively engage the student in the experience of understanding, decoding, and answering a test question. Several suggestions for achieving this goal are described below, although there are certainly other creative ways to engage students using multiple choice questions.

Taking Mini-Tests After you give a lecture or series of lectures on important course materials, pass out a mini-exam of 10-15 questions that are representative of the type that would be on a course exam. Allow class time for students take and score their exams. Then give the students an indication of what the scores would mean if this were a real exam. You should also spend time going through each question and ask students to explain or justify reasons for correct and incorrect answers. You can also discuss any tips or tricks for answering multiple choice questions.

It is recommended that this strategy be used several times during a course because it prepares students for each exam, builds confidence for test-taking, and identifies areas of weakness. To keep student interest you might vary the strategy by having students compare answers with nearby students during their scoring. This variation gets students working with each other on the course content. You can then call on groups of students to explain their answers to test questions, thus promoting a good class discussion on content issues.

Writing Exam Questions You can invite students to submit written multiple choice questions that you would consider for inclusion on a course exam. This strategy gives you an opportunity to explain what you look for in test questions and show examples of ones you are likely to put on exams. You can tell the students that you are more likely to add a question that requires higher-level thinking rather than just recognition or recall. To write the questions, the students have to read the text materials, review your lectures, and think about the content. The incentive for students to do this extra work is the possibility that their question, or your modified version of it, would be on the test and they would know the answer.

Using Exam Gripes If you follow the practice of returning exams to students you can use this activity to turn multiple choice testing into an active learning experience. After you show students the answer key, you can invite anyone who disagrees with an answer to write a short explanation for why that answer is correct rather than incorrect. This strategy allows students to vent any exam gripes in a constructive way. Collect these written responses and read them after class. Then give credit to any student who wrote a persuasive argument. It is probably best to give credit only to the student making a good case because that person did the work, not the whole class. You can also use the incorrect written explanations for distractors in new multiple choice questions that you write.

Conclusion

Multiple choice tests are probably the predominant method of assessment in principles of economics courses. The reason has to do with the many advantages of this method, including the ease of scoring, the ability to sample the content domain, and greater test reliability. No matter what the advantages, however, the soundness of the tests and the questions still depend on the quality of input from the instructor. Economics teachers need to know how to write good multiple choice questions and how to prepare a well-constructed test. They also need to know what to look for in the follow-up analysis of the test data. This chapter outlined basic points of multiple choice test construction so that economics instructors can prepare mid-term or final exams that accurately measure student knowledge of principles of economics.

NOTES

1. The examples in this chapter are based on multiple choice tests in principles courses, but the general points apply to all undergraduate economics courses.

2. Reliability is measured on a scale from .00 to 1.00, with higher numbers indicating a more consistent measure (see test analysis section). A study of college tests of English composition (Breland, et al., 1987) found that the reliability of single essays read once ranged from .36–.46, and only rose to the range of .53–.62 after being read three times. The reliability of the multiple choice tests were in the range of .84–.92. For a further discussion of this issue with standardized achievement tests, see Wainer and Thissen (1993).

3. There are many other taxonomies of the cognitive domain. The most widely-used was outlined by Benjamin Bloom and others (1956) and has six levels: (1) knowledge; (2) comprehension; (3) application; (4) analysis; (5) synthesis; and, (6) evaluation.

4. Multiple choice tests in economics have been criticized because of possible gender bias. For recent research on this issue, see Hirschfeld, Moore, and Brown (1995) or Walstad and Robson (forthcoming).

5. Several studies have found high correlations between scores on multiple choice and essay tests in various subjects (Breland, et al., 1987; Wainer and Thissen, 1993; Walstad and Becker, 1994), and suggest that multiple choice tests may provide more reliable and cost-efficient measures.

6. In large classes, you may want to produce several forms of an exam to restrict opportunity for cheating. Test software lets you scramble the order of questions. Research by Spector and Gohmann (1989) indicates there is no difference in performance between students who take a scrambled test or students who are tested with questions in the order in which the material was covered in the class or the text.

7. You should beware of the cognitive level of test bank questions. Karns, Burton, and Martin (1983) found in six principles of economics textbooks that the large majority of the questions were written at the knowledge and comprehension level of Bloom's taxonomy (see footnote 3).

8. Be careful when interpreting alpha, or when comparing alphas across tests. It should be remembered from studying the formula that alpha can be increased by increased the number of test questions or by administering it to a more heterogeneous group. The opposite changes tend to produce decreased in alpha.

REFERENCES

Bloom, B.S., Englehart, M.D., Furst, E.J., Hill, W.H., and Krathwohl, D.R. (1956). *Taxonomy of educational objectives handbook I: Cognitive domain.* New York: David McKay.

Breland, H., Camp, R., Jones, R.J., Morris, M.M., and Rock, D. (1987). *Assessing writing Skill.* New York: College Entrance Examination Board.

Ebel, R. (1979). *Essentials of educational measurement.* Englewood Cliffs: Prentice Hall.

Hirschfeld, M., Moore, R.L., and Brown, E. (1995). Exploring the gender gap on the GRE subject test in economics. *Journal of Economic Education,* 26(1), 3-15.

Karns, J.M., Burton, G.E., and Martin, G.D. (1983). Learning objectives and testing: An analysis of six principles of economics textbooks, using *Bloom's Taxonomy. Journal of Economic Education,* 14(3), 16-20.

Nunnally, J.C. (1972). *Educational measurement and evaluation.* New York: McGraw-Hill.

Saunders, P. (1991). *Test of understanding in college economics: Examiner's manual,* 3rd ed. New York: Joint Council on Economic Education.

Spector, L. and Gohmann, S.F. (1989). Test scrambling and student performance. *Journal of Economic Education,* 20(3), 235-238.

Wainer, H. and Thissen, D. (1993). Combining multiple-choice and constructed-response test scores: Toward a Marxist theory of test construction. *Applied Measurement in Education,* 6(2), 103-118.

Walstad, W.B. and Becker, W.E. (1994). Achievement differences on multiple-choice and essay tests in economics. *American Economic Review,* 84(2), 193-196.

Walstad, W.B. and Robson, D. (forthcoming). *Journal of Economic Education.*

CHAPTER 20

ESSAY QUESTIONS AND TESTS

Arthur L. Welsh

Phillip Saunders

Although objective-type tests such as multiple choice and true-false examinations have become very common in large enrollment principles of economics courses (Siegfried, Saunders, Sintar and Zhang, 1996), essay questions and tests still have strong advocates at the principles level, and they are more common in advanced undergraduate courses (Becker and Watts, 1996). Indeed, for many economists the essay test is the only appropriate type of examination, notwithstanding the fact that it has been subjected to over a half century of criticism by testing experts. The purpose of this chapter is not to completely resolve the differences economists might have in choosing between objective tests and essay tests, nor is it to intrude into the debate among experts in the field of testing and measurement. Rather, the somewhat more modest goals of this chapter are to review the strengths and weaknesses of essay examinations, and explore situations in which they can be used to advantage. The chapter then discusses some general guidelines to use in preparing essay questions and tests, and concludes with some suggestions for grading student answers. Careful preparation and grading can overcome some of the weaknesses of essay examinations, and help instructors take advantage of more of their strengths—not only in testing student knowledge, but also in influencing student study habits.

Strengths of Essay Tests

The greatest strength of the essay exam is that, if carefully constructed, it permits us to *assess and develop higher level cognitive skills* such as synthesis and evaluation in ways that are not possible in multiple choice examinations. While multiple choice questions can be written which require the use of sophisticated cognitive skills to arrive at correct answers, we can never be certain that individual students actually use these skills, since there are no intellectual "tracks" or "footprints" left by either the skilled or the unskilled student.

A student answer on a multiple choice question tells us *what* the student thinks the answer is. The answer on an essay question tells us *why* the student thinks that is the answer. In many cases, of course, the *why* can be very significant. Jerry Petr, for example, has supplied us with a set of two student responses to the following question: "Assume that a monopolistic publisher has agreed to pay an author 15 percent of the total revenue from the sales of a text. Will the author and the publisher both want to charge the same price for the text?" This question, following a unit on profit maximization under monopoly, is supposed to get the student to differentiate between profit maximization and revenue maximization, and, if written in multiple choice or true-false format, would require an answer of "no" in some form or other.

Consider, however, two possible student responses to this question in essay form. Student "A" says, essentially, "No; because the author gets 15 cents on every dollar of price, ($1.50 on a $10 book—$3.00 on a $20 book) s/he will want to charge a higher price than the publisher thinks would be good for sales." Student "B" says, "Yes; even though the author would be better off in the short run by urging the publisher to produce until marginal revenue is driven to zero, thereby maximizing total revenue, the intelligent author knows that long run existence of his/her publisher would be better served by maximizing profit at a lower volume, and lower revenue, where marginal revenue equals marginal cost." In this example, the students' intellectual "tracks" are obviously more revealing of underlying economic sophistication than the simple affirmative or negative answer to the question.

In addition to what they can reveal about students' knowledge and thought processes, essay questions can also *encourage the development of writing skills*. If one thinks that training in expression, organization of content, and techniques of outlining and summarization are important, one will probably want to use at least some essay questions on their examinations. It has been our experience that students who know in advance that they will be required to write out answers study differently than those who know that they will be required only to select answers. No matter how many times we tell our students that our multiple choice questions will require interpretation and application and not just memory we have found that it is only when we tell them that they will also have to write out answers and explain things that they really begin to look for relations between concepts and try to integrate their understanding of various points. And, of course, there is the obvious point: writing is writing is writing. If we want students to develop writing skills, we must give them opportunities to write. (See Chapter 15.)

A third strength claimed for essay tests is that they are superior to objective tests in *eliciting students' opinions and attitudes*. Economists who make a strong distinction between positive and normative economics may not be too interested in opinions and attitudes for grading purposes. For purposes of relating their instruction to their students "learning set" (see Chapter 8), however, information about student attitudes and opinions can be helpful. Since there are other ways of eliciting information about student attitudes and opinions besides essay tests, however, we doubt that many economics instructors use essay examinations for this purpose.

A fourth strength of the essay test is one, perhaps, that we don't always fully acknowledge to ourselves. It is simply the fact that *good essay exams are more easily prepared than good multiple choice exams*. This does not always imply that a good essay question is easier to write than a good multiple choice question. It simply means that an essay test with four good questions takes less time to prepare than an objective test with 25–30 good multiple choice questions. It has been suggested by experts in testing and measurement that this feature of the essay test is what keeps it popular.

Weaknesses of Essay Tests

Despite the fact that essay tests are the best instruments for measuring certain objectives, one of the most common weaknesses in actual practice is that instructors often *fail to exploit their potential advantage*. Instead of challenging students to analyze and evaluate, our questions are sometimes trite and ambiguous in form. A good essay question requires at least as much specificity and thought from its creator as from its respondents.

A second weakness, and one that is hard to overcome, is that essay questions are *time consuming to score*. Unlike multiple choice or true-false questions, they cannot be assigned to a computer to score. With large classes and/or frequent testing, the opportunity costs to an instructor of grading essay answers can be considerable.

Two other weaknesses of essay examinations are limited content sampling and inconsistent scoring.

Limited content sampling simply means that four essay questions are not likely to probe student understanding of as many concepts as forty multiple choice questions. A partial antidote for this problem is to draft a larger number of more sharply focussed essay questions. And, of course, "limited content sampling" diminishes as a problem if we admit that any reasonably sized segment of our course material may contain only a few major concepts suitable for essay probing, along with a lot of other material more amenable to objective testing.

The problem of *inconsistent scoring* of essay answers is the problem of human fallibility. Our evaluation of written work is "subjective" and can vary from one reading to another and from one evaluator to another. We are sometimes influenced by the legibility of handwriting, cleverness or awkwardness of phrasing, grammar, punctuation, and other factors which may be extraneous to a student's economic understanding. There are ways by which the careful instructor can minimize the problem of imprecise scoring, however, and they will be discussed below.

When to Use Essay Tests

Putting together and administering examinations is an important part of a teacher's responsibilities. It is primarily through the use of examinations that we inform our students about what we think is really important and obtain feedback on how well or poorly they are achieving. If examinations are to provide accurate information for the instructor and be fair to students, the format should be selected with great care. Unfortunately, such care is sometimes lacking in many economics courses. All of us, of course, do some thinking about test format before we put our exams together; but, too often, our thinking is not as precise as it might be. Generally, we have an idea of the broad content areas we are testing for. However, we tend to be less aware of the type of student knowledge we are attempting to measure. It is because of this that we sometimes misuse the essay test and fail to exploit its advantages.

If our essay questions begin with words like "who," "what" and "where," we are misusing the essay format. Such questions usually do not get us beyond simple memorization or recall, and these skills can be tested for more efficiently by objective tests. If our essay questions test the student's ability to select ideas, organize these ideas, and present them in his or her own words, however, then we are exploiting the superior advantage of the essay test over other formats.

Keep in mind that the key consideration in selecting a test format (essay versus objective) is a precise knowledge of what it is you want to measure. Now, let us turn to some practical things to consider when preparing essay questions and tests.

Steps to Improve Essay Questions and Tests

Devote More Time to Planning the Test We generally have an idea of the broad content areas for which we are testing. In improving our test planning, however, we should go beyond "broad content areas." A useful first step is to specify in some detail the content we wish to cover and then to prepare the examination to meet these specifications, allowing sufficient lead time to permit careful editing and last minute revisions.

A simple matrix, sometimes called a *table of specifications* is often helpful in planning the test. In the left-hand column of the matrix we list the content areas we wish to test, i.e., elements of national income accounting, real vs. nominal magnitudes, price elasticity of demand, etc. In the horizontal categories we describe the intellectual or cognitive levels for each content item. For example, we may only want our students to be able to recognize the differences among GDP, NI, PI and DPI—fairly low levels of cognitive understanding. On the other hand, we move up the cognitive ladder if we want to measure how well students can relate the idea of a chain-weight price index to a real life situation in macroeconomics. The idea here is to get students to apply the concepts they learned to perhaps a novel situation. This, of course, requires a more sophisticated thinking process than mere memorization of terms.

There are several things that a simple test specifications matrix can do for us: (1) by stating the content categories we are forced to specify the content we wish to examine; (2) the cognitive categories show us at a glance the type of student behavior to be tested (and whether the essay test is the appropriate format!); and (3) since presumably not all content areas are equally important, we get a clue on how essay questions should be structured to focus on the more important content areas.

Devote More Time to Constructing Questions We have already mentioned that one of the strengths of essay tests is that they are easier to prepare than objective tests. But, remember, we were talking about preparing *good* essay tests as opposed to good objective tests. Good essay questions—the features of which we will describe below—are not easy to write. If essay questions are intended to elicit the behaviors we reserve for these types of tests, then sufficient time and care should be given to their preparation.

In discussing when to use the essay test we also noted that essay questions which begin with words like "who," "what," and "where" constitute a misuse of the essay format. The reason questions like these persist is that they take virtually no time to write. Consider the following:

1. Who are the members of OPEC and what are their current aims?
2. What are the conditions for perfect competition?
3. Where are most of the world's current supplies of oil and gas located?

One can think of scores of questions like these in a short period of time, but they are of limited educational value. What we should be seeking instead are essay questions which call for contrasts and comparisons, causes and effects, statements of relationships, analyses and synthesis, and the like. Moreover, we should try to motivate our students by posing challenging and interesting introductions to our questions. For example:

Currently the Federal Reserve seems preoccupied with the problem of inflation. Some critics of Fed policy, however, believe that Fed actions are too timid to tame inflation while others believe that the Fed is overreacting to inflation fears and risks bringing about an early recession.

If you were chairman of the Fed, how would you respond to your critics? Restrict your answer to an analysis of the current economic situation and the likely effect of the Fed's policies on short-term employment, prices, and economic growth.

or:

You were required to read the following books:

An Inquiry Into the Nature and the Causes of the Wealth of Nations—Smith
The Theory of the Leisure Class—Veblen
Value and Capital—Hicks
The New Industrial State—Galbraith

Which of these books gives the most complete account of the workings of the market economy? Briefly summarize what you found in that book. How do the findings of the other books differ from those in the book you selected?

and:

The following two headlines might have appeared in newspapers somewhere:

"J.M. Keynes, Socialist Economist, Dies at the Age of 63"
"J.M. Keynes, Savior of Capitalism, Dies at the Age of 63"

Select either headline and defend it by giving your understanding of Keynes's main arguments expressed in the *General Theory*.

Keep in mind that the foregoing questions are illustrative only; they are simply meant to indicate that essay questions should not be, nor need not be, trite. But searching questions require time to think about and compose.[1]

Provide Adequate Instructions for the Students Even though some students may not know the answer to a question, every student should know what question is being asked. Oftentimes we need instructions calling the student's attention to what we expect in the way of content coverage and detail. Don't be afraid to use detailed instructions in order to keep students on track. Failure to do this can result in some students attacking the problem the way you intended, while others, for legitimate reasons, do not. The upshot of this situation is that there is no fair way to compare students' answers.

Consider the following questions:

1. You are the President. What economic policies would you pursue?
2. You are advising the President of the U.S. What economic policies would you recommend be currently pursued with respect to employment, the price level, and the rate of real economic growth? Restrict your analysis to the instruments of fiscal and monetary policy and how conscious changes in these policy instruments might affect these goals.

Neither of these questions is technically perfect, but clearly the second is more explicit than the first. The first question gives the student great latitude for discourse; the only limitation being that it be restricted to "economic policies." The second question, while longer, directs the student but also allows latitude to demonstrate synthesis and evaluative skills.

Another pair of questions is:

1. Discuss the publicly-financed income maintenance system in the United States.
2. Discuss the publicly-financed income maintenance system in the United States. In your discussion, identify the two main elements in the system. Give a specific example of a program in each element, and compare and contrast each element with respect to: basic underlying rationale, source of financing, eligibility for benefits, and relative size.

Which question would you prefer to answer if you were a student? Which one would you prefer to grade if you were an instructor?

Several Short-Answer Essay Questions May Be Preferable to a Few Long-Answer Questions An examination covering the first third or half semester is typically no more than fifty minutes in length. In such a limited period of time only a fraction of the content you might wish to test for can be included. It becomes important, then, to specify carefully the content you are testing for and to design your exam accordingly.

Three or four long, or extended, answer essay questions are probably the most that can be used in a typical exam situation. Unless these questions are very well thought out and tightly phrased, the risk of unreliability due to limited content sampling becomes very real. While content unreliability can result in any type of examination of any length, it is *more likely* to occur in tests with few questions—especially the long-answer essay test.

To get around the problem of content unreliability—and thus minimize the risk of drawing unwarranted inferences about students' knowledge—it is sometimes wise to use ten to twelve short-answer essay questions in place of three or four extended-answer essay questions. By spacing the questions on the examination form you can indicate the desired length of each answer. One type of short-answer essay question combines the essay with the multiple choice exam. You can do this by asking students to write several sentences explaining the process by which they selected one option on a multiple choice question and explaining why each of the other options they rejected were "incorrect." This type of exercise is not only useful in gaining insights into students' analytical processes but is also a good method for determining whether the multiple choice question has weaknesses you might have overlooked.

Examples of two such questions that we have used are:

With the same overall level of aggregate demand, which combination of fiscal and monetary policy might do the most to increase the rate of economic growth? *Why?* (Circle the alternative and explain below.)

A. "Easy" fiscal policy and "easy" monetary policy.
B. "Tight" fiscal policy and "easy" monetary policy.
C. "Easy" fiscal policy and "tight" monetary policy.
D. "Tight" fiscal policy and "tight" monetary policy.

The following table gives the number of tons of apples and bananas that can be produced in Country X and Country Y by employing the same amount of productive resources.

	Apples	Bananas
Country X	10	5
Country Y	8	2

Under these conditions, *Country X* would find it advantageous to: (Circle one alternative and explain below.)

A. export apples and import bananas.
B. export bananas and import apples.
C. export both apples and bananas and import nothing.
D. import both apples and bananas and export nothing.

Another form of "mini-essay" that can sometimes be used to improve content sampling and also help improve future multiple choice questions is the "true-or-false-*and-why*" question. If the bulk of the grading is based on the "why" part of the answer rather than on the "true or false" part, considerable insight can be gained into students' thinking, and a fairly large number of questions can be used. Some student answers to this type of question can also be edited and made into options for future multiple choice questions.

One of the most difficult problems in constructing multiple choice questions is to come up with plausible wrong answers, or "distractors." While it's difficult for instructors, who know the right answer, to think of plausible wrong answers, students can often provide us with more than we might want to consider. Seeing what students write on "true-or-false-*and-why*" questions can provide you with a good source of short, plausible wrong answers in constructing good multiple choice questions.

Another form of short answer essay question that permits a wide range of content sampling and also permits an evaluation of different levels of knowledge is a set of terms for the students to "define-and-explain-the-significance." As this form of question is used by Professor Jerry Petr at the University of Nebraska, students are required to write two sentences about each term on the list. The first sentence is to be used to "define" the term; this is often a matter of recall or mastery. But the second sentence is to "explain the significance" of that term in the context of the course. The ability to place a concept in context requires rather higher level cognitive skills, skills which are not reflected in a response which says " 'Externalities' are significant because we study them in economics courses." A number of such terms ("elasticity," "concentration ratio," "crowding out," "currency depreciation" are all examples) can be incorporated into an examination without making unreasonable time demands on the student.

Keep in mind that the short-answer essay can improve content reliability but it does not guarantee that result. Many short-answer questions, for example, which cover a narrow range of the subject matter may not adequately sample the universe of understanding you wish to measure. Thus, it is vitally important that serious prior thought be given to content coverage *before* you actually write your exam questions.

Make Sure Sufficient Time is Allowed for Student Response There are three main considerations to keep in mind when allotting time to answer a question. The first concerns the breadth of response you intend. If long, written responses are your intention, you should use few questions or extend the testing period. Since the latter is usually not possible, the number of items must be reduced. But remember that this may cause you a content sampling problem.

A second consideration concerns the depth of response, or complexity. If an in-depth treatment of a particular topic is required, then the extended essay is most appropriate and sufficient time to complete the task is required. It is the in-depth question which often provokes student complaints—and they are not all groundless. We tend, at times, to overestimate our students' abilities and maturity levels, and believe that they can accomplish complex tasks in a short period of time. This is a mistake we should try to avoid. A good way to do this is to actually write out an answer yourself. After you see how long it takes you, add a time allowance of 15–20% for students who will come to the question less prepared to formulate an answer than you are, and use this as a guide. (As pointed out below, your written answer can later serve as a basis of a carefully worked out scoring key.)

Lastly, we should clearly indicate the number of points assigned to each question and each part of complex, multi-part questions on an exam. Some concepts and principles, and some relations among them, are more important than others, and we rightly attach more weight to questions requiring use of the more important ones. Our students should know at the outset of the test which questions and which parts of complex questions have the greater value so they can budget their time accordingly.

The Use of Optional Essay Questions Should be Avoided Permitting students to answer any three of five questions on an essay test, or two of three, or whatever combination, is common practice. Perhaps the reason for this is that the instructor may feel vaguely uncomfortable with the content sampling and wishes to broaden it with optional questions. But whatever the reason, it is a practice to avoid, with minor exceptions. Keep in mind that the purpose of a test is to assess student performance in responding to a representative sampling of the course content. An examination in which individual students can select different questions is no common examination at all. Since the questions presumably deal with different content matter, any attempt to apply the same grading scale to dissimilar tests is unfair to students and, therefore, generally unwise. Students may also spend so much time trying to decide which questions to answer that they do not leave enough time to adequately answer the ones they finally do select.

As noted above, there are possible exceptions to this rule. At some institutions a "common" examination is given to multiple sections taught by several instructors. While all instructors are required to teach a "common core," latitude may be given to the various instructors to emphasize additional material according to their wishes. In such a situation, optional questions in conjunction with a common core exam, may be appropriate to accommodate class variations. Another closely related exception is the case where students are doing independent learning under the tutelage of different instructors and a common exam is given to all. Again, optional questions may be appropriate to capture variations in content emphasis and approach of different instructors.

Grading Essay Questions

Prepare an Answer and a Scoring Key   The importance of writing out the answer and making a key for marking exams should be obvious; the key should indicate the elements desired in an acceptable answer and the credit points assigned to each element, thus reducing the chances of unreliability in scoring. Let's assume, for example, that we have presented the following statement to students and asked them to indicate whether they agree or disagree, to identify the main issue(s) involved, and to show by way of examples their supporting argument.

Question: "Clean air, clean water, green grass and redwoods are all good things, but so are electricity, newspapers, houses and bread, and I don't see any reason to believe that the market wouldn't give us the right combination of them all."

Model Answer: *Disagree.* The problem of third-party costs and third-party benefits (externalities) makes it unlikely that a free market based only on private costs and benefits would provide optimum combinations of all goods. Goods with third-party costs (negative externalities) would tend to be overproduced, and goods with third-party benefits (positive externalities) would tend to be underproduced.

If burning coal to produce electricity fouls up the air, for example, an unrestricted free market would not count the cost of air pollution and this cost would not be covered by the price paid by the consumers of electricity. Part of the cost of electricity is thus shoved off on "third parties" and, since the price charged consumers is lower than it would be if it covered all costs this would tend to cause overconsumption and overproduction by the parties directly involved.

Likewise goods that have third-party benefits such as neat, trim lawns are likely to be underproduced in a free market. Since the person who improves the appearance of his lawn can't effectively charge all of the passersby who derive aesthetic enjoyment or charge his neighbors who benefit from the general neighborhood improvement, he is likely to devote less time to improving his lawn than would be the case if he could charge for the third-party benefits of his private lawn improvements.

If we're satisfied with our written answer we can now assign credit points to the elements in the answer we feel are most important. For this question an instructor might assign fifteen points, weighted as follows: three points for disagree; three points each for noting third-party costs and third-party benefits (or negative and positive externalities); and three points each for examples showing third-party costs and third-party benefits and their consequences.

Why this particular assignment of points? It is largely *subjective*; what the instructor thinks is important based on what he or she has emphasized in class. If you were to prepare an answer for this question and assign credit points, in all likelihood your results would differ somewhat from this example. Because of this, it becomes especially important that all instructors agree on a suitable answer and a scoring key on common departmental examinations.

A well thought out scoring key not only facilitates more objective scoring, but can also help instructors achieve a greater degree of discrimination among students' responses. For example, some instructors are loathe to give a student zero credit on an essay question unless the question is left blank. In the absence of substance some instructors can find redeeming merit in anything the students put down on paper and give them two or three credit points. On the other end of the grading scale, these same instructors may embrace the notion that students are inherently incapable of a "perfect" answer and assign as a best score one that is two or three points below the maximum allotted.

The difficulty with adding points at the lower end of the scale and shading them at the upper is that one automatically restricts the range of scores. A ten-point question with a 0–10 theoretical range becomes for all practical purposes a 2–8 range or even a 3–7 range. By restricting the range, scores tend to cluster and the question loses much of its discriminating power; that is, it does not reveal significantly different performance levels among students with good and poor answers.

Of course, the range of scores may be narrow because the question is too difficult or too easy. This will happen sometimes but can be overcome with experience. However, restricting the range of scores because one does not have an adequate scoring key is avoidable.

Don't Make the Scoring Key too Rigid Before grading examination questions it is a good practice to glance through some of the students' responses. Sometimes students come up with valid points you may not have thought about, or you might have worded your question in such a way as to lead students toward an unintended—but valid—answer.

Suppose, for example, you asked students to "describe the process of inflation and identify the groups in society which suffer from price inflation." You then write out your answer to the question and assign credit points. After glancing through some of the students' responses you notice that some students are answering on the basis that the price inflation was anticipated by all groups in society, while other students assumed that the price inflation was unanticipated. You had "unanticipated" in mind. Are your answer and key valid? Probably not, since your question is ambiguous on this point.

The ideal solution is to construct questions which leave no room for unintentional ambiguity. Regardless of how hard one might try, however, mistakes do happen. In such situations recognize the error as yours and not the student's, and prepare an alternate key.

Also, in some situations, you may want an essay question that permits or encourages different responses depending upon what assumptions are made. You may even want to test for students' ability to recognize and respond to this point. In these cases an answer key should be constructed to reflect this situation. (See below.)

If you want to use your examinations as learning devices as well as grading devices, it is a good practice to distribute your preliminary, tentative answer key to the students as soon as they hand in their answers, before you have had a chance to read them. Our experience is that these answers are read with an intensity that is rare in other, more conventional study situations. Regardless of what students have written on their own exams, they concentrate on a set of good answers to what are, hopefully, the most important questions in the course while the questions are fresh in their minds. This is a rare opportunity to focus student learning; having a carefully prepared, but reasonably flexible, answer key enables you to take advantage of it.[2]

An example of a flexible answer to a "true-false-*and-why*" question that we have used for learning as well as grading purposes is the following.

Question: "A change in the stock of money will lead to a proportional change in the price level." (Source: The "Classical" Quantity Theory of Money)

Model Answer: True, or False, or Uncertain depending on the assumptions made about V and Q in the classical equation $M \cdot V = P \cdot Q$. The statement would be true *if* the velocity of circulation (V) and real output (Q) *both* remain constant. It would be false or at least uncertain if V or Q changed. Realistically, V is not always constant, and real output also varies, so there is more empirical evidence for a false or an uncertain answer than a true answer. But, for grading purposes, a person who says that the statement is true if one assumes a constant V and Q will get full credit if these assumptions are clearly specified.

Grade Each Question for All Students before Moving to the Next Question
Grading one student's entire exam before moving to the next exam can result in unconscious scoring bias. If, for example, the first few responses on a student's

exam are excellent, there is sometimes a tendency to award more credit on the next question than is perhaps warranted by the answer. The reverse situation holds also. Thus, grade each question *seriatim*.

Don't Look at the Student's Name before Grading the Exam Knowing the identity of the student whose exam you are grading can be a source of unconscious scoring bias. Instructors often gain quick impressions of who their better and poorer students are. In grading exams there is sometimes a tendency to legitimize prior impressions by reading more into the answers of "better" students than is actually there. The opposite holds true for "poorer" students. One can minimize the potential for bias by not looking at the name on the examination until all questions are marked, or by having students put only identification numbers on their answers.

Summary

The essay-type test can be an effective and useful device for assessing student thought processes and their ability to write effectively. Well written essay questions can probe higher level cognitive skills and require students to synthesize and evaluate ideas. Moreover, unlike objective questions, essay questions require students to supply an answer rather than select one. Essays are also a superior method of eliciting student opinions and attitudes, although most instructors do not seek to do this extensively. Finally, good essay tests generally take less time to prepare than good objective tests, chiefly because fewer questions are involved in a typical essay examination.

Criticisms of the essay format center around four general points: (1) they are often used inappropriately; (2) they are time consuming to score; (3) they are more susceptible to content unreliability than objective tests; and (4) they are vulnerable to human scoring error.

A common problem concerning examinations in general is that too little planning takes place prior to writing them. We should know beforehand the precise content we wish to cover on our exams and the cognitive processes we wish to measure. Once we have determined this, we can apply some general guidelines in preparing our exams. A list of these guidelines would include the following: (1) devote more time to constructing questions; (2) provide adequate instructions for the students; (3) consider using several short-answer questions rather than a few extended-answer questions; (4) allow sufficient time for student response; and (5) avoid the use of optional essay questions.

When grading essay questions keep the following in mind: (1) prepare an answer to each question and a scoring key; (2) don't make the scoring key too rigid, and be prepared to alter it if it becomes necessary to do so; (3) grade each question for all students before moving to the next question; and (4) don't look at the student's name before grading the exam.

NOTES

We are indebted to Jerry Petr for some of the ideas and examples used in this chapter.

1. One of our favorites, originally inspired by Michael Sattinger, is:
   Read the following three passages and answer the questions below.
   Exodus, Chapter 30, verses 12-15. "Each who is numbered in the census shall give this: half a shekel according to the shekel of the sanctuary (the shekel is twenty gerahs), half a shekel as an offering to the Lord. Every one who is numbered in the census, from twenty years old and upwards, shall give the Lord's offering. The rich shall not give more, and the poor shall not give less, than the half shekel, when you give the Lord's offering to make atonement for yourselves."
   Leviticus, Chapter 27, verses 30 and 33. "All the tithe of the land, whether of the seed of the land or of the fruit of the trees, is the Lord's; it is holy to the Lord. And all the tithe of herds and flocks, every tenth animal of all that pass under the herdsman's staff, shall be holy to the Lord."
   Deuteronomy, Chapter 16, verse 17. "...every man shall give as he is able, according to the blessing of the Lord your God which he has given you."
   Questions:
   A. In terms of "*vertical equity,*" how does the Lord's tax system seem to be changing as one moves from the second to the third to the fifth books of the old testament? (i.e., What kind of a tax is indicated in the passage from Exodus? What kind of tax is a tithe? What principle of taxation is implied in the passage from Deuteronomy?)
   B. If you were chief angel in charge of economics, which of these three kinds of taxation would you favor? Why? (Explain fully the reasons you favor one kind of taxation over another. Make clear the difference between any analytical concepts and any value judgments you use in your explanation.)
2. It has also been our experience that this practice reduces student complaints about grading. Students looking at the model answer almost always implicitly grade themselves harder than we do. Thus, they often have a sense of relief when they get back answers with partial credit. Without a prior look at a model answer, students with only partial credit are often prompted to ask "why were points taken off." Once they have seen a model answer that usually contains things that might have been included that they didn't think of, however, they are less inclined to ask this question.

REFERENCES

Becker, W.E. and Watts, M. (1996). Chalk and talk: A national survey on teaching undergraduate economics. *American Economic Review Proceedings*, 86(2), 448-454.
Siegfried, J., Saunders, P., Sintar, E., and Zhang, H. (1996). How is introductory economics taught in America? *Economic Inquiry*, 34, 182-192.

CHAPTER 21

USING VIDEOTAPING FOR TEACHER DEVELOPMENT AND SELF-EVALUATION

Michael K. Salemi

Alexander J. Cowell

Videotape is a superior medium for providing feedback to teachers. It is useful both in the training and development of new teachers and for self-evaluation by experienced teachers. Videotape is useful because it provides a literal record of what went on in the classroom. It permits the teacher to see what the students see. No other medium permits teachers to watch their own classroom teaching, as many times as necessary, to determine what worked well and what did not.[1]

A practical advantage of videotape is that it is convenient and inexpensive. Colleges and universities of all sizes have video cameras capable of producing tapes that can be watched on the standard home videotape player. Today's portable equipment is lightweight, convenient and produces clear images from available light. This means that the teacher's regular classroom may be used for taping.

Videotape is a powerful tool, one that must be used with care. Most teachers, novices especially, are frightened at the prospect of seeing themselves on videotape. They are inclined to be embarrassed and self-conscious about their appearance and the sound of their voice. The powerful impact of videotape makes it a two-edged sword. On one hand, it is usually easy to get teachers to take their videotaped sessions seriously. On the other, it requires careful planning and management to make the videotape experience constructive.

This chapter suggests how to use videotape successfully in a teacher development program. The first section sets out the ways in which videotape can be used in such a program. The second and third sections discuss specifically how to use videotape to provide constructive feedback to both new and experienced teachers. The fourth section provides a specific example of the teacher training program run by the Department of Economics at the University of North Carolina. The last section suggests how videotape can be used for self-evaluation.

Using Videotape in Teacher Development Programs

There are several ways in which videotape can be used as part of a training program for new teachers or a development program for experienced teachers.

First, videotape can be used as it would be in the typical classroom—to bring information to the participants. Programs for new teachers do more to improve teaching performance when the participants find it easy to connect the principles of good teaching offered in the program with actual classroom situations where they can be employed. Videotape is an effective way to make this important connection. A session on teaching styles can be enhanced by a videotape providing examples of both a formal, professorial style and an informal, conversational style. A session on questioning techniques has greater impact when participants can view a tape of a teacher using follow-up questions to probe the students' understanding and to prompt them to dig deeper for answers. A session on lecturing skills can illustrate those skills by showing several ways of presenting, say, the "revenue test" for the elasticity of demand.

The use of "trigger tapes" as a discussion-starting strategy is a second important use of videotape in teacher training programs. Trigger tapes are collections of short episodes. Each episode is an enactment of a potentially troublesome teaching situation. One type of trigger tape sets up the situation but does not show its resolution. Instead the narrator asks questions intended to begin discussion among the participants about the nature of the problem and strategies for correcting or resolving it. A second type illustrates poor teaching practices and asks participants to discuss ways of improving the performance.

Consider two examples. Novice teachers are rarely prepared for the first time a student, under stress, breaks down in their office. While they may have received good advice for dealing with such a situation, they are unlikely to recall it when faced with reality. By using a trigger tape depiction of such a breakdown, new teachers can experience the emotion of the situation and practice responding to the distraught student. Good teachers know that it is important to listen carefully when students ask questions. A trigger tape segment showing an instructor answering the "wrong question" can drive this point home and stimulate useful discussion about how to listen carefully.

Trigger tapes can focus on content as well as on teaching skills. One of the hardest concepts to explain to beginning economics students is the application of demand and supply analysis to the foreign currency market. A trigger tape might show a weak presentation where an instructor confuses the forces that underlie each schedule. Participants might then discuss strategies for presenting the material clearly and correctly.

One useful trigger tape was produced by the department of economics at the University of North Carolina at Chapel Hill. It depicts a number of "critical moments" that teaching assistants can face when teaching principles of economics. The tape helps new TAs think through issues such as the level at which to pitch recitations, how to stimulate student participation, and the types of questions students are likely to ask. Trigger tapes must be updated from time to time so that out-of-date hair styles or attire do not detract from the taped scenarios. Departments that have on-going teacher development programs should consider producing their own trigger tapes in order to address the specific needs of their novice teachers.

The third way that videotape can be used in teacher training and development programs is as part of the microteaching process. Microteaching is a small group training procedure that uses videotape to provide feedback to a trainee who is attempting to master a specific teaching skill. The typical microteaching exercise has three steps. In the first step, the supervisor demonstrates or models the skill. In the second, the trainee practices the skill and the practice session is videotaped. In the third step, the supervisor replays the tape for the trainee and the group and leads a discussion in which suggestions are given by the group members to the trainee.

For example, microteaching can be used to teach participants how to ask follow-up or probing questions in class. In the first step, the person leading the training session defines follow-up questions, explains why they are used, and then shows how to use them. (See Chapter 14 for an explanation of follow-up questions.) In the second step, participants practice asking follow-up questions. Each begins the practice session by explaining some concept and quickly asks the group a question. When other participants respond, the instructor follows up with another question designed to stimulate further participation. In the third step, the videotape is replayed and the group members offer suggestions—perhaps pointing out questions that worked well and places where probing opportunities were missed.

Microteaching is more effective than many other methods for teaching new techniques such as questioning skills. Often teachers are reluctant to try these techniques in the classroom simply because they have had no opportunity to practice them and are reluctant to try them out in a "game situation." Microteaching provides intensive practice and nearly instantaneous feedback. The trainee is able to practice the technique until s(he) does it well and feels comfortable with it.

The fourth use of videotape in teacher training and development programs is the one to which the rest of this chapter is devoted—the use of videotape to obtain feedback on the effectiveness of one's teaching.

Types of Videotape Critiquing Programs

The first factor that differentiates programs is the type of teaching performance that is taped and critiqued. Short, simulated lectures and actual class sessions are the most common types. Some programs use formal, objective procedures to review the tape; most use an informal, subjective approach. Programs also approach critiquing in different ways. Some programs count on participants to critique themselves; others use critiquers.

Videotape critiquing can be part of a short workshop or conference. In that case, participants are typically videotaped while giving ten minute lectures.[2] Such critiques are useful. They provide an instructor with basic feedback on voice level and quality, blackboard skills, and body language.

Videotape critiquing is far more valuable when it is based on an actual in-class performance. Semester-long training programs such as those offered by the economics departments at Indiana University and the University of North Carolina at Chapel Hill critique participants on the basis of one or two hour long class sessions. The UNC program is described in detail below.

Programs differ also as to the formality of their videotape reviews and instructor critiques. At one extreme are programs that simply provide participants with videotape of their class and permit them to view it privately. No review and no formal critiquing occurs. At the other extreme is the program that was used by the University of Minnesota in the 1970s.[3] There, a specialist undertook an elaborate, numerical review of each videotape to document how an instructor used class time. The critiquer introduced that objective data as part of the instructor's critique.

Choosing a critiquer involves tradeoffs. A department can invite specialists to its campus to conduct a critiquing program. This option frees the department from the costs of developing in-house expertise but, since the program is concentrated into a few days, often rules out critiques based on actual classroom performances. The department may be able to use on-campus critiquers provided by its teaching and learning center. Those critiquers are knowledgeable about teaching practice but are rarely trained in economics and are thus unable to comment on the content of the class session.

There are also trade-offs involved in choosing how formal a critiquing program will be. Providing instructors with tapes of their class sessions is inexpensive, but there is no guarantee that they can use the tapes to improve their teaching. Reviewing tapes with the Minnesota procedure provides objective data on each instructor's performance, but at a cost of two to three hours of analysis per class. At UNC, we have found that it is not important to provide instructors with a detailed statistical analysis of how they used their class time. It is important, however, to conduct a critique.[4] Our "semiformal" approach is described later.

Maxims for a Successful Videotape Critiquing Program

A successful videotape critiquing program improves instruction. It helps instructors improve by providing them with useful information and a framework for evaluating that information. A successful program follows several rules—implementation of the rules may vary but the rules themselves will not.

First and foremost, the program must, as far as possible, be non-threatening to the participants. If an instructor feels threatened by videotaping, (s)he is likely to be nervous during the taped class and give a sub-par teaching performance. The resulting tape will not be representative and it will be difficult to provide the instructor with accurate feedback and helpful suggestions. If the instructor feels threatened by the critique, (s)he will be more concerned with self-defense and less open to suggested improvements. If, on the other hand, the instructor is comfortable with videotaping and critiquing, the tape will be more representative of a normal teaching performance and s(he) will be more receptive to the critiquer's suggestions. Then the process can be a powerful tool for development.

Several strategies can be employed to minimize the threat associated with the taping and the critique. One strategy is to conduct an orientation session designed to show that the critique can be a rewarding experience. In the session, the critiquer can explain that the goal of taping and critiquing is to develop rather than evaluate participants. The critiquer can also show participants a videotape of a former program participant and explain what points he would make in the critique.[5] This strategy could be taken one step further by showing the participants a videotape of the critique itself. The point is that participants see in advance that they will not be assessed or graded, but will be involved in a discussion about teaching strengths and weaknesses and options for improvement.

Another way of making a training program "participant friendly" is to make all the arrangements for taping and critiquing in consultation with the participant. As far as possible, the critiquee should choose the class session for the critique.

Another threat-minimizing strategy is to assure participants that the taping and critique will lead to a reasonable and manageable plan for improvement. Part of this strategy is emphasizing those teaching practices that worked well for the instructor. It is as important to reinforce effective teaching practices as it is to change ineffective ones. Another part is limiting the critique to the two or three areas for improvement that appear to be most important. When participants know in advance that they will receive some praise and a manageable agenda for change, they are more likely to relax during the taping and remain open to suggestion during the critique.

The second maxim of a successful videotape critiquing program is that the videotapes and the results of the critique are confidential. The principle here is that teacher development and teacher evaluation are incompatible objectives. Videotape critique will be a more effective tool for improving instruction when the participant trusts the critiquer and does not feel compelled to defend the teaching practices recorded on the videotape. It is far easier to create an atmosphere of trust when the critiquee knows that s(he) will not be evaluated on the basis of the tape or the critique.

The third maxim of a successful videotape critiquing program is that steps are taken to help instructors watch their tapes in a structured way that will help them assess their own performance. It is not enough for instructors to gain a general impression of their style and effectiveness. The desired outcome is improved instruction so that instructors should watch the tapes in a way that helps them decide what to change.

A useful device for introducing structure is to have instructors write down before the taping, on a form like that in Figure 21-1, the objectives and teaching plan for the class session.[6] After the class, but before viewing the tape, the instructor should also complete a self-evaluation, like that given in Figure 21-2. While watching the tape the instructor should be invited to identify those teaching techniques that worked best. S(he) should also be asked to identify a few places in the tape that indicate a need for improvement and to suggest some alternatives. Finally, the instructor should reevaluate how well the class objectives were met and decide where improvements are most needed.

Since improved instruction is the most important objective of videotape critiquing, a fourth maxim for such a program is to use a contract for change. Instructors should be asked from the beginning to agree that they will implement in their classes the improvements that they identify as most important in their videotape critiques. In some cases they might agree to seek help with specific problems from teaching specialists on their campus. The contract might be a formal one but will more likely amount to an informal agreement between the critiquer and the critiquee. If the instructor is taped again at a later date, the second critique should begin with a review of the original contract for change.

By asking instructors to make all the important decisions, the critiquing program helps them begin a process of self-evaluation and improvement that can continue after the videotape program is over. The instructor should decide what worked and what didn't. The instructor should decide whether class objectives were met. The instructor should decide where improvement is most needed. The instructor should decide to make a commitment to change in the indicated ways.

There is the question of what to do with an instructor who does not take the critiquing process seriously and ignores needed change. A second critique may help by pointing out to the instructor that the same problems exist. This is about as far as a development-oriented program can go. An instructor who will not cooperate may be a problem better dealt with by the school's separate evaluation program.

The final maxim is that the participants in the training program should be informed of maxims one to four. A training program will be most effective if participants cooperate willingly. Cooperation is more likely when participants understand at the outset that tapes are confidential information, that they will have a say in the schedule, that the purpose of the program is development and not evaluation, and that the program is designed to help them make decisions, not to make decisions for them.

FIGURE 21-1   PRE-VIDEOTAPING SURVEY

1. You are asked to complete this survey for the class which is being taped. When is this class session?

    Section 304, Econ 10, September 13, 2:00 pm

2. What are the objectives for the class? What should the students know or be able to do by the end of the class?

    The objective for this class is to engage students in a discussion of scarcity, choice, and opportunity cost, the most important concepts introduced in chapter three. The students should learn from the class the definitions of those concepts and how to apply them in a discussion of the allocation of water to the competing uses of irrigation and production of textiles. They should be able to draw a production possibilities frontier and explain how it shifts when less rainfall occurs or when water quality improves.

3. What is your teaching plan for the class? What materials, if any, will you use?

    I will begin class by defining scarcity and explaining that a scarcity of inputs implies a tradeoff between outputs. I will give as an example the scarcity of student time and draw myself a ppf where study time is on one axis and recreation time is on the other. I will then ask the students how to draw the ppf for the example given above and lead them through its construction. I will then ask the students how the ppf will shift in a number of cases.

Videotape Critiquing Models

The Teacher Training Program at the University of North Carolina In the Department of Economics at the University of North Carolina, videotape critiquing is one part of the department's annual Teacher Training Program (TTP). The TTP consists of a series of lectures, discussions, and practicums, a set of written assignments, and videotape critiquing.

The TTP sessions are organized and conducted by a regular faculty member as part of his/her departmental committee chores. The videotaping and critiquing is done by a senior graduate student chosen and trained by the faculty member. Although mandatory for all new teaching assistants and faculty, the program is very popular so that attendance is regular and participation spirited. The lectures, discussions, and practicums occur at the beginning of the participant's first teaching assignment. Videotaping occurs midway through that first semester.

The first teaching assignment for most of our graduate students is to be a teaching assistant for an economics principles course. There are typically four TAs assigned to each principles professor. The TAs are responsible for conducting weekly recitations to groups of about twenty-five students each. After serving two or more semesters as a principles TA, graduate students are assigned to teach their own course in summer school and to be an assistant for an advanced course or a TA coordinator for principles.[7]

Videotaping and critiquing are conducted mid-way through the first semester. A follow-up critique is conducted in the second semester as the TA teaches his/her recitations for the second time.

Preparing to Videotape the Class Session The first step in the UNC critiquing process is to prime the participants. New TAs will differ in their approach to teaching for the first time, but most are anxious about their "First Day". This anxiety is often compounded by the knowledge that at some point they are to be videotaped giving one of their classes. As part of the Teacher Training Program, the experienced graduate student responsible for administrating the videotaping and providing the critique gives a 90 minute seminar on the Videotaping and Critique. This seminar is designed to inform the participants about the videotaping process, to answer questions that participants have, and to help alleviate their fear of being videotaped while leading a recitation. This is an example of what is meant by the "Final Maxim", that the participants of a training program should be informed.

Towards the end of the seminar, three video clips are shown. First, participants are shown a five-minute long segment of a videotape of one of their (now experienced) peers, as an example of what is considered to be a good recitation. This videotape segment is one that was actually used in a critique in a previous year, and is shown with the permission of the instructor. Following this first segment, the seminar leader would point out why this videotape segment is thought to be an example of good teaching practice. The last two clips are humorous examples of classroom recitations that have gone awry. Humor can be one means of dealing with pre-videotape anxiety.[8]

The next step of the program is to schedule the class session to be taped. The TAs are consulted to determine an appropriate week and the recitation section in which they prefer to be taped. Classes where exams are given or reviewed or which immediately precede a holiday are not appropriate for taping.

Prior to the taping, each TA completes a survey (Figure 21-1) in which the TA states the objectives and teaching plan for the recitation. We use the survey to reinforce the idea that teachers should begin planning by asking what students should be able to accomplish as a result of the lesson. We also use it to emphasize that self-development requires, as a first step, that the teacher set some objectives.

Videotaping the Class Session Next comes the taping of the class. We urge the TAs to tell their classes a week in advance that they will be videotaped and to explain why. The students tend to be more relaxed and more responsive when they understand the purpose of the taping. They are also pleased to learn that the department has a program designed to improve instruction.

We use standard "consumer" equipment: a VCR, a standard battery powered "camcorder", a tripod, and a TV monitor.[9] Most often, the camera operator brings only the camcorder and tripod to the classroom. In some applications it makes sense to use the TV monitor, rather than the tiny camera monitor, during taping in order to better observe the class and stay alert to what is going on.

The camera operator for our program is the same experienced graduate assistant who critiques the videotape. This is not essential and a large program might prefer either to hire an undergraduate as operator or to ask for help from the campus media center. In our case, it is simpler to consolidate tasks and the same senior TA tapes, critiques, reads and comments on participants' written exercises, and assists with the TA seminars.

It is highly desirable that the taping occur in the TA's regular classroom. The technical quality of the tape is clearly less than that obtainable in a media lab. But the tape is *much more* useful because it gives a *much more* accurate picture of the TA's in-class behavior and the interaction between the TA and the students. The equipment we use is so compact and quiet that most instructors report that after a few minutes they largely forget that it is there.

While taping, the camera operator should obey a number of simple rules. Above all, the operator should be as unobtrusive as possible. S(he) should set up the equipment and check the sound level well before the beginning of class. Tape and lighting quality are verified by using the built-in playback facility (available as a feature in most product lines). There is a tradeoff involved in deciding where in the classroom to position the camera. To be able to record the facial expressions of students who are asking and answering questions, the ideal position for the camera is on one side about half way toward the back of the room. Because this positioning tends to distract some students, we have on occasion chosen to tape from the rear of the classroom.[10]

Most of the time the camera operator focuses the camera on the instructor, taking care to tape the instructor's physical reaction to student questions and answers since "body language" may affect students' willingness to participate. The operator should use the zoom lens to vary the shot from a head-and-shoulders closeup to a shot that takes in a width of about ten feet. S(he) should also get a clear shot of several seconds' duration of whatever is written on the blackboard. From time to time the operator should pan the class so that the instructor will later be able to reflect on the attention level and reaction of the students.

FIGURE 21-2   POST-VIDEOTAPING SURVEY

Please fill out this survey after your taping and before your critique.

1. Did your students meet their objectives? How do you know?

    I think so. My example went over nicely and a number of students asked questions and participated in a discussion it. But they had some trouble understanding how to shift the ppf.

2. How well did your teaching plan work? Did you stay with the plan? If not, why? Which aspects of the plan worked best? Less well?

    My lecture on the ppf went well. But I was surprised by the number of questions that the students asked about my simple example. Also, no one volunteered when I asked how to draw the ppf for the water quality example. I explained how but ran out of time before I could give them much practice on shifting the ppf.

Please fill out the checklist (Figure 21-3) and use it as a guide when answering the next three questions.

3. What were the two greatest strengths of your performance? Explain.

    I think I did a good job of maintaining eye contact with the students. By maintaining eye contact, I was able to address my answers to the whole class and not just to the person asking the question. I also made good use of gestures. I also think my ppf examples were good illustrations of the concept.

4. What were two weaknesses of your performance? Explain.

    I think I repeated myself too often when I introduced scarcity and went off on a tangent about the invisible hand. Also, I think I might have asked better questions about the water example. I looked at the blackboard after class and found that my writing and drawing were a little sloppy.

5. How will you overcome the weaknesses mentioned above?

Preparing for the Critique After the taping, both the instructor and the critiquer prepare for the critique. The instructor fills out a self-evaluation survey (Figure 21-2). This self-evaluation is one of the most effective tools of the training program at UNC. The are two reasons for this. First, critiques are more effective when instructors have first evaluated their own performance because they learn during the critique whether their self-assessment is realistic. Second, videotape critiques are more likely to have a permanent impact if they teach instructors how to critique themselves. The self-evaluation provides the instructor with a set of criteria on which to judge his or her performance.

The critiquer prepares for the critique by reading the teaching plan and the self-evaluation and then watching the tape. A novice may need to watch the tape twice: once to get a general impression of the session and a second time to plan the critique. An experienced critiquer will generally watch the tape only once unless the session presents some special problems.

In addition to gaining an overall impression of the session, the critiquer should gather three kinds of specific information. First, s(he) should be prepared to point to two or three parts of the performance that were particularly good. It is at least as important to reinforce good teaching practices that the instructor employs as it is to identify areas for improvement.

Second, the critiquer should identify sections of the tape that bear directly on the objectives that the instructor set out for the class. These are sections that the critiquer plans to discuss with the instructor. An example of the type of videotape segment that may be used is given below. Detailed notes of the videotape are extremely useful so that the critiquer can later recall how to use these segments. Date/time clock readings in the margin of the notes link the notes to the associated segments and help cue the tape. By the time the critiquer has finished viewing the tape, s(he) will usually have accumulated two to four pages of notes on letter-size paper.

Finally, the critiquer should decide on one or two areas where the instructor might improve. For example, s(he) might decide that the instructor should listen to student questions more carefully and should ask more follow-up questions. S(he) would therefore present suggestions for improvement that flow naturally from the tape segments on which the critique has been focused and, ultimately, from the objectives set by the instructor for the class. If possible, the critiquer would relate these suggestions to the instructor's self-evaluation.

Above all, the critiquer should recognize that the decision to change is the instructor's. At most, the critiquer can facilitate change. The critiquer must be prepared to adjust to the attitude of the instructor. If the instructor seems resistant or defensive, the critiquer should be prepared to make fewer suggestions for change. If the instructor is receptive, the critiquer should be prepared to do more.

Providing the Critique The critique itself is designed to be informative yet concise—a typical critique will last between twenty and thirty minutes. The critiquer's first duty is to explain the ground rules of the critique, and to reassert that the critique is confidential. In order to establish a dialogue about the class session with the instructor, a good way of leading into the discussion is for the critiquer to ask the instructor what s(he) thought of the recitation. This provides a natural bridge to a review of the instructor's objectives for the class and the critiquer may then compare these to the instructor's post-class self-evaluation. The critiquer would then bring in the main points from his or her notes on the recitation. Once the critiquer has introduced his or her main points, there is the opportunity to show the selected segment(s) from the videotape. Such a segment would illustrate selected features of the presentation.

An example should help to clarify the sort of videotape segment that might be used in a critique. Suppose an instructor has stated that the objective for a class is that students practice using demand and supply analysis by solving comparative statics exercises. Early in the class the instructor sets the first practice problem. One or two students unsuccessfully attempt to work through the problem. Thereafter, the students no longer volunteer. After a brief pause, the instructor solves that problem, reviews the rules for shifting demand and supply schedules, and goes on to solve some other practice problems.

The critiquer should plan to focus on the tape segment that shows the instructor giving up the questioning strategy and beginning to lecture. S(he) should plan to ask why the instructor abandoned the questioning strategy. S(he) should also ask the instructor to think of some ways to make the questioning strategy work even though students have stopped volunteering. If possible, the critiquer should show the instructor another segment of the tape where things went better—one, perhaps, where the instructor managed to restate the original problem in a simpler way and stimulate additional participation.

Once the segments of the videotape have been shown, the instructor may have one or two comments, and these are then discussed. To provide closure to the critique, the critiquer and instructor agree upon a contract for change. They agree on two or three areas where the instructor will seek to improve. Only two or three areas are highlighted so that the instructor comes away with a manageable agenda for change. The critiquer's ideal plan would have been to show important contradictions between the instructor's objectives and the taped performance, but the decision making is left to the instructor. If the instructor is not persuaded, the critiquer should plan to drop the issue rather than to place the instructor on the defensive.

The critiquer always offers the instructor the opportunity to borrow the tape or watch it again. Invariably, instructors take this opportunity and also take a copy of the critiquer's detailed notes to review with the tape. This reinforces the idea that it is ultimately the instructor's responsibility to motivate improvement themselves.

The Follow Up to the Videotaping Critique As mentioned above, every TA for a principles course will have an assignment for at least two semesters. For all principles TAs, a brief follow-up critique is given mid-way through the second semester. The follow-up was introduced to help participants review their progress.

Although no videotaping takes place in the follow-up, it is an integral part of the videotaping process, and deserves a summary here.[11]

To prepare for the follow-up, the critiquer usually needs to review the videotape and notes from the first semester. The follow-up is less formal than the first critique so that the instructor has the option, but is not required, to fill out pre- and post-class self-evaluations. At a pre-arranged time, the critiquer sits in a recitation given by the instructor. No videotaping occurs. The critiquer is there to determine whether the instructor is improving in the few areas that s(he) agreed to work on in the first critique. The critiquer should also watch for the good practices that the instructor used in the taped class. It is as important to reinforce good practices as it is to monitor needed change.

The critiquer and the instructor then meet either immediately after the class, or within two days of the class. The follow-up critique focuses on the points highlighted in the first semester and touches on any other aspects of teaching that the critiquer or the instructor wish to raise. The follow-up critique is confidential, and this is made clear to instructors.

The Harvard Model A second model for videotape critiquing closely resembles microteaching and was used for some years by the department of economics at Harvard. In this model, videotape critiquing is used as part of an intensive training program for new TAs. TAs are instructed to prepare a short lecture suitable for presentation in the principles course. They are then taped while delivering that lecture to the training group. A critiquer replays the tape immediately and makes suggestions to the TA. TAs modify their teaching plans and are re-taped the following day giving the same lecture.

There are several benefits to the microteaching approach. First, TAs receive rapid feedback on their lecture technique which permits them to make needed adjustments and assess the success of those adjustments. This feedback appears to work well since the second-day tapes usually show significant improvement. Second, the program is easy to implement. One need only arrange to use videotape equipment for two or three days each year. Third, the program is particularly valuable for teaching a specific skill. For example, if a TA's blackboard writing was poorly organized in the first taping, the critiquer can point this out and suggest specific improvements. At the second taping, the critiquer will see whether the TA understood how to correct the problem and then can provide additional instruction as needed.

There are likewise some disadvantages to the microteaching approach. Above all, it does not provide feedback on an instructor's actual in-class performance. It cannot realistically simulate, for example, how instructors adjust their presentation when students signal that they do not understand. Nor can it show how well instructors field spontaneous questions. Because it does not provide sustained reinforcement, instructors may revert to their previous practices once the program has ended.

FIGURE 21-3   POST-VIDEOTAPING CHECKLIST

Please indicate by checking the appropriate boxes your own assessment of the class which was videotaped.

		Very pleased	O.K.	Would like to Improve
1.	**Delivery**			
	a. I spoke clearly		x	
	b. I used good vocal inflection and was not monotone.		x	
2.	**Enthusiasm**			
	a. I appeared interested in the lesson.	x		
	b. Students appeared interested.			x
3.	**Poise and self-confidence**			
	a. I appeared confident and natural.		x	
	b. I was free of distracting mannerisms.		x	
	c. I kept eye contact with students.	x		
4.	**Lecture skills**			
	a. My explanations were coherent.		x	
	b. I made good use of examples.			x
	c. I used the blackboard well.			x
	d. I showed mastery of the subject.		x	
	e. My notation was clear and precise.		x	
	f. The pace of the class was appropriate.			x
5.	**Discussion skills**			
	a. I made good use of questions.		x	
	b. I fielded questions well.			x
	c. I used follow up questions well.			x
	d. I listened carefully to answers.		x	
6.	**Planning**			
	a. My lesson was well organized.	x		
	b. I emphasized important ideas.	x		

Overall, it would seem sensible to think of the microteaching model as a complement to, rather than a substitute for, in-class videotaping. (Klinzing and Klinzing-Eurich also reach this conclusion.) One benefit of using both types of video feedback is that experience with microteaching at the beginning of a TTP should lower the TA's anxiety about the full scale taping and critiquing to come later.

Using Videotape for Self-Evaluation

This section is addressed to those readers who do not have access to video tape critiquing services or who prefer not to involve someone else in the critiquing process. Much of what has been said in the previous sections is relevant to the use of videotape for self-evaluation. Our recommendations are summarized in a five step approach.

A Five Step Approach to Videotape Self-Evaluation

1. Request your media center, teaching resources center, or anyone owning a "camcorder" and tripod to tape one of your classes. Show them the suggestions for taping given above.
2. Fill out the pre-class questionnaire (Figure 21-1).
3. After the class is over and before you watch the tape, fill out the self-evaluation (Figure 21-2). You are now ready to watch the tape.
4. Watch the tape with an eye toward making a list of the three parts of your performance that worked best. Write these down and ask yourself why they worked. At the end of the tape, write down two (and only two) parts of your performance that you believe could be improved.
5. Reread the pre- and post-class forms and remind yourself why you liked the parts you liked and why it is important to change the parts you didn't like. Write down a manageable plan for change.

It is a good idea to keep the videotape and watch it again at a later date, possibly in preparation for repeating the self-evaluation process. In this way you can monitor whether your plan for change has been effective and adjust it if necessary.

Summary

Our own experience in the UNC TTP confirms that videotaping and critiquing improves instruction. The participants regularly report that they find the videotape critiques to be helpful. And our critiquers notice improvement when they conduct follow-up critiques in the second semester. For example, a common habit of novice instructors is to lecture to the students rather than lead them in discussion. Once this has been identified in the videotape and discussed in the critique, it is often evident in the follow-up that the instructors are doing a better job of involving students.

Videotape is a powerful way to provide feedback to teachers. The medium is so powerful, that steps should be taken to insure that the videotape experience is a positive one. Our approach is to inform participants at the outset that videotaping and critique are part of a development program and will not be used for evaluation. We then take participants through a series of steps that make review of the videotape by the participants one part of a self-evaluation process. Throughout, we encourage participants to recognize their own teaching strengths when the tape reveals them and to make a plan for improvement that is reasonable and manageable.

NOTES

We thank Steve Cobb, Matt Klena, Edward Neal, Phillip Saunders, and Joan Worth for making many useful comments on an earlier draft of this chapter.

1. There is a growing body of research documenting that using videotape to provide feedback to teachers improves instruction. See, for example, Klinzing, Hans G. and G. Klinzing-Eurich, "The effects of self-confrontation via TV and of additional training components: group discussion, discrimination training, and practice in a scaled-down situation on the indirectness of teacher trainees," (paper presented to the annual meeting of the American Educational Research Association, New Orleans, La., April 23–27, 1984). For documentation that videotaping improves instruction in a microteaching environment, see Frager, Alan M. "Videotape technology and teacher training: a research perspective," *Educational Technology,* v. 25, n. 7, 1985, 20-22; and Ajayi-Dopemu, Y. and Talabi, J.K. "The effects of videotape recording on microteaching training techniques for education students," *Journal of Educational Television,* v. 12, n. 1, 1986, 39-44.

2. See Hansen, W. Lee, P. Saunders, and A. L. Welsh, "Teacher Training Programs in College Economics: Their Development, Current Status, and Future Prospects," *Journal of Economic Education,* Spring 1980, 11, 1-9.

3. See William E. Becker et al., "Development and Evaluation of Teaching Skills through the use of Videotape," Chapter 11 of Saunders, Phillip, A. L. Welsh, and W. L. Hansen, (eds.) *Resource Manual for Teacher Training Programs in Economics,* Joint Council on Economic Education, New York, 1978.

4. There is literature documenting that videotape critiquing improves teaching. Juliette Venitsky in a paper prepared for the 1982 Annual California Great Teachers Seminar entitled "Using Videotape for Self-Improvement" argues that effective use of videotape requires positive feedback, the provision of immediate and private feedback and the provision of multiple opportunities be taped and critiqued.

5. The critiquer must always obtain prior approval to show the tape of a participant to anyone, especially to the participant's faculty and graduate student colleagues.

6. See Chapter 8 for an introduction to instructional objectives.

7. The department is in the process of expanding the TTP to provide additional instruction for senior graduate students who are assigned to teach their own courses. A

graduate student who completes both modules of the TTP will have an opportunity to complete an independent study and earn a teaching credential in the form of three hours of graduate credit in economics.

8. The second clip shows a three minute part of a recitation that did not go particularly well. The third is a simulation of an instructor who has prepared poorly for class, and then stumbles through the consequences. We use both with permission.

9. Some camcorder features are necessary for in-class recording. These are: a date/time clock; a built-in replay function that permits the operator to check recording quality on the fly; a tripod mount; an option that allows for internal microphone over-ride with external microphone sockets; easily accessible zoom and pan adjustments; and automatic and manual light settings. These features are available on standard home camcorders. The Panasonic AG170 camcorder that we use at UNC has these features, for example.

10. All of our videotaped class sessions are held in classrooms that hold a maximum of 40 students, are sufficiently well lit and have no acoustic peculiarities; hence, the equipment outlined above is adequate. There are occasions when a standard home camcorder is insufficient. For those who may be videotaping larger classes, it is necessary to position the camera near the front of the room and advantageous to over-ride the built-in microphone and to use instead the mixed input from two microphones. Position one directional microphone near the rear of the class to capture the instructor's voice. Position a second near the front of the room to record students' questions, responses, and comments. Experimenting with microphone positions and mixer settings may be necessary to obtain a clear record of student comments.

11. Depending on the available resources of the department and university, departments may wish to consider a second videotaping session and critique for the follow-up. A second taping would stretch the resources here at UNC. Also the marginal benefit of the second taping would be considerably lower than for the first taping, and so we choose not to tape instructors again in the second semester.

CHAPTER 22

USING STUDENT AND FACULTY EVALUATIONS TO IMPROVE ECONOMICS INSTRUCTION

William B. Walstad

Phillip Saunders

Two important reasons for evaluating economics teaching are to diagnose areas for improvement (often called formative evaluation) and to aid in personnel decisions on salary increases, promotion, and tenure (often called summative evaluation). In both of these cases instructors can rely on student, self, and colleague evaluations. The timing and content of the instruments used and the strategies and procedures employed, however, should differ depending on the purpose for which the results will be used. In this chapter we will emphasize formative evaluation for improvement, but we will also discuss the collection and interpretation of summative evaluation data.[1]

Student Evaluation of Teaching

Many departments and universities use a common end-of-course evaluation questionnaire to collect data from students for summative evaluation purposes.[2] In these situations individual instructors may have little influence over the questions asked or the data collection and reporting procedures used, and they may find the results of little use in helping them improve their teaching. Nevertheless, there are some generally accepted principles and procedures that should be employed when common questionnaires are used (Centra, 1993), and individual instructors interested in improving their instructional effectiveness (and their summative student ratings) can supplement them with activities of their own. We will first note some findings from the extensive literature that has developed on the use of student evaluation questionnaires, and then discuss a variety of student evaluation methods that individual instructors can use to improve their instruction before a course is completed or a personnel decision is made.

Reliability and Validity A major concern with student evaluation of teaching is whether it provides reliable and valid information on teaching effectiveness. Many questions have been raised over the years about how to define and measure a relatively vague construct such as "teaching effectiveness." The reviews of research studies on student evaluations in many disciplines indicate that they do provide reliable and valid information about teaching performance, even if they are not perfect measures (McKeachie, 1994; Cashin, 1995).[3]

Reliability refers to the consistency, stability, or generalizability of the items on the form for measuring teaching. The consistency evidence comes from studies showing high correlations among the ratings that students give an instructor. The correlation rises as the number of student raters increases (e.g., .69 for 10 students and .90 for 40 students). Studies also have found that the student ratings are stable over time. Students who gave an instructor a high rating one year will tend to give the instructor a high rating when surveyed years later. Student ratings of teaching also measure *general* teaching effectiveness rather than *specific* teaching skill. Studies show that the correlation in the student ratings of the same instructor teaching the same course are higher than the ratings of the same instructor teaching a different course.

The validity of student ratings as a measure of teaching effectiveness is more difficult to establish given the problem of defining what constitutes effective teaching. Multiple sources used for the validity evidence, however, indicate that student ratings are positively associated with learning outcomes, other ratings of the instructors, and teaching behaviors. For example, reviews of studies have been conducted where instructors taught multiple sections of courses that used the same syllabus, textbook, and same *external* exam. Positive correlations were found between the exam grade and students' self-ratings of their achievement in the course (.47), overall course evaluation (.47), and overall instructor evaluation (.44). The positive correlations were also found when controlling for student, instructor, course, or school variables.

Perhaps more important for the purposes of this chapter were the positive correlations between the exam grades and student ratings of instructors on different dimensions of teaching. Positive correlations were found between the exam grade and such factors as: (1) teaching skill, .50; (2) preparation, .57; (3) clarity of objectives, .35; (4) teaching structure, .74; (5) understandableness, .56; (6) knowledge of the subject, .34; (5) teacher rapport, .34; (6) availability to students, .36; (7) respect for students, .23; (8) interaction with students, .22; and, (9) encouraging discussion, .36. What these findings indicate is that teaching behaviors and practices have a direct effect on student learning. As students learn more they will give more positive evaluations. *Thus, the instructor has substantial control over the outcomes from student evaluations by the positive teaching behaviors and practices they exhibit in the classroom.*[4]

Another way to assess the validity of student ratings is to compare them with other evaluations of instructors. Positive correlations in the range of .29 to .49 have been found between student ratings and the instructor self-ratings of their teaching performance. Similarly, positive correlations have been found between student ratings of instructors and those supplied by colleagues (.49 to .69), alumni (.40 to .75), administrators (.47 to .62), and trained observers (.50 to .76). Several studies also report positive correlations (.73 and .93) between student comments written about an instructor and their overall numerical rating.

In most cases, the primary purpose of the common end-of-course evaluation form is to provide comparative data for administrators when making salary or promotion and tenure decisions. What is most often used for this purpose are the summary items that ask students to rate the "overall effectiveness of the instructor," the "overall value of the course," or "the amount learned in the course." *These summary items are of limited value to an individual instructor for improving their teaching; but, if interpreted carefully, they can provide useful information to a department or university administrator when making personnel decisions.*

Other Considerations Reasonable caution and judgement should be used by administrators when making comparisons across instructors. Even valid and reliable ratings are not perfect measures of teaching effectiveness and are subject to interpretation and measurement error. They are best thought of as general indicators of instructional effectiveness that need to be supplemented with other information. In many cases, there may be no meaningful difference in the overall ratings that most instructors receive from students because ratings tend to be skewed in a positive direction, thus limiting the range of the scale. The difference in a rating of 3.8 and 4.0 on a five point scale, for example, is minor and should not be used for ranking instructors, but a difference between 2.5 and 4.0 is likely to be important.[5]

Furthermore, other factors may need to be controlled when comparing ratings across instructors. These factors include: (1) *Rank.* Regular faculty tend to be rated higher than graduate assistants or adjunct faculty; (2) *Expression.* The more enthusiastic and expressive the instructors, the higher their ratings; (3) *Motivation.* Instructors are generally rated higher in courses where students are more interested in the subject (e.g., take the course for general interest or as an elective); (4) *Expected grades.* There tends to be a positive, but low, correlation between expected grades and student evaluations; (5) *Course level.* Graduate classes tend to rate more highly than undergraduate, and seniors rate higher than freshmen; (6) *Difficulty of the class.* Some studies find that the harder the course the more positive the evaluation, indicating that students like a course that challenges them; (7) *Evaluation procedures.* Faculty receive lower evaluations if they are anonymous rather than signed, and higher evaluations if students know they are used for personnel decisions rather than for diagnostic purposes (Cashin, 1995).

Other instructor or student characteristics that might be expected to influence student ratings appear to have no consistently significant effect. Neither the sex nor age of the instructor seems to change student ratings. The personality of the instructor appears to make no contribution to student ratings. There seems to be no significant relationship between students' rating of teaching and the research productivity of the professor.[6] Student characteristics such as age, sex, grade level, previous GPA, or personality apparently have little effect on student evaluations. Even such factors as class size, the time of day for the class, or the administrative period when the student ratings are collected do not seem to be factors influencing the results (Davis, 1993; Cashin, 1995).

Of particular importance to economists, particularly if interdepartmental comparisons of instructors are being made at the college or university level, is a study showing that economics was one of the seven academic fields consistently rated lowest on both course and instructor effectiveness scales for the 45 academic fields covered in the SIR and IDEA national data bases (Cashin, 1990). It is not clear why different academic fields appear to be consistently rated differently by students, but this makes it important for economics departments to establish their own norms on common student evaluation questions. In making comparisons, it is important to compare ratings of economics instructors with ratings of other economics instructors and not instructors from other disciplines that are consistently rated higher by students.

The big point that needs to be emphasized, of course, is that end-of-course student evaluations are but one source of information on teaching effectiveness. Other faculty can provide valuable information and insight about teaching performance, and individual instructors can use a variety of techniques to obtain useful information from their students. The best evaluation strategy for teaching improvement involves a conscientious and consistent effort to get feedback throughout the course to check for understanding and solicit opinions about different dimensions of instruction. This information can then be used to shape instruction and increase student learning.

Feedback from Students

Feedback from students gives you insights that you can't get in other ways, either from colleagues or your department chair. If you give students the opportunity, they will let you know, for example, if they can follow the points in your lecture on monetary policy and understand how changes in monetary policy affect the national economy. Students can also give you feedback on the clarity of your presentation, their interest in the topic, the difficulty of your exam questions, and a host of other factors that affect their learning in the course and perception of you as the teacher.

None of this is worthwhile, however, unless you are willing to receive and use the student comments to diagnose problems and improve instruction.

Student feedback is especially important for new faculty members because they tend to try to do more than students can handle—put too much economic content in the lectures, go too fast over difficult material, make homework assignments too complicated, and select a textbook that is too difficult to read. The reason newly-minted Ph.D.s tend to overwhelm students is that they are most familiar with what they recently learned in graduate school and are thinking at that level of complexity, and thus are most comfortable with teaching as they were most recently taught. They may have forgotten how to simplify an economic explanation, use words in place of equations or graphs, or illustrate a point with a practical example that will make sense for an undergraduate who is new to economics. They also may have forgotten that they *elected* to study economics whereas most freshmen or sophomores are taking a principles class as conscripts or reluctant volunteers. These new students prefer instruction that is concrete rather than abstract, and they want to see the connection between what is covered in the classroom or textbook and what is happening in the "real" world. Regular student feedback will greatly assist the new instructor in adjusting his or her teaching practices to the reality of the undergraduate classroom and the types of students they are teaching.

Focus on Understanding One of the first things that most instructors want feedback on is whether students are understanding the material. A variety of classroom assessment techniques are available for this purpose (Angelo and Cross, 1993). These techniques help the *instructor and student* bridge the gap between what is taught and what is learned well before students are tested or graded. They provide the instructor with vital information for determining what, how much, and how well students are learning. Any problems that you identify can be addressed in the next class session, not after the exam. These techniques let students know that you care about whether they are learning the material, which may affect their end-of-course ratings.

1. *One-minute papers.* At the end of a class session, ask students to write a short one- or two-minute paper in response to two questions: (1) "What was the most important point that you learned in today's class session?" (2) "What questions do you have that remain unanswered?" Reading these short papers will give you direct feedback on what students are thinking and their unanswered questions, information which you can then use in designing your teaching in the next class session.

2. *Muddiest Point.* This assessment technique is similar to the one-minute paper, but asks students to answer the question "What was the 'muddiest point' in my lecture today?" The reasons for the "mud" are also sought by asking the student to attribute the problem to such factors as your unclear presentation, a lack of opportunity to ask questions, a lack of student preparation, problems with the textbook, or something else. You can take corrective actions in the next class.

3. *Summaries.* After covering a topic in class, have students write a short summary of the topic and what they think they learned. If students cannot restate

in their own words something that they learned that makes sense to you, then it should be clear to both you and them that there are learning problems that need to be addressed in future class sessions. You can also promote group work by having them check their understanding with each other before turning in the summary to you.

4. *Applications or Examples.* Many different concepts or ideas are presented in economics courses. One of the best ways to check for student understanding is to give students a sheet of paper and ask them to give you an example or an application of an economic concept after you've discussed the concept in class. This technique gives feedback to the student and to you. If students cannot supply an example or application, then they probably do not understand the course material. The other benefit is that students get to see the connection between abstract concepts and the world in which they live.

5. *Analytic Memo.* For more in-depth assessment, you can ask students to write a short, one-page memo on a topic. This memo can be written for the company president, a political leader, a Federal Reserve official, or someone else involved in making an important economic decision. The memo would outline the economic problem, discuss possible alternatives, and recommend a solution. If they can't write a clear and convincing memo, then they have not mastered the material or see the different points of view on the issue.

Many other short and insightful classroom techniques can be designed for assessing student understanding in the course. You're limited only by your imagination.[7]

Solicit Student Opinions The other type of feedback that the instructor wants to get from students are comments on what they think about your course and how you teach. Several methods—both formal and informal—can be used to obtain this information. You should also tell students that you want both *positive* and *negative* comments. The positive ones let you know what you are doing right and should continue, and the negative ones let you know what you might consider changing. After you get their opinions, you should make it a practice to explain to students the changes that you plan to make in the course based on their comments and why. This practice gives students the sense that they have an important role in the success of the class and that what you are asking them to do is worthwhile.

1. *A mid-course evaluation.* Many instructors have students complete a mid-course evaluation form that either they prepare or is available from the campus teaching center. The evaluation form would ask students a series of questions about course organization, the clarity of instruction, course assignments and materials, their interest in the course, and exams and grading practices. Marsh (1984) found that "instructors who received midterm feedback were subsequently rated about one-third of a standard deviation higher than nonfeedback instructors on the total rating" and particularly on items such as "instructor skill," attitude towards the subject," and "feedback to students." Marsh also found that when feedback was

coupled with consultation between the instructor and a more experienced professor, there was even more improvement in instructor evaluations.

2. *Index card comments.* An informal method of obtaining feedback is to periodically pass out index cards to students during the last ten minutes of class. Ask them to answer some general questions about the course or your teaching. Answers to questions such as "What do you like about the course?," "What do you like about my teaching?," or "What would you like to change in the course?" may give you new ideas for improving your teaching.

3. *Suggestions mailbox.* You should let students know that you welcome suggestions for the course. The suggestions can be submitted at any time in a designated mailbox. The place for leaving comments might be a manila envelope that you put at the back of the classroom or one that you attached by your office door. You can also tell students to leave comments in your office mailbox. If you and the students are connected by e-mail, then use this electronic media to get student comments.

4. *Student interviews.* One of the best ways to get to know your students, and also get feedback from them is to schedule a ten-minute interview with each one during the course. In the interview you can ask students what they think of the course, what they like about it, how it can be improved, or any problems that they are having with the materials. The basis of your questions might come from the written comments that students have submitted to you in previous evaluations. The personal contact with the student signals that you care about them, and can help "break the ice" between student and instructor.

5. *Class advisory committee.* You might establish an advisory committee for the class that would consist of several students. These students would either be randomly chosen or volunteer to serve. You can meet with the student committee three or four times during the course, before or after class, or during your office hours. You can tell the other students that if they have any comments about the course, your teaching, or the course content, they can either direct them to you or the members of the class advisory committee. Bonus points can be assigned for service on the committee, and you can also rotate membership during the course.

6. *Letter to the next student.* At the end of the course, have students write a letter to a student who will be taking the course the next time it is offered. The letter should describe what they learned, assess the instructor's teaching, and make recommendations to students about what they should do to be successful in the course. These letters would be anonymous, and would be summarized for future students or distributed to them the next time you teach that course.

7. *A special evaluation form.* At the end of the course, you may want to prepare an evaluation form for students to complete that is different from a department-wide form. This assessment technique requires that you design a numerical and written form that meets your needs and addresses characteristics of your course. The questions on the form might ask students to evaluate your lecturing, course content they found most or least interesting, the quality of the class discussions, the textbook or reading, group work, course assignments, tests, etc. The questionnaire

need not be overly long and should not duplicate what is covered in the standard departmental forms. This type of evaluation is highly recommended, especially for new instructors, because you will get the specific feedback you need, both positive and negative, to guide your teaching next time you teach the course.

Student Criticisms Of course not all student comments will be accurate or valid. Students may focus on very minor points that have little to do with instruction, or they can whine about assignments that are perfectly legitimate for you to ask them to do. They may complain about the difficulty of your test questions in an effort to get you to lower your standards and increase their grades. They may also be brutally frank and pointed in their comments in an effort to hurt your feelings ("You are the most unfair teacher I've every had."). You have to learn not to let the comments affect your personal or professional judgment of students. It will be your task throughout a course to sort out the valid comments from the ones that are petty, misdirected, or a blatant attempt to manipulate you.

There are some complaints that are made quite often by students about economics courses. You should be prepared for these comments when you solicit opinions or check for student understanding, and in many cases you can counter the negative sentiments they express.

1. *Economics is too abstract.* Economics requires analytical reasoning and manipulations of several variables at one time. Students, especially at the principles level, may not have encountered this type of thinking in the other courses they are taking. To help students overcome the sense that the subject (and by association, you) are too abstract, you need to give many concrete examples and applications of economic theory so they see the connection to the "real" world. One way to do this is to ask students to give you another example after you've illustrated a point with an initial one in class. In general, attention paid to students' "prior learning set" and learning theory, as discussed in Chapter 8, should help reduce some of the perceived abstractness of the subject that makes it difficult for students to learn.

2. *I didn't expect: (a) to have to study this much; (b) this to be on the test; etc...* Expectations affect students' ratings. You need to be continually aware of what students expect and whether that is realistic. This realization does not mean that you need to make the course less difficult or cater to student whims. Rather, you should explain to students what you expect throughout the course and give them opportunities to discuss their expectations or check their understanding. Many of the previously described feedback exercises will give students a chance to realign their unrealistic expectations with reality, or give you a chance to reduce their frustration with learning economics.

3. *Economics has too many graphs.* Open up any undergraduate economics textbook at any level and there will be many graphs and charts. Most students taking economics courses are ill-equipped for understanding graphical material. Graphs must be handled with care when you present them in class or ask students to read material using graphical explanations. Chapter 10 offers a perspective on

why students find graphs so difficult and some suggestions for good graphing practices.

4. *You grade too hard.* Students tend to focus on grades and forget about learning when they take an economics course. You need to put the grades in perspective and show them what they have learned in the course. This objective can be achieved by using pre- and posttest assessment activities to compare performance. You need to let students know what your grading practices and standards are so they have a better basis for judging the fairness of your grades.

Whatever comments that you get from students about your teaching or the course, the valid messages will generally outweigh the invalid ones. The net results from soliciting feedback is that you get useful diagnostic information to become a better instructor.

Self Evaluation of Instruction

Instructors who want to become more effective teachers must first be willing to conduct a self-evaluation of their teaching and develop a plan for self-improvement. To do so, they should also identify other people who can help them. Most departments or colleges have faculty who have won teaching awards or who are keenly interested in various aspects of teaching. Beginning faculty should make contact with these people so that they will have someone to talk with about teaching issues, and perhaps at a later stage, invite them to conduct an informal peer review of their course or become their teaching mentor. There also are teaching consultants on most campuses outside of the department or college who will assist individual instructors and conduct workshops on new techniques or approaches for their courses.

The discussion that follows offers several practical suggestions for evaluating an instructor's teaching. By following these suggestions, an instructor will be more prepared for a formal review by the department chair, a personnel committee, or the college faculty, and more likely to receive a positive recommendation in a personnel decision.

Teaching Questionnaire The self-analysis of teaching is perhaps easiest to begin by focusing on one course that you teach before looking at all the other courses or your overall teaching activity. A sample questionnaire is found in Appendix 22-1. Completion of the questionnaire encourages you to evaluate your teaching more objectively and from a more comprehensive perspective than you would do on a daily or weekly basis. You can complete the questionnaire and review it by yourself, or arrange to discuss the responses with a campus teaching consultant or another faculty member.

The questionnaire gives you an opportunity to evaluate different aspects of your teaching. The questionnaire asks you whether course goals and objectives are clearly stated. You get a chance to assess the teaching material you use for the course and the appropriateness or level of difficulty for your students. Also included are questions related to teaching practices and methods, the relationship with students, grading and evaluation, and interest in teaching. Most of the chapters in this volume address one or more of the items on the survey.

At the end of each questionnaire are several general questions to answer: (1) "What are your major contributions to teaching this course?"; (2) "Are there any problems or limitations with teaching this course?"; (3) "What aspects of your teaching for this course would you like to improve?"; and (4) "How do you plan to make those changes?" These questions are the most important because they force you to reflect on what you do well in your course and what you can change.

It will be worthwhile for you to complete a course questionnaire for each course you teach because there can be significant differences in teaching practices and course conditions. You might do a great job of teaching an advanced course in your area of specialization, but do a poor job teaching a principles of economics course. You might also use different teaching techniques in different courses, so completing a course evaluation gives you a better sense of the range of your teaching and concerns you have at different levels of instruction.

Videotapes and Visitations Another easy step for self-assessment of instruction is to videotape a class and review it. Videotaping is relatively unobtrusive and can be done by a work-study student or teaching assistant. You can view the tape alone, with another faculty member, or with a teaching consultant. You can videotape the class on several occasions and observe your changes in teaching. Videotape analysis is one of the most effective ways that you can change your classroom teaching behaviors and is discussed in detail in Chapter 21.

Another way to get constructive feedback on a "live" example of your teaching is to invite another faculty member or teaching consultant to visit your class. The class session that you have the visitor attend should be fairly typical and it should be chosen so that you are as relaxed as possible. You can simply ask your colleague for their comments on what they see you doing—things you do to help students learn and ways that the class session might have gone better. The peer can comment on your enthusiasm for teaching, how well you explained an economic concept, how you handle questions from students, the rapport they observe between you and the students, and other aspects of your teaching. This visitation process gives you the opportunity to discuss particular teaching problems and get possible solutions. At the same time, another colleague gets to know you better as a teacher.[8]

Teaching Portfolios One of the best ways to conduct a self-evaluation of your teaching is to prepare a teaching portfolio (Seldin, 1991). The portfolio gives you an opportunity to describe your teaching goals, strengths, and accomplishments in a form that best reflects how you view your teaching and that can be easily reviewed by others. In the process of preparing the portfolio you will have a chance to reflect on your teaching and assess what you have done and what you might like to do in the future. Thus, the preparation of a teaching portfolio lets you assess your teaching and create a personal statement about it that can be read by administrators or peers.

The procedure that most faculty use in preparing a portfolio is relatively straight-forward and involves several steps. First, you need to prepare a statement about your teaching responsibilities. It should include an explanation of the courses that you currently teach or have taught in the past. You can also describe what teaching-related activities you do outside of the classroom, such as serving as an advisor for student groups or presentations on your teaching to other faculty. Second, you need to select items to describe in your written portfolio that are most directly related to your teaching responsibilities, such as course syllabi, sample tests, or student ratings. Third, you need to provide a brief written description of each item in the portfolio that would highlight your activities and achievement for that item. For example, you might describe the activities or project you've done to improve your teaching of an intermediate theory course. Finally, you need to provide the documents that support your statements about teaching initiatives or results in the appendices. These documents might be letters from students about your teaching, sample homework assignments, or articles you've written about your teaching.

Perhaps the most difficult step in preparing a portfolio is deciding what items to include in it. Most portfolios contain material that you prepare, material from others, and outcomes from your teaching. The items you are most likely to prepare, and which constitute the majority of the written portfolio are: (1) a statement of teaching responsibilities; (2) an explanation of your teaching philosophy and methods; (3) an overview of the courses you teach (content, objectives, readings, and assignments, and tests); (4) a description of teaching innovations and their results; and, (5) a discussion of what you have done to improve your teaching and a plan for how you will continue that process. The material from others that you would include would be your interpretation of student ratings of your teaching with comparative data over time. You would also attach letters or testimonials from students and alumni about the quality of your teaching, and describe awards or honors that you've received for your teaching. If you have pre- and posttest data on standardized tests that show improvement in student learning in your course, you should write a description of those results.

The portfolio can be updated and revised continuously as formative evaluation evolves, but the "official" version submitted for summative evaluation should be about ten single-spaced pages of text. Any supporting documents (e.g., course syllabi) can be attached as appendices or exhibits. To keep the size of the portfolio limited you might attach a statement that the supporting materials are available for review upon request in those cases where it is not essential for the reviewers to see the original materials. Examples of teaching portfolios from many disciplines and a description of how they are used to improve teaching can be found in Seldin (1993).

Peer and Colleague Review of Teaching

After you've completed a self-analysis of your courses, reviewed your classroom teaching on videotape, and prepared a teaching portfolio, you are in a good position for a peer or colleague review of your teaching. Peer review has long been used in academe to evaluate scholarly work. Faculty regularly comment on the academic writings of colleagues and make suggestions for changes. They also formally evaluate their colleagues when selecting grant recipients or when making promotion and tenure decisions. Peer review can make a similar contribution to the improvement of teaching (Centra, 1993; Braskamp and Ory, 1994). Peer review of teaching, however, is more useful for certain purposes than others.

Classroom visits by colleagues is one of the most controversial methods of collecting information about teaching for personnel decisions, but peer observation has enjoyed more success as a strategy for teaching improvement. In addition to classroom visits, colleague review of an instructor's course materials (syllabi, reading lists, problem sets, handouts, graded exams, etc.) can be a valuable source of information for both summative and formative evaluation. In all cases, peer and colleague evaluation is likely to be most effective if it is preceded or conducted in conjunction with a continuing and ongoing process of self assessment by individual instructors. If instructors are unwilling to think about what they are doing in the classroom, or make a conscientious effort to improve their performance, then evaluative comments from students, peers, or even the department chair are not likely to have much effect.

The review process can be informal or formal depending on the circumstances. Informal reviews designed to offer advice and comments about your teaching can be conducted at any time, and are best done several times before you are considered for tenure or promotion. This formative evaluation is done solely to give you constructive feedback suggestions, usually orally, and is simply an extension of your self-analysis. Any faculty member can do the review for you, although it would be best to select someone who is known as a good teacher and who you think will give you the best insights into your teaching.

By contrast, the department chair may assign qualified faculty members to prepare formal written reviews of your overall teaching abilities and teaching performance when you are being considered for a high-stakes personnel decision. If you have the option of selecting faculty members to prepare summative reviews, you should consider inviting someone you worked with on an informal review to prepare the formal review that is shared with other faculty members or with campus administrators.

What is needed for a peer review, either informal or formal, is detailed information and documentation about your teaching. Most of this information you will have pulled together when you prepared your teaching portfolio. These items will include course syllabi, handouts, assignments, tests, graded papers, student evaluations, letters from alumni, teaching projects, a classroom videotape, and other relevant material. The written items should be organized into binders in a logical order for inspection by another faculty member. You will also need to arrange to have the faculty member visit your class to observe your teaching firsthand or supply them with a videotape to review. You might also be asked to complete a questionnaire on your teaching. The final part of the review consists of a discussion between you and the reviewer about your teaching that gives you the opportunity to explain what you are doing and gives you suggestions for improvement. If you have made a conscientious effort to do a self-analysis, the peer review is likely to confirm a good rather than a critical report.

Readings, Workshops, and Discussion Groups One of the most challenging aspects of being an economics professor is keeping yourself current with changes in the discipline. To do so requires that you continually read the research literature and attend professional meetings. The situation is no different with teaching. No one, not even the most experienced teachers, can rest on their laurels even if they received positive peer reviews or teaching awards. Students, technology, courses, and teaching methods change, all of which may affect your performance in the classroom. Good teachers think about teaching issues and want to find out new ways to help students learn, and they achieve those objectives in part by reading and attending workshops. In fact, if you want to conduct an informal test of whether a professor is genuinely interested in teaching, ask the person to discuss one recently read article on teaching or describe a recently attended workshop on a teaching topic.

One of the best sources for what other economics professors are doing to improve their teaching is the *Journal of Economic Education.* Each of the quarterly issues contains articles discussing content issues, economics instruction, research on economics teaching, and information about economic education. Articles in the *Journal* have discussed many different kinds of teaching methods and practices in economics courses at all instructional levels (Becker and Watts, 1995).[9]

Workshops on new techniques in teaching are offered on most campuses that cover different topics. These workshops can be a source of inspiration and help for trying new teaching methods or learning about technological applications for the classroom. Attending one or two of these workshops a year may give you some new ideas for your teaching and let you find out what other concerned teaching professors are doing. You should make a policy to schedule time each year to go to workshops on topics that might cover problems you are having in class (e.g., "how to get students motivated") or on new methods for teaching (e.g., "using learning groups").

Over the past six years, there have also been a series of national teaching workshops designed specifically for economics professors. The topics discussed in these workshops cover general teaching methods and approaches, such as lecturing, discussion, active learning, cooperative groups, writing, and testing and evaluation, but illustrate their direct application to economic courses. The economics professors who have attended, many of whom are experienced teachers, have given them high ratings (Salemi, Saunders, and Walstad, 1996).

There is no reason why you need to wait until a formal workshop is offered to get teaching ideas. You can be proactive and organize a teaching discussion group with other professors in your college. Plan to meet with the group once a month to talk about teaching issues and problems. The format can be informal and the topics can vary from month to month. All you need to get the group discussion started are some introductory comments on a topic, a short reading, or a presentation by a guest speaker. The real value of the group is that it becomes a support group and idea laboratory for your teaching. You also get to know your colleagues better, which may be useful for other collaborative or assessment activities such as work on common projects, team teaching, mentoring, or peer review.

Common Projects When faculty work together on a common project, they are likely to share insights about teaching with each other. There are many possibilities for working on projects with other faculty, especially in courses with multiple sections such as principles of economics. You can work with all faculty teaching the course on a common final. You can develop a series of homework assignments that must be completed by all students. Students can be required to write papers using common guidelines that you prepare with other faculty teaching the course. A joint review session can be held for all sections of an economics course. Students from one class can be asked to comment on writing from another class.

Consider, for example, the value of the collaborative work in preparing a common test for a principles course. To write the test, you and the other professors teaching the course must outline the course goals and objectives so that you can develop content specifications for the examination. A lively debate is likely to arise from a discussion of the economic topics to include on the exam, the importance of each topic, and the cognitive level of test questions. The test preparation process will lead to a discussion of coverage of selected topics and a description of various teaching practices that are used to help students learn particular economic concepts. By working on a common test or project, each instructor is in a better position to evaluate his or her teaching in relation to the team.

Working on a common project is more costly in terms of time than teaching the course by yourself because it will require time to sort out different views and reach a conclusion. Nevertheless, there are substantial benefits from collaborative projects. The insights gained and observations shared might be used to improve your teaching of the course the next quarter or semester. You also get to know another faculty member better, and can ask the other faculty member for advice about your teaching problems. In the future, the colleague might be willing to conduct a formal peer review of teaching that is required for your promotion or tenure decision, or at least be willing to serve as a credible reference on the quality of your teaching.

Team Teaching You can take the collaboration one large step further and team teach a course with another professor, if there are opportunities for course experimentation and flexibility at your institution. Team teaching means cooperative planning and teaching and not just presenting a series of guest lectures. Team members plan the course together and consider the objectives, materials, teaching strategies, and assessment techniques. This process encourages discussion on developing and improving the course. A team member can provide immediate feedback on the effectiveness of the various teaching strategies when he or she watches you teach. A team member also can provide suggestions for new instructional activities. Team teaching offers an opportunity to talk about teaching and to see other teachers in action that rarely occurs in most universities.

Conclusion

The major conclusion that emerges from this discussion of the evaluation of teaching is that it should be an continuous process. There are many effective and low-cost ways to get feedback from students. You should adopt some of these methods and use them to make the adjustments to teaching that will help students learn and raise their opinions about your instruction. You need to be willing to conduct a self-analysis of teaching that can be used to prepare a teaching portfolio or a plan of action. You should work with other faculty to improve your teaching either by having them review your work or collaborating with them on special projects.

Good teachers are not born, they are made. One key input in the production process is the evaluation of teaching. It needs to be used on a regular basis so you get information gathered from students, yourself, or colleagues. By continually monitoring your teaching and making the necessary changes, you will receive a positive evaluation when a high-stakes decision is made.

NOTES

1. This chapter has benefitted from ideas presented in Davis (1993), Marlin (1990), McKeachie (1994), and Niss (1990).

2. For example, the SEEQ (Students' Evaluations of Educational Quality) developed by Marsh (1984) assesses student opinions on nine dimensions of teaching (learning/value; enthusiasm; organization; group interaction; individual rapport; breadth of coverage; exams/grades; assignments; and workload). The fact that there are at least four items used for rating each dimension contributes to the quality of this measure, but results in a large number of questions for summative purposes. See Aigner and Thum (1986) for a version of the SEEQ form used at the University of Southern California.

Two other well-constructed and often-used rating forms are IDEA (Instructional Development and Effectiveness Assessment) (Cashin and Sixbury, 1992) and SIR (Student Instructional Report) from the Educational Testing Service. Most evaluation forms contain multiple questions or items that assess about six factors related to teaching: (a) course organization and planning; (b) clarity and communication skills; (c) teacher-student interaction and rapport; (d) course difficulty and workload; (d) grading and examinations; and, (f) students' rating of their learning (Centra, 1993). Many economics departments, however, develop their own common forms rather than use a standardized measure such as SEEQ, SIR, or IDEA. The quality of these forms vary considerably because they are not developed by experts and are often limited in scope.

3. The reliability and validity evidence in this section is taken from Cashin (1995).

4. Similar conclusions have been drawn when examining the results from studies of student evaluations of teaching in economics. (See Chapter 11)

5. The means should be interpreted in light of the variation, or lack of it, in the data. In this respect, information on the standard deviation and median of ratings will be useful.

6. See Yunker and Marlin (1984) for a review of the literature and an economic analysis of the relationship of teaching performance and research productivity.

7. For other ideas, see Chapter 15.

8. There are methods and forms for conducting classroom visits. See Seldin (1981), Centra (1993), and Braskamp and Ory (1994), or Chapter 21 for videotape forms.

9. The *Journal* website is *http://www.indiana.edu/-econed/index.html*.

REFERENCES

Aigner, D.J. and Thum, F.D. (1986). On student evaluation of teaching ability. *Journal of Economic Education*, 17, 107-118.

Angelo, T.A. and Cross, P.K. (1993). *Classroom assessment techniques*, 2nd ed. San Francisco, CA: Jossey-Bass.

Becker, W.E. and Watts, M. (1995). Teaching methods in undergraduate economics. *Economic Inquiry*, 33, (October), 692-700.

Braskamp, L.A. and Ory, J.C. (1994). *Assessing faculty work: Enhancing individual and institutional performance*. San Francisco: Jossey-Bass.

Cashin, W.E. (1990). Students do rate different academic fields differently. In M. Theall and J. Franklin (eds.), *Student ratings of instruction: Issues for improving practice* (pp. 113-121). San Francisco: Jossey-Boss.

Cashin, W.E. (1995). Student ratings of teaching: The research revisited. *Exchange*. Center for Faculty Evaluation & Development, Kansas State University, Idea Paper No. 32.

Cashin, W.E. and Sixbury, G.R. (1992). Description of database for the IDEA *Diagnostic Form*. Center for Faculty Evaluation & Development, Kansas State University, Technical Report No. 7.

Centra, J.A. (1993). *Reflective faculty evaluation: Enhancing teaching and determining faculty effectiveness*. San Francisco: Jossey-Bass.

Davis, B.G. (1993). *Tools for teaching*. San Francisco: Jossey-Bass.

Marlin, J.W. (1990). Student evaluation of instruction: Decipher the message. In P. Saunders and W. B. Walstad (eds.), *The principles of economics course: A handbook for instructors* (pp. 236-254). New York: McGraw-Hill.

Marsh, H.W. (1984). Students' evaluations of university teaching: Dimensionality, reliability, validity, potential biases, and utility. *Journal of Educational Psychology*, 76, 707-754.

McKeachie, W.J. (1994). *Teaching tips: Strategies, research, and theory for college and university teachers*, 9th ed. Lexington, MA: D.C. Heath.

Niss, J. (1990). Utilizing peers to improve the instructional process. In P. Saunders and W.B. Walstad (eds.), *The principles of economics course: A handbook for instructors* (pp. 255-269). New York: McGraw-Hill.

Salemi, M., Saunders, P., and Walstad, W.B. (1996). Teacher training in economics: Past, present, and future. *American Economic Review*, 86(2), 460-464.

Seldin, P. (1981). *Successful faculty evaluation programs.* Crugers, NY: Coventry Press.

Seldin, P. (1991). *The teaching portfolio.* Bolton, MA: Anker Publishing.

Seldin, P. (1993). *Successful use of teaching portfolios.* Bolton, MA: Anker Publishing.

Yunker, J.A. and Marlin, J.W. (1984). Performance evaluation of college and university faculty: An economic perspective. *Education Administration Quarterly*, 20, 9-37.

APPENDIX 22-1

Faculty Self-Assessment of Economics Instruction

Instructor _____ Course _____ Year _____

Directions: The following statements are designed to help you think about your teaching behavior and the course you teach. Complete the questionnaire either by yourself or with a faculty colleague. You should evaluate your response to each statement using the following scale:

1 = Strongly Agree   4 = Disagree
2 = Agree   5 = Strongly disagree
3 = Uncertain   6 = No Opinion/Not Applicable

Course Preparation

1. I have clearly stated objectives for this course.
2. I keep the course materials current and up to date.
3. I allocate sufficient time to organize and prepare for teaching this course.
4. I have written a syllabus that is a useful guide for students.
5. I am aware of the many factors that may affect a course (e.g., class size, room conditions, availability of equipment, textbook orders, course requirements, and student background).

Course Content/Difficulty

6. I have thought carefully about what economic content to teach.
7. I limit the course content to a manageable amount for students.
8. I teach the course at an appropriate level of difficulty for students.
9. I have reviewed the textbook for its content coverage and pedagogy.
10. I develop effective materials to help students learn difficult content.

Teaching Practices

11. I state objectives for each class session.
12. I am organized when I teach a class.
13. I explain material clearly to students.
14. I make clear connections between class sessions.
15. I convey enthusiasm when I teach about a topic.
16. I give good examples and applications to illustrate points.
17. I explain to students how to make best use of the textbook.
18. I use different approaches to motivate *all* students to learn.

Teaching Methods

19. I primarily lecture in this course.
20. I encourage class discussion in this course.
21. I use writing to enhance learning within class sessions.
22. I make good use of active learning techniques in class sessions.
23. I encourage group work and collaborative learning in or out of class.
24. I like to conduct experiments and simulations in this course.
25. I use technology to enhance student learning in this course.
26. I like using a variety of methods to teach economics.

Students

27. I invite student questions during my classes.
28. I give clear answers when students ask a question.
29. I encourage students to ask for help or visit me when they have a problem.
30. I clearly communicate the course expectations to students.
31. I have a good rapport with students, in or out of class.
32. I solicit student opinions about my teaching during the course.
33. I show *all* students that I'm genuinely interested in their learning.

Grading/Evaluation

34. I have established clear grading standards for this course.
35. I let students know what is expected of them in this course.
36. I regularly check for student understanding.
37. I keep students informed of their progress.
38. I test students using different types of examinations.
39. I give effective written assignments.
40. I am satisfied with student learning in this course.

Interest in Teaching

41. I like to read articles or books to improve my teaching.
42. I enjoy attending workshops or conferences on teaching.
43. I often discuss teaching issues with my colleagues.
44. I often think about new ways to improve my teaching.
45. I will review and revise this course after teaching it.
46. I have demonstrated my interest in teaching to my colleagues.

Open-ended questions

47. What are my major contributions to teaching this course?
48. Are there any problems or limitations with my teaching in this course?
49. What aspects of my teaching for this course would I like to improve?
50. How do I plan to make these changes?

INDEX